SUNRISE WITH SEAMONSTERS

PAUL THEROUX

PENGUIN BOOKS

Penguin Books Ltd, Harmondsworth, Middlesex, England
Viking Penguin Inc., 40 West 23rd Street, New York, New York 10010, U.S.A.
Penguin Books Australia Ltd, Ringwood, Victoria, Australia
Penguin Books Canada Limited, 2801 John Street, Markham, Ontario, Canada L3R 1B4
Penguin Books (N.Z.) Ltd, 182–190 Wairau Road, Auckland 10, New Zealand

First published in Great Britain by Hamish Hamilton Ltd 1985
Published in Penguin Books 1986

Made and printed in Great Britain by
Richard Clay (The Chaucer Press) Ltd,
Bungay, Suffolk
Typeset in Plantin

PENGUIN BOOKS

SUNRISE WITH SEAMONSTERS

Paul Theroux was born in Medford, Massachusetts, in 1941, and published his first novel, *Waldo*, in 1967. He wrote his next three novels, *Fong and the Indians*, *Girls at Play* and *Jungle Lovers*, after a five-year stay in Africa. He subsequently taught at the University of Singapore, and during his three years there produced a collection of short stories, *Sinning with Annie*, and his highly praised novel *Saint Jack*. His other publications include *The Black House* (1974), a novel; *The Great Railway Bazaar: By Train Through Asia* (1975), an account of his adventurous journey by train from London to Tokyo and back; *The Family Arsenal* (1976); *The Consul's File* (1977); *Picture Palace* (1978; winner of the Whitbread Literary Award); *A Christmas Card* (1978); *The Old Patagonian Express: By Train Through the Americas* (1979); *World's End and Other Stories* (1980); *London Snow* (1980); *The Mosquito Coast*, which was the *Yorkshire Post* Novel of the Year for 1981 and the joint winner of the James Tait Black Memorial Prize; *The London Embassy* (1982); and *The Kingdom by the Sea* and *Doctor Slaughter* (1985).

Paul Theroux divides his time between Cape Cod and London.

To my Parents,
Albert and Anne Theroux
With Love

"Words, words, words! There were no deeds," interrupted Rudin.

"No deeds! What kind of —"

"What kind of deeds? Supporting a blind old granny and all her family by your hard work — remember Pryazhentsev? There's a deed for you."

"Yes, but good words can also be deeds."

— Ivan Turgenev, *Rudin*
(translated from the Russian by Marcel Theroux)

Contents

Introduction

For the past twenty years I have been writing with both hands. I thought: I'll write a few more pieces and then I'll work on my novel. I never dared to entertain great hopes for my novels – or my travel books, either. But I always expected to be fairly paid for my journalism, which these fifty pieces are. This was specific labor of short duration that would finance my more ambitious, or at least more time-consuming, books. I assumed that one day I would gather some of these pieces together, but I never guessed it would be other than a motley collection, and certainly not a book in any symmetrical sense. This was, mainly, writing for money – paying bills.

I think I was wrong. For one thing, the money for this work was not much. I had thought of including the fee I got for each piece: "The Killing of Hastings Banda," *Esquire*, 1971 – $600; "Malaysia," *Vogue*, 1973 – $70; "A Circuit of Corsica," *The Atlantic*, 1977 – $350; and so forth, as an instructive joke and a severe warning to anyone who intended to make a living this way. But then I decided that it would distract attention from the pieces themselves, and the price-tags might demean them. Anyway, these pieces hardly paid my bills. It was my books that saved me from dropping back into the schoolroom, or into the even more dire profession of writing applications for grants and fellowships ("My creative writing project is a novel about . . ."). And as for the question of symmetry, I hope this book is something more than a rag-bag anthology. I have waited this long so that it might have the proportions of a better book – four dimensions and even a kind of narrative.

The early pieces sound a little forced and clumsy to me. I was twenty-two or twenty-three, and if the prose is harshly old-fashioned, then so was the setting. I wrote most of the early pieces in Africa – the old Africa, with muddy roads and dusty faces; "Yes, Master," the elderly "houseboys" would say. This was Malawi, an ex-British Protectorate that was to turn into a franker kind of black dictatorship. It was not merely that there were no African members of the Blantyre Club, or that I had a cook and a gardener and they earned about $15 a month between them; and it was not the signs in the butcher shops advertising "Boys' Meat" (cheap mutton you were supposed to buy for your "houseboy"); no, stranger and more startling, it was the sight of African women who fell to their knees in the dust by the roadside as I passed on a motorcycle or a car, because of my white face – but it was whiter for having seen that. It was the Africa of leper colonies and Home Leave; and it was not regarded as inhuman but only bad manners for a white person to say, "Exterminate the brutes!"

I remember another day in Mozambique, in a terrible little country town, getting a haircut from a Portuguese barber. He had come to the African bush from rural Portugal to be a barber. What was so unusual about that? Mozambique had been a colony for hundreds of years – the first Portuguese claimed it in 1489. If I had asked, I am sure this barber would have said he was following in the footsteps of Vasco da Gama. He did not speak English, I did not speak Portuguese, yet when I addressed his African servant in Chinyanja, his own language, the Portuguese man said, in Portuguese, "Ask the bwana what his Africans are like." And that was how we held a conversation – the barber speaking Portuguese to the African who translated it into Chinyanja for me; and I replied in Chinyanja which the African translated into Portuguese for the barber. The barber kept saying – and the African kept translating – things like, "I can't stand the blacks – they're so stupid and bad-tempered. But there's no work in Portugal." It was grotesque, it was outrageous, it was the shabbiest, darkest kind of imperialism. I could not believe my good luck. Twenty years ago in parts of Africa it was the Nineteenth Century, and living there I was filled with an urgency to write about it. I like the word "pieces". I wrote about it in pieces.

It has given me, in an overlapping way, two writing lives; in one I have been writing books, a lengthening shelf of them, and in the other life I have been writing these pieces. I regarded a book as an indulgence – I mean a "vision" but the word sounds too pompous and spiritual. These pieces I meant to be concrete – responses to experiences, with my feet squarely on the ground; immediate and direct, written to fulfill a specific purpose, and somewhat alien to the meandering uncertainties of the novel. They were also a breath of air. In the middle of writing *Picture Palace* I went to San Clemente and wrote about Nixon (and some of *Picture Palace* I wrote in the San Clemente Motor Inn); and the piece reprinted here which is an introduction to the O.U.P. paperback edition of *His Monkey Wife* I wrote during a break from *The Kingdom by the Sea*. In the middle of *The Mosquito Coast* I went down the Yangtze River from Chonqing to Shanghai and wrote about it for a British newspaper (a fuller account of the trip appeared as a small book, *Sailing Through China*). I never really minded writing with both hands. I usually needed a break – I am sure *The Mosquito Coast* is the better for my experiences in China. I require a certain amount of undemanding interruption in order to maintain my concentration. I start every day by writing letters, and even when I am working on a novel I answer the phone.

I have often found the writing of occasional pieces to be valuable in unexpected ways – inspirational even. Not simply going to California or reading Joyce Cary or looking in Vermont for traces of Kipling's family feud – each experience a pleasure all its own; but rather carrying out an ambiguous assignment and in so doing making discoveries that change my outlook for good. These are the excitements of a writer's life. Writing about the New York subway was one of the most illuminating experiences I have ever had, and the memory of riding all those trains continues to suggest to me new ways of looking at the metropolitan world. Going to my high school reunion was another such memorable experience: it altered my thinking about myself and the past. I saw that it was not education that made me a writer, but perhaps its opposite – my sense of incompleteness, of being outside the currents of society and powerless and unprivileged and anxious to prove myself; that, and my membership in a large family, with childhood fantasies of travel and, in general, being if not a rebel then an isolated and hot-eyed punk. For years I felt that being respectable meant maintaining a sinister complacency, and the disreputable freedom I sought helped make me a writer.

In the course of writing these pieces I was forced to draw conclusions, sometimes brutal ones. If I had not been asked to write them – most of them are responses to editorial requests – I would never have had to face these truths. I needed that discipline and I needed the encouragement of regular work – of writing. I was put in touch with the world, and drawn away from my desk, and given the illusion of writing as a profession: so I felt businesslike and orderly and purposeful. I needed all those illusions to keep up my morale.

I had once thought that these pieces fell naturally into categories: Travel, Photography, Books, Writers, Family, and Trains. I realized that I habitually mixed these topics together: travel was not only an experience of space and time, but had its literary and domestic aspects as well. Travel is everything, and my way of travelling is completely personal. This is not a category – it is more like a whole way of life. And it is impossible to write about a subway without alluding to *The Wasteland*, or to deal with Burma without mentioning Orwell. My piece about my family – "My Extended Family" – owes a great deal to my having lived in Africa. They are all personal.

There was only one arrangement of this book that made any sense. Set out chronologically these pieces seemed to me to form a narrative of having lived through two interesting decades in a number of different countries; and not just lived through, but grown up in. This is what I was writing when I was also writing my books. Even if they don't shed light on those books – but I think they do – perhaps they explain why I never had time for anything else; why I am so poor at tennis and inexperienced as a film-goer, and why I raise my voice so quickly when the Guggenheim Foundation ("We regret to inform you . . .") is mentioned. That is what I mean by a narrative. For example, it ought to be easy to understand, after thirty-eight pieces and seventeen years (and seventeen books), and no Fellowship, why the thirty-ninth piece in 1980 was an attack on patronage.

And I think I was wrong about book reviewing. I wrote 356 book reviews in this time. None of them is included here. It seemed to me that they were insubstantial and that to include them would be asking for trouble. I believed that they were likely to antagonize any reviewer of this book. "I can do better than that," I imagined a reviewer murmuring, and I saw him doing precisely as he had said, demolishing me in a stylish way. It is a hard living – book reviewing – and except in the rarest cases it is seldom a livelihood. That was another misapprehension of mine twenty years ago – that if all else failed I would be able to make ends meet this way. I suppose I might have managed, hacking away on the Entertainment Page, where book reviews generally appear these days.

I must say I have very little time for the academic who regards a book review as a "publication", to be listed in his or her curriculum vitae in the hopes of securing tenure. A book review is, or ought to be, a notice – a response. It is not an essay, not even a piece. If it is reprinted at all it ought to have a certain period charm. How else can it be justified? The sheer fun of the vicious attack, the mocking review or the assault on a bubble reputation are not long-lasting. Something more judicious is needed, and in rereading my book reviews I saw that it was usually lacking. I was writing "notices". If a book was good I wanted it to have readers; if it was bad I tried to discourage interest in it. If I felt it was overrated I tried to get its true measure.

But as all my book reviews have turned out to be ephemeral things, I begin to wonder why I went to such trouble. A book review was a two-day job – one day to read the book, another to write the review. The book reviewer does not choose the books: they are sent to him by the literary editor. That is part of the book reviewing code; and another part of it is that the reviewer resists influence and usually reacts violently against hype. It is to my mind one of the most decent areas of journalism and probably the worst paid. There are foolish and vain and self-serving book reviewers, but I have never known a corrupt one, nor have I been aware of any suggestion that a book reviewer was in the pay of a publisher.

There is immense value in reviewing, though there is no denying that it is often a great nuisance, too. The reviewer is forced to judge a work; he must articulate his reaction; he must learn to read intelligently. I think reviewing tends to make a writer a bit more open-minded, less self-regarding and precious. It could be argued – I certainly believe it – that reviewing is one of the duties of the profession, too, and a much greater necessity for a writer than teaching how to write at a university, or leading seminars on literary culture. I have a comradely feeling for novelists who review books, and those who don't – who turn their refusal into a sort of loathsome boast – I find lazy and contemptible.

And yet I cannot bring myself to reprint all that stuff. I know they would have a weak warmed-over flavor, and I am satisfied that they have served their purpose. Looking through them, just before I decided to chuck them all, I was somewhat startled by their dated ferocity. This is the beginning of my review of *Fear of Flying:*

> With such continual and insistent reference to her cherished valve, Erica Jong's witless heroine looms like a mammoth pudendum, as roomy as the Carlsbad Caverns, luring amorous spelunkers to confusion in her plunging grottoes. On her eighth psychoanalyst and second marriage, Isadora Wing admits to a contortion we are not privileged to observe and confesses, "I seem to live inside my cunt," which strikes one as a choice as inconvenient as a leaky bedsitter in Elmer's End . . .
> This crappy novel . . .

At the time of the Royal Wedding in London, when Prince Charles married Lady Diana Spencer, an ambitious Australian who was also one of the nastier television critics, wrote a slurping poetic tribute to the prince. Perhaps he deserved this:

> It is not true that all bad poetry springs from genuine feeling. Look at this book, for example. It is about as awful, as lame and as lifeless as can be, and yet it clearly springs from spurious feeling, self-boosting facetiousness and cack-handed social climbing which, in Clive James's couplets, turn into fawning mockery, as he hitches his trundling wagon of assorted poetic styles to the Royal Coach in the hope of someone catching sight of his bumpy head and inefficient eyes, so he can wave hello in his own way . . .

It went on in this way for eight more paragraphs.

Another waspish review, far too long and far too cruel to quote, was the one I wrote of John Updike's *Rabbit Redux*. I read the book and wrote the review when I was in Indonesia, living among some of the poorest people I have ever seen in my life. This was on the fringes of Djakarta. In my lap was the complacent Rabbit Angstrom and his hysterical wife and the sexual tangles that Mr Updike seemed to be insisting were serious problems; and out of the window – I could see them by glancing up – were people living in cardboard shelters, drinking black water and actually starving to death. To say that I took a dim view of Rabbit is an understatement; I said it was immoral and asinine. I am sure I over-reacted, but I still think it is a silly book.

I had my fill of reading bad books and giving damaging reviews. I decided that if a book was no good I did not want to read it, much less review it, and for the past eight years or so I have stuck to that. No one is sure whether reviews play much of a part in the selling of a book, and this uncertainty is a salutary thing – it has at least kept book reviewing honest. One of the happiest results of a book review I wrote was my receiving, a few years ago, a copy of the local newspaper of Wilton, Connecticut. Just under the paper's title, at the top of page one – where you might expect to find a quotation from Deuteronomy or one of Pudd'nhead Wilson's Maxims – was the line: "*I never knew a snob who was not also a damned liar*" *– Paul Theroux*. From a book review – bless them! I thought then, maybe someday I'll collect those reviews. But I have read them all. Some made me laugh, some made me cringe. What a lot of work! But they have served their purpose. There are none here.

The past tense and reminiscing tone of this Introduction might make it seem as if in a fit of renunciation, the way you clean out a drawer, I have put it all behind me and given up writing pieces. But, no, I am still at it.

P.T.

December, 1984

The Edge of the Great Rift

[September 1, 1964]

There is a crack in the earth which extends from the Sea of Galilee to the coast of Mozambique, and I am living on the edge of it, in Nyasaland. This crack is the Great Rift Valley. It seems to be swallowing most of East Africa. In Nyasaland it is replacing the fishing villages, the flowers, and the anthills with a nearly bottomless lake, and it shows itself in rough escarpments and troughs up and down this huge continent. It is thought that this valley was torn amid great volcanic activity. The period of vulcanism has not ended in Africa. It shows itself not only in the Great Rift Valley itself, but in the people, burning, the lava of masses, the turbulence of the humans themselves who live in the Great Rift.

My schoolroom is on the Great Rift, and in this schoolroom there is a line of children, heads shaved like prisoners, muscles showing through their rags. They are waiting to peer through the tiny lens of a cheap microscope so they can see the cells in a flower petal.

Later they will ask, "Is fire alive? Is water?"

The children appear in the morning out of the slowly drifting hoops of fog-wisp. It is chilly, almost cold. There is no visibility at six in the morning; only a fierce white-out where earth is the patch of dirt under their bare feet, a platform, and the sky is everything else. It becomes Africa at noon when there are no clouds and the heat is like a blazing rug thrown over everything to suffocate and scorch.

In the afternoon there are clouds, big ones, like war declared in the stratosphere. It starts to get gray as the children leave the school and begin padding down the dirt road.

There is a hill near the school. The sun approaches it by sneaking behind the clouds until it emerges to crash into the hill and explode yellow and pink, to paint everything in its violent fire.

At night, if there is a moon, the school, the Great Rift, become a seascape of luminescent trees and grass, whispering, silver. If there is no moon you walk from a lighted house to an infinity of space, packed with darkness.

Yesterday I ducked out of a heavy downpour and waited in a small shed for the rain to let up. The rain was far too heavy for my spidery umbrella. I waited in the shed; thunder and close bursts of lightning charged all around me; the rain spat through the palm-leaf walls of the shed.

Down the road I spotted a small African child. I could not tell whether it was a boy or a girl, since it was wearing a long shirt, a yellow one, which drooped sodden to the ground. The child was carrying nothing, so I assumed it was a boy.

He dashed in and out of the puddles, hopping from side to side of the forest path, his yellow shirt bulging as he twisted under it. When he came closer I could see the look of absolute fear on his face. His only defense against the thunder and the smacking of rain were his fingers stuck firmly into his ears. He held them there as he ran.

He ran into my shed, but when he saw me he shivered into a corner where he stood shuddering under his soaked shirt. We eyed each other. There were raindrops beaded on his face. I leaned on my umbrella and fumbled a Bantu greeting. He moved against a palm leaf. After a few moments he reinserted a finger in each ear, carefully, one at a time. Then he darted out into the rain and thunder. And his dancing yellow shirt disappeared.

I stand on the grassy edge of the Great Rift. I feel it under me and I expect soon a mighty heave to send us all sprawling. The Great Rift. And whom does this rift concern? Is it perhaps a rift with the stars? Is it between earth and man, or man and man? Is there something under this African ground seething still?

We like to believe that we are riding it and that it is nothing more than an imperfection in the crust of the earth. We do not want to be captive to this rift, as if we barely belong, as if we were scrawled on the landscape by a piece of chalk.

Burning Grass

[October 22, 1964]

In July, it was very cold in Malawi. On the day that Malawi gained her independence the wind swept down from Soche Hill into the Central stadium bringing with it cold mists. The Africans call this wind *chiperoni* and dread it because they don't have enough clothes to withstand its penetration. They also know that it lasts only a few weeks and that once this difficult period is gotten through they can go out again into the fields and dig furrows for planting.

Independence was very dark, yet despite the cold winds the people came to see their newly designed flag raised. The Prime Minister told everyone that Malawi is a black man's country. The cold seemed to turn everything, everyone, to wood; even the slogans were frozen, the gladness caged in trembling bodies.

Through August it became warmer. The violet flames of the jacaranda, the deep red of the bougainvillaea, the hibiscus, each bloom a delicate shell – all suddenly appeared out of the cold of the African winter.

In September, two months had passed since that winter, two months since that freezing Independence Day. And now, in this dry season, the people have begun to burn the grass.

September 8 was the first day of school. On this same day three members of the cabinet were asked to resign. Shortly afterward all the ministers but two resigned in protest. The Prime Minister, "the Lion of Malawi," was left with only two of his former ministers. Two months after independence the government smoldered in the heat of argument.

The custom of burning grass dates back to prehistoric times when there was a great deal of land and only a few farmers; much of the land could lie fallow while the rest was burned. It was thought that the burning was necessary for a good crop the following year. The scientists say this is not true, but there are only a handful of scientists in this country of four million farmers. So each year, in the dry season, the grass is burned. A few weeks ago I saw thin trails of blue smoke winding out of valleys and off the hills to disappear in the clouds. And at night I saw the flicker of fires at a great distance. A short time ago the fires were not great; I could still see the huge Mlanje plateau, a crouching animal, streaked with green, disappearing into Mozambique.

Last night I walked outside and saw the fires again. It can be terrifying to see things burning at night, wild bush fires creeping up a mountain like flaming snakes edging sideways to the summit. Even behind the mountains I could see fires, and off into the darkness that is the edge of Malawi I saw the glowing dots of fires just begun. They could burn all night, light the whole sky and make the shadows of trees leap in the flames. During the day the flames would drive the pigs and hyenas out of their thickets; the heat and smoke would turn the fleeing ravens into frightened asterisks of feathers

Today the portent was real. Early this morning the radio said there would be heavy smoke haze. I looked off and Mlanje, Mozambique, even the small hills that had always lain so patiently in the sun, were obscured by the smoke of the bush fires. The horizon has crept close to my house. The horizon is still blue, not the cold blue of the air at a distance, but the heavy pigment of smoke and fresh ashes lingering low over the landscape, close to me.

In this season the ministers who have broken from the government are making speeches against the Prime Minister. They are angry. They say that this government is worse than the one it replaced. They say that in two months the Prime Minister has kept none of his promises; the ministers have spread to all the provinces where, before great numbers of people, they repeat their accusations. The air is heavy with threats and indignation; the people are gathering in groups to talk of this split in the government. They take time off from burning the grass to speak of the government now, after two green months, in flames.

Fire in Africa can go out of control, out of reach of any human being, without disturbing much. It can sweep across the long plains and up the mountains and then, after the fire has burned its length, will flicker and go out. Later the burned ground will be replaced by the woven green of new grass. For a while very little will clear; the smoke will hang in the air and people will either dash about in its arms blindly or will be restless before it, anxiously waiting for it to disperse.

We all know that the horizon will soon move back and back, and another season will come in Malawi. The prolonged fires will delay planting but planting will certainly begin; perhaps the harvest will be later than usual.

Yet now we have the flames and we must somehow live with the heat, the smoke, the urgency of fires on mountains, the terror of fires at night, the burning grass, the dry fields waiting to be lighted, and all the creatures that live in the forest scattering this way and that, away from the charred and smoky ground.

Winter in Africa

[July 2, 1965]

Ptolemy guessed that there was snow on the equator, but it was not until 1848 that Johann Rebmann actually saw it. Rebmann noted in his diary that it was a "dazzling white cloud" on Mount Kilimanjaro; his guide told him that it was called "beredi", cold.

The idea of snow on the equator was ridiculed even after Rebmann's discovery and it was some time before it was a proven fact. Late in the nineteenth century it was discovered that the snow on the Ruwenzoris (Ptolemy had called them "the Mountains of the Moon") provided the water which formed one of the sources of the River Nile.

Ptolemy was more realistic about these matters than most people were, or are. It can be very cold in Africa.

In the tiny country of Malawi the winter is severe, though paradoxical, and the inhabitants of this country are both eager and hesitant to greet it. May, June and July, the cold months, are also the harvest months. This is the season when the village silos – huge baskets on legs – are filled to the brim with corn, the staple food of the Malawian. The oranges and tangerines are ripe; the second bean crop, the tobacco and tea are all being harvested and auctioned. This is the season when there are jobs, a season of feasting in the cold.

On the plateaux the cold wet winds sting the countryside with a mixture of fog and rain. These winds whip sideways against the face, tear and flatten the elephant grass, and yank swatches of thatch from the roofs of the mud houses. Yet one rarely hears complaints about this cold season – food is a great blessing in a poor country. Few mention the discomfort and perhaps this is the reason no one has popularized the African winter.

As an English teacher I can tell the season by the changing conditions of the exercise books. In the rainy season, spring, the books are damp, the ink has run, and the point of the red grading pencil gets soggy and usually breaks. Winter arrives in Malawi and the students' exercise books are charred at the edges, the stacks of books reek of woodsmoke and dampness. Sometimes moons of candlewax appear on the pages.

This is the circumstantial evidence of the season, of the conditions under which those essays on truth or *Treasure Island* are written. One corrects the compositions and a small room materializes. The room is either of cement or mud and has a grass roof; in the corner of the room a boy or girl squints at an exercise book under the feeble flickering light of a candle or the low flame of a wick stuck in a dish of kerosene. The kerosene lamp gives off a deep yellow light and fills the room with thick smoke. In the center of the room a pile of smoldering coals in a pit warms the student and a sleeping family.

In the townships just outside the large cities of Central Africa – Salisbury, Blantyre, Lusaka – winter can be dismal. It is not a time of harvest since the persons that live in the townships in those millions of cement sheds are civil servants, mechanics, shopgirls and students. Even if there were time to plant and care for a garden there would be no space for the garden. The townships stretch row on row, symmetrical treeless towns, long files of tiny white one-room or two-room houses. Rusting signboards appear at intervals on the dirt roads that run in a grid in the townships. And early in the morning, before dawn, a stream of people winds its way among the unnamed roads. The school children, many without shoes, run stiff-legged in the cold; the girls march in clumps, hugging themselves in their long clothes.

At the assembly, held outside the school in the morning, the national anthem is sung by three hundred shivering children. Their teeth chatter and they hop up and down between choruses to keep warm. If anyone owns shoes this is the season for them. The leather shoes are patched, sewn, and some are in shreds; some wear plastic shoes – made in Rhodesia or Japan – which are uncomfortable and very little protection against the cold.

In class the wind sounds like someone crawling slowly around the corrugated roof, a heavy man trying to break through the tin. After school there is a vigorous soccer game. No one dares to stand still, the players dash about the field – a ballet on the grass with a backdrop of trees tossing in the fog.

In the villages after supper the people can be seen crouching around fires to warm themselves. A student of mine once suggested that independence in Malawi came at a perfect time of the year. He said the day of independence comes in July, with winter at its coldest, and the people who would naturally be together around the fires would have a good opportunity to discuss the meaning of the freedom they had won for themselves.

There are places in Africa that are colder than Malawi. In Basutoland (Lesotho), where the national costume is the blanket, the people can expect snow, sometimes two or three feet of it. Freezing winds sweep across the Karoo table land of South Africa, batter the Great Rift escarpments in Kenya and Uganda.

Winter in Africa? Yes, just as sure as there is snow on the equator. Winter in Africa is much more than a word. And though we may not associate cold with this continent, it is there as conspicuous and intense as the heat, and perhaps as unpublicized as the peace that also exists in Africa.

The Cerebral Snapshot

[October 5, 1965]

It is my good fortune that I've never owned a camera. Once, when I was in Italy, I saw about three dozen doves spill out of the eaves of an old cathedral. It was lovely, the sort of thing that makes people say *if only I had a camera*! I didn't have a camera with me and have spent the past two-and-a-half years trying to find the words to express that sudden deluge of white doves. This is a good exercise—especially good because I still can't express it. When I'm able to express it I'll know I've made the grade as a writer.

And recently I was driving through Kenya with a friend of mine. It was dusk, an explosion of red shot with gold, and the setting sun and the red air seemed to be pressing the acacias flat. Then we saw a giraffe! Then two, three, four – about ten of the lanky things standing still, the silhouettes of their knobby heads protruding into the red air.

I brought the car to a halt and my friend unsheathed his camera and cocked it. He snapped and snapped while I backed up. I was so busy looking at the giraffes that I zig-zagged the car all over the road and finally into a shallow ditch.

The giraffes moved slowly among the trees like tired dancers. I wanted them to gallop. Once you've seen a giraffe galloping – they gallop as if they're about to come apart any second, yet somehow all their flapping limbs stay miraculously attached – you know that survival has something to do with speed, no matter how grotesque, double-bellied and gawky the beast may be.

My friend continued to fire his camera into the sunset, and pretty soon all the giraffes had either loped away or had camouflaged themselves in the trees. Both of us, rendered speechless by beauty, nodded and we continued along the road.

After a while my friend told me that we should have stayed longer with the giraffes. Why? Because he didn't get a good look at them.

"See," he explained calmly, "if you take a picture of things – especially moving things like giraffes – you don't really see them." He said he would have had trouble explaining what the giraffes looked like except that he had seen some in the Chicago Zoo. I could only agree and I told him about my Italian dove episode.

The next day, when we saw another herd of giraffes, he pushed his camera aside and we both sat there – it was a blazing Kenyan noon – and watched the giraffes placidly munching leaves and glancing at us, pursing their lips in our direction.

No camera is like no hands, a feat of skill. And if you know that sooner or later you will have to explain it all, without benefit of slides or album, to your large family, then as soon as you see something you start searching the view for clues and rummaging through your lexical baggage for the right phrases. Otherwise, what's the use? And when you see something like a galloping giraffe which you can't capture on film you are thrown back on the English language like a cowboy's grizzled sidekick against a cactus. You hope for the sake of posterity and spectators that you can rise unscratched with a blossom.

Some writers frustrated by prose turned to get-rich-quick schemes, action paintings or mushrooms. Goethe botanized, Melville wore black, Dostoevski gambled all his money away, and Mark Twain had many flirtations with printing machines and photography. All writers look for a way out of writing. But writing is like serving a jail sentence – you're not free until you've done your time on the rock-heap. Taking fine pictures won't give any lasting freedom to a writer.

(And neither will plagiarizing. I was once in a writing course in which there was a boy who wrote superb poems. Of course the teacher gave him a hint or two, touched the poems up here and there, but said affirmatively that the boy was well on his way to becoming a very good poet. Everyone competed with the boy and we all improved ourselves by his good example. Alas, our poems never were as good as those of the boy. On the last day the class met it was revealed that the boy had lifted his poems from somebody else's translations of Juan Ramón Jiménez, the Nobel Prize winning Spanish poet.)

A poet-friend of mine who lives in Amherst, Mass., has a rattletrap camera that is more of an oddity than anything else. It is a very old box camera, and before my friend takes a picture he must measure distances carefully and read the yellowed directions about five times. Chuckling privately to himself he snaps the picture. Cranking the film forward takes more time and having the pictures sent to be developed requires all the mystery and care of an income-tax return.

But it is really not the pictures that intrigue him. It is the fun of owning an infernal machine (when he is not actually snapping the picture he holds the camera as if it were a time bomb). After he had taken some pictures of me he announced that none of them looked like me and he suggested that we refrain from taking any more pictures. This was fine with me because, as I have said, no camera is like no hands.

Ignoring cameras is also good for the eyes. I have often sat staring at something wide-eyed, feeling a fabulous clicking in my skull, snapping everything in sight and, occasionally, things that aren't in sight. Afterwards, strenuously gesturing and leaping out of my seat, I have described these phenomena to my friends.

This is also good exercise. What I have told may not always have been the pictorial truth – a camera may easily have seen something different. But when you see a sunset or a giraffe or a child eating a melting ice-cream cone there is a chemical reaction inside you. If you really stand as innocent as you can, something of the movement, entering through your eyes, gets into your body where it continues to rearrange your senses. Also – and for a writer this bit of information is priceless – a picture is worth only a thousand or so words.

State of Emergency

[June 12, 1966]

Yesterday I finally got down to marking the political science papers from the correspondence students, and yesterday an uprising started in Kampala. The students would like their papers back. I don't blame them; the papers have been sitting on my desk for two weeks.

Yesterday was a bad day for marking papers. Today is not much better. The Kabaka (or King) of Buganda was President of Uganda until a few weeks ago; under the new constitution all political power has been taken from the hereditary monarchs of Uganda. The Kabaka once controlled the richest and most powerful Kingdom in Uganda, that of Buganda. But Milton Obote, former Prime Minister, has taken over as President.

While I was grading papers yesterday there was some shooting in the streets near the Kabaka's palace, about a half a mile from my office; roadblocks were put up, streets and pavements torn apart, and railroad ties and telephone poles ripped up. Travelers were deputized by the Kabaka's people and made to dig up the roads and help make effective roadblocks against government troops.

The Special Forces and riot squads rushed around with night sticks and Sten guns. And rumors, like locusts emerging, flew about the city. I couldn't grade papers yesterday. I had to buy some food in case the shops closed. They might not reopen for a week or more. I only looked over a few papers.

This morning I was determined. I sat down at my desk. The weather is beautiful in Kampala, the rains have just stopped after about six weeks of downpours, and everything is emerald in the sun; the herons in the large tree outside on the lawn are flapping around and tending to their fledglings. But no distractions this morning! I must get those papers graded.

The first paper, the first question. *What is a Nation?* "A nation," runs the quite elegant handwriting, "is a group of people of common consciousness and like-mindedness." I check it right. He has understood the lesson.

And then I hear a small pop. Then another. I look across to the Kabaka's palace on one of the hills opposite and see nothing. I can see a few open streets from my window. There is no traffic. I hear the pop-pop-pop of an automatic rifle. Are they gunshots? I ask the secretary – she lives near the palace. She tells me that she had trouble getting through the army lines when she came to work in the morning. She saw five truckloads of government troops. Some were battling with the people of Buganda. I turn back to the paper. "The difference between Government and State is that the Government is not permanent while the State never changes . . ."

The people of Buganda are proud. They love their king, they are polite and wise and seldom get ruffled. It is undignified, they might say. It was one of their kings, the first Kabaka Mutesa, who welcomed the first white men, Speke and Grant, into Uganda in 1862. The wide avenue leading to the palace is still called the We-Love-The-Kabaka road in the vernacular. This is the road where most of the fighting is taking place this morning. Back to the papers.

The question was, *What are the advantages and disadvantages of decentralization of power in a state?* I check some of the answers: "When many people exercise responsibility many of them will be interested in the government . . ." I look up again. I have just heard more rifleshots, this time a long volley, some louder than others.

The fighting seems much heavier today. It is hard to concentrate on the marking; and now students who are enrolled in evening classes are dropping in to say that, because of the curfew, they won't be in class tonight. Will I pass their names along to the teacher?

A few weeks ago Uganda was a Federal State with each king acting as lawgiver and tax-collector for his particular kingdom. More recently the federal constitution was suspended and Uganda made a Republic. The Kabaka and the other monarchs, people said, would be angry; no longer would they have any power. But they have loyal subjects, as loyal as any medieval farmers standing in the rain on a muddy road to watch their lord pass in a gilded carriage. But I have it all before me in one of the papers: "Federal government is that in which a number of states join together, each state keeping control of some matters, but allowing the Central Government to control national defense and foreign affairs."

Uganda is no longer a Federal State. I hear some objection to it, out the window, across the valley where there is shooting.

The Kabaka has issued what amounts to an ultimatum: he will give Obote's government until May 30 to leave his kingdom and change his mind about the constitution. We can assume that the state of emergency will last until then. I may even be grading papers until that date, perhaps these same papers.

Grading papers is not hard work and, after all, some students seemed to have grasped the principles pretty well; they are teachers and they do all their studying by mail. The last question has provided some very good answers: *Why We Should Study Political Science – a short essay.* I can let one of my students speak: "As we live by the government we have to know our place and the part we have to play in political matters. This will also enable us to sort out current affairs and understand them when we read the newspapers . . ."

Meanwhile there is shooting here in the capital of the state emergency. I'm a teacher. I presume I don't belong on the street making barricades or breaking them down. But the smoke from the palace, which the office boy has told me has just burned down, has something to do with politics; and the soldiers on the street; and the persistent pop-pop of the guns – that's politics, too. But it's not political science, and I'm a teacher; my correspondence students have just sent in their exams. I have papers to mark.

Leper Colony: A Diary Entry

[1966]

Leprosaria: it could be a tuber, a jungle vine, a thing from the bush with dark petals and fruit, ovoid, bitter to the taste.

The lepers are idle and so they fight with knives and they knit wool caps, and they crouch and applaud when the white priests pass.

Bats have the faces of pigs and three hang in the privy and squeak; soft mouse-fur, kite-strutted wings, bones showing in skin. And they live, heads hanging down in the warm cesspit.

And all around the place elephantine baobabs, gray: exploded creatures plastered hastily back and patched with the rough stubbled hide; stiff ears protrude from stumps of shoulders; they stand like dead sentries, fat, useless jugs.

Khate: the Chinyanja word is a call for help if ever there was one; choke, clear your throat with a *khate* or two. The fishermen say it and then point toward those trees.

There is leprosy which causes a "tiger's mouth" in the flesh between the thumb and forefinger; the toes and fingers shrink back and hang down; the skin, hard, scaled like a night thing living among the stones; and the nose absorbed into the face, tilted up and monstrous, almost bat-like. There is nerve leprosy which clouds the eye and aims it off, which makes claws of hands and stills the jaw; limbs are clubs to thump dirt pits for trash, to wish for knives.

For three days the *Nyau*, the image-dance, drums through the bush, ticks pulse and thunder; and because the dancers are lepers they go longer and naked. The image they have chosen is a car made of sticks and cloth – the soul of the dead man lives there for three days, conjured by dwarfish lepers dancing, whirling their stumps of hands.

Ugly, the *khate* a thousand times over; creeping back into huts and ditches and sleeping on mats; flies and dung-ugly geckoes; even children with the dead furred rash and small faces sucking bladder breasts, toying with green reeds.

Night, and a woman in labor wails in the leprosarium; her fingers are gone and she cannot grip tight, but only hangs, leprous, pregnant with pain; one last gasp signals the tearing of the bulbed head down hard against the membranes; fluid from one wounded body, a child, smooth seed from the ravaged husk, brought among the drums and into the night of this cursed community; out of its freakish crust the world exudes the novelty of perfect form.

Scenes From a Curfew

[1966]

It was not odd that the first few days of our curfew were enjoyed by most people. It was a welcome change for us, like the noisy downpour that comes suddenly in January and makes a watery crackle on the street and ends the dry season. The parties, though these were now held in the afternoon, had a new topic of conversation. There were many rumors, and repeating these rumors made a kind of tennis match, a serve and return, each hit slightly more savage than the last. And the landscape of the city outside the fence of our compound was fascinating to watch. During these first days we stood in our brightly flowered shirts on our hill; we could see the palace burning, the soldiers assembling and making people scatter, and we could hear the bursts of gunfire and some shouts just outside our fence. We were teachers, all of us young, and we were in Africa. There were well-educated ones among us. One of them told me that, during the Roman Empire under the reign of Claudius, rich people and scholars could be carried in litters by *lecticarii*, usually slaves, to camp with servants at a safe distance from battles; these were curious Romans, men of high station who, if they so wished, could be present and, between feasts, witness the slaughter.

But the curfew continued, and what were diversions for the first few days and weeks became habits. Although people usually showed up for work in the mornings, work in the afternoons almost ceased. There were too many things to be done before the curfew began at nightfall: buses had to be caught, provisions found, and some people had to collect children. We visited the bars so that we could get drunk in the company of other people; we played the slot machines and talked about the curfew, but after two weeks it was a very boring subject.

The people who never went out at night before the curfew was imposed – some Indians with large families used to matinées at the local movie houses, the Africans who did manual labor, and some settlers – felt none of the curfew's effects. And there were steady ones who refused to let the curfew get to them; they were impatient with our daily hangovers, our inefficiency, our nervous comments. Our classes were not well-attended. One day I asked casually where our Congolese student was – a dashing figure, he wore a silk scarf and rode a large old motorcycle. I was told that he had been pulled off his motorcycle by a soldier and had been beaten to death with a rifle butt.

We left work early. In the afternoons it was as if everyone was on leave but couldn't afford to go to Nairobi or Mombasa, as if everyone had decided to while away his time at the local bars. At the end of the month no one was paid because the ministry was short-staffed. Some of us ran out of money. The bar owners said they were earning less and less: it was no longer possible for people to drink in bars after dark. They would only have been making the same amount as before, they said, if all the people started drinking in the middle of the morning and kept it up all day. The drinking crowd was a relatively small one, and there were no casual drinkers. Most people in the city stayed at home. They were afraid to stay out after five or so. I tried to get drunk by five-thirty. My memory is of going home drunk, with the dazzling horizontal rays of the sun in my eyes.

The dwindling of time was a strange thing. During the first weeks of the curfew we took chances; we arrived home just as the soldiers were drifting into the streets. Then we began to give ourselves more time, leaving an hour or more for going home. It might have been because we were drunker and needed more time, but we were also more worried: more people were found dead in the streets each morning when the curfew lifted. For many of us the curfew began in the middle of the afternoon when we hurried to a bar; and it was the drinkers who, soaked into a state of slow motion, took the most chances.

Different prostitutes appeared in the bars. Before the curfew there were ten or fifteen in each bar, most of them young and from the outskirts of Kampala. But the curfew was imposed after two tribes fought; most of the prostitutes had been from these tribes and so went into hiding. Others took their places. Now there were ones from the Coast, there were half-castes, Rwandans, Somalis. I remember the Somalis. There was said to be an Ethiopian at the Crested Crane, but I never saw her; in any case, she would have been very popular. All these women were old and hard, and there were fewer than before. They sat in the bars, futile and left alone, slumped on the broken chairs, waiting, as they had been waiting ever since the curfew started. Whatever other talents a prostitute may have she is still unmatched by any other person in her genius for killing time and staying on the alert for customers. The girls held their glasses in two hands and followed the stumbling drinkers with their eyes. Most of us were not interested in complicating the curfew further by taking one of these girls home. I am sure they never had to wait so long with such dull men.

One afternoon a girl put her hand on mine. Her palm was very rough; she rubbed it on my wrist and when I did not turn away she put it on my leg and asked me if I wanted to go in the back. I said I didn't mind, and she led me out past the toilets to the back of the bar where there was a little shed. She scuffed across the shed's dirt floor, then stood in a corner and lifted her skirt. Here, she said, come here. I asked her if we had to remain standing up. She said yes. I started to embrace her; she let her head fall back until it touched the wood wall. She still held the hem of her skirt in her hand. Then I said no, I couldn't nail her against the wall. I saw that the door was still open. She argued for a while and said in Swahili. "Talk, talk, we could have finished by now!" I stepped away, but gave her ten shillings just the same. She spat on it and looked at me fiercely.

Anyone who did not crave a drink went straight home. He took no chances. There were too many rumors of people being beaten up at five o'clock by drunken soldiers impatient for the curfew to start. As I say, the drinkers took the risks, and with very little time to spare dashed for their cars and sped home. For many the curfew meant an extra supply of newspapers and magazines; for others it meant an extra case of beer. A neighbor of mine had prostitutes on his hands for days at a time, and one of the girl's babies in a makeshift cot. Many people talked about rape.

The car accidents were very strange, freak accidents, ones that could only happen during a curfew. One man skidded on a perfectly dry road and drove his car through a billboard six feet wide; dozens of people, as if they had been struck blind, plowed straight across the grass of rotaries. And there were accidents at intersections: not hitting oncoming cars, but smashing into the rears of the cars ahead of them. These rear-end collisions were quite numerous and there were no street sweepers to cope with all the broken glass. It was hard to go a hundred yards without seeing shards, red plastic and white glass, sprinkled on the road. Overturned cars on the verge of the road are rare in Africa, but they became very common around Kampala. Accidents in Africa are usually serious; few end with only a smashed headlight or simple bruises. Either the car is completely ruined or the car and driver disappear. We had some of these fatal accidents during the curfew, but there was also, for the first time, a rash of trivial accidents: broken lights, smashed fenders, bent bumpers, bruised foreheads. I think these were caused by the driver glancing around as he drove, half expecting to see angry people about to stone him, or troops aiming rifles at him. I know I tried to pick out soldiers as I drove along, and I always watched carefully for roadblocks which were so simple (two soldiers and an oil drum) as to be invisible. But it was death to drive through one.

There were so many petty arguments those days. In the bars there were fights over nothing at all; with this, a feeling of tribe rather than color. It was not racism. It was a black revolt; northern Ugandans were killing Bugandans, and neither side was helped to any great extent by anyone who was not black. The lingua franca in Kampala was bad Swahili instead of the usual vernacular which was Luganda. At any other time Swahili would have been a despised language, because only the fringe people used it – refugees, Indians, white men, foreigners. But after the curfew began it was mainly the fringe people who took over the bars.

The curfew reminded many of other curfews they had sat through in their time. During the day, in the bars, if the curfew was mentioned, old-timers piped up contemptuously, "You think *this* is bad? Why, when I was in Leopoldville it was a lot worse than this . . ." Sometimes it was London, Palermo, Alexandria or Tunis, or, for the Indians, Calcutta, Dacca or Bombay during the Indian emergency. It brought back memories which, though originally violent, had become somewhat glamorous in the long stretch of intervening time: days spent in haggard platoons in the Western Desert, in the dim light of paraffin lamps in Congolese mansions, in London basements with the planes buzzing overhead, in Calcutta with the sound of blood running in the monsoon drains. These men enjoyed talking about the other more effective curfews, and they said that we really didn't know what a curfew was. They had seen men frightened, they said, but this curfew only bored people. Still, I knew then that some time in the future I would recall the curfew – perhaps recall it with the same fanciful distortions that these men added to their own memories. It is so strange. I was in Africa for five years; I remember nothing so clearly as the curfew.

The cripples who sold newspapers at the hotels and down by the Three Stars Bar no longer had to shout and point at their stacks of papers. As soon as the new papers arrived they were sold. The ones from Kenya and Tanzania were in demand since they were printing all the facts and even some of the rumors. The local papers which showed some courage during the first weeks were banned or their reporters beaten up. They now began all their curfew stories, "Things are almost back to normal . . ."

More and more people began tuning to the External Service of Radio South Africa, and after a time they didn't even apologize. People traded rumors of atrocities (the gorier the story the more knowledgeable the storyteller was considered). No one except the anthropologists chose sides. The political scientists were silent (it was said that as soon as the tribal dispute started half a dozen doctoral dissertations were rendered invalid). We waited for the curfew to end. But the weeks passed and the curfew stayed the same. At night there was stillness where there had been the rush of traffic in town, the odd shout, or the babbling of idle boys in the streets. Barking dogs and the honk and cackle of herons in our trees replaced the human noises. The jungle had started to move in. Every hour on the hour the air was thunderous with the sound of news broadcasts, but after that, at our compound, you could stand on the hill and hear nothing. Lights flashed soundlessly and to no purpose. Nothing outside the fence moved. Viewed from that hill the curfew seemed a success.

"This is your friend?" asked the Somali girl in Swahili.

The Watusi next to her ignored the question. He turned to me, "*C'est ma fille, Habiba.*" When I looked at the girl he said in Swahili, "Yes, my friend Paul – *rafiki wangu.*"

"*Très jolie,*" I said, and in English, "Where'd you find her?"

"*Sur la rue!*" He laughed.

For the rest of the evening we spoke in three languages, and when Habiba's friend, Fatma the Arab, joined us the girls spoke their own mixture of Swahili and Arabic. Gestures also became necessary.

I did not know the Watusi boy well. We had spoken together, our French was equally bad, but it was interlarded with enough Swahili and English for us to understand each other. And that was a strange enough *patois* to create a bewildered silence around us in the bar. I knew he was from Burundi; he claimed a vague royal connection – that was one of the first things he had told me. I had bought him a drink. His name was Jean. His surname had seven syllables.

He leaned over. "She has a sister," he said.

At six o'clock we drove to the Somali section of town, a slum like all the sections inhabited by refugees. Even the moneyed refugees – the fugitive *bhang* peddlers, the smugglers – seemed to prefer the anonymity of slums. Habiba's sister came out. She was tall, wearing a veil and silk trousers, but with that sable grace – long-necked, eyes darting over the veil, thin, finely made hands, a jewel in her nostril – that makes Somali women the most desired in Africa. Jean talked to her in Swahili. I smoked and looked around.

There were about a dozen Somali families in this compound of cement sheds; they leaned against the walls, talked in groups, sat in the deep mud ruts that coursed through the yard, eroded in the last rain. Some men at the windows of the sheds sent little boys over to beg from us. We refused to give them any money, but one begged a cigarette from me which he quickly passed to a tough-looking man who squatted in a doorway.

Habiba came back to the car and said it was impossible for her sister to come with us. The men would be angry. The Somali men, forced by the curfew to meander about the yard of their compound, the ones sending little boys to beg from us and chewing the stems of a green narcotic weed (the style was the hillbilly's, but the result was delirium) – those refugees with nothing to do and nowhere to go might lose their tempers and kill us if they saw two of their girls leaving with strangers. They could easily block the drive that led out of the compound; they would have had no trouble stopping our car and beating us. They had nothing to lose. Besides, they were within their rights to stop us. Habiba had a husband, now on a trip (she said) upcountry; technically these other Somali men were her guardians until her husband returned. Two dead men found in a drain. It would not have been a very strange sight. Corpses turned up regularly as the curfew was lifted each morning.

Habiba got into the car and we drove away. I expected a brick to be tossed through the back window, but nothing happened. Several men glared at us; some little boys shouted what could only have been obscenities.

Take a left, take a right, down this street, left again, chattered Habiba in Swahili. I drove slowly; she pointed to a ramshackle cement house with a wooden verandah pocked by woodworm and almost entirely rotted at the base. Some half-caste children were playing nearby, chasing each other. The racial mixtures were apparent: Arab-African, Indian-Somali, white-Arab. The texture of the hair told, the blotched skin; the half-African children had heavy, colorless lips. We entered the house and sat in a cluttered front room. There were pictures on the walls, film stars, a calendar in Arabic, and other calendar pictures of huntsmen in riding gear and stiff squarish dogs. And there was a picture of the ruler whose palace had been attacked. No one knew whether he had been shot or managed to escape.

Some half-castes and Arabs drifted in and out of a back room to look at us, the visitors, and finally Fatma came. She was unlike Habiba, not ugly, but small, tired-looking and – the word occurred to me as I looked at her in that cluttered front room – dry. Habiba was very black, with a sharp nose, large, soft eyes and long, shapely legs; Fatma was small, ageless in a shrivelled way, with frizzed hair and one foreshortened leg which made her limp slightly. Her eyes were weary with lines; she could have been young and yet she seemed to have no age. She was cautious – now seated and carefully smoothing her silk wrappings, not out of coyness but out of the damaged reflex of pride that comes with generations of poverty. Even the small children in that room looked as concerned as little old men. I felt like a refugee myself who, moving from slum to slum, took care in an aimless, pointless way. Fatma offered us tea.

At that moment I changed my seat. I moved into a chair with my back to the wall. I know why I did it: I was sitting in front of a window and I had the feeling that I was going to be shot in the back of the head by a stray bullet. During the curfew there was always gunfire in Kampala. That was four years ago, and in Africa, but I am still uneasy sitting near windows.

"No time for tea," Jean said in Swahili. He pointed to his watch and said, "Curfew starts right now."

Fatma left the room and Jean nudged me. "That girl," he said in English, "I support her."

"*Comment?*"

"*La fille est supportable, non?*"

We had only fifteen minutes to get back. We drove immediately to a shop and bought some food and a case of beer, then hurried back to my apartment and locked ourselves in. It was precisely seven when we started drinking. The girls, although Moslems, also drank. They said they could drink alcohol "except during prayers".

As time passed the conversation lapsed and there was only an occasional gulp to break the silence. We had run through their life stories very quickly. Habiba was eighteen, born in Somalia. She came to Uganda because of the border war with Kenya which prevented her from living in her own district or migrating to Kenya where she was an enemy. She married in Kampala. Her husband was away most of the time; in the Congo, she thought, but she was not sure. Fatma's parents were dead, she was twenty-two, not married. She was from Mombasa but liked Kampala because, as she said, it was green. The rest of the conversation was a whispered mixture of Arabic and Swahili which the girls spoke, and the French-English-Swahili which Jean and I spoke. Once we turned on the radio and got Radio Rwanda. Jean insisted on switching it off because the commentator was speaking the language of the Bahutu, who were formerly the slaves of Jean's tribe. That tribal war, that massacre, that curfew had been in 1963.

Jean told me what ugly swine the Bahutu were and how he could not stand any Bantu tribe. He squashed his nose with his palm and imitated what I presumed to be a Hutu speaking. He said, "But these girls – very *Hamite*." He traced the profile of a sharp nose on his face.

The girls asked him what he was talking about. He explained, and they both laughed and offered some stories. They talked about the Africans who lived near them; Fatma described the fatal beating of a man who had broken the curfew. Habiba had seen an African man stripped naked and made to run home. She mimicked the man's worried face and flailed her long arms. "Curfew, curfew," she said.

Jean suddenly stood and took Habiba by the arm. He led her to a back room. It was eight o'clock. I asked Fatma if she was ready. She said yes. She could have been a trained bird, brittle and obedient. She limped beside me into the bedroom.

At eleven I wandered into the living room for another drink. Jean was there with his feet up. He asked me how things were going. We drank for a while, then I asked him if he was interested in going for a walk. If we went to sleep now, I said, we'd have to get up at four or five. We switched off all the lights, made sure the girls were asleep, and went out.

The silence outside was absolute. Our shoes clacking on the stones in the road made the only sound and, at intervals, the city opened up to us through gaps in the bushes along the road. Lights can appear to beckon, to call in almost a human fashion, like the strings of flashing lights at deserted country fairs in the United States. The lights cried out. But we were safe inside the large compound; no one could touch us.

When we were coming back to my apartment an idea occurred to me. I pointed to the dark windows and said, choosing my words carefully, "Supposing we just went in there without turning on any lights . . . Do you think the girls would notice if we changed rooms?"

"*Changez de chambres?*"

"*Je veux dire, changez de filles.*"

He laughed, a drunken sort of sputtering, then explained the plan back to me, adding, "*Est-ce que c'est cela que vous voulez faire?*"

"*Cela me serait égal, et vous?*"

Habiba was amused when she discovered, awaking as the act of love began, that someone else was on top of her. She laughed deep in her throat; this seemed to relax her, and she hugged me and sighed.

Jean was waiting in the hallway when I walked out an hour later. He was helpless with suppressed giggling. We stood there in the darkness, our clothes slung over our shoulders, not speaking but communicating somehow in a wordless giddiness which might have been shame. At the time I thought it was a monstrous game, like a child's, but hardly even erotic, played to kill time and defeat fear and loneliness – something the curfew demanded.

Tarzan is an Expatriate

[1967]

Consider the following quotation, from *The Man-Eaters of Tsavo* by Lt.-Col. J. H. Patterson, D.S.O.

". . . Shortly I saw scores of lights twinkling through the bushes; every man in camp turned out, and with tom-toms beating and horns blowing came running to the scene. They surrounded my eyrie, and to my amazement prostrated themselves on the ground before me, saluting me with cries of '*Mabarak! Mabarak!*' which I believe means 'blessed one' or 'Saviour' . . . We all returned in triumph to the camp, where great rejoicings were kept up for the remainder of the night, the Swahili and other African natives celebrating the occasion by an especially wild and savage dance. For my part I anxiously awaited the dawn . . . "

There is a human shape that stands astride this description and a thousand others like it. It is the shape of Tarzan, prime symbol of Africa.

My knowledge of Tarzan is that of a person who, fifteen years ago, spent Sunday afternoons on the living room floor on his elbows reading that serious comic inspired by Edgar Rice Burroughs' novels. Tarzan may be gone from the comics; I have no way of knowing. But I do know that he is here, in Africa, in the flesh. I see him every day.

The Tarzan I remember was a strong white man in a leather loincloth, always barefoot; and he was handsome, a wise mesomorph, powerful, gentle and humorless. The animals all knew him. He spoke to them cryptically, in a sort of private Kitchen Swahili (two of the words he frequently used were *bundolo* and *tarmangani*). The animals replied in bubbles which only Tarzan understood. Although he was known as Tarzan, "The Ape-Man," he was undeniably a man and bore not the slightest trace of simian genes.

There was Jane. She aroused me: her enormous breasts strained the makeshift knots on her monkeyskin brassière; she was also barefoot, an added nakedness that in the case of a woman is certainly erotic, and she walked on the balls of her feet. She was watchful, worried that Tarzan might be in danger. When she sniffed trouble she had a sexy habit of thrusting out those breasts of hers, cocking her head to the side and cupping her hand to her ear. Boy, the odd epicene child, appeared on the living room floor one week and stayed, as pubescent as the day I first laid eyes on him: a slender, hairless little boy scout with his child-sized spear.

And my Tarzan, real or the result of a dim recollection dimmed even further by my being remote in time and place, defined his society and implied its close limits when he said, pointing, "Me Tarzan . . . You Jane . . . Him Boy . . . "

In spite of the fact that there was a green parrot with his claws dug into Tarzan's shoulder, a monkey holding his hand and a lion faithfully dogging his tracks, Tarzan did not admit these creatures to his definition. In the most politic way, by not mentioning them, he excluded the animals from the society of the intimate white three. There was no question of equality: the fact remained that the animals simply were not the same and could therefore never have the same rights as the humans. Tarzan did not aggravate the situation; he asserted his authority over the animals very passively. When there was trouble the animals rallied round, they served Tarzan, grunted their bubble-messages and assisted him. Except in a time of jungle crisis Tarzan had little or nothing to do with them. Distance was understood. Tarzan never became bestial; he ate cooked food and, to my knowledge, never bit or clawed any of his enemies or buggered his functionaries. Yes, of course he swung on vines, beat his chest and roared convincingly, but these gestures were not an expression of innate animalism as much as they were the signal of a certain solidarity with the animals; as gestures they demonstrated futility as well as sympathy, and it was this sympathy that made them seem genuine. But, still, even the skillful pose which the gestures ultimately comprised was not a pose which anyone could bring off. Only Tarzan could beat his chest and win respect. Others would be laughed at.

Having defined his society (a small superior group; white, human, strong) Tarzan still recognized that he was in the jungle. His definition therefore was an assertion of exclusiveness which, coupled with the fact that he did not want to leave the jungle, seemed to indicate that he wanted to be a king; or, if "king" is objectionable, then he wanted to be special, lordly, powerful. We have established the fact that he was not an "ape-man" and we know that he was above the lion and the elephant, both of which are known as King of the Jungle, according to who has faced them (the lion-hunters plump for the lion, the elephant-hunters for the elephant). Above all, he had conquered the animals with an attitude, an air; no force was involved in the conquering and so it was the easiest and most lasting victory. This gave rise to Tarzan's master-servant relationship with the animals rather than a master-slave relationship (the slave does not know his master, the servant does; the servant is overpowered by an attitude, the slave by a whip).

Tarzan was contemptuous of all outsiders, especially those who were either hunters or technicians. When the old scientist and his daughter lose their way in the bush and are confronted by Tarzan, it turns out that Tarzan is wiser than the scientist and Jane has bigger breasts than the daughter; if there is a boy involved, he is a simpleton compared with Boy. The animals feared the botanist in the cork helmet, the anthropologist in the Landrover; Tarzan had either hatred or contempt for them. But though he hated these people who had a special knowledge of the jungle fauna and flora, Tarzan was still interested, in a highly disorganized way, in preserving wildlife and keeping the jungle virgin. Tarzan knew about the jungle: each root, tree, animal and flower, the composition of soil, the yank of the quicksand, the current of rivers. He had conquered by knowing and he was knowledgeable because he lived in the jungle. There was very little brainwork in this. It was a kind of savage osmosis: he took the knowledge through his skin and he was able to absorb this wisdom because he was in Africa. All that was necessary in this learning-experience was his physical presence.

He did not harm the animals; this was enough. He knew everything any animal knew; he lived among the animals but not with them. The animals traipsed after him and sometimes he followed them; still the relationship was a master-servant one, with an important distance implied (no one, for example, ever suspected Tarzan of bestiality). He did not kill as outsiders did; at most he wounded or crippled, though usually he sprang an ingenious trap, embarrassing the enemy with helplessness instead of allowing him the dignity of a violent jungle death. He led a good vegetarian life, a life made better because he had no ambition except to prevent the interruption of his passive rule. He was indolent, but still there was nothing in the jungle Tarzan could not do.

The phrase *in the jungle* is important. Take Tarzan out of the jungle and he would be powerless. His element was the jungle and yet he was not of the jungle. He was clearly an outsider, obviously a man; much more than Robinson Crusoe who was inventive, impatient and self-conscious, Tarzan was the first expatriate.

We should not wonder why Tarzan came to the jungle. The reasons Tarzan had could be the same as those of any white expatriate in Africa. There are five main reasons: an active curiosity in things strange; a vague premonition that Africa rewards her visitors; a disgust with the anonymity of the industrial setting; a wish to be special; and an unconscious desire to stop thinking and let the body take over. All of these reasons are selfish in a degree. Mixed with them may be the desire to do a little good, to help in some way; but this is desire together with the knowledge that the good deeds will be performed in a pleasant climate. This, in the end, is not so much a reason for coming as it is an excuse. The wish to be special (and rewarded) is dominant; the need for assertion – the passive assertion, the assertion of color – by a man's mere physical presence eventually dominates the life of the expatriate. Tarzan must stand out; he is non-violent but his muscles show.

Curiosity is the first to go. It may draw a person away from home but in Africa it diminishes and finally dies. When the expatriate feels he knows the country in which he is working he loses interest. There is a simple level at which the expatriate learns quickly and easily about his surroundings (and no one is more in his surroundings than the expatriate; the lack of privacy is almost total, but privacy is something upon which very few in Africa place a high value). He learns the settler anecdotes and racial jokes, the useful commands for the servants, the endless dialect stories about the habits of Africans and the rules of conduct which are expected of him as a white man in a black country. All of this information is slanted toward white superiority, the African as animal and, again, the kind of assertion that is based on color. A sample Kenyan story concerns a white man who sees an African walking a dog. "Where are you going with that baboon?" the white man asks. "This isn't a baboon, it's a dog," says the African. "I'm not talking to you!" the white man snaps. There are the expatriate truisms: never give an African anything; Africans really don't want anything; if you run over an African on the road you must drive away as fast as you can or you'll be killed by the murderous mob that gathers (this is not refuted even by the staunchest liberals); Africans smell, have rhythm, don't wash, are terribly happy and so forth. There are the vernacular commands, all of which can be learned in a matter of a few days: "Cut the wood," "Dry the dishes," "Mop the floor," "Get bwana's slippers," "Don't be sulky to Memsahib." The rules of conduct for whites are aimed at keeping up expatriate morale: never argue with a fellow expatriate in the presence of an African; always offer a lift to whites you see walking in the road; never be a loner or exclude other whites from your society, especially in up-country places; feel free to drop in on fellow expatriates – expect them to drop in on you; when traveling, get the names of all the whites on your route; develop an anti-Indian prejudice; fornication, conversation and general truck with Africans must be covert and kept to a minimum – sleeping with tribeswomen is bad for the morale of expatriate wives. The jokes, the racial stereotypes, the vernacular commands, the rules of conduct – all of these tell the expatriate that he is different, he is superior, he is Tarzan. This information is sought by the recently arrived expatriate; his confidence is built on such information. When he knows enough so that he won't blunder unknowingly into liberalism and so that he is able to dominate everyone except those in his rigidly defined society, he stops seeking.

He wants to do more than merely stay alive; he *does* want to be special, visible, one of the few. But this is the easiest thing of all, and so surprising in its ease that the result is a definite feeling of racial superiority. His color alone makes him distinct. He does not have to lift a finger. The great moment in the life of every expatriate comes when he perceives that, for the first time in his life, people are watching him; he is not anonymous in a crowd, in a line, in a theater or a bar. With the absence of strict segregation he is even more distinct: he is *among* but not *with*, drinking in a bar where there are many Africans he will stand out. His color sets him apart and those he is among nearly always respect him and keep their distance: the Indian shopkeeper rubs his hands and scurries around trying to please him; the African carries his shopping for twenty cents, singles him out in a crowd and offers to wash his car while the expatriate watches a film, takes his place for a penny in the stamp line at the post office and a hundred other things.

The realization that he is white in a black country, and respected for it, is the turning point in the expatriate's career. He can either forget it or capitalize on it. Most choose the latter. It is not only the simplest path, it is the one that panders most to his vanity and material well-being. He may even decide to fortify his uniqueness by carefully choosing affectations: odd clothes, a walking stick, a lisp, a different accent; he may develop a penchant for shouting at his servants, losing his temper or drinking a quart of whisky a day; he may take to avocados, afternoon siestas or small boys. When the expatriate goes too far with his affectations, his fellow expatriates say he is a victim of "bush fever". But they know better. What the expatriate is doing is preparing his escape, not out of the jungle, but escape to retirement – that long sleep until death comes to kill – within the jungle. Having proven his uniqueness by drawing attention to his color, by hinting through his presence that he is different, by suggesting through a subtle actionless language that he is a racist, and perhaps demonstrating one or two feats of physical or intellectual strength, he retires to a quiet part of the jungle and rests. He is fairly sure that no one will bother him and that he will be comfortable.

Reward is a certainty. I speak about East and Central Africa. There are very few expatriates in these parts of Africa who do not make more money here than they would make at home. The standard of expatriate living is always very high: here the watchful parrot is a Nubian night watchman for the house, and the rest of Tarzan's useful animal servants have their equally talented counterparts in the cook, houseboy, steward, driver, gardener, and so forth. There is a functionary at every turn: carpenters, tailors, garage mechanics, baby-sitters and carwashers – each of whom will work for a song. They have been trained by other Tarzans; there are always more candidates to be trained who are jobless, poor with large families and small gardens and not the slightest notion of either comfort or salary. It is easy to train them, to keep them employed and, especially, to dominate them. If they work poorly they can be fired on the spot. It is unlikely that the Labour Office will get after the former employer and intercede on the fired man's behalf. If the Labour Office did care to make an issue of it, it would probably lose. In the parts of Africa I have lived whites do not lose arguments.

There are further rewards, equally as tempting for Tarzan as the servants and functionaries. There are baggage allowances, expatriation allowances, subsidized housing, squash courts, golf courses, swimming pools and mostly white clubs. The sun shines every day of the year on the flowers. There are holidays: a car trip to Mombasa, climbing and camping in the snow-covered Mountains of the Moon with a score of bearers, a visit to the volcanoes of Rwanda or the brothels of Nairobi, a sail in a dhow, a golfing vacation in the Northern Region. One day's drive from where I write this can take me to pygmies, elephants, naked Karamojong warriors (who, for a shilling, will let themselves be photographed glowering into the lens), leopards, the Nile River, a hydro-electric dam, Emin Pasha's fort, palatial resorts, Murchison Falls or the Congo.

The expatriate has all of these rewards together with a distinct conviction that no one will bother him; he will be helped by the Africans and overrated by his friends who stayed in England or the United States. He is Tarzan, the King of the Jungle. He will come to expect a degree of adulation as a matter of course. He is no longer hurrying down a filthy subway escalator, strewn with ads for girdles, to a crowded train in which he will be breathed upon by dozens of sweating over-dressed people; he is no longer stumbling up another escalator to his home where his children are croaking and shrieking on the floor. Tarzan had his vine, the expatriate has his car and, very likely, driver. The idea of using public transportation does not occur to the expatriate: it exists for the public, not him. Africans will wave to him as he drives by in his car; some, in up-country places, will fall to their knees as he passes. He will have few enemies, but even if he had many, none would matter. Everyone else is on his side. He is Tarzan.

There is the death of the mind. The expatriate does not have to think; he has long since decided that nothing should change, the jungle should not alter. In Africa he is superior and should remain so. Most agree with him; all the people he works with agree with him; Africans with money and position are the most convinced of all that change means upsetting the nature of society.

These Africans have come around to the expatriate point of view; they have been conquered with an attitude and a little money; they settle tribal disputes by saying to the tribesmen, "Let's be English about this" and ask the expatriate's indulgence in not being critical of the brutal and bloody suppression of a tribe or opposition party or minority group. "These are difficult transitional years for our developing country," is the excuse for these purges.

The expatriate does not enter any fray; he takes Tarzan's view: it is wrong — because it is unnatural — to try and settle jungle quarrels. It proves nothing. The animals may chatter and squabble, but this is of no concern to Tarzan; this is nature at her purest and should not be interfered with.

The mind dies and Tarzan discovers flesh. The suspicion about Africa that the expatriate had in a cold English or American suburb is confirmed in a Mombasa bar or a Lagos nightclub when three or four slim black girls begin fighting over him. They also fight for the fat bald man sitting in the corner, for the Italian merchant marine jigging in the center of the floor, with his pants down, for the Yugoslavian ape-man who has just stumbled in and is now tearing the pinball machine apart. The expatriate has gone away from home to give his flesh freedom. He never guessed how simple the whole process was. What makes it all the simpler is that there is no blame attached. Even if there were blame or reprisals, only the embassy would suffer. The expatriate is soon ardently dealing in skin and this, with the death of the mind and the conscious assertion of color, is the beginning of the true Tarzan Complex. The expatriate has been served, waited on, pandered to, pimped for and overpaid; he has fed the image of his uniqueness and his arrogance has reached its full vigor.

There is a plain truth that must be stated as well. This Tarzan, like the Tarzan of the comics, is not an objectionable man. He is not Mr. Kurtz, "Mad" Mike Hoare or Cecil Rhodes. There is very little that can be called sinister about him. There was little duplicity in his reasons for coming to Africa, but overthrowing the government by force is the furthest thing from his mind. What is most striking about him is his ordinariness: he is a very ordinary white person in an extraordinary setting. He is a white man starting to wilt, sweating profusely, among millions of black men, frangipanis, wild animals and bush foliage.

The liberal has it both ways. He enjoys all the privileges of Tarzan and still is able to say that he is a nationalist. He is the reversible Tarzan. His speech is entirely at odds with his actions: he bullies his servants in one breath and advocates class struggle in the next. When there is trouble he becomes Tarzan, with all of Tarzan's characteristic passivity. He does not fight, and yet the schizoid nature of his existence drives him occasionally to apologize for a brutal black regime. The archetypal Tarzan never apologizes; he accepts the behaviour of the animals insofar as it does not bother him, Jane or Boy. The liberal Tarzan denies that there are differences in the jungle and insists that his color means nothing. But his life is much the same as the Tarzan expatriate, and his motives for coming to Africa are likewise the same. He is the most fortunate liberal on earth.

He makes a virtue of keeping silent while the jungle is spattered with gunfire. He knows he will lose his job and have to go home if he criticizes the ruling party. Although he may say he is concerned with freedom, he knows that certain topics are taboo: in Kenya he cannot defend the Asians when they are under attack; in Tanzania, Malawi and a dozen other countries he cannot be critical of the one-party form of government; in Uganda he cannot mention that, one year ago, there was a forcible and bloody suppression of the largest tribe in the country. He believes that he has won over the Africans by saying the right things and praising the injustices. But the African attitude toward him, because it is based on color, is no different from the attitude toward the average non-political expatriate.

The liberal's paradise seems to be a place where he can hold leftist opinions in a lovely climate. Sub-Saharan Africa is one of these paradises: the old order does not alter, the revolutions change nothing and still to be white is to be right; being British is an added bonus. The liberal quacking may continue, and the liberal may pretend that he is not Tarzan, but he is Tarzan as much as any tightlipped civil servant admiring his jacarandas. The Tory Tarzan keeps silent; the liberal Tarzan says "Hear, hear" when the preventive detention legislation is passed.

A person should not agree to work in a country that demands silence of him. This rids the person of any human obligations and helps him to become Tarzan, the strong white man who has what he wants at the expense of millions of people who serve him in one way or another; he has everything, those around him have nothing. The very fact that silence is a condition of getting the job should indicate, especially to the academics, that the government is not ready for him. With this release from any feelings of sympathy or any real obligations toward the people he is among, the expatriate has a lot of free time to think, but no set standard for reflection except the excesses of past Tarzans. In this climate, with no sensible limits on thought, fascism is easy. This is the extreme no one expected before he came. The simple selfishness that was a part of all his reasons for coming to Africa had nothing to do with fascism, but within the slowly decaying condition of mind that is realised after years of sun and crowds, disorder and idleness, is a definite racial bias. It is not a scientific thing; rather, it is the result of being away, being idle among those he does not know. His voice gets shrill, unrecognizable, but he cannot speak; he has taken a vow of silence; his bad temper increases. An extended time in this unnatural pose can make him hateful; a black face laughing in the heat or screaming, a knot of black people merely standing muttering on the street corner can make him a killer.

The sun should make no one a fascist, but it is more than the sun. It is a whole changed way of looking and feeling: "I now understand *apartheid*," says the Israeli hotel-owner who has spent two years in Nigeria; "Frankly, I like the stupid Africans best," says the white army officer in Malawi; "I wouldn't give you a shilling for the whole lot of them," says the businessman in Kenya; "Oh, I know they're frightfully inefficient and hopeless at politics — but, you know, they're terribly sweet," says the liberal English lady. If I stay here much longer I will begin to talk like this as well. I do not want that to happen. I do not want to be Tarzan and cannot think of anything drearier or more stupid and barbarous than racism. The last thing I want to be is the King of the Jungle, any jungle, and that includes Boston as much as it does Bujumbura.

Somewhere along the way there was an understanding reached between Tarzan and his followers. Either it was a collaboration (don't bother me and I won't bother you) or it was true conquering that was in some ways permanent. There must have been this understanding or there would not be so many Tarzans today. I refuse to collaborate or conquer and further refuse to sit by while the double talk continues. Someone must convince the African governments that fascism is not the special property of the Italians and Germans, and ask why independent African rule has made it infinitely easier for Tarzan, complete with *fasces*, to exist undisturbed and unchallenged.

Cowardice

[1967]

In the old days, young boys with nothing to do used to stand around drugstores talking excitedly of picking up girls. They now have other choices – they can pick up guns or protest signs. I tend to take the druggist's view: have an ice cream and forget the choices. I intend to give in neither to the army nor to the peace movement.

I am now certain of my reason for thinking this: I am a coward.

It has not always been this way. I used to think I was a person of high principles. The crooked thing about high principles is that they can live in thin air. I am fairly sure mine did. For the past five years my reaction to anything military was based on borrowed shock.

I still believe that war is degrading, that it gets us no place, and that one must not hurt anyone else. The pacifists say this and the government calls them cowards. The pacifists protest that they are not cowards. I feel no kinship with the government. I have some sympathy for the folk who call themselves pacifists because I believe many of them to be as cowardly as I am. But I see no reason to be defensive about it. Certainly they should not have to put up with all that humiliation on the sidewalk. As cowards they should be entitled to a little peace. They should not have to waste their time and risk arrest scrawling slogans on the subway or walking for hours carrying heavy signs. Guns may be heavier, but why carry either one?

A soldier shuffled nervously in front of me while I stood in line at the East Side Airlines Terminal in New York two years ago. He turned abruptly and told me that he was going to Oakland, California. I told him I was going to London and then to Uganda. Harmless talk – the kind that travelers make with ease. He surprised me by breaking convention and continuing what should have been an ended conversation. After Oakland he would be going to Vietnam. I clucked at his misfortune and as we both thought presumably of death he said, "Somebody's got to go."

But not me, I thought. I got my ticket confirmed and a week later I was in Africa, far from the draft board, even farther from Vietnam. Five years ago I would have hectored the soldier with some soul-swelling arguments. I was a pacifist and a very noisy one at that.

When I was told that I must join the ROTC at the University of

Massachusetts in 1960 I refused. Then I tried to think why I had refused. I had no friends who were pacifists but I did not need a manual to tell me that I hated violence. I dreaded the thought of marching or taking guns apart; I quietly resolved never to go into the army, the ROTC, or anything that was vaguely military. The thought of wearing a uniform appalled me and the thought of being barked at frightened me. I wanted to write a book and be left alone. In two hours I was a pacifist, a month later I was the only healthy non-Quaker at the University exempt from ROTC. A few years later I was arrested by the campus police for leading a demonstration (that was in 1962 when demonstrations were rare and actually bothered people). I bunched together with a dozen more pacifists, organized some more protests, and, the year I graduated, ROTC was put on a voluntary basis by a faculty committee. Although the committee was composed of friends of mine it was not really a put-up job. ROTC was just not consistent with high principles.

Before I was excused from ROTC I had to meet an ad hoc committee: the colonels of the army and the air force ROTC, the chaplain, and the provost. The army colonel, a man with a passion for writing patriotic letters to the student newspaper, listened to my woolly tirade against the military (quotations from Jesus, Norman Mailer, Tolstoy, and Eugene V. Debs). He rose, his medals jangled at me, and he thundered: "What do you know about war!"

It couldn't have been plainer, but for a pacifist it is an easy question to answer. "Nothing, but . . ." And then the atrocity stories, a smattering of religion, and a few abstract nouns. I could have appealed to the governor if they had not let me out of ROTC. The governor was coming up for re-election and would not have wanted to appear a jingo by making me take ROTC or a communist by excusing me. The committee quietly released me from my obligation.

If I had told them I was a coward they would not have wasted a minute with me. I would have been given regulation shoes and told to keep them clean; I would have been expected to know all the parts of an M-1 carbine; I would have had to stab sandbags with a bayonet every Tuesday after entomology class. So I did not tell them I was a coward, although that would have been the honest thing to do. The colonel, a man experienced in these matters, insinuated that I was one, but good taste prevented his speaking the word.

The ROTC has never done much more than bruise a man. Its contribution has been to teach college boys marching. Ironically, the people who object to ROTC end up marching many more miles than the sophomores on the parade ground. Peace movements are successful usually because they are so militaristic in organization and attitude. The language of the peace groups is always military-sounding: fighting, campaign, movement, ranks, marches – even freedom awards, for valor. There is keen envy among the groups: which college has the most picketers, the bloodiest and most agonizing signs, which men have the most handsome beards. Tempers are short among demonstrators; they have ridden a long way to be grim. The protester from the Amherst area gets off near the White House and begins grousing: "Jesus, we just got here and they expect us to start picketing!"

I was persuaded by a friend to picket in Times Square against nuclear testing one cold night in 1962. We had to report to a cigar-smoking gentleman who gave each of us a sign and instructions: "Walk clockwise, single file around the army recruiter booth. Remember, don't talk, don't stop walking, and if you want to leave just raise your hand and I'll get someone to carry your sign. Let's practice walking without the sign first, then we'll start. Okay, everyone line up here . . ."

The little man did not carry a sign. He was the sergeant, we were the privates. He marched beside us and used his big cigar as a swagger stick. Every so often he would tell someone to pipe down or walk straight. We got off to a rough start, but soon got the hang of it, convincing me that, if nothing else, we responded well to discipline and would all have made pretty good soldiers.

Many pacifists I have known are scared out of their wits that they will be drafted. Is this fright caused by seeing moral laws broken and all Gandhi's hunger strikes made worthless by a man's head – or let's say, a pacifist's head – being blown apart? Is the fright a fear of death or a fear of failed principles? Is the refusal to join in the slaughter inspired by feelings of cowardice or moral conviction? I am thinking of pacifists who have been taught their fear after being beaten up, threatened by armed boys, and seeing brutality up close.

I lived in a crowded suburb of a large city in the United States and I had to pass through an alley – the lights at the opposite end: salvation – to get a bus when I went to the movies. The last time I passed through that alley five figures came toward me. I knew they wanted to beat me up. I stood still and hoped they would pass by, although what I imagined – being surrounded, having the youngest one push me down in the snow and punch me while I curled up and groaned, hearing them laugh and then running away, until my throat ached – actually happened, and the next ten minutes were a blur of cruelty. I was frightened but I would not let anger take the place of my fright.

This is really what a coward is, I believe: a person who is afraid of nearly everything and most of all afraid of anger. His own anger is a special danger to him. He accepts his solitary hardship and pays the price of withdrawing. He knows that each attempt to deal with violence may require summoning all the inhuman bravado he can contain. The bravery is a cover. Its weight intimidates the flesh beneath it. Since bravery implies a willingness to risk death, the fear to be brave becomes the fear to die. I am unable to understand what could make me risk death: neither patriotism, a desire to preserve anything, nor a hatred of anyone could rouse me to fight.

I have always wondered how people do things which require risk, whether there is not a gap in their consciousness, a suspension of judgment while the dangerous act is performed. I have never felt this release, even momentarily, from the consequences of risk. Remembered incidents intrude: street fights I could not bear to watch, threats I walked away from, vicious glares that made me sick, and some time ago being in a bar in Washington, D. C., where a woman on a stool kept calling the dishwasher a nigger. She leaned on the bar and slobbered: "You a nigger, ain't you? You know you are; you nothin' but a nigger. You ain't no Creole like you say. You a nigger . . ." And the Negro behind the bar whistled and looked at no one. I wanted to shout at the woman. But with a fear that quickly became nausea I left.

Leaving is a cure for nothing, though if one goes to the right spot one may have time to reflect usefully on why one left. Four years ago I joined the Peace Corps, was sent to Malawi, in Central Africa, and taught school. Unlike most people in their early twenties, I had personal servants, a big house, and good public relations. My relatives said I was really sacrificing and doing good work (there is a school of thought that assumes if one is in Africa one is, *ipso facto*, doing good work). I was happy in my job. I was not overworked. And I had joined the Peace Corps for what I now see were selfish reasons: I had thought of responsibilities I did not want – marriage seemed too permanent, graduate school too hard, and the army too brutal. The Peace Corps is a sort of Howard Johnson's on the main drag into maturity. Usually life is pleasant, sometimes difficult, occasionally violent. A good time to find out whether or not you are a coward.

Violence in Malawi became common. The resignation of several high-ranking politicians and the firing of a few others threw the country into a nightmare of suspicion late in 1964. Many people suspected of collaborating with the ex-cabinet members were choked or hacked to death. One day I was walking home along the dirt road that led to my house. I saw smoke. Up ahead I saw three Youth Leaguers dashing into the bush. I knew they had just burned something, but I was not sure what it was. I was sure that it was serious and became worried. Just over the hill was a truck in flames. The cab of the truck was crackling and I could make out stiff black shapes in the holes of the flames. I detoured around the burning truck and went home. At home I had a drink, locked the door, and went to bed.

About a week later I was on a train and going North to the lake shore.
At each stop, boys, Youth Leaguers anywhere from ten to forty years old,
got on the train and demanded to see the party cards of the African
travelers. If a person did not have a card he was beaten. An old man next
to me was dragged out of his seat, thrown to the floor, and kicked. Just
before they dragged him out of the seat he looked at me (we had been
talking about how terrible it was this thing was happening and I said that
it made me very angry) and his hand reached out for my sleeve. I moved –
a timid reflex – against the window and he missed my sleeve. They quickly
got him onto the floor. His screams were terrific and he wept as they
kicked him. No one in the car moved. Several minutes later, another and
another were thrown to the floor and beaten. Outside the train a man was
being chased and punched as he ran through a gauntlet of people. His
hands were pushed against his face for protection. He reeled across the
platform and bumped into a fence. I saw him huddled against the fence –
the boys hitting him with sticks – as the train pulled away. I could not tell
if he was screaming. I had closed the window. By the time the train had
gone about a hundred miles, the car was almost empty; most of the
occupants had been dragged out and beaten. I stepped out at my station
and walked to a taxi. It was hard to suppress an intense feeling of relief.
The cards that the men were being asked to produce were sold by the
Youth Leaguers for two shillings. Many refused to buy them because they
did not believe in the present regime and would not compromise their
principles.

In August of 1965 I drove a car through the Northern region of
Malawi. I passed through fourteen roadblocks and reached the border-
post at about ten in the evening. The gate – the customs' barrier – was
closed. I saw some men standing near it. My headlights were still on and
the windows of the car were rolled up. The men appeared to be saying
something but I could not hear them. Only after a few moments did I
realize that my headlights were shining into their eyes. I shut off the
engine and rolled down the window. As soon as the window was open a
crack I heard the loud shouting of the men. They stood where they were
and ordered me out of the car. They raised their rifles to my face. When
the guns were pointed at me my body started to shake, my legs felt as if
they had gone suddenly boneless. I was numb. I knew I was about to be
shot. I was waiting to be murdered. *If they're going to shoot me let them
do it quickly!* flashed through my mind. The feeling of standing there on
that border – a border that had been raided four times, resulting in the
deaths of many more people than even the large number reported in the
press – in the darkness, the bullets crashing into my shirt, bursting
through my back with a fist-sized lump of flesh and clotted blood, my
body dropping into the sand by the light of a fizzing lantern, the men

standing over me and firing into my inert body, my head broken open . . . It was unbearable. And my papers were in order, my passport was in my hand high above my head. But the guns! The shouting! I was so afraid that I think I could have been moved to action – I felt capable of killing them, or attempting it. Yet this would have been absurd because I had done nothing wrong. The guns remained pointed into my face. The feeling persisted: I wanted to shoot them or be shot. I wanted something to happen, something violent that would settle the whole affair.

They told me I must walk toward them. This I did, all the while trying to prevent myself from lunging at them in an attempt to incite them to shoot me and get it over with. But they did not shoot me. They swore at me and took me into the police station. I pleaded with them to let me through the barrier (I felt that as long as I remained on their side of the border I was guilty of something). I convinced them and that night drove until two in the morning along the narrow bush track into Tanzania.

When my Peace Corps stretch was over I decided to stay in Africa. I realized that there was violence in Africa, but I started to understand it. I had reached two conclusions: one, the violence was either tribal or political – I had no tribe and was not involved in politics and so the violence was not directed against me; two, life in Africa is simple, provincial, dull generally but with stirrings here and there, evidence of growth that I might help with. Day-to-day life in Africa is much like day-to-day life in New Hampshire: people strolling in the sunshine or standing around the local bar spitting on the sidewalk; there is gossip about love affairs and car-buying, there is time for talking or reading or writing. Sometimes there is trouble at the castle and the gun-shots echo down through the huts. Trouble happens around powerful people, politicians and chiefs. I live among neither.

On my way to work, gliding through the green in my car, I think: *you can be drafted today.* I am twenty-five; I have bad eyes, but am otherwise physically fit. I have no wife. My job as a teacher here in Uganda may exempt me from the draft, but there is no guarantee of that. My draft board knows where I am. President Johnson has said that he will again increase the number of troops in Vietnam. The war is a jumble of figures: the number of troops and planes, the number of bombings and raids, the number of dead or wounded. The numbers appear every day in the Uganda papers as cold as football scores. I add flesh and blood to them and I am afraid.

As a coward I can expect nothing except an even stronger insistence that I go and fight. *Fight whom?* A paradox emerges; the coward recognizes no enemies. Because he wants always to think that he will not be harmed (although he is plagued by the thought that he will be), there is no evil in his world. He wills evil out of his world. Evil is something that

provokes feelings of cowardice in him; this feeling is unwelcome, he
wants to forget it. In order to forget it he must not risk hating it. Indeed,
the coward hates nothing just as he loves nothing. These emotions are a
gamble for him; he merely tolerates them in others and tries to squash or
escape them in himself. He will condemn no one when he is free from
threat.

The word coward is loaded with awful connotations. It does not
ordinarily lend itself to inclusion in logical discourse because it quickly
inspires two assumptions. The first is that cowardice does not indicate
how we really feel; the second is that we have principles which are in no
way related to, and always more powerful than, our feelings, our flesh.
The first assumption implies that the feeling of cowardice is somehow
fraudulent; a coward is discounted as authentic because of the word's
associations: it is allied to "tail" (Latin: *cauda*), one of its synonyms is
"fainthearted" or, more plainly, "womanish". To accept this definition is
to reach the conclusion that the coward's head will clear, that he will
cease to become weak if he thinks a bit. The second assumption is that
one's principles will overcome one's feelings. I would suggest, if my flesh
is any indicator, that this is not the case.

Talking a mixture of rubbish and rhetoric to get out of ROTC,
picketing the Military Ball, sympathizing with those Californians who
were dragged down cement stairs by the police, their spines bumping over
the edges, seeing some logic in Wolfgang Borchert's simple advice to
pacifists ("Sag, 'NEIN'!") – these are ego-inspired feelings; the ego fights
for air, rejects absorption, anonymity, and death. Since we have perhaps
far less dogma cluttering our lives than any other people in history, these
ego-inspired feelings which can move us to acts of protest may prove
essentially good, the principle of non-violence made out of a deep feeling
of cowardice may prove the truest. It is bound to have its opposite
motives: Cardinal Spellman's blessing of the war in Vietnam was one of
these acts of the ego and certainly not the result of any biblical dogma he
had been taught.

All of this goes against existing laws. It is illegal to be afraid to go into
the army. If I tell the draft board to count me out because I am afraid, they
will answer, "That's impossible . . ." But it is not impossible, it is only
illegal, I will say; I saw a man die, I saw a man kicked to death, I held the
crumbling blue body of a drowned man in my hands . . . This is feeling; I
will be asked for principles, not feelings. Fear is selfish and so no amount
of fear, even if it stems from observed violence, is acceptable grounds for
exemption.

Yet ours is not a military-minded nation; this is clear to everyone. The
president of a Chicago draft board was quoted as saying a few months
ago: "I've been threatened half-a-dozen times. Guys say they're gonna kill

me if they see me on the street . . ." Is it the thought that war is degrading and immoral that makes this half-dozen take the trouble to threaten the life of their draft board president? Or is it something else? We know we are terrible soldiers, that we are not bold; we have placed our trust in the hardware of war. ("Thank God for the atom bomb," my brother's sergeant said when he saw the platoon marching higgledy-piggledy across the parade ground.)

I say "we" – I mean "I". If I allow myself to be drafted into the army I will be committing suicide. The army is to a coward what a desert is to an agoraphobe, an elaborate torment from which the only escape serves to torment him further. The coward marches with death; the agoraphobe stalks the rolling dunes in search of an enclosure.

I sit here in a cool dark room in the middle of Africa thousands of miles from the people in the city hall who want to draft me. I sit down in the middle of it all and try to decide why I do not want to go. And that is all anyone can do, try to be honest about what he feels, what he's seen or thinks he's seen. He can offer this disturbing vision to those who are not sure why they are unwilling. Folksongs and slogans and great heroes are no good for us now, and neither is the half-truth that is in every poem or every melodious sentence that hides barbaric notions.

When I think of people trying to convince themselves that high principles result from merely hugging answers I think of the reverse of the old fairy story: a princess in her hunger kisses a handsome prince and turns him into a toad. The answers will not come by forcing ourselves upon dogma. The issue is that we should admit once and for all that we are frightened. We will not have told ourselves a lie and, after this truth which is a simple one, maybe even ugly, we can begin to ask new questions.

Seven Burmese Days

[1970]

An Indian merchant in Rangoon recently gained considerable local fame by paying (so one version of the story goes) 210,000 *kyats* for a five-year-old Alfa Romeo which the Revolutionary Government of Burma was auctioning off. "And the funny thing is," my informant, an Asian diplomat, said with only the faintest trace of a smile, "the engine block cracked after two weeks." I was so intrigued by the high price (at the official rate of exchange it's about $46,000) that I asked several other people if they had heard of the Indian and the Alfa. Everyone I spoke to had heard, and other, lower prices were quoted, but the difference was only a few thousand dollars. Even if the Indian had bought his *kyats* from a pouch-wearing Tamil money changer on a Singapore pavement, at three or four times the official rate, that is still a lot of money to pay for a used car with a defective engine block.

Burmans, and foreigners in Burma, compulsively quote prices. In a country where no overt political talk is tolerated, it is a form of political discussion. "See this motorbike?" I was asked (it was a ten-year-old Triumph). "Guess how much?" I named a fair price. The Burman cleared his throat with pleasure, spat, and took me by the wrist. A month before he had paid 4500 *kyats* (approximately $935) for the battered machine. Then he lifted my wrist and said, "Omega" – a nice eye for watch brands: another Burmese characteristic – "how much?" I told him it wasn't for sale. We were standing at the foot of Mandalay Hill, before two towering stone lions and a sign FOOT WEARING IS FORBIDDEN. I took off my shoes – "Stockings too," said the Burman apologetically – and socks, and began climbing the holy stairs. He kicked off his rubber sandals and followed me, muttering, "Omega, Omega."

And spitting. "Foot wearing" is forbidden, but bicycles are not – provided they are pushed and not ridden – and neither is spitting. Dodging great gouts of betel juice, I climbed, and soon others joined us. A troop of boys quickly took up the Omega chant. On every landing there was a temple, a soft-drink stall ("Dagon Pure Orange – Bottled in Rangoon With Distilled Water"), and a sugar-water machine which squeezed split canes in a contraption that resembled an old laundry wringer. Halfway up the hill I stopped, had a Super Soda, and examined some statuary in wire cages, life-sized plaster figures, brightly painted and horrific as a Tiger Balm ointment tableau: a supine figure sticking his tongue out at a crow perched on his chest and tearing bright blue intestinal coils, yards of shiny hose, from a gaping hole in the man's belly; another satisfied man with a cutlass, squatting next to a disembowelled deer. I slipped a coin into a cast-iron machine, and three figures in a window were set into motion: a clockwork man swept a path with a wire broom, a clockwork saffron-robed monk shuffled on the path, and a clockwork devotee raised and lowered his clasped hands to the monk.

We set off again, stopping once for a boy to piss on the sacred hill (according to legend, Buddha climbed the hill and pointed down at what was to become the Center of the Universe, later Fort Dufferin, and now Burmese Army Headquarters for the Northwest Command). In the temple at the top of the hill, where there is a massive gold Buddha smiling toward the army barracks, I collapsed onto a bench in the 106-degree heat. I was surrounded by Burmese quoting ridiculously high prices for my watch. Very clearly I said, "My *mother* gave me this watch," and in a moment they were gone.

They had told me how much they had paid for their *longyis*, how much their shirts cost; I turned the conversation to politics for, since the textile industry is nationalized and all the prices are determined by the government, surely this was a political matter. They were silent. One said, "We can't say," and that was that. I had broken the rules by mentioning politics; one must mention only high prices for government goods. In a Burmese house in Mandalay, I asked about former Premier U Nu. "That," said my host, "is a political matter." He smiled; end of conversation. His son, a law student, broke in: "Burmese people! Happy people! Never solly, always jolly!" He told me afterward that his father had been destroyed financially by General Ne Win, the present Premier, and had decided to spend the rest of his life "in meditation".

Mandalay, according to the official Revolutionary Government *Guidebook* (printed in Calcutta by Sri L. C. Roy at Gossain and Company, 7/1 Grant Lane), "is now inevitably putting on a mantle of modernity." I was dining one evening in Mandalay with some doctors. Outside the hotel, on the dirt road (the *Guidebook*: ". . . curiously enough, alphabetically named A, B, C, D etc.") where that morning I had seen a dead dog, its hindquarters in a paper bag, a tonga clattered past – a pony cart with two tiny kerosene lamps aglow next to the driver. The doctors worked at the Mandalay General Hospital (built in 1924), and their talk was of amoebic dysentery and hepatitis. I asked about cholera. The doctor next to me said, "This isn't the season . . . but it's coming."

"We have been suffering, oh, we have been *suffering*," said a doctor across the table. He poured himself a glass of warm Mandalay Pale Ale. "Suffering. Not for a decade, but for a century, I should say. For a *century*."

I was interested, and asked him to explain. This produced a silence at the table. A fork scraped, and finally there was a voice: "Mr Paul, where are you domiciling?"

In Rangoon (the *Guidebook*: ". . . Mandalay has not the fast tempo of Rangoon"), crouched on the steps of a huge mock-Edwardian building, were a languid prostitute and three pimps. "Go-betweens," said the Burman with me. I made a feeble joke about the girl, wondering aloud whether she had been nationalized yet. "Social and economic upheaval," said the Burman, raising his hands. I asked about the buildings around us: so many, so empty! "Social and economic upheaval," he said. I asked about the disenfranchised Indians; his reply was the same.

The decrepitude of the buildings in Rangoon is almost grand. The surfaces are shabby, but the shapes are extravagant, and the workmanship is obvious (Corinthian columns support one veranda; another, very graceful, is of wrought-iron lyres); their dereliction has splendor. Some have spires and others a score of ambitious balconies with pockmarked balusters or flowery balustrades, peeling yellow shutters, and lines of motionless laundry hung out to dry – the clothes-lines strung from the blossom of a cornice to the studs of that ornate pillar. Dates and names are given in medallions at the top of each building: 1903, 1914, 1922, 1927; Irrawaddy Chambers, Dawson's Bank, and The Chartered Bank (both painted out but legible). The defunct Burman Herald Building is high and whitewashed, and black metal urns decorate the parapet of the roof. The General Hospital is a seedy palace with towers and spires, bridges and buttresses and yellow cornices, and parked in front are three tongas, a 1936 Chevy, and fifty patients. The High Court and the Secretariat, both with domes and spires, red brick, yellow trim. And dozens with names like The Suleiman Building, The Abdullah Building, Arya Samaj Hall, The Neogy Building; those signs are painted out too, and green government signs in white Burmese script are hung on the porticoes: National Bank, Revolutionary Government Reading Room, National Teak Marketing Board. On Sule Pagoda Road, there is a bizarre three-story building with mullioned windows, crazily framed and blacked out, lozenge-shaped openings in crenellated towers, red battlements. This building bore two painted-out plaques – J. E. de Bain and The Castle – and one green government signboard – National Insurance Company.

On Bogyoke Aung San Street (formerly Montgomery) the Central Jail is being pulled down. The workmen were surprised to get a visitor and willingly showed me around the six enormous cell blocks which radiate in clumsy spokes from a central courtyard and administration building. They pointed out scratchings on the cell floors made in the teak planks by bored prisoners, the Burmese equivalent of tick-tack-toe. One man told me the place was one hundred and seven years old – the seven gave the date a certain credibility; in fact, I couldn't imagine the Burmese pulling down a building less than a hundred years old. The only market in Mandalay is the Zegyo Bazaar, designed and built in 1903 by an Italian, Count Caldrari (who was also the first secretary of the Mandalay Municipality). I stole a small sign from over a cell door in the Central Jail. It reads: 56' by 26½' by 12' – CUBICAL CONTENTS 17967 – ACCOMMODATION FOR 28. It is only a short hop from the Central Jail to the Pegu Club, now an Officers' Mess of the Burmese Army. The Pegu Club was to Rangoon what the Selangor Club was to Kuala Lumpur and the Tanglin Club to Singapore (but these two are still going strong). The sentry said that he would have let me look around, but as it happened, a senior officer (the sentry bulged his eyes to illustrate how senior) had just arrived and was inside.

"What is your country?" is a question the stranger will ask as you pass him on the street (also: "Change money – good price?" and "Want girl? Chinese, Burmese, Indian, anything?"). To frustrate Omega-hunters and those (many it seemed) who desired to buy my trousers when I refused to sell my watch, I said that I came from Singapore. They know that Singapore is mostly Chinese, and the Burmese have opinions about the Chinese. "Chinese, let me tell you about the Chinese," said a Burman whose name was U Georgie. "They save a lot of money, a *lot* of money." He made a wrapping motion with his hands and then threw the invisible wrapped thing away. "Then they throw it away. Gambling." He looked at me. "How do the Chinese make money? Easy. A Chinaman wants a cheroot. He sees a broken one in a monsoon drain. He picks it up and wipes it off. He smokes it. He saves a few *pyas*. Easy. And Indians. Do you know what the Indians do with their women . . .?"

All the Burmese have racial opinions, but this is not unusual in a country with such a mixed population and with cities yet divided into ethnic districts: Chinatown in Rangoon; a walled-in Gujarati community in Mandalay announcing its vegetarianism with a sign BE KIND TO ANIMALS BY NOT EATING THEM; Tamil and European districts, the most elegant being the American compound for Embassy personnel. (There is an American Club and a private American commissary which stocks peanut butter and cornflakes. The lowliest person at the American Embassy has a car and a driver – officially, Rangoon is "a hardship post".) Whole towns in Upper Burma are populated with Nepalese – the remnants, children and grandchildren, of demobbed colonial soldiers.

A very large number of town-dwelling Burmese speak English. I met several enterprising fellows who had started English Institutes (they were civil servants; their "Institutes" started classes at six in the evening). In Nyaungu, signs in English announce a literacy campaign; the English is for the many tourists who visit Nyaungu's ruins. (It is expensive to be literate in Burma – a cheap Burmese paperback costs at least one U.S. dollar.) I complimented one pavement bookseller on his English; pleased with the compliment he recited this sentence: "I am enduring exposure . . . to the sun's powerful rays . . . before I reach my destination." He removed his spectacles and repeated it, looking at the sky.

Much of their English may be learned from British and American films. On the train to Mandalay I met the manager of a Bhamo cinema. "Cowboy films are very popular," he said. An Anthony Quinn Western ran eighteen days, four shows a day, in his cinema. "Maybe the Burmese like Anthony Quinn," I said. No, said the manager: *The Visit* (Anthony Quinn and Ingrid Bergman) ran only two days. He was returning to Bhamo after a week of film-going in Rangoon and was anxious to discuss the films he had just seen: *What a Way to Go* (an all-star cast, including Shirley MacLaine, Paul Newman, Robert Mitchum); *Our Man Flint* ("America's Playboy Hero!"); *The Adventurers* (Alain Delon, from the book of the same name by Harold Robbins); *King Kong Escapes* (directed by Ishiro Honda); *Five for Hell, Cosa Nostra, An Arch Enemy of the FBI* ("The Untold Story of the FBI's Crackdown on the Kings of Crime . . ."). There are many Indian and Burmese films, and there is a fairly large Burmese film industry (the pictures of film stars adorn the temples they have visited), but all Burmese films have to include at least sixty per cent socialism (a Burman's statistic: I didn't question it).

Not surprisingly, the cinema manager had an American accent. He was on his way back to Bhamo to screen *That Darn Cat*, which he had picked up from the Film Distribution Board of the Revolutionary Government. We were having a lively talk about films, and I was marveling at his knowledge of directors and actors. The train had just stopped at Toungoo, where we had each picked up a supply of cold Mandalay Pale Ale which we were drinking (he through a straw) in the Buffet Car of the train. Our talk was interrupted by the train guard, who told the manager to take his beer elsewhere: it was forbidden to drink beer in the Buffet Car. The reprimand was in Burmese, but the tone was unmistakable and I started to creep out with my bottles. Both train guard and manager were deeply hurt; both motioned me to my seat and urged me to drink. And the manager said, "You are an exceptional case."

Tourists are welcome, treated with enormous courtesy, invited to Burmese homes, photographed, and squired around and given special privileges. I was told that I needn't worry about getting a seat on the plane from Mandalay to Nyaungu because if the plane was full I would be given the seat of a Burmese who would be ordered out and requested to wait for the next plane. This sounds much worse than it works out in practice: on the Fokker Friendship from Mandalay to Nyaungu I was the only passenger. The pretty stewardess spent the trip eating her lunch (which she invited me to share) from a palm leaf. I asked her how she liked her work. "Sometimes," she said, "I get fed up."

Package tours fly in daily from Bangkok, and the tourists are whisked by plane from town to town where waiting Japanese buses take them from sight to sight; then lunch from a hamper packed in Rangoon; then a hotel (average price about $13 a night, with breakfast). "See Burma in Four Days," is the boast of one travel agency in Bangkok.

"Wake up, Father, here's the plane," I heard an elderly American lady say to her sleeping husband at the airport in Nyaungu. The man was curled up on the bench next to her. One sees the package tourists in most of the large towns; they have an exhausted, cheated look in their eyes, and many seem beyond caring what Burma has to offer. It was fun to watch the American man, sixty-five if he was a day, playing solitaire with his back to the blood-red sun spectacularly dissolving into the Irrawaddy at Pagan. But not all the tourists come in packages, and most of Burma's visitors fit V. S. Naipaul's description, in *An Area of Darkness*, of the "new type of American whose privilege it was to go slumming about the world and sometimes scrounging, exacting a personal repayment for a national generosity".

I witnessed an American girl being asked by two Burmese whether they could buy a piece of batik cloth from her. Their price seemed fair; she was burdened by a bulging rucksack; but she was unreasonably indignant. I asked her why she didn't sell. "When I go to a place," she said, "I don't expect to give people things. I'm a guest – I expect them to give *me* things." Her next stop was to be Calcutta.

In Pagan I spent some hours with an American hippie. Here was no scrounger; he had just come from New Zealand and Australia, where he had been, he said, "dealing" (selling drugs). He showed me a wad of money and a sheaf of air tickets. One ticket was for Switzerland, "where we have a villa". He wore only a pair of shorts, and his hair was fixed with what my mother used to call bobby pins. I learned a little bit about current LSD prices from him after he pointed to my head and said, "You got this temple here . . . you should find out what's inside it." I noted his figures: a dealer gets one ounce of acid; this costs $2,000 but is good for making 4,000 tablets ("tabs", "hits") which can be sold for five to seven dollars apiece. He was thoroughly contented with his lot; his grievance was with Asians, whom he had come to dislike. He explained this to a Burmese architect who was in Pagan to supervise the building of a luxury hotel: "I used to think you Asians knew where it was at . . . and now I been all over Asia and, like, now I can see you're all fucked in the head."

The architect became attentive.

"Like . . . " – his speech came in bursts and grunts; his fuddled brain couldn't seem to keep track of more than four words at a time –". . . I try to talk to you . . . you know, I try to" – a batting motion with the hands – "I try to *hit in* . . . but, Jesus, you're heavy" – a weighing gesture – "You Asians are really heavy . . . hung up on gadgets . . . heavy . . . I can't talk to you. You're too . . . heavy . . . "

Then why was he in Pagan?

"Getting . . . some really good vibrations," he said. "There were some . . . good people here . . ."

"Yes, Buddha," said the architect.

He was off to Katmandu very soon, he said. But surely Nepalese were Asians? No, he said, he was going to Katmandu to visit the Hog Farm, an American commune which had just been set up there by a man called "Wavy Gravy".

The tourist trade, just beginning, might manage to accomplish what Kubla Khan, centuries of Chinese invasions, British colonialism, and the Japanese occupation could not do – make the Burmese solly instead of jolly. I was talking to the barman in the long bar of the Strand Hotel; I was wondering what was the name of the song the Bengali orchestra was playing in the empty lounge (was it "Roses from the South"?), and he was saying, "I don't know, but it's an old tune." A tall American walked in resolutely and shook a fistful of chits in the barman's face.

"You've made a mistake. I've just worked it out. I've been drinking with my friends for half an hour and the bill comes to twenty-five American dollars. That's impossible."

The barman put on a pair of glasses and examined the chits. "Almost a hundred *kyats*. It's correct."

"That's highway robbery."

Wearily, the barman took a tattered drink menu and handed it over. "Here are the prices. You work it out. You'll see it's correct."

"You're cheating me! This is outrageous."

"I am not cheating you," said the barman, weariness giving way to annoyance. "This is a government hotel. Those are government prices."

"Then you should get a new government!" The American threw down the required amount and left as the barman, raising his voice, said, "They'll lock you up for that."

In Asia a city should be judged not by the number of rats scuttling in its streets but on the rats' cunning and condition. In Singapore the rats are potbellied and as sleek as housepets; they crouch patiently near noodle stalls, certain of a feed; they are quick, with bright eyes, and hard to trap.

In Rangoon I sat in an outdoor café toying with a glass of beer and heard the hedge near me rustle; four enfeebled, scabby rats, straight off the pages of *La Peste*, tottered out and looked around. I stamped my foot. They moved back into the hedge; and now everyone in the café was staring at me. It happened twice. I drank quickly and left, and glancing back saw the rats emerge once more and sniff at the legs of the chair where I had been sitting.

At five-thirty one morning in Rangoon, I dozed in the hot, dark compartment of a crowded train, waiting for it to pull out of the station. A person entered the toilet; there was a splash outside; the door banged. Another entered. This went on for twenty minutes, until dawn, and I saw that outside splashing and pools of excrement had stained the tracks and a litter of crumpled newspapers – *The Working People's Daily* – a bright yellow. A rat crept over to the splashed paper and nibbled then tugged; two more rats, mottled with mange, licked, tugged, and hopped in the muck. Another splash, and the rats withdrew; they returned, gnawing. There was a hawker's voice, a man selling Burmese books with bright covers. He shouted and walked briskly, not stopping to sell, simply walking alongside the train, crying out. The rats withdrew again; the hawker, glancing down, lengthened his stride and walked on, his heel yellow. Then the rats returned.

Cheroots are handy in such a situation. Around me in the compartment smiling Burmese puffed away on thick green cheroots and didn't seem to notice the stink of the growing yellow pool just outside. At the Shwe Dagon Pagoda I saw a very old lady, hands clasped in prayer. She knelt near a begging leper whose disease had withered his feet and abraded his body and given him a bat's face. He had a terrible smell, but the granny prayed with a Churchillian-sized cheroot in her mouth. On Mandalay Hill, doorless outhouses stand beside the rising steps, and next to the outhouses are fruit stalls. The stink of piss is powerful, but the fruitseller, who squats all day in that stink, is wreathed in smoke from his cheroot.

A shortage of cheroots might provoke an uprising; no other shortages have yet done so. Food is cheap and seems to be plentiful; and inexplicably in the Dry Zone, four hundred miles long and seventy-five broad, where it had not rained for over five months, one sees Burmese pouring pailfuls of water over their heads to cool themselves (I tried it: one shivers with cold for a minute and then dries and continues to gasp and perspire in the heat). In Mandalay the source of water is the moat which surrounds what used to be the Golden City: the moat is a bright putrescent green, and I was advised by a Burmese doctor not to touch it but to go on drinking Super Soda.

There are shortages of everything else: spare parts, electrical equipment, anything made of metal or rubber, and worse, cotton cloth. In the YMCA in Rangoon one is given a room; the fan is broken, cockroaches scuttle in the adjoining shower stall, and on the bed is a dirty mattress. The mattress cover is torn; there are no sheets, no pillowcases. The manager is helpful; he says, "Sleep downstairs in the dormitory. There are no sheets there either, but it only costs two *kyats*." I demanded sheets. "Expensive," he says. But the room is expensive! He demurs: "All the sheets are at the laundry."

And the sheets are at the laundry again in Mandalay, at Maymyo, at Nyaungu, and Pagan. But on the lines of wash in these towns there are no sheets.

There are Germans here, a Burman told me, studying ways of increasing textile production. In the meantime, I said, you could import cloth. "No, no! Burmese socialism! We import nothing!" And yet, in the Rangoon Airport, while I was waiting for my suitcase, I saw four large wooden crates. The stickers showed that these had just arrived, airfreight from Japan, and each contained 1,200 yards of blue poplin. For whom? And why airfreight? No one knew. And the tourists' buses and tourists' cornflakes and the brand-new bull-nosed Dodge army trucks that one sees Burmese army officers using for ferrying their families to the temples: made in Burma?

I was in Rangoon at the suffocating height of the Burmese summer, which may account for my impression of the city being one of lassitude and exhaustion. But Richard Curle used those same words when he visited in 1923. In *Into the East* (preface by Joseph Conrad) he speaks of the city over which hovers "so queerly the breath of stagnation". The rats and pariah dogs wait for the cool of the evening to scavenge; during the day only the crows are active, soaring in the blazing sun, in a perfectly cloudless sky. It must have been a bustling place in the 'twenties, as those dates on the medallions show and as Curle maintains (" 'Boy, give me a chit,' resounds here and there . . ."); but the medallions have been painted out, and the green signs of the Revolutionary Government have begun to fade and peel. The city is moribund, flanked by a coffee-colored river on which there is not a shadow of a ripple; and most of the buildings in Rangoon are demonstrably more decrepit than the eleventh-century temples at Pagan.

But the people – generous, hospitable, curious, so alert and quick to smile, neatly dressed in a place where all cloth is at a premium – they are in such contrast to the dead city that it is as if they have, all of them, just arrived and are padding down those sidewalks for the first time. Their appreciation of the city's few beauties is acute: the Shwe Dagon Pagoda, the several lovely cathedrals, the Scott Market, the flowering trees in Maha Bandoola Park – clusters of heavy yellow blossoms hanging in bunches on the laburnum trees like grapes on a vine. In Maha Bandoola Park there is an obelisk, the Independence Monument. "Look at it closely," said my Burmese friend.

I looked. "Very pretty."

"Look again," he said. "You see? It's not straight. It bends."

The remark was, I decided, profoundly political. He had said that he drank beer once a year, one bottle. I asked whether he had had this year's bottle yet, and when he said no, we went to the Strand Hotel – both of us for the first time (but he had lived several blocks away for thirty-five years) – and squandered three dollars on two small bottles of pale ale. A few hours later the palm court violins were playing a melody from "Bittersweet" and down Strand Road clattered a 1938 Nash.

The Novel is Dead, Allah Be Praised!

[1971]

The guest lecturer has at least two things in common with a condemned man, the experience of enormous meals and the knowledge that whatever outrageous thing he says cannot matter much to his fate: he'll be gone in the morning. A lecture-tour through Indonesia by an American professor of literature preceded my own by several months. But the professor was not forgotten; he had, it seemed, a standard spiel which made a profound impression on Indonesian students and writers who repeated it to me on many occasions in Sumatra and Java. After my own talk had ended, skinny brown arms shot up, and the signalling questioners usually asked the same thing.

"Sir," one would begin, "I have enjoyed very much the talk you have given us today about novels. But I am confused. Don't you think the novel is dead?"

Fighting down "Don't be ridiculous!" I said, "Not exactly" and explained in a hasty summary of the lecture I had just given why I thought it wasn't, ending, "What gave you *that* idea?"

"Professor E said the novel is dead." This inspired nods and murmurs and many beatific smiles, of the sort that accompany the ejaculation, "Allah be praised!"

The first time I heard this I had a feeling Professor E might be in the audience, an expatriate lecturer whose judgement had run amuck (Indonesia is the home of that word) in the stifling heat. I was patient and conceded that while the novel was far from dead, the form was certainly changing; and I waffled on about Sterne and Joyce and the dazed Frenchman whose novels, with unglued bindings, can be shuffled like a pack of cards. When I learned that Professor E had been a visitor – indeed, was now back in the States – and that I needn't worry about demoralizing his students, I denounced him. Still, the professor's academic rope-trick, his vanishing (to the applause of simple folk) along a feeble strand of literary argument that defied all logic, was a hard act to follow.

And God help the person who follows me. During one of the first lectures I gave I confessed that I knew very little about Indonesian writing; afterward, a friendly Javanese lady put a book into my hands and said I should read it. It was titled *Six Indonesian Short Stories* (New Haven, 1968), and that night before going to sleep I read all six. Five were undistinguished, but a sixth, called "Inem", by Pramoedya Ananta Toer, had many virtues. At the lectures which followed this discovery I mentioned the writer's name, praised his vision and — because my mention of the man provoked only silence — recounted his story. I thought it was strange that such a good writer should be neglected. One evening I found out the reason. I had been enthusing about him and urging the students in the audience to read him; then I asked, "Is Pramoedya still alive?"

There was an uncomfortable silence. I asked the question again. A man in the front row said, "Yes, he is alive. But —"

"But he is in prison," another added joylessly. "He has been there since 1966."

Not just behind bars I read later, but on the remote prison island of Buru, east of Celebes, in the Banda Sea. He had been jailed by General Suharto; in 1947 he had been jailed by the Dutch.

The writers who are not in prison are doing other jobs, anything but writing. A man is introduced as a poet. I ask him how his poems are coming along. "Not so well," is the reply. "I haven't written a poem since 1962." He smiles and adds, "But I signed the Culture Manifesto — you know the Culture Manifesto? Against Soekarno. All the writers signed it."

In Djakarta there is a cultural center of modern construction, the Taman Ismail Marzuki, which an American compared — appropriately — to the Lincoln Center in New York. The design is similar, it is as new and huge, and it may have cost nearly as much. Here, in the floodlit courtyard, before the shimmering buildings, the three theaters and the reflecting pools, it was explained to me why there were few writers in Indonesia. "Before the *coup* in 1965," said one of the center's officials, "there were so many writers! They were suppressed by the communist regime, but still they wrote — plays, poems, novels, everything! If you will come here six years ago you will meet them and talk to them. Then the *coup*. The communists were kicked out. But," he said, raising a finger, "now there were so many jobs in the government. The writers and intellectuals took those jobs. Now, no one writes. When they were suppressing us we had time and we felt like doing it. These days we have no time for writing."

"This is a poor country," another says, shaking his head and tapping a clove cigarette on a pudgy knuckle. "Writing takes money. We do not have enough money to buy even a few sheets of paper! I used to write short stories, I had a few *rupiahs*. Now when I get home from work — I've got three jobs — I'm too tired."

It is a common argument: we are too poor to write, too busy to read. I repeated what I had been told about the spate of writing in the early 'sixties, when the country was poorer and there was heavy censorship. Well, it was explained, there was a necessity for it then: it was political. Then, they had a subject; now, there is no subject. And yet no writer – or rather, former writer, since they have all gone into early retirement – could explain why there had been no novel or story concerned with the massacres (perhaps half a million throats cut). Surely *that* was a subject? One teacher said, "It is too early to write about that. Maybe . . . sometime." The massacres took place at the end of '65 and in early '66.

The non-writing argument was contradicted by one lady who told me: "There are *many* writers in Indonesia. We have *many* novelists. Go to the publishers and there you will see big piles of manuscripts – this high! But they don't want to publish them because no one will buy them. No one reads in this country."

Some people read. I spoke to many students who had read *Love Story* ("The English is easy enough for us to understand"); *The Godfather*, in Indonesian translation, is being serialized in the largest newspaper in the country, *Indonesia Raya* ("This government is controlled by the business *mafia*," a Djakarta journalist said at a party, and everyone in the room who heard, laughed out loud: the word was well-known). At another level, the Indian epic, *The Ramayana*, appears as a comic book. The newspaper industry is flourishing: there are scores of daily newspapers in all the cities, and even Surabaya is said to have about forty-five morning newspapers. There are so many newspapers, in fact, that there is a shortage of certain letters of type, and one often comes across the Indonesian remedy for this in a sentence like: "Presidenl Nixon reileraled lhis morning his delerminalion lo slop lhe war in Vielnam . . ." Occasionally the lack of a critical letter and the substitution of another makes an unfortunate word.

Some Indonesians appear to be widely read. In Bogor I had a lively discussion with a young man who was doing a dissertation on Eugene O'Neill; another in Surabaya said he was influenced by Albert Camus. In Medan, in North Sumatra, a short-story writer said his reason for writing was "to promote Islam" (one of his stories: a Muslim entering a brothel hears the call for prayer from the local mosque; he decides not to enter the brothel and instead goes to pray). He told me that Saki and O Henry "are not *authors* – they are *story-tellers*!" At the Taman Ismail Marzuki, an ex-novelist asked me: "One of your most famous writers is Margaret Mitchell. Author of *Gone With The Wind*. I have read this book. Also I have read a lot of literary criticism from America. Why is it that I never see the name of Margaret Mitchell?"

This question was followed by: "Why are all American novels written by Jews?"

One of the unexpected bonuses of travelling in Indonesia and irrigating oneself with many bottles of Bintang Beer, is that one forgets one's replies to these questions. For example, I noted the following students' comments in my diary, but none of my replies: "Poem cannot be discuss. If you like poem, okay. If you don't like, okay. But not necessary to discuss." And: "Is conflict necessary to story? If so, internal or external?" And: "Before I can tell you about this poem" (one of Roethke's) "I must know who is this poet? Where does he live? What is his life like? I must have some information, then I will tell you my opinion of this poem."

The novel is very much of the West; so is the activity of reading for pleasure. The Indonesian response to literacy is to translate *Hamlet* and *Macbeth* into colloquial Indonesian and stage them at their multi-million dollar cultural center – I believe they were paying an elaborate compliment to the American donors; it is to stock the library of the University of Indonesia in Djakarta with thirteen copies of *Don't Forget To Write*, by Art Buchwald, and moldering sets of Thackeray, Dickens and Scott. For many, literacy is a skill which, once mastered, needs never to be proven again. The man who wrote an anti-communist poem in 1962 is a poet; his role is indisputable: he will recite his poem for you. The 'fifties novelist, now a civil servant, is still regarded as a novelist: there is his sixty-page novel, affectionately dedicated to you. Only the writer in jail has ceased to be a writer, because he has ceased to be a person.

Ten years ago there were three literary magazines in Indonesia; now there is one, *Horison. Horison*, published in a country of a hundred and twenty million people, has a circulation of five thousand. It loses money; the editor says its funding "is a secret". That means the CIA's Department of Literary Appreciation. As in much of Southeast Asia, there are two cultures, one devouring the scrappy newspapers, bathetic feature films and pop concerts; the other going to traditional dances, thrilling to gong-orchestras and staying up all night to watch shadow-plays. And these cultures may not be all that separate, for they certainly meet when *The Ramayana* is presented as a comic book.

It is understandable, then, that the lecturer travelling through Indonesia will have the feeling he is pestering his audience most of the time, practising a form of cultural imperialism which, like urging the Balinese soloist to sing a national anthem, is not just a waste of time but may eventually diminish a more satisfying art form. If no one writes novels, it is possible that no novels are needed; and it is probably true that *Love Story* is closer to a traditional Javanese tale than, say, *Emma* or *Portrait of a Lady*. After a while I no longer found it odd that Professor E's ludicrous judgement that the novel is dead should find such approval in the non-writing republic, and I felt like a wet blanket for insisting on the contrary.

But this is not the whole story. The student of O'Neill, the admirers of Mario Puzo, Camus, Margaret Mitchell and that talented short-story writer on his prison island in the Banda Sea have to be reckoned with. Thinking back on them I recall a strange sight I witnessed in Djakarta: a naked boy, burned black by the sun, with wild eyes, clutching a post which was stuck in the middle of a wide canal. Some people washed in the canal and others pissed, and on both sides there was heavy traffic, cars, tri-shaws, men on bicycles. But the boy clung motionlessly to his perch, and I doubt that anyone saw him.

The Killing of Hastings Banda

[1971]

> It is the privilege of early youth to live in advance of its days in all the beautiful continuity of hope which knows no pauses and no introspection.
>
> Joseph Conrad, *The Shadow-Line*

We weren't supposed to get rain during the dry season in Malawi, but it was pelting down that October morning in 1965 when two men drove up to my school compound in a Jeep and demanded to see me. I had just left the school, having finished an early class, and was wobbling through the rain on my bike to collect the mail. The Jeep pulled up beside me on the muddy road and the door swung open. The man in the driver's seat said, "Get in, Paul. We've got some bad news for you." He said it somewhat mechanically, as if he had rehearsed it, the way people do when they learn in advance they have to deliver bad news.

"You're being deported," he said.

Any other Peace Corps schoolteacher might have become indignant and asked, "What for?" But I did not speak. I dropped my bike into a puddle and climbed into the Jeep. At my house I packed a small suitcase, and at the bank I changed all my money into traveler's checks. I boarded a plane four hours later – this may be something of a record, I believe – for Salisbury, Rhodesia, with an escort.

The little plane nosed its way shuddering through the downdrafts, passing lamb-wisps of cloud; soon we were in sunlight, cruising over a sea of clouds. I could think of four reasons for my deportation . . . four different reasons.

There was Heinz. He had phoned me in January and asked me to have lunch with him. He represented a new German magazine, he said, and had just come to Malawi from Rhodesia where the editors of the left-wing *Central African Examiner* (then banned by the Smith regime) were saying complimentary things about me.

I should explain that the previous year there had been an attempted *coup d'état* in Malawi. I knew several of the men involved as well as many sympathizers. One sympathizer was Mr David Rubadiri, a former headmaster of my bush school and later a delegate to the United Nations. At the time of the attempted coup the level of debate was not high. I remember seeing "Elvis for Prime Minister" chalked on the blackboard of my classroom the morning after the Prime Minister, Dr Banda, sacked his entire cabinet and threatened them with prison (Malawi had been independent for two months). I knew I could do better than plump for Elvis, so I began writing anonymous pieces about Malawi politics for the *Examiner*. Sporadic violence followed the abortive *coup*: Dr Banda's Young Pioneers beat up some people and killed others who were suspected of being in league with the rebel cabinet ministers. They clubbed villagers into joining Dr Banda's party, and they shouted "stoogie" and "Capricorni" at anyone who expressed doubt about Dr Banda or concern for the death of democracy. My articles were reasonably well-informed, and I wished to God that my name could appear on them. But that candor would have meant my immediate expulsion from the country.

Heinz ate a big lunch and encouraged me to do the same, and when we were finished he explained his mission. People in Germany, he said, were so ignorant about Africa. They still believed it was a savage place, and all they knew were the few facts that appeared in the German newspapers. His magazine planned to dispel this ignorance by having correspondents send monthly letters and reports giving detailed information about matters that never reached the press.

What he wanted was what, in the art of journalism, is known as "a thumb-sucker" – a background piece. He said I would be paid an honorarium (it was more than my Peace Corps salary) for my work.

He said that Germany and the world were quite progressive these days. His parting words were, "Sings are different now. We do not sink like our fazers sot."

I agreed, and that evening wrote my first article for him. A few weeks later he wrote:

"Many thanks for No. 1! Some interesting facts: How could ex-ministers make a trip through the north without being captured? I heard, just in the north, there are about 200,000 people not supporting B, not obeying to governmental orders or instructions?

"What about C, is he still in the country, what is he doing?

"Could you please give a short analysis on the inner-political situation now; it seems there has changed something after Dr B's successful trip to Europe.

"Alles Gute und recht viele Grüsse."

I became a keen correspondent. I wrote reports on sewage disposal; I wrote one on overcrowding in townships and several on the raid in February of a border post by the ex-ministers' guerrilla soldiers. Dr

Banda, the Prime Minister, was always good copy; after the border raid, he said, referring to the leader of the guerrillas: "I want him brought back alive. If not alive, then *any other way!*"

One month I had other things to do. I wrote nothing. But my honorarium arrived at my bank. Another month passed; I couldn't think of anything to say about Malawi. Again I was paid. I felt guilty about this and so put an article together from pieces I had read in the local newspaper. The reply to that article did not come from Heinz:

"Thank you very much for your Report No. 10. This time it did not yield much information for the editorial staff, as the subject you treated was already known to us for some time, the African and international press, which we carefully analyze, having already dealt with it in detail. I would therefore deem it expedient if you confined your reports and continued informing us on the background of the development in this country. To be sure, it is possible that for some time nothing happens at all in Malawi, but then you naturally need not send us a report. I would, however, ask you to remember that we already know everything divulged by the Malawian, Rhodesian, Zambian and Tanzanian newspapers as we get them by airmail.

"Hoping that you will understand this and comply with our wishes, I remain –"

. . . *it is possible that for some time nothing happens at all in Malawi,* the gentleman said. But so much was happening! I can't remember ever having been so busy.

I was at a new school and was an English teacher. We had no books at the school that we could use for English lessons. The textbooks were very few, and what books we did have were an embarrassment. Why was it that there, in Central Africa, we had so many copies of a dramatized version of *Snow White?* We had a roomful of grammars from Kansas, many Enid Blytons and a chewed-up set of the Waverley novels that had been sent to us by the English-Speaking Union in London. We had a multitude of books from the USIS (*Machines That Made America, Yankee From Olympus,* and many of the *From Log Cabin to White House* variety), but we had nothing really suitable for African children learning English. In a year the students' English had not improved. Sentences such as "I wish to confabulate with you" and "I was oscillating with my girl friend" were common.

To remedy the situation – this was about the same time as Heinz contacted me – I decided to write my own English textbook, a chapter a week. Each lesson was composed of a reading passage with a Malawi background, a dialogue adapted from the passage, an exercise in sound discrimination (the students confused *l* and *r*, *m* and *n*, and *s* and *sh*) and the correction of a common Malawi error in English ("I foot to school,"

"I hear the flowers smelling," "I was caught by a cold"). As the months passed the book became more ambitious and eventually I collaborated on some sections with a man who was a trained linguistician. He said he thought the book could be published.

One day during a session of the Malawi Parliament my collaborator showed me a page from *Hansard*, the parliamentary report. He said, "We're finished."

Dr Banda had given a long speech in Parliament attacking the teaching of English in Malawi. He used his secretaries as examples of the result of bad teaching.

"These girls do not know English," he said. "If you ask them what a gerund is they wouldn't be able to tell you." The same went for subordinating conjunctions, adjectival phrases, semicolons, and the rest. Malawians needed grammar very badly, said Dr Banda. "These girls do not know how to use a comma properly!" The trouble was with the teaching: teachers in Malawi didn't know the first thing about English grammar. No one knew what an adverb was anymore! No one cared. "Hear, hear," and "Shouts of 'Shame' ", and "Loud Applause" were scattered parenthetically through the official record of Dr Banda's speech.

My collaborator was worried. There was no grammar in our book: we had deliberately omitted it and concentrated on verb patterns and sentence structures. In his speech, Dr Banda had referred to this as "the nonsensical linguistic approach". But prior to the speech my collaborator, who was an inspector of schools, had arranged for an interview with Dr Banda to tell him about our English book, which was the first of its kind in Malawi.

It was too late to put in sections on grammar. With some apprehension my collaborator went through with the interview, and it was, predictably, a disaster. Dr Banda leafed through the typescript and said, "Where is the grammar? I want my people to know grammar! There is no grammar in this book! They must know what a clause is, what a phrase is . . ."

But I had less and less time to work on the book. For one thing, the German magazine was occupying my thoughts, even if I wasn't doing much writing for it. I had also recently struck up a correspondence with my old friend Mr Rubadiri, who said that he was disenchanted with the United Nations and very angry with Dr Banda for his casual arrests and his disorderly Young Pioneers. And I had started a newspaper.

I got the idea for the newspaper when a second piece I wrote for the Germans was returned to me with a note saying that they had read it before in the international press. The newspaper was modestly titled *The Migraine*; generally I printed the articles of mine that were rejected by the Germans, and the Peace Corps office helped to mimeograph it. Three or four other volunteers were on the editorial staff; we had an excellent cartoonist and a number of good writers. Copies were sent free to all the Peace Corps volunteers in the country.

The July issue of *The Migraine* coincided with a migraine of my own. I received word that Mr Rubadiri had just denounced Dr Banda in New York, that he had resigned his post at the UN, and that he was leaving to take up a new job in Uganda. His denunciation was rather incautiously timed. Mr Rubadiri's mother was still in Malawi and so were most of his personal effects, a large car and an enormous library of books. Shortly after Mr Rubadiri arrived in Uganda I got a note from him asking me if I could find it in my heart to help his mother flee the country, and also would I mind driving his car to Uganda with his set of best china, a dinner service for twelve?

Mr Rubadiri's mother was a tough old bird. The Young Pioneers had threatened to set her house on fire and beat her up for what her son had said about "The Messiah", as Dr Banda was called. Mr Rubadiri had implied that Dr Banda was a betrayer of the revolution and a lackey of the Portuguese; Dr Banda called Rubadiri a stooge. Mrs Rubadiri said the Young Pioneers didn't scare her a bit and that she planned to write down all their names and get even with them when her son was back in power.

Before she left the country, Mrs Rubadiri sold me the car for a token few pounds and my name was entered as Present Owner in the car's logbook. She was in such a hurry – and who could blame her? – there was no time to get a new logbook; my name appeared under that of David Rubadiri, now considered to be a political criminal. In addition to the car I got a crate containing the dinner service. I told Mrs Rubadiri that her son could expect me in Uganda toward the end of August.

I needed a vacation. I couldn't think of anything to write for the Germans, and my bank account was swollen with unearned cash: there was quite literally no place to spend it in Malawi, and having done nothing to earn most of it I didn't feel right about spending it; *The Migraine* was not very popular ("Too negative," said one Peace Corps official); and the business about the grammar in the textbook was getting me down.

What made the car journey to Uganda something of a challenge were the many roadblocks on the Great North Road in Malawi, where Young Pioneers stopped cars, searched them for smuggled arms and looked for spies and infiltrators – they were looking in fact for friends of people like Mr Rubadiri. Also a distance of 2,500 miles separated my home outside Blantyre from Mr Rubadiri's in Kampala. The drive would be difficult, but the greatest danger was my name in the logbook.

I was hesitant to drive that distance alone. I persuaded a friend to come along to share the driving. There was only one thing that remained to be done before I left. President Johnson had just escalated the war in

Vietnam by sending in 20,000 more troops: I wrote an article about this for *The Migraine* condemning Johnson's decision and also mentioning the recent fiasco in the Dominican Republic. That finished, we set off in the car for Kampala with the crate of dishes.

The drive in Malawi was harrowing. We were stopped at fourteen roadblocks and threatened by gun-toting Young Pioneers. At one roadblock a bottle of wine we were carrying blew its cork, making a loud bang and rattling the armed boys. We also took several wrong roads, trying a shortcut through the Luangwa Valley and crossing a disturbed area where the Lumpa sect, fanatical Christians led by a fat black lady named Alice Lenshina, were attacking police posts. Each Lumpa carried what they called "A Passport To Heaven" which guaranteed a *kraal* in Paradise; when the police opened fire the Lumpas rushed headlong into the blazing guns. Skirting the Lumpas, we circled back into Malawi and had more fearful moments at the northern frontier, which had been attacked on three occasions. Few people drive at night in Africa, and when we arrived at midnight at the border post the Young Pioneers thought we were raiding them. I hid the logbook. We were guarded at gunpoint while the car was searched. But it was dark and very cold, and the Young Pioneers gave up their search after a few minutes. Two thousand miles of Africa's worst roads remained, but we had no more problems. We saw lions and giraffes and Masai warriors; we had a glimpse of Mount Kilimanjaro. It was a marvelous trip, though the new car was a bit banged up by the time we reached Kampala.

On the other hand, we had broken only one small plate in the large dinner service. I transferred the car to Mr Rubadiri's name and he did me a favor. I told him about my writing for the German magazine and asked him if he would mind being interviewed by me: would he explain his attitude toward African independence, Malawi's relations with Portugal and South Africa, and Dr Banda? He agreed and we had a long, lively talk which I typed and sent to Munich. I had justified that month's payment at least.

Then he asked a favor of me. I would be flying back to Malawi and on the way stopping for an hour in Dar es Salaam; would I deliver an envelope to a Mr Yatuta Chisiza who would meet me at the airport in Dar? I said yes, of course.

"Ah," said the bearded Mr Chisiza with relief when he received the envelope. I was sure it was filled with money. "When does your plane leave?"

"In an hour or so," I said.

"Have a beer," he said. Though it was only ten in the morning, I obliged. He was leader of the guerrilla band, one of the most hated men in Malawi. He was reputed to have been trained in China.

"How was the drive?" he asked.

"So you know about Rubadiri's car."

"Everybody does!" he said. "That was a wonderful job!"

"We spent most of the time bluffing our way through roadblocks," I laughed, though I had been scared stiff at the time.

Mr Chisiza unfolded a map on the table. "Show me where they are," he said. And when I did, he said, "So many! They must have put up a few more since the last time we were there."

"So you still go to Malawi now and then?"

"Now and then." He smiled.

My plane was announced. I finished my beer and started walking toward the door.

"I wonder if you'd do me a favor or two," said Mr Chisiza.

"That depends," I said.

"It won't be any trouble." He said I was to deliver two messages in Malawi: one was to tell a Mr M that his two boys were fine, that they had gotten safely over the Tanzanian border and had started school; the other was to tell a certain Greek fellow that on October 16th he should deliver his bread to Ncheu, a town thirty miles from Blantyre.

My readiness to say yes to favors may suggest a simplicity of mind, a fatal gullibility; but I was bored, and the daily annoyance of living in a dictatorship, which is like suffering an unhappy family in a locked house, had softened my temper to the point where anything different, lunch with a stranger, the request for an article, the challenge of a difficult task, changed that day and revived my mind. The risk was usually obvious, but it always seemed worth it – better that than the tyranny of the ordinary.

I knew that Mr M's boys must have been in Mr Chisiza's army which had attacked the border post. Furthermore, when someone mentions delivering bread on a certain day in a certain place many hundreds of miles away, I know as well as the next man that the order is a euphemism for a plot. But passing on a simple message requires no personality; if there was a plot, I knew mine was a blameless involvement; neither message was much of a revelation: I was available.

That was about the middle of September. In the next four weeks my luck started to change.

I took my time delivering the messages. Mr M worked, I was told, for Radio Malawi. He was pointed out to me; I made sure he was alone in his office and then introduced myself and said, "I'm just back from Dar es Salaam. Your boys are fine – both of them are in school."

Mr M covered his face and began sobbing. He said, "Oh, thank God!" and got up and shook my hand a number of times. Calmer a few minutes later, he said that he thought his boys had been killed. His wife had just been arrested in the north.

"That's terrible," I said. "Aren't you worried about yourself? Banda's men might be after you."

"No," he said. He had just written a song called *Brother, Pay Your Taxes* which Dr Banda liked very much — Malawi was close to bankruptcy — and Mr M thought that if he kept writing songs he would be in the clear for a while.

Then Mr M asked: "Would you do something for me?"

He needed some money, he said, to go up north by plane — there wasn't much time — and see if he could get his wife released from prison. I could hardly refuse. His tears had moved me, and the indignity of having to write a song called *Brother, Pay Your Taxes* for a government which had imprisoned his wife was really intolerable. From the large bank balance of the mounting German funds I gave him seventy-five pounds and wished him luck; and I told him that it might be better if we never saw each other again.

Mr M had cried when I told him his news. The Greek baker trembled and went pale when I told him about the delivery he was to make in Ncheu. He took me into his back room and asked me to repeat it. He held his head in his hands. He did not say, "Thank God," but he might very well have said, "Oh God." He held his head tightly and did not look at me, and I noticed that he was wearing a wig, glossy stiff animal-like hair, the shape of a fancy bathing cap.

"Stay here," he said. "I'll be right back."

When he was out of the room I looked around. My eye was caught, as most people's are, by a bookshelf. But on this bookshelf there were three or four books with their spines turned to the wall. Thinking I might get some clue to my errand, Mr Chisiza's odd message, I whipped them around and read their spines. The first was titled *Defeating Baldness*, the rest were about hair restoring, head massage, and how to thicken your hair.

The Greek returned no less nervous than when he left. I remembered Mr Chisiza had said that I should tell the Greek to give me the drink he owed him. I did so, as good-humoredly as I could.

"He should buy *me* a drink," the Greek snapped. He asked me my name. I told him, and said that I was just an English teacher in the Peace Corps and that I didn't want to get involved in anything.

"How can I get in touch with Chisiza?"

Mr Chisiza had told me his alias ("Ali Abdullah") and his box number in Dar es Salaam. I remembered the alias because it was so different from his real name, and the box number was easy because it was a historical date. I told the Greek.

"Do me a favor," said the Greek.

"Sorry," I said.

"Write to him and tell him I can't deliver the goods," said the Greek. "I got a wife and three kids. I got a business to worry about. The CID are watching me — they know I helped those guys get out of the country last year."

I refused. But I wonder what I would have done if the Greek had been an African? I think I might have helped him out; I might have pitied him. Though it wasn't pity that made me help Mr Rubadiri. He was an important man, a United Nations delegate, and his request pushed me to do something which I could construe as humane. The same went for the German articles: I was clarifying the African position; I was a kind of nationalist. My little helps were consistent with the mood of that decade in Africa, of engaging oneself and being available for the purpose of national development. The image of the Azania-like joke republic committing farcical outrages upon itself was temporarily antiquated then; it was a time when the admission to the United Nations of a country like Gambia (which is a riverbank) or Rwanda (half a dozen volcanoes) would not raise a smile.

That decade is over; what was engagement is now detachment, a prevailing spirit of passionate disregard. And no less for the Africans themselves. I find it hard to believe that a German magazine at present would look for its contributors among the European section of a community in Africa. More frankness would be found among Africans. And now a delegate to the United Nations would not know a school teacher in his country: the time has passed when diplomats are picked from a nation's headmasters. And a black guerrilla fighter asking a white American to pass messages for him? Such things don't happen today: Azania reasserted itself at the close of the 'sixties — not in the European mind, but, much more significantly, in the African one. The next *Black Mischief*, if not the next Evelyn Waugh, will be wholly African.

The Greek asked a favor. I had no trouble refusing. My refusal was racial: he didn't count. I said, "I told you I don't want to get involved. I was supposed to give you this message. It's between you and him. It's not my affair."

"But you're in touch with him," said the Greek. "I'm not. I didn't know he was in Dar. They said he was in China."

"I'm not in touch with him," I said. "I happened to see him at the airport in Dar, that's all."

"You haven't ever written to him?"

"No," I said, "and I don't intend to."

"How do you spell your name?" asked the Greek.

Which made me suspicious. So I gave him a wrong spelling. Mine is an easy name to misspell.

A week later he invited me out to eat. But I had to turn him down. I had a new problem.

The Germans, in reply to my interview with Mr Rubadiri, had written me the strangest note. It was in an opaque envelope, of the sort used by Swiss banks, with no return address. The large sheet of notepaper was not headed. The message read as follows:

"I wish to thank you most sincerely for your letter of August 21st and for Item No. 17 which can be considered as being particularly interesting. This kind of 'poetry' is of special importance both for me and for all members of the redaction staff. If you could go along this line with your poetry it could be tremendously interesting for all of us over here. Thanks a lot."

I happened to know the German Ambassador to Malawi. His daughter was to marry one of my good friends. I asked him about the magazine.

He had never heard of it. "A German magazine about African affairs, you say?" He was somewhat angry that he had never been sent a copy, because he was supposed to be up-to-date on such publications. He said he would check on it.

In the weeks that followed a further problem cropped up: *The Migraine*. The long-delayed issue with my editorial about Vietnam had come out only to be seized and confiscated by the American Ambassador, Sam P. Gilstrap. The full text of my editorial was cabled to the State Department. And in due course the Peace Corps' representative, Mr Michael McCone, was sent back to Washington for what was considered a lack of judgment.

Nothing was done to me. The editorial board of *The Migraine* was summoned to the Embassy.

"I wrote that editorial," I said. "If anyone should be sent home it should be me, don't you think?"

"You didn't know what you were doing," said Ambassador Gilstrap. "But McCone should have known better." And then he blustered: How could I have written that? What possessed me? How could I be so stupid?

"Any human being would write what I did," I said, though I saw how feeble this justification was.

"I don't agree with you," said Ambassador Gilstrap.

"May I ask why?"

"Because I don't think you're a human being, that's why!"

A moment later he apologized for this remark, but he added, "McCone is out, and as long as I'm the Ambassador here he's not coming back. This is a very serious matter. What if your article got into the hands of the Egyptians?"

The Egyptians?

"They'd use it for propaganda to prove we're not united."

"Who says we're united?" I asked. "Everyone knows there's a lot of opposition to the Vietnam war."

"Not *here*," said Ambassador Gilstrap. He sat forward and knotted his fingers and fixed me with a stare. "Boy, I'm going to tell you one thing and I want you to remember it. You're not in Nebraska now! If I read anything more like this I'm sending you home, too. I won't hesitate." He nodded and said, memorably, "I will *prevail*!"

"Today," said Dr Banda, "I am going to talk about the teaching of English . . ." It was October 12th, the opening of the new University of Malawi; as Chancellor of the University Dr Banda gave the opening address, which was in the form of a lecture.

He spoke about the importance of grammar; it was a long lecture in the course of which he mentioned that some months previous he was shown a typescript of a textbook with no English grammar in it. "Some people in Malawi," he said, were "masquerading as teachers" and "trying to fool my people!" McGuffey the grammarian might have applauded this speech, though there was little applause from the members of the diplomatic corps, the first-year students or the civil servants, who listened in great bewilderment. Toward the end of the speech Dr Banda said, "I am sure you all know Mendel. Mendel's example is one to follow. He had to work very hard to compose his *Messiah* and you will have to work like Mendel to learn English grammar."

This was my first indication that Dr Banda had a reasonably good memory; he had forgotten Handel's name, but I guessed he knew mine. He remembered the textbook, and I wondered if there would be any repercussions. I found little consolation in his closing remarks, which were to the effect that he planned to make personal visits to the English classes of all large schools to appraise the teaching of parsing and grammar. The psychology of dictators is unique in that in their determination to make people obey them they see treason in variation. It is an attitude they are trying to eliminate, rather than a single act. The man who refuses to teach English grammar is disaffected; his decision is political, he is traitorous.

It was a few days later that I saw the German Ambassador again. I went to his house with my friend Fred, who was engaged to his daughter.

The Ambassador was having dinner when I arrived. He rose from the table and beamed. "Ah, Paul! Come right in! Shall I call you brother?" He shook my hand. And he explained: for a year I had been working for the German equivalent of the CIA.

I was in suspense, but the suspense was not to last. On the 20th of October I was deported. Expelled is a better word, since it suggests speed. The only inconvenience I recall is of being unable to cram my traveler's checks into my pocket. I had several thousand dollars in fives and tens, and I couldn't fold the plastic wallet in half.

Because of the speed of the deportation, onward plane reservations were impossible. We would have to stay in Rhodesia a few days.

And it was in a Chinese restaurant in Salisbury that I learned why I had been deported from Malawi. Wes Leach, my escort – but he was also a friend – had been silent on the plane. There were times when I saw him eyeing me furtively, as if he believed I would make a desperate bid for freedom by leaping from the Dakota into Mozambique. I suppose I looked rather desperate, for I had been going over all the possible reasons for my deportation: was it the German secret service? Or had Sam P. Gilstrap prevailed? Or was it the textbook? Or, perhaps – but this was so complicated! – Mr M was really working for Dr Banda . . . or perhaps the Greek?

Wes was reluctant at first to tell me. He said he did not know much. He urged me not to ask. I nagged him. He gave in. The American Embassy, he said, had received a call from Dr Banda's office saying that Dr Banda wanted to speak to the chargé d'affaires.

"What if I told you," said Dr Banda to the chargé, "that one of your Peace Corps chaps tried to kill me?"

The chargé winced, but said he didn't think it was likely.

"It is likely, and it is true," said Dr Banda. He showed the chargé a file.

In the file (it may have been marked *Hastings Banda/Assassination Attempt*) there were a number of letters: half were from Ali Abdullah in Dar es Salaam, and the rest were from me. The letters described the plot to kill Hastings Banda.

The Greek, in order to clear himself for having helped the rebel ministers initially, informed the Criminal Investigation Department after I delivered the message about the bread van. Using my name, a correspondence was struck up with Mr Chisiza who was assured that it would all be smooth sailing. A dozen gunmen were dispatched from Tanzania; the bread van they expected to take them to Zomba was waiting on the road, in the appointed place. But behind the bread van were a score of soldiers from the Malawi army. The gunmen were ambushed and all were killed.

Dr Banda said to the chargé, "If you don't remove this chap I will have him imprisoned."

In Washington, I had long talks with the Peace Corps ("How could you do this to us?") and with the State Department ("When," they asked expectantly, "is the lid going to blow off Malawi?"). I thought my passport might be taken away, but my brother, who is a lawyer, said, "Let them try." The Peace Corps fined me for "six months' unsatisfactory service" and made me pay my air fare from Blantyre to Washington; the State Department men simply raised their eyes to the ceiling and whistled at the end of my tale – my *abridged* tale: I didn't mention grammar or Germans – and one said, "You can consider yourself a very lucky fellow."

Others were not so lucky. Mr McCone was sent to Sarawak, Mr Chisiza was shot and killed trying to enter Malawi a year later, Mr Rubadiri is still in Uganda. Some of the former ministers got scholarships from the CIA to study in American universities; the rebel soldiers still live in Dar es Salaam, and from time to time they save enough money to make a raid in Malawi. Mr M disappeared, and the Greek was eventually deported.

Hastings Banda is alive and well. They say his facial tic worsened after 1965. Last year I read in a Singapore newspaper that Banda gave a speech in which he said that after this year he wants no more Peace Corps volunteers in his country. That piece of news didn't surprise me in the least.

This is a little lesson in restraint. I didn't have very much then, but I might have learned some since. For example, I've waited half a dozen years to explain this complicated story. Sometimes it seems as if it happened longer ago than that, and to another person.

Lord of the Ring

[1971]

Ernest Hemingway imagined himself, as all his admirers now do, a heavy-weight, a literary hard puncher and even physically a formidable opponent. He valued the attributes that the American male (and the Karamojong warrior) value. His biographer shares the attitude and the metaphor: "He ... dealt, almost singlehanded, a permanent blow against the affected, the namby-pamby ..." He took enormous pleasure in flooring a muscular Negro with his bare fists, and delivering a manuscript he could say, "I'll defend the title again against all the good young new ones." He spoke of the discipline needed for writing as similar to that for successful boxing; he was proud of his good health, doing exercises, running, swimming and rising early while he was engaged on a book; and he saw his writing career in terms of the ring: "I started out very quiet and I beat Mr Turgenev. Then I trained hard and I beat Mr de Maupassant. I've fought two draws with Mr Stendhal." He had the humility to add, "But nobody's going to get me in the ring with Mr Tolstoy ..." His line was that he could lick practically any man in the house.

He was a destroyer and so are many of his characters: even the gentle Santiago recalls a triumphant arm-wrestling match (with a muscular Negro); others of his characters are fighters, inclined towards pugilism. One sees the glamor: his destroyers come in pairs and all eyes are on them; it is one big man against another, and implies competition, ultimately a winner and a loser. We are to admire the winner (Hemingway, not Turgenev; Santiago, not the Negro). But the very reverent biographer concedes bullying: "Throughout the month of May, Ernest's behaviour was often that of a bully." Professor Carlos Baker is referring to Hemingway ruining his friend's catch of a large marlin by firing a tommy-gun at some circling sharks which, maddened by the taste of their own spilt blood, devour most of the marlin. Later in that same month Hemingway beats up Joseph Knapp, a New York publisher. Both of these incidents, tidied up to make the gunner heroic and the fight with the rich intruder a justly-deserved victory, are retold in *Islands in the Stream*, with the *envoi*, black calypso singers immortalising the fist-fight with a song as, in 1935, they "celebrated Ernest's victory with an extemporaneous song about the 'big slob' from Key West."

The boxer recalls his famous matches, the novelist his novels; a boxer is bigger than any of his fights and though writing is hardly a competitive art, much less a sport, the novelist postured deliberately to be bigger than any of his novels. The question of "style", a favourite boxing word, is fundamental to a discussion of Hemingway's work; not style as a literary value but style as a posture, emphasising the face, the voice, the stance. Hemingway blamed the bad reviews of *Across the River and into the Trees* on his photograph that appeared on the dust jacket ("Makes me look like a cat-eating Zombie"); the voice is familiar ("You got very hungry when you did not eat enough in Paris . . ."); and the stance? Always the boxer's: "Am trying to knock Mr Shakespeare on his ass."

The reputation is all, and counts for more than the writing. Asked who is the most popular American writer in the Soviet Union, the Russian journalist says, "Papa." The note of friendly intimacy is common: it is the man that matters. The American writer produces a good book and acquires a reputation. The reputation displaces the idea of literary quality: the idea of the author is much more important than the ideas in the work. Interesting, the number of academics who care so deeply about the man's adventures and leave the work unread, or see blasphemy in a low evaluation of it. Hemingway claimed to dislike academics, but those who flattered him were welcomed at his haunts and in his house; he yarned them, feeding them lines, took them on his boat, and wrote them candid letters. In the letter refusing Carlos Baker permission to write a biography, Hemingway mentions ("with almost bewildering frankness") how he practised *coitus interruptus* with his second wife. (The fact appears in Professor Baker's recent biography, *Ernest Hemingway – A Life Story*.)

Since the aggressive narcissism of commerce and the vanity of money are the driving forces of reputation-making, the progress of the reputation is best described in the language of the stock-exchange. A writer appears on the market; he has considerable long-term upside potential; he gets a divorce and hits a slump, his plane crashes in a jungle and this is a technical rally; he tumbles and bottoms out, he meets resistance at the buyer level, then rallies again and inflates the firms up and meets a negative critical flow, and so forth. This does not have much to do with writing, but Hemingway's reputation grew without much reference to his work, and in the years since his death, aided by the urgent whisperings of fact-finders and anecdotalists, it has rallied and consolidated sideways. Now a "new" novel has been found; it was written twenty years ago and apparently abandoned by the author. It is technically his last novel and its publication is a triumph for those obsessed with the man.

The novel has no literary importance, but its personal candour is essential. This is of course the basest motive for reading; contemptuous of the art of fiction, the reader is interested in the book only in so far as it gives access to the author: "This is just a story but Ernest Hemingway is writing it . . ." The satisfactions are finding out how Hemingway drank and handled a boat, and spoke, and made love, and treated his friends. These revelations are considered important, for once the reputation is made and the novel is a study rather than a pleasure (or a bore), the hero of the novel is its author. Fortunately for Hemingway his life began to be studied before he failed as a novelist, so it was never acceptable to say, "This novel is bad." The novels were aspects of the man, and the man's heroism was never questioned.

Islands in the Stream is divided into three parts. In 1951 Hemingway said that parts 2 and 3 were "in shape to publish", but he did not publish them. The novel (to use the publisher's term; it is really nothing of the kind) is set in the Caribbean and seems originally to have been intended as a study of the sea. Previous titles of the sections were *The Sea When Young, The Sea when Absent,* and *The Sea in Being,* retitled in the present edition as "Bimini", "Cuba" and "At Sea." The sections are loosely linked by the common subject of the sea and by the main character, Thomas Hudson, who is "in appearance, manner, and personal history . . . clearly based on Ernest himself" (according to Professor Baker). There was a fourth section, and Thomas Hudson was not the hero of it. This was the story of an old man, Santiago, who caught a marlin and battled to save it; it was published (Hemingway had some reservations about its length) as *The Old Man and the Sea.* Professor Baker reports that Hemingway was very enthusiastic about the unpublished parts of the book he was calling *The Island and the Stream,* but rather than publish it he turned from it and wrote *A Moveable Feast,* his last book, parts of which are prefigured in the reminiscences of Thomas Hudson. Hudson, in his youth, also lived with his wife and small child over a sawmill in Paris in the 1920s, and had a cat named F Puss and liked the bicycle races and drank in cafés with James Joyce and Ezra Pound.

Here, perhaps, is the reason Hemingway never published *Islands in the Stream*. It was autobiography – this is clear from the duplicated recollections in *A Moveable Feast* – but he wanted it to read as fiction. He wrote it at an age when most novelists turn to autobiography, but rather than reveal the novel as that, he published the story of Santiago and spent the last three years of his life writing a straightforward reminiscence, to which he added ambiguously in the Preface, "If the reader prefers, this

book may be regarded as fiction . . ." It is hard to say whether he would
have published the present novel, had he allowed himself to live a few
years longer. This is crucial because a writer can only be held responsible for what he publishes himself and stands by; he can't be blamed for
writing a bad book that he chose to leave in a bottom drawer.

Thomas Hudson is a painter. He has been divorced and he lives in
different places in the Caribbean. He seems to have a separate personality for each place. In the first section of the book, on the island of
Bimini, he is a reticent friend, a quiet drunk and a devoted father; he
fishes with his three boys and does a little painting of the Winslow
Homer variety. The second section is set largely in a bar in Havana; here
Hudson is a bar-fly, drinking and betting, and talking at some length to
an elderly prostitute; he does no painting. A sea chase occupies the
whole of the third section; Hudson is a bullying, Bogartesque ship's
captain pursuing Germans along the coast of Cuba. Three episodes,
hardly stories, and except for Hudson, who alters but does not grow, the
episodes bear no relation to one another. The three boys, Hudson's
children, are all dead by the time the second section opens, possibly to
give Hudson nothing to live for, though more likely because Hemingway couldn't think of any way of working them into the conversation
with the elderly prostitute or the pursuit of the Germans. The artless
novelist has his reasons for disposing of characters, usually no more
complicated than the eldest boy's in *Jude the Obscure*, when he hanged
himself and his siblings: "Done because we are too menny."
  Hudson gets little satisfaction (but evidently lots of cash) from his
painting. He is, for most of the book, an aggressive self-absorbed man
for whom killing a big fish and disembowelling a German are ways of
proving one's manhood. It is the philosophy of combat – perversely
based on killing one's friend, for the noblest combat is destroying
something beautiful, something one values. "In the worst parts, when I
was tiredest, I couldn't tell which was him and which was me," says
Dave, one of the sons, after the fish had been caught and killed.
Incapable of creation, these characters see beauty in destruction;
considering themselves men in the proverbial sense of the word, their
ambition must be to win: to kill the lion, to floor the Negro, to catch the
fish, to have always the winning hand. Achievement is irrelevant here
(Hudson's painting is all but dismissed as daubing) because achievement
implies solitary creation. Winning is another matter: one wins by
beating one's opponent. Thus, most strangely: "Am trying to knock Mr
Shakespeare on his ass."

"All fights are bad."

"I know it. But what are you going to do about them?"

"You have to win them when they start."

Failure is losing, because losing is humiliation, unbecoming to a man: "Get it straight. Your boy you lose. Love you lose. Honor has been gone for a long time. Duty you do." That is Hudson at his lowest point, a loser. He recovers, but others are not so lucky, for the last loser deserves it, as the winner deserves his success. The loser's mortality proves more than the winner's physical superiority – it implies the winner's immortality. So much for the fist-fight between Roger and the wealthy yachtsman, which Roger wins, saying, "That guy was no good, Tom." And Thomas Hudson agrees: "You taught him something." The implication is that the yachtsman has been taught that he will never win a fist-fight with a man Hemingway conceives to be morally superior. In this case the man should know better: Roger is a writer and the sniveling yachtsman he defeats is a publisher.

Hemingway insists on the rightness of the philosophy. Consequently there is an interminable repetition of the words fine and good and true and wonderful and brave and necessary, all applied to bullying and mean-spirited and unworthy acts, "a wonderful chase," "a fine shot," "a beautiful kill". A sententious utterance, implying if not employing one of these words, closes each incident. After Dave hooks the swordfish and yanks on him for six hours (and twenty-five pages of the book), the motto is, "But there is a time boys have to do things if they are ever going to be men." An odd thing for a painter to say; but Thomas Hudson is no creator.

There is a great deal of killing in the book, practically all of it gratuitous, as when the swordfish is killed or Thomas Hudson shoots a land crab that appears on his path (". . . the crab disintegrated . . . Poor old crab, he thought . . .") or the Germans are shelled. Murder is necessary and it is a shame it makes one feel bad:

> Then why don't you care about anything? he asked himself. Why don't you think of them as murderers and have the righteous feelings that you should have . . . Because we are all murderers, he told himself. We all are on both sides, if we are any good, and no good will come of any of it.
>
> But you have to do it. Sure, he said.

We all are on both sides: "I couldn't tell which was him and which was me," says Dave when the fish is dead; and "He was a pretty good guy," Willie says of the German he's blown to bits. The philosophy demands the sentimentality of pity. And grief is self-pity. Here is Hudson revealing the death of his son to the mother of the boy, his ex-wife:

> "That isn't it," she said. "Tell me, is he dead?"
> "Sure."
> "Please hold me tight. I am ill now." He felt her shaking and he knelt by the chair and held her and felt her tremble. Then she said: "And poor you. Poor, poor you."
> After a time she said: "I'm sorry for everything I ever did or said."
> "Me, too."
> "Poor you and poor me."
> "Poor everybody," he said, and he did not add, "Poor Tom."

A very large number of suicides, by various means, are mentioned in the novel as well, remarked upon with a kind of queer joy. Obeying the perverse logic of destruction, the destroyer as hero, it is consistent that after subduing or killing every powerful thing on earth, the man, to maintain the image of his invincibility, kills himself. The warrior runs upon his own sword. Self-slaughter is the only acceptable end for the destroying hero; any other death is humiliating defeat. Hudson does not commit suicide. At the end of the book, wounded by Germans for whom he has developed an eager affection, he is full of self-love and self-loathing which, combined, turn to pride and a satisfied self-pity. Motto: "You never understand anybody that loves you."

The Hemingway Stamp, that cauliflower earmark that characterises his worst fiction, is everywhere apparent. Hudson reflects on catnip: "There still should be some catnip in the shelf of drawers of the cat room if it hasn't gotten too dry and lost its force. It lost its force very quickly in the tropics and the catnip that you raised in the garden had no force at all." Hudson has a drink: ". . . strong with the real Gordon's gin that made it alive to his tongue and rewarding to swallow . . . It tastes as good as a drawing sail feels, he thought. It is a hell of a good drink." The descriptions of food and wine are given lovingly, while lovemaking is reduced to utter vagueness: "He did something . . . She did something else . . ."

The novel is offered as something of a departure for Hemingway, with "a rich and relaxed sense of humor." But nearly all the humor depends on seeing bullying or ridicule as comic: attempting to set a dock on fire, humiliating the yachtsman or taking the mickey out of a tourist or "a fine old whore," or teasing a sleepy-headed servant. In each case there is a victim who is weak or passive; he is made a figure of fun and one is meant to find him contemptible and so laughable. The humor has Thomas Hudson and his friends in stitches, and in many places Hudson says how much he is enjoying himself, but he is an embittered, heartless, unquestioning and deluded man. Physical superiority is what Hudson cares about but he is old and life is unbearable for him.

The disappointment and the sour regret give the novel the tone of a suicide note. It is sad to think that Hemingway wrote it, and understandable that he left it in a bottom drawer.

A Love-Scene After Work
Writing In The Tropics

[1971]

One of the most pathetic illustrations in all literature about the difficulty of holding a job and writing a novel at the same time occurs in Anthony Trollope's *Autobiography*. He has been sent to Scotland "to revise the Glasgow Post Office", and in order to assess the labors of the letter carriers he must trudge alongside them all day as they deliver. He is determined to do a good job; when a letter carrier goes to the top floor of a house, Trollope follows. It is mid-summer and hot. "The men would grumble," Trollope says, "and then I would think how it would be with them if they had to go home afterwards and write a love-scene."

Any person who has tried to work and write understands that remark. Trollope knew a further difficulty: writing in the tropics. *The West Indies and the Spanish Main* was written in Trinidad, Jamaica, Costa Rica and Cuba, on board ship, in stuffy hotel rooms, in terrible heat. And he was working in the West Indies – surveying the postal service. Trollope was an unusual man, a great whist player, an avid horseman, a curious and observant traveler, a devoted civil servant (framer of postal treaties, inventor of the pillar box). He was a prolific novelist and a hard-working editor. Trollope's energy is a rare thing, and so is his candor: "But the love-scenes written in Glasgow, all belonging to *The Bertrams*, are not good."

A job, especially one that requires alertness, always menaces the novel. A job overseas is different; there are many advantages in being an expatriate worker, but there are more disadvantages, and after working abroad for nine years as a teacher in the seasonless monotony of three tropical countries I have decided to chuck the whole business and never take a job again. I have to admit that some of my objections are petty. I am made unreasonably angry when one of my unsmiling superiors, summoning me through his secretary, bites on his pipe, and mispronouncing my name, demands that I must do this or that. I suppose the rudeness angers me; it is the Singaporean's least endearing quality. But it is a Chinese rule. The most powerful are the least polite; a promotion means a diminution in civility, which is a quality – not a virtue – of the very low. The weak have no choice but to be polite.

"Excuse me, sir," says a student. "Eddie Fang says you are a novelist. Are you going to write a novel about Singapore?"

"No thanks," I reply. "But you've lived here your whole life – why don't you write one?"

"Can't." He flinches and adds: "There's nothing to write about."

There have been excellent English schools in Singapore for a hundred years. Singapore claims to have the best school system in Asia. English is the official language. No Singaporean has ever written a novel in English. Once there was a girl here who wrote poetry, but she went to Iowa and never came back. The highlight of the UNESCO-sponsored Festival of Books in Singapore was a children's fancy-dress contest; Raffles, Cinderella, Robin Hood and Lord Krishna were winners.

"Well, if there's nothing to write about, then how am I supposed to write a novel about Singapore?"

"Eddie Fang said you used to live in Africa. And you wrote some books about Africa. So I thought –"

Sometimes during a conversation like this (I am asked the question twice a week) I say, "I'm writing a novel about a writer in Singapore who wants to write a novel about Singapore and can't." No one laughs at that.

No one laughs at much. The Singapore government, which is a mixture of paranoia and paternalism – inspiring the fearfulness of childhood, when authority always seems irrefragable in its strength – exhorts her citizens to be busy. The Singaporeans' play looks like work; people made into children are fearful about breaking rules, and very tense they become very humorless. They don't want to be caught laughing – anyway, what's so funny? Humor is the sort of independent mimicry that requires the same rebelliousness writing does. Humor also emphasizes differences in people, in their speech and habits; it has a tendency to distort gleefully in order to express a truth. At Morning Coffee, which is a tropical ritual observed as thoroughly as Afternoon Tea is in a temperate climate, I tell a joke. The several Chinese at the table fall silent, although the joke is quite harmless. If it was about physical deformity or race they might laugh. Then one says, "That's very interesting," and looks grave. My Indian friend giggles; like me, he's an expatriate. He offers a joke of his own. The Chinese stare at him.

A few days later the Indian asks me if I plan to stay in Singapore. I tell him I intend to leave, to quit teaching entirely and take up writing full time.

"So you vant to be another Faith Baldvin?" he says, and titters into his coffee cup. But he is not mocking. He also reads Oliver Goldsmith for pleasure.

Conrad said (in "A Glance at Two Books", *Last Essays*): ". . . a book is a deed . . . the writing of it is an enterprise as much as the conquest of a colony." This means a daily effort of laborious concentration. It cannot be haphazard, weekend flurries of composition, and who can get up as early in the morning as Trollope? By stages one encloses oneself in one's novel, erects a barrier that shuts out the real world to duplicate it. Obviously, if one is married and has a job and children and friends, one can't write one's book as if one is serving a prison sentence, going into isolation and emerging when the work is done. On the other hand, one doesn't write a book by observing a landscape or hearing a phrase at a party and then going home and scribbling the observation in the margin of the text. "Are you writing a book about Singapore?" the student asks. I'm not; if I do it will be elsewhere.

Mornings in the tropics – an hour or two – are for teaching, afternoons for sleeping; the lighted pause of early evening is spent in a bar or drinking on a veranda. Writing at night is out because of the heat, and the desk lamp attracts insects that make shadows as they strafe the pages. But also, teaching in the tropics is undemanding, hours are fewer, classes smaller, and I've given all my lectures before. I can dig out last year's lecture on *The White Devil* or Middleton's comedies and with a little planning I can free myself during the best hours of the day, the glittering spring-like morning, from seven to ten or eleven. I write in longhand so I can memorize everything I've written; committing a novel to memory makes it possible to think about it, extend it, and correct it in any idle hour.

I consider myself to have been very lucky. Both in Uganda and Singapore my bosses were writers themselves; they were interested in my work, and I think they made some allowances for me. Mr Moore used to ask me how my poems were coming along, and Mr Enright and I used to commiserate in the Staff Club; he would look around at the drinkers, when we were talking about writing, and say, "They think it's easy!"

The best job for a writer, a job with the fewest hours, is in the tropics. But books are hard to write in the tropics. It is not only the heat; it is the lack of privacy, the open windows, the noise. Tropical cities are deafening. In Lagos and Accra and Kampala two people walking down a city street will find they are shouting to each other to be heard over the sound of traffic and the howls of residents and radios. V. S. Naipaul is the only writer I know of who has mentioned the abrading of the nerves by tropical noise (the chapter on Trinidad in *The Middle Passage*). Shouting is the Singaporean's expression of friendliness; the Chinese shout is like a bark, sharp enough to make you jump. And if you are unfortunate enough to live near a Chinese cemetery – only foreigners live near cemeteries, the Chinese consider it unlucky to occupy those houses – you will hear them mourning with firecrackers, scattering cherrybombs over the gravestones.

Sit in a room in Singapore and try to write. Every sound is an interruption, and your mind blurs each time a motorcycle or a plane or a funeral passes. If you live near a main road, as I do, there will be three funerals a day (Chinese funerals are truckloads of gong-orchestras and brass bands playing familiar songs like "It's A Long Way To Tipperary"). The day the Bengali gardener mows the grass is a day wasted. Hawkers cycle or drive by and each stops; you learn their individual yells, the bean-curd man with his transistor and sidecar, the fish-ball man on his bike, the ice-cream seller with his town crier's bell (a mid-afternoon interruption), the breadman in his Austin van, leaning on the horn; the elderly Chinese lady crouching in her *sam foo* and crying "*Yeggs!*" through the door, the Tamil newsboy, a toddy alcoholic, muttering "Baybah, baybah". Before the British forces left there was a fish-and-chip van; it didn't beep, but there were yells. The Singaporean doesn't stir from his house. He waits in the coolness of his parlor for the deliverers to arrive. The yells and gongs, at first far off, then closer, console him. It is four-thirty, and here comes the coconut-seller ringing his bicycle bell. He has a monkey, a macaque the size of a four-year-old, on the crossbar. The coconut-seller is crazy; the buyers make him linger and they laugh at him. A crowd gathers to jeer him; he chases some children and then goes away. After dark the grocery truck parks in front of your house; the grocer has a basket of fish, a slaughtered pig, and the whole range of Ma-Ling canned goods ("Tripe in Duck Grease", "Chicken Feet," "Lychees in Syrup") and for an hour you will hear the yelp and gargle of bartering. You have written nothing.

The heat and light; you asked for those in coming so far, but it is hotter, though less bright than you imagined – Singapore is usually cloudy, averaging only six hours of sunshine a day. That persistent banging and screeching is an annoyance that makes you hotter still. You are squinting at the pen which is slipping out of your slick fingers and wondering why you bothered to come.

Slowly, it happens, a phrase, a sentence, a paragraph. Nothing comes out right the first time, and you are not so much writing as learning a language, inching along in what seems at times like another tongue. A characteristic of writing in the tropics is this recopying, rewriting, beginning again, and understanding that it will take a long time, whatever you write: it has taken me a week to get this far with this little essay. It is not impossible to finish, just hard, because many things have to be in your favor: it can't be too hot, it must be quiet, two or three hours have to be totally free of interruption; your health must be good and your mood fairly bright – a late night, an argument or a hangover means a lost day.

But the fact of being in a foreign place has made you small. You are not a public figure (public figures who are habitually vocal are deported), simply an English teacher. The bookstores do not stock your novels, or anyone's. No one is going to ask you to lecture at the National Library on "The Future of the Novel"; the worst that can happen, if it is known you are a writer, is that you'll be asked to edit the church newsletter. You are unaware of any sense of celebrity or reputation. That happened last year, in another country, when your novel appeared; and there hasn't been a murmur since. Everything has to be proven anew, and if you need humility, look at the bookshelf behind you where your novels, even last year's, have become mildewed and discolored in the humidity: they could be the books of a dead man. No one where you live has the slightest idea of what you are doing. To write you have withdrawn, like any conscientious hobbyist; and ceasing to live in the place you may be lonelier: your world is your house, your family, your desk; abroad is a bar.

It is a form of eccentricity, but in the tropics the eccentric is common, and far from being held in contempt, he is regarded as rather special and left alone. At Makerere University in Uganda, one head of department was never seen. He didn't teach his classes; he was never sober; he was said to be a great character. He had many defenders. There was a professor of philosophy in Singapore who used to saunter down the street in his pajamas, reading difficult books. This was his uniqueness. He was watched but never pestered. Expatriates by the very fact of their having come to the tropics are considered by the locals to be somewhat crazed, and the expatriate who fails to be a person in any subtle sense can still, with a little effort, succeed as "a character". This requires a specific obsession, a singular tic of personality. Your distinguishing mark might be your continual absence ("Oh, *him* – he's *never* around"), and if not doing your job is your affectation, then you may proceed with other things. What does it matter if anyone sees this as dereliction? You are an expatriate on contract, not an exile; you intend to go home eventually. Gain a modest reputation for being unreliable and you will never be asked to do a thing. The students will become used to receiving their essays late.

The students demand less than American ones; the system, Oxbridge in equatorial decline, forces them to work alone. They are as insular as their parents and subservient to the government; their civic-mindedness takes the form of fashion shows for charity. They are intelligent, nervous, inexperienced and poorly read. Many would like to emigrate to Australia (Singaporeans talk reverently about Australia, the way people from

Massachusetts used to talk about California: "Plenty of opportunities there, and a really nice climate"). Like students in developing countries everywhere their speech is a mixture of the bookish and the political ("whilst we go from strength to strength", "timorous Claudio is part and parcel . . ."). Some in essays sound like Jacobeans. One discovers Irving Ribner and tears him to shreds; another who has never heard of the First World War writes about Wildred Owen. There is no American literature. "Richard Cory" is said to be an old English ballad, and Herman Woo and Heidi Chin think the eponymous hero's name "ridiculous and comic". Except for the archaic phrases the students write clearly, in mission school copperplate; they speak less well, and in a tutorial sometimes spell out the word they want to say. Lady Macbeth is "roofless" or "rootless", and Dickens is very good at "crating a crackter". It is easy to laugh at such lapses, until one reminds oneself of the émigré scientists in the States – brilliant men in their fields – pronouncing their original sentences all wrong. Chinese students are plagued by glottal stops and certain consonants, and they always speak very fast. In a tutorial a girl holding a leatherbound book reads aloud to prove a point she has just made:

> *Must dow esplain da ting I hate most on erf,*
> *Da treason, da shame, da assident of my berf?*

In a lecture on *Tamburlaine* I repeat the line, "Holla, ye pampered jades of Asia!" They smile earnestly in recognition. What will become of them? It is a foreigner's question. Their parents have saluted four different flags, some more; in twenty-five years, when these students are middle-aged, what flag will be flying over the Singapore City Hall? It is futile to speculate, but not less worrying for the person who has spent three years among them, who knows many as friends and who has come to understand that the student who says, "Must dow esplain . . ." is no fool.

I never traveled much in the United States, but I remember my two older brothers making a train journey from Boston to Ohio when I was seven or eight – in the late 'forties. Somehow we had the idea that people in Ohio suffered from a lack of iodine because of the scarcity of fish. The Ohioans were afflicted by goiters, and people walked around Cleveland with bulbous growths on their necks. I was too young to go to Ohio, but I remember my brothers' stories: about their meal on the train, how the waiter brought their change back on a plate (a *plate*!), the flatness of Ohio, and they *had* seen some people with goiters, and one elderly lady called my brothers "Yankees". They had their rolls of film developed; the results were blurred and banal, every one was a disappointment: Ohio, which sounded so foreign, looked like Massachusetts.

Growing up, I mistrusted anyone who had not traveled. I thought of becoming a White Father, not out of any piety but from a desire to be sent to Africa. I thought of becoming a doctor: then I could have a useful occupation overseas. When I was nineteen or twenty I applied for a job in a Lebanese university, and having fabricated much of the application, was called for an interview in a Boston hotel. The interviewer was kind, asked me my age, then smiled and said I wouldn't do: Beirut was a rough city, and "there is always some kind of trouble in the Arab quarter". I finally left in the spring of 1963, and I have not been back in the States for more than a few weeks at a time, a total of about four months in nine years. Now I want to go back for good, not because it is too difficult to live abroad – only writing is hard in the tropics – but perhaps because it is too easy. Africa, for all its mystery and strangeness, unquote, is really a very simple place to live. Africans are candid and hospitable, and make it easy for you to live among them. The Chinese in Singapore appear not to see you; the students do not greet you or each other. Anonymity is simple.

Living among strangers in a foreign place I am like an unexpected guest waiting in a tropical parlor. My mind is especially alert to differences of smell and sound, the shape of objects, and I am apprehensive about what is going to happen next. I sit with my knees together in the heat, observing the surfaces of things. At the same time, the place is so different I can indulge myself in long unbroken reflections, for the moments of observation are still enough to allow the mind to travel in two directions: recording mentally the highly-colored things one sees is simple; the mind then wanders. The reflection may be a reminiscence of early youth, a piecing-together of an episode out of the distant past; it is not contradicted or interrupted by anything near. In a foreign country I can live in two zones of time, the immediate and apprehensible, and in that vaguer zone I thought I had forgotten. Since I do not write autobiographically, I am able to see the past more clearly; I haven't altered it in fiction. That detail of the goiters in Ohio, the forsythia bush behind our Medford house, our large family; slowly, in a foreign place, the memory whirrs and gives back the past. It is momentarily a reassurance, the delay of any daydream, but juxtaposed with the vivid present it is an acute reminder of my estrangement.

And it may be wasteful and near senility, this reaching back that living abroad allows. Certainly trivial details can be strongly visualized: twenty-five years ago I pulled myself up the side of my grandfather's rainbarrel and looked in and saw mosquito larvae twitching near the surface like tiny seahorses. I had not thought of it until yesterday, in a suburb of Singapore. I wonder at its importance.

Most of a writer's life is spent in pure idleness, not writing a thing. Up to now I have used this idleness to poke in places with bewitching names, Sicily, the Congo, Malaya, Burma, Singapore, Java; this distraction could be a form of indulgence, but I can't think what else I should have done. I know it is a mistake to stay away from home too long, and it is foolish if one calls oneself a writer to go on teaching. The professions are separate; I admire the people who can write love-scenes after work. I can't, and it is unprofitable to pose as if I can. I told a colleague I was leaving. She was concerned. She believes my subjects are little countries. She said, "But if you live in Europe or America, what will you write about?" We'll see.

V. S. Naipaul

[1971 and 1982]

I had been in Africa for a little over three years, writing every day; I was full of ideas, full of books and plans. This was in Uganda. I was a lecturer in the Department of Extra-Mural Studies at Makerere University. We ran weekend courses for adults in upcountry towns (now, most of those adults are dead and their towns burned to the ground). One day in 1966, a man on the English Department said, "V. S. Naipaul is coming next week. He's joining the department. He'll be with us for about six months."

He never gave a lecture; I don't think he set foot in the department, and towards the end of his term he moved into a hotel in western Kenya. He hated the house he had been given. "Everybody gets those houses," a woman told him. He said, "I'm not everybody." He refused to put a nameboard on his house; and then he had an idea: "I'll have a sign saying 'Teas' and as you go up the road past the houses you'll see 'Smith,' 'Jones,' 'Brown,' 'Teas!' " He was asked to judge a literary competition. None of the entries was good enough for first or second prize: the single winner got third prize. He had some writing students; he invited them to his house and, one by one, urged them not to write. He gave the university's name a Scottish pronunciation, something like *MacArayray*. He said African names baffled him. "Mah-boya" he said for Mboya, "Nah-googy" for Ngugi, and an Englishman named Cook he called "Mah-Cook," because the man wore an African shirt and was full of enthusiasm for bad African poems. Naipaul bought a floppy military hat and a walking stick. He walked around Kampala, frowning. "See how they make paths everywhere — every park is crisscrossed with paths!" he said. "They do exactly as they please, that's why they're so happy," he said of the Africans. "But the English here are shameless. They're inferior, you know. Most of the men are buggers. That's why they're here." He liked referring to Ghana as "The Gold Coast" and Tanzania as "Tanganyika" and towards the end of his stay in East Africa, when Indians were being persecuted in Kenya and Uganda, he advised the Indian High Commissioner to cable his government urging a punitive mission. "Anchor a few battleships off Mombasa. Shell the coast. Mah-boya will change his tune."

I had never met anyone like him. We were introduced at one of Mah-

Cook's poetry sessions. Afterwards, Naipaul asked me casually what I had thought of it. "Awful," I said, and from that moment we were friends. I told him how much I enjoyed his books. This pleased him, and if I gave him a line I liked he could give me the next one. He knew his books by heart, having copied them out in longhand two or three times – that was his writing method. He was impressed that I had read so many of his books – no one else in Kampala had. "No one reads here," he said. "They're all inferior. Obote puts a bronze plaque of his face over the Parliament Building and everyone thinks it's wonderful. He's a dictator! This country is slowly turning back into bush!"

He said he found writing torture. This surprised me, because his books were humorous and full of ease; the imagery was precise and vivid, the characters completely human. I did not know then that to write well one went slowly, often backwards, and some days nothing at all happened. "Writing should be transparent," Naipaul said. But it took great strength and imagination to make light shine through it. I had read *An Area of Darkness, The Mystic Masseur* and *Mr. Stone and the Knights Companion* and *A House for Mr Biswas*. I admired them and reread them, feeling only discouragement for myself, dismay at seeing my own writing.

I wondered what Naipaul read himself. He showed me his books – two of them, Martial in Latin and The Holy Bible. He tapped the Bible and said, "It's frightfully good!"

One day he asked me what I was writing. It was an essay, I said, on cowardice. "It explains why I feel cowardly." He looked at it, scrutinized it, asked me why I used this word and not that word, challenged me and suggested I rewrite it. I rewrote it four times. When I was finished he said, "You should publish it. Send it to a good magazine – forget these little magazines. Don't be a 'little-magazine' person. And write something else. Why don't you write something about this dreadful place?"

He was the first good writer I had ever met and he was then, in 1966, working on one of his best books, *The Mimic Men*. It is almost impossible for me to overestimate the importance of Naipaul's friendship then. I was 25, he was 34. He said he felt very old; he seemed very old. "I'm not interested in meeting any new people," he said. "I should never have come here to this bush place. You've been here for three years – you see how writing keeps you sane? If you hadn't been writing you'd have become an infy" – it was his word for inferior – "like the rest of them."

His praise mattered, and when he gave advice I took it. He demanded that I look at punctuation, at the shape of a paragraph. "And you need to be calm to write well. Be detached – detachment is very important. It's not indifference – far from it!"

It was like private tuition – as if, at this crucial time in my life (I had just finished my first novel), he had come all the way to Africa to remind me of what writing really was and to make me aware of what a difficult path I was setting out on. When we were together he was very sensible and exact, and he could be terribly severe: Never do this, never do that. "Never give a person a second chance," he said. "If someone lets you down once, he'll do it again." He talked often about writing, the pleasures and pains. He was proud of the fact that he had never had another job. The American Farfield Foundation had financed this Uganda trip, but Naipaul said he was losing money by staying.

"At this stage of your life your writing will change from week to week. Just let it – keep writing. Style doesn't matter – it's the vision that's important, and writing from a position of strength." He was right. I began to notice an improvement, a greater certainty in my writing. It was Naipaul who showed me that Africa was more comedy than tragedy, and that perhaps I should spend more time writing and less time organizing extra-mural classes. He said, "Never take people more seriously than they take themselves."

With me he was a generous, rational teacher. But in Kampala his reputation as a crank was growing. "I hate music," he said. "African music is frightful. Listen to them." He went around saying that Africans were wasteful and unresourceful: "Look at the Italians – they can make cheese out of dirt." Every now and then he shocked a room full of people by describing in detail his punitive mission of Indian gunboats. He claimed that there were very few African writers who were not in some way plagiarists; and several were exposed, though not by Naipaul.

"Those are the ones that frighten me," I heard him say one day to a Makerere lecturer. He pointed to a long-legged African walking on flapping sandals under the blue-gum trees.

"What about him?" the lecturer asked.

"He's carrying a book," Naipaul said. "The ones that carry books scare the hell out of me, man."

He asked me to take him to a brothel. He sat on the veranda, drinking banana gin and smiling in refusal when a girl came near. He said, "I see perfect integration here."

When he finished his novel, he wanted to travel. "Let's go to Rwanda," he said. Naipaul had a car, and even a driver, but his driver had let him down in some way and, in a kind of vengeance, Naipaul did the driving and the African driver sat in the back seat, scowling in remorse. In the event, we took my car to Rwanda, and I did the driving. One day we made a wrong turn and ended up in the Congo. Border guards detained us. They wore colorful shirts and they carried guns. When they sent us away, Naipaul said, "Did you see their uniforms? Did you hear their bad French? Let's get out of here."

We went to Goma, on Lake Kivu. There were a few Indian shopkeepers there. Naipaul talked to them, asking them about business, the future, and were their children going to school? Afterwards, he said, "They're all dead men." The hotels were empty except for the large Belgian families which ran them and ate enormous meals, quarreling and shouting the whole time. Rwanda was still a colonial place, with decaying villas and savage guard dogs. A dog snarled at us one night as we were out walking. Naipaul said calmly, "What that dog wants is a good kick."

In Kigali, the dusty capital, the hotels were full. I inquired at the American Embassy and was told that Naipaul and I could use the embassy guest house. This brought from him a melancholy reflection. "Look what it means to come from a big powerful country — you Americans are lucky," he said. "But I come from a ridiculous little island."

We had one argument on the trip. I picked up an African who was hitchhiking. Naipaul had said, "Let him walk." But the African was in the bush; there was no transport at all. I sometimes hitchhiked myself. Naipaul was very angry; the African was a lazy, sponging good-for-nothing, preying on the conscience of an expatriate. But it was my car.

Later in the trip we stopped at a hotel in a remote town. It was the only hotel. Naipaul said, "I'm not having dinner tonight." I was surprised – he hadn't eaten anything all day. He said, "I was here once before. I had a row with the manager. The waiters had dirty uniforms, and one put his thumb in my soup."

He was fastidious about food, a strict vegetarian. He would not buy food at a market if it was uncovered. He would go hungry rather than eat meat. But he was curious about other people's eating habits, and on one occasion he bought a pound of fried locusts for his African driver and took delight in watching the African eat them.

He was certain that the Indians in Uganda and Kenya would soon be expelled. He often asked Indians about their prospects in Africa. His questions were always direct and challenging. I was with him once when an Indian in Kampala told Naipaul that he was all right, and he explained that he had an elaborate plan for staying.

I was convinced the man would be safe.

Naipaul shook his head. "He was lying."

Doubt, disbelief, skepticism, instinctive mistrust: I had never found these qualities so powerful in a person, and they were allied to a fiercely independent spirit, for his belief in himself and his talent never wavered. He was merciless, solitary, and (one of his favorite words) unassailable. No one had a claim on him.

At last, he left East Africa. I stayed for two more years. We remained friends; we had some common interests. It did not matter to me that he had never mentioned my books. Once in an interview he was asked which writers he liked. He began by saying, "It would be easier to say who I don't like – Jane Austen, Henry James . . ."

Nowadays I seldom see him – we have not met for three or four years. During the pointless Falklands War, Naipaul made a public statement. "When the Argentines say they are going to fight to the last drop of blood," he said, "it means they are on the point of surrender."

I laughed! That was the surprising, provocative voice I had heard all those years ago in Africa. He was sometimes wrong, he was often shocking or very funny. He had woken me and made me think.

"When I speak about being an exile or a refugee I'm not just using a metaphor, I'm speaking literally," Naipaul said in 1971, and that same year, as if to dramatize the statement, he lived in Wiltshire, the West Indies, South America and New Zealand. Some people still think of him as a Trinidadian, but when he flies to Port-of-Spain he has to produce an air ticket showing that he intends to leave. So much for being a Trinidadian. One considers his movements over the past thirty-two years and concludes that since he left Port-of-Spain in 1950 his life has been a series of onward bookings – or, speaking literally and figuratively, flights.

In *The Middle Passage* he mentions that when he was in the fourth form he made a vow to flee Trinidad within five years. He fled after six. Ten years later he returned to the West Indies, examined half a dozen places, rejected them all and fled again. Back in London, which he considered a neutral territory, "a good place for getting lost in, a city no one ever knew," he felt confined: "I became my flat, my desk, my name." He fled England; he sought India, and for a year was a resident. He traveled all over the Indian subcontinent, and in Srinagar wrote *Mr Stone and the Knights Companion* – the only novel in which he depicts English life. The end of his Indian experience was another flight, back to England via Madrid. "I had learned my separateness from India," he wrote in *An Area of Darkness*, "and was content to be a colonial, without a past, without ancestors." He is a tireless but reluctant traveler, like an unsponsored explorer without a compass in his work as in his life – for his characters share his homelessness; the awkward questions are "Where are you going?" and "Where are you from?"

Vidiadhar Surajprasad Naipaul was born in the country town of Chaguanas in Trinidad in 1932 of a large Brahmin family which originated in India, in the state of Uttar Pradesh. At the age of seven he was taken to Port-of-Spain to live, and there he received his early education. One guesses that his upbringing was very similar to Anand's (Biswas's son) in *A House for Mr Biswas*, and there is much in Anand's nature that is in Naipaul's: "Though no one recognized his strength, Anand was among the strong. His satirical sense kept him aloof. At first this was only a pose, an imitation of his father. But satire led to contempt, and [at . . . Shorthills] contempt, quick, deep, inclusive, became part of his nature. It led to inadequacies, to self-awareness and a lasting loneliness. But it made him unassailable."

In 1950, Naipaul came to England and was for four years at University College, Oxford. He married Patricia Hale, who had been a fellow student, in 1955, and published his first novel, *The Mystic Masseur*, in 1957. He has published eighteen books since then. Do a little arithmetic and you see that he was furiously reviewing fiction for the *New Statesman* (and was known as a particularly brutal critic) when he was in his mid-twenties; he wrote one of his masterpieces (he regards his first three novels as "an apprenticeship"), *A House for Mr Biswas*, at the age of 29, *Mr Stone* (which is about a Londoner of 62) at 30, *An Area of Darkness* at 32, *The Mimic Men* at 35. *The Times* described him as "the youngest of the W. H. Smith Award winners, and a quarter of a century light of the average". Naipaul explains what is already a shelf of his collected edition ("The Russell Edition" – his publisher has remained the same) by saying, "I was driven by an enormous tension." Even in the early books he gives the impression of being an older, reflective man, of wide experience and considerable learning, capable of wise judgment, with a mature style characterized by an exactitude of phrase. And yet he is now only fifty, and quite relaxed; he disliked Oxford scholarship; he bears only a passing resemblance to any of his heroes, and though he says in interviews that he feels his real work is behind him and that he visualizes simply "going silent", he is still game and on the move.

He is a small, finely-made man with an expressive mouth that can draw itself into a sad grimace, eyes that become hooded and oriental with fatigue, and thick black hair which he flings back when he gives his deep, appreciative laugh. His hands are delicate and his wrists are the size that make a watch slip and flop like a bracelet. He speaks in carefully framed sentences and his voice is precise, and sometimes sharp, except when he pauses to say, "Do you see what I mean?" He often says, "But you knew that, didn't you?" when imparting a totally unexpected piece of information. He is a brisk walker, hard to keep abreast of, as he takes his unusually long marching strides. He eats well, but not hugely; he likes good restaurants and hotels, and can give a thorough report on most places he has eaten in – the decor, the condition of the waiters' uniforms, the treatment, the service ("Try the Lake Victoria," he told me in Uganda. "They warm their cups"). He is a reasonable vegetarian, out of preference rather than any Hindu stricture. I once asked him about it. It was a personal matter; he didn't caution me or proselytize.

He made a face and said, "Biting through sinew. I couldn't do it."

Writing demands an immense amount of physical stamina, and Naipaul's books exhaust him. His health is unreliable, occasionally frail – he is plagued by asthma and insomnia – but he can be energetic, even athletic: he does callisthenic exercises every evening, and in East Africa he was so disturbed by the punyness and heavy drinking of the other expatriates he stopped drinking and took to running a mile every day on a Kampala track in the tropical heat. His chief aversion is to noise and he considers most music as disquieting as the sound of a pneumatic drill. With this concern he is an inveterate double-glazer and he used to subscribe to a magazine called *Noise*. In his flat in Kampala, a place he detested for its raucousness, he drew my attention to a radio blaring upstairs and said through gritted teeth, "Listen to the bitches!" He abandoned the place soon after for a hotel in Kenya, miles from the nearest town, "where you might hear the odd Kikuyu shout, but that's all."

His contempt is severe; he mocks humbug and is impatient with the ignorant and the inept. He can manage his impatience tactfully. "Is this your poem?" he asked an African student who had submitted a hand-written piece of verse ("A New Nation Reborn") to him for comment. "Yes? Well, I've read it and I want you to promise me to give up poetry immediately. Don't be depressed. Look at me, I've never written a poem in my life! I'm sure your gifts lie in quite another direction. But you have beautiful handwriting."

But in Dar es Salaam he lost his temper and identifying an African who attempted to needle him as "our friend from the Gold Coast" created a very anxious moment. He is skillful at depicting rage in his books. For example, Singh's "blind, damaging anger" at the house-warming party in *The Mimic Men*, when the Roman-style house is wrecked; Mr Stone and Mr Biswas, whose tempers isolate them; and in one of the autobiograph-ical parts of *In A Free State* he describes his confrontation with the rowdy bullying Italian tourists at Luxor (he defies the tourists and disarms the Arab). He loses his temper in India and analyzes the quality of the rage: "It was brutal; it was ludicrous; it was pointless and infantile. But the moment of anger is a moment of exalted, shrinking lucidity, from which recovery is slow and shattering."

Normally, Naipaul is a gentle and affectionate man, with a brilliant intellect, a remarkably decisive mind and a genius for inspiring friend-ship. His marriage is a confident, supportive influence, and intensely private, based on the respect which comes out of deep love. Pat Naipaul is devoted to her husband and awake to his moods; she has traveled great distances with him, knows his work better than any critic, and with some of *The Loss of Eldorado* acted as a patient and scholarly collaborator.

Though she is never mentioned in his books (in *An Area of Darkness* she is referred to once, with what seems calculated vagueness, as "my companion"), she is behind every word he writes.

If Naipaul had a country he would have made a useful diplomat for difficult postings. He has traveled to the interiors of India and Africa and South America, and crossed North America; he has reported on them. He speaks French well and Spanish with a Castillian accent (his Hindi is said to be shaky). He can move quickly and set himself up comfortably. He has had more home addresses than any man I know, but these addresses are impermanent: his household effects are nearly always in a warehouse.

Other people's stairs are steep, other people's bread is salty, said Dante of exile. For a writer there is a special curse in having to work among unfamiliar books and surroundings, on someone else's table, staring at another man's taste in wallpaper ("I see you put my wallpaper in *The Mimic Men*," a Kenyan hotel-owner wrote to Naipaul). Once, Naipaul had a house in Stockwell. It was in poor condition when he bought it, but (Georgian, detached, in a quiet crescent) it had possibilities. He redecorated it, furnished it, put in double-glazing, central heating – and went to Africa. Less than two years after returning from Africa he sold the house, moved into a hotel, then into a friend's house, and finally went to California. It makes moving for him something like the colonial ideal on a small scale, setting a place on its feet and then withdrawing from it. The Srinagar "Hotel Liward," where Naipaul was a guest (he gives it a chapter of *An Area of Darkness*), actually improves with his residence, as he puts idling employees to work, reminding them of their duties, encouraging them in their skills.

Both in his writing and in his daily life he is a perfectionist. Never late himself, he punishes the unpunctual. If you are late for dinner he might start without you; then you arrive when other guests are eating, beginning your first course when others are halfway through their second: the embarrassment is all yours, and you're left holding the grapefruit, as it were. I stayed with Naipaul in London. We were invited out to dinner; the host's car was to be sent to collect us, and Naipaul had autographed one of his novels as a present. But the car was an hour late, and the signed novel was left behind. An African had an appointment with him in Nairobi. The African was very late; he had, he said, run out of petrol. "He was lying," said Naipaul afterwards. "Everyone's late here – what else could he say?" In East Africa, a place noted for its unpunctuality, Naipaul insisted things should start on time, and eventually, where he was concerned, they did.

"I still have a great instinct towards great happiness and delight and pleasure," Naipaul says. He will share his enthusiasms (on which he has read all the literature) with any friend who shows an interest. He is knowledgeable about cricket, movies of the 'forties, snuff, architecture, fine wine, Indian art and politics, exploration, military strategy and topography, and printing (once on the Oxford train he breathed on the window and sketched half a dozen styles of typeface for me); and he is an astute graphologist as well.

"He's a tormented man," Naipaul said of a man who appeared to me rather unflappable.

I doubted this. How did he know?

"His handwriting." Naipaul winced. "Tormented."

Mention someone's name and Naipaul's first reaction might be, "An interesting hand. Even upside down it's still revealing."

His wit makes him a delight to know. When two Chinese, both named Wong, were deported from East Africa at a time when Europeans were getting preferential treatment, Naipaul commented, "Well, two Wongs don't make a white." Everyone he has met remembers something of him. The West Indian lady says, "Man, I'll never forgive him for saying, 'A banana a day keeps the Jamaican away' "*; a lady he stayed with in the States remembers, "He said he would never live in a place where he couldn't get Gloucester cheese"; the host in Africa respects him for insisting on Schweppes soda, the hotel-owner in Kenya says, "When Naipaul stayed here I had to buy a new cookbook, a vegetarian one." "A very curious man," says a doubtful English lady. "He said he'd given up sex." A literary person recalls him saying that *Mr Stone*, the story of an English clerk on the verge of retirement, is "my most autobiographical book." In a Soho *trattoria* he leaned across the table and said to me, "Don't you think the British government should sell knighthoods at the post office?"

He writes steadily, but slowly ("to achieve a writing which is perfectly *transparent*"), on unnumbered pages, using few notes, staying with a book without a break to the end. Though he does little revision in the conventional sense he might, as he did with *The Mimic Men*, throw away 20,000 words. After typing a book he often recopies it by hand (*Mr Stone* takes up the whole of a thick yellowing Indian ledger) and then types it again. Understandably, the writing of a book exhausts him like a sickness,

*Note: What Naipaul actually said was, "Sadly, I reject Mrs. Macmillan's consolation that electricity will put an end to 'the long dark evenings in which ... the only possible recreation is sex.' Electricity or no electricity, there will soon be two million Jamaicans. It is hard to see what anyone can do except eat more Jamaican bananas without complaining. And perhaps – who knows? – a banana a day will keep the Jamaican away." (*New Statesman*, 4 Jan., 1958) and after each book he has a period of recovery, a convalescence during which he reads, usually puffing a plump Amboseli meerschaum, in his pajamas and dressing gown. "I dress for dinner," he explained to me once, and he laughed. But of *Mr Biswas* he wrote, ". . . he was given strength to bear with the most difficult part of the day: dressing in the morning, that daily affirmation of faith in oneself, which at times was for him almost like an act of sacrifice."

He has considerable courage, a refined sense of order and an unswerving literary and moral integrity; his eye, attentive for the smallest detail, can give an apparently common landscape or unremarkable physique many features. The decision to begin the long labor of writing a novel, with all the penalties of solitude, is an enormous one. "You do your work; you do it over long periods of total isolation," Naipaul says. "It's a rather horrible life . . . You become crankish — I used to wonder why all the writers I got to know were all so crankish. I understand more and more; it's the sheer solitude and loneliness of the job!" While writing *Mr Biswas* Naipaul used to console himself with a fantasy: "I would imagine that a man would come to me and say, 'I'll give you a million pounds, if only you will stop writing; you must not finish this book.' But I knew I would have to say no." And he adds, "Well, today I wouldn't say no."

But he probably would. The designation *Writer* in his passport (a British passport but no more an indicator of his nationality than Conrad's was) describes him perfectly. He has never been anything but a writer; "I have never had to work for hire; I made a vow at an early age never to work, never to become involved in people in that way. That has given me a freedom from people, from entanglements, from rivalries, from competition. I have no enemies, no rivals, no masters; I fear no one."

Kazantzakis' England

[1972]

"And what's more," says Nikos Kazantzakis in his travel book, *England*, speaking of Englishmen traveling, "wherever they go, even the most backward, distant country, they are able to settle down comfortably, because everywhere, they carry England with them." But this is true, in varying degrees, of more people than the English. Consider the yams in Brixton market, the Bank of Baroda in Southall, or the exclusive American supermarket/PX at the US airbase in Ruislip. Like the *bidet* in the Congolese hotel, it indicates who is living – or who once lived – close at hand. All immigrants are colonists in the sense that they carry something of their national culture with them: ideas of comfort, religion, business and appetite are part of their luggage, you might say. The traveling Englishman's first act in the distant country was to give definition to the new landscape by naming – or re-naming. In Malaya he found an agreeable place and called it the Cameron Highlands; he remembered a king or an explorer or a trader on a road sign, and in front of his own veranda'd bungalow put up a board saying "Hillcrest" or "Cluny Lodge". It is an English trait – the colony, a blank landscape waiting to be dramatized with names, gave this passion full vent – and part of the comfort Kazantzakis speaks about derived from the familiar names. After the naming came the rituals and institutions, the club, the church, the school, the team, the drama group – English enthusiasms, enclosing and protecting the community. To seek admission to these was to seek to be English.

Kazantzakis was surprised and delighted by a great deal that he saw on his visit to England in 1939; much he found alien and strange: Sheffield (and the "appalling, depressing" "grime-stained" cities of Birmingham, Liverpool and Manchester) "pained" him:

> . . . faces smeared with smoke; smudges of coal on naked, girlish legs; factory after factory, all looking alike; horrid brick apartment houses; tormented expressions. The workers grave, severe, their eyes blue steel. This was the first and last time I would see them. But it was all I could do to stop looking at them.

He knew England through her literature, but he suggests that the literature had not prepared him for this horror (perhaps revealing a gap in his reading, an inexperience of the English novel). He read Shakespeare, "and this is the amazing thing – there is no human type so different from the Shakespearean hero as the contemporary Englishman". Kazantzakis repeated that he was from Greece, a hot indolent place, and though Greece's links with England have always been unique and strong, he thought of himself as an "Oriental":

> I sometimes think that we of the Oriental, tormented, pain-steeped ports, where the air has been permeated with desires for thousands of years, are like crafty old men going to the innocent, barbarous, ephebic North, our eyes forever seeking, greedy, yet slightly tired and derisive, as though knowing everything. The races of the Orient are old ladies, heavy and primordial.

It is almost an English assessment of a particular kind of foreigner. And Greece is not far away. East Africa and Singapore are farther, but for a person like myself who has lived happily in these former English territories, England is not a strange place; it holds no terrors and few disappointments; a visit is like a return. Then, one must conclude that the English were more than successful in carrying their country abroad, for the England they carried was understandable to me, an outsider. If I had a surprise on arriving in England it was the unexpected confirmation of the accuracy of the literature and a convincing justification of reminiscences I heard in tropical bars. I had doubted certain things. I found descriptions of English sunlight and spring flowers hard to believe; I tended to think that a man's memory of a particular rural landscape exaggerated its color and emptiness, and could not help but feel that behind every English hill was an English factory belching smoke, and that the English people I knew overseas were escaping to a suitable climate, or else castaways from that rainy island who had chosen to live in a fantasy of Englishness that was permitted in a cut-price colony. And if the memory was not falsified, and the literature was accurate, why should the Englishman travel so far? Why not go home? The answer is in the small East African settlement, the club, the church, the school, moved intact from the mother country and offering protection. It is also something very different from this, a factor Mr Kazantzakis doesn't mention: the Englishman's appreciation of foreignness – he produced a whole library of the literature of expatriation. That appreciation is like another distinctly English trait, the pleasure in coping with adversity – hostility in awful climates – as real in the fenced-off compound in the tropics as in Britain during the winter power cuts when the householder's mood was curiously triumphant.

The English sense of order, the result of an habitual reflex rather than a systematic decree, gives the impression of a tremendous solidity and balance. It was carried abroad and it reassured those who could enter into it. English attitudes traveled without changing much, and to a large extent this accounts for some of the Englishman's isolation. The English overseas are accused of living a rather narrow existence, but the point is that they associate themselves deeply with a locality: in this sense all Englishmen are villagers. It shows in the special phrases they use when they are away, among "natives" or "locals."

"We've lived here for donkey's years, but we've never been invited to one of their houses," says the Englishman, adding, "though we had them around to tea."

"They're very secretive and awfully suspicious," says his wife.

"They *seem* very friendly, but they're not interested in us. They lack curiosity."

"They keep to themselves."

"An odd lot. I can't say I understand them."

You might think they are talking about Kikuyus or Malays, but they aren't. They are Londoners who moved to Dorset eight years ago and they are talking about ordinary folk in the village. I knew the locals: I was neutral – just passing through, stopping for five months. The locals had strong opinions on outsiders who had settled in that part of Dorset.

"They come down here and all the prices go up," one old man said. He might have been a Kenyan, speaking of settlers. There were other objections: the outsiders didn't bother to understand the village life, they kept to themselves, acted superior, and anyway were mostly retired people and not much use.

Expatriates and natives: the colonial pattern repeated in England. There was a scheme afoot to drill for oil on a beautiful hill near a picturesque village. The expatriates started a campaign against it; the natives said very little. I raised the subject in a pub one night with some natives of the area, asking them where they stood on the oil-drilling issue.

"That bugger –", one said, mentioning the name of a well-known man who had lived there for some years and was leading the campaign. "I'd like to talk to him."

"What would you say to him?" I asked.

"I'd tell him to pack his bags and go back where he came from."

So one understands the linguistic variations in England, the dialect that thickens among the natives when an expatriate enters a pub. No one recognizes him; the publican chats with him; the talk around the fireplace is of a broken fence or a road accident. The expatriate is discussed only after he leaves the room: Where does he live? What does he do? The natives know the answers, and later when he buys a round of drinks they will warn him about the weather ("We'll pay for these warm days!"). It is a form of village gratitude, the effort at small-talk. But in England a village is a state of mind. "Are you new in the village?" a friend of mine was asked by a newsagent. This was in Notting Hill.

"In our own day the peasants have almost disappeared from England . . . The few peasants left are silenced and terror-stricken." If Kazantzakis meant countrymen, rustics and workers on the land – or if he gave them more precise occupations (thatchers, crofters, shepherds) – he might have looked closer and seen them. Sheep-shearing is still an annual springtime event in much of rural England, even if it is not so festive as in Act IV of *The Winter's Tale*. Kazantzakis steered clear of farms and small villages, though he appears to have been a house guest at the manor of some titled people in what is now the Green Belt. For the most part he stuck to large cities and traveled on the main thoroughfares that connect them. He was enthralled by London and saw much of its charm in the fact that it is a "work of chance". The industrial cities of the midlands and north nearly undid him, and the four cities I mentioned previously he called "the four great circles of hell". Though he was careful in describing each city, he depended on apocryphal stories for his condensed English history, and one wonders how precise his eye was for racial characteristics. In the London streets he saw "centuries, clearly reincarnated in the highly diverse passers-by . . . Viking giants . . . daydreaming Celts . . . Norman gentlemen . . . ancient Iberians, restless and rapacious", as well as "kindhearted Saxons with their athletic flesh, their short bull-like necks, and the everlasting pipe wedged between their broken teeth". He saw no other races. His attitude is like a kind of commitment.

The English were candid with him, but the candor Kazantzakis reports seems as unEnglish as the rhythms of their speech – though the strange and pompous effects are undoubtedly a result of the speech having been turned into Greek and back again into English. One young man told him, "I've never been interested in analyzing the various bloods flowing through my veins . . . It's enough to have them flowing regularly and strongly. In case they ever vie among themselves, no one should learn of it." And another cried at him, "Can you understand me, you descendant of Themistocles?"

Only once did he have a conversational setback. He was at the country house attempting to talk to "two bony girls".

"Have you read Demosthenes?" I asked them with provincial naîveté just to see their reaction.

They both burst out laughing.

There was a gulf between us and I felt an unexpected bitterness, as though I had been left behind and the young people had passed me by. I felt ashamed of having read Demosthenes once upon a time."

A number of people told him (and he showed signs of agreeing) that the English are devoid of imagination. They meant it as praise and quoted Cecil Rhodes saying, "The world belongs to the English because they have no imagination." Kazantzakis found the English tough, prosaic, self-absorbed, polite, gentle, full of confidence and praising what is most homely. He met an old pensioner who discussed Shakespeare with him. The pensioner said that Shakespeare gave "a humane and characteristically English ending . . . to his demonic life" when he "bought houses and land, and became the pillar and pride of the little town where he was born . . ."

It is an unusual judgement. Kazantzakis did not dispute it. He indulged in a whimsical sally, comparing the dead Shakespeare's unwritten tragedies to the unhatched eggs you find in the entrails of a chicken you've just killed. "The pensioner shrugged his shoulders, and out of politeness refrained from making a reply. These Orientals! he must have been thinking to himself."

Kazantzakis took the English at their own assessment. In a nation of sweet-eaters he met only wine bibbers. Where is the rebel, the complainer, the shy egotist, the crank, the conspirator, the hobbyist? Kazantzakis' single encounter in this direction was with a Scottish Hindu who told him a very long story about Vivekenanda, and he maintained that England's contribution to humanity (with the Magna Carta and Shakespeare) is the Gentleman. He means more than a polite person – he means someone comparable to the Italian *cortegiano*, the Spanish *hidalgo*, the French *honnête homme*. They are, all of them, vanished breeds; but this is not to undervalue the English character. Kazantzakis reacted strongly to England, and his opinions – always somewhat idealized – reflect a great deal of English influence. What is clear in his dated, but valuable book, is that one must look in out-of-the-way places, both on land and in literature, for clues to the English character, and not all the places or books will be English in the usual sense of the word. Kazantzakis's England, the home of empire, where gentlemen read Shakespeare, was to change. But there was another England. The Greek, a classicist, didn't notice it.

Malaysia

[1973]

There is a sultan in Malaysia whose nickname is "Buffles" and who in his old age divides his time between watching polo and designing his own uniforms. His uniforms are very grand and resemble the outfit of a Shriner or thirty-second degree Mason, but he was wearing a silk sports shirt the day I met him on the polo ground. The interview began badly, because his first question, on hearing I was a writer, was, "Then you must know Beverley Nichols!" When I laughed, the sultan said, "Somerset Maugham came to my coronation. And next week Lord Somebody's coming – who is it?"

"Lewisham, Your Highness," said an Englishwoman on his left.

"Lewisham's coming – yes, Lewisham. Do you know *him*? No?" The sultan adjusted his sunglasses. "I just got a letter from him."

The conversation turned quite easily to big game hunting. "A very rich American once told me that he had shot grizzly bears in Russia and elephants in Africa and tigers in India. He said that bear-meat is the best, but the second best is horsemeat. He said that. Yes!"

We discussed the merits of horsemeat.

The sultan said, "My father said horsemeat was good to eat. Yes, indeed. But it's very *heating*." The sultan placed his hands on his shirt and found his paunch and tugged it. "You can't eat too much of it. It's too heating."

"Have you ever eaten horsemeat, Your Highness?"

"No, never. But the *syces* eat it all the time."

The match began with great vigor. The opposing team galloped up to the sultan's goal with their sticks flailing.

The sultan said, "Was that a goal?"

"No, Your Highness," said the woman, "but very nearly."

"*Very* nearly, yes! I saw that," said the sultan.

"Missed by a foot, Your Highness."

"Missed by a foot, yes!"

After that *chukka*, I asked the sultan what the Malay name of the opposing team meant in English.

The sultan shook his head. "I have no idea. I'll have to ask Zayid. It's Malay, you see. I don't speak it terribly well."

But there are Malay words everyone knows. There is *gong*, and *sarong*, and *mata-hari*, which are charming; and there is *amok*, which is terrifying. And though the customary greeting in Malaysia is *Salaam aleikum* ("Peace be to you!"), the Malays are capable of working themselves into a perfect frenzy. In a few short weeks of 1969, two thousand Chinese were killed in riots following a disputed election. On the other hand, there is a non-Muslim tribe in the southern Malaysian jungle which is completely pacifist: they have never fought or quarrelled with anyone and violence is unknown to them. They fit in quite well. In a country where the ruler barely speaks the language it is no surprise to find a primitive tribe of semi-naked pacifists. However, it was not that long ago that the now-retired headhunters of East Malaysia ate their last missionary.

Traveling through Malaysia I used to wonder who the real natives were. The Europeans I met called the Chinese natives; the Chinese referred to the Malays as natives, and the Malay phrase for the little jungle dwellers (who make a graceful living selling orchids and parrots by the roadside) is *orang asli* – "natives". There is a community of Portuguese in Malacca which claims to have been there for five hundred years, and one is almost convinced. Malacca's pedigree is very old: there are an ancient Portuguese cathedral and fort, and Dutch civic buildings, and – notice the national priorities – an English club. In the Malacca antique shops you can buy furniture carved by "Straits Chinese" (whose food is probably the best in the country) 150 years ago and more.

The least interesting town in Malaysia is the capital, Kuala Lumpur, which a French traveler called – with good reason – "Kuala *L'impure*", but it is a convenient stopping-off place, and from there you can easily travel by train or road to the Cameron Highlands. Here, the air is as cool as an autumn day in England; below you, in Tapah and beyond, people are gasping in the heat and swatting mosquitoes, but you are thousands of feet up, in a temperate climate, where strawberries grow and beds need blankets and rooms log fires. There are country walks in the highlands, but you walk with a memory of danger: one day an American tycoon took a stroll after lunch and was never seen again. From the Cameron Highlands, the island of Penang is not far, and after driving the hundred hairpin bends to Tapah the train is a reward. First Class on Malaysian Railways includes a wood-paneled compartment which you have to yourself, with a comfortable bed, and at Butterworth you're woken by a man in a sarong with breakfast – tea, a biscuit and a banana.

After the 1969 riots, American soldiers from Vietnam stopped coming to Penang for "Rest and Recreation Leave", and a local newspaper reported: "A survey shows that nine leading hotels, as well as 300 trishaw drivers and 200 'social escorts' will be affected." But Penang is rising again, and new hotels and holiday bungalows are being built on its Neapolitan-looking coastline. The food in Penang is superb, but eating habits tend to be unusual: the Chinese eat chicken feet and fish-lips, but are nauseated by cheddar cheese; the Malays eat practically anything except pork (though during Ramadhan, the Muslim fasting season, they can be fined by the so-called "Religious Police" for eating in daylight hours), and in Indian restaurants one is given a scrubbed palm leaf as ceremoniously as if it was a warmed plate – it serves the same function.

The vegetation all over Malaysia is unearthly. Orchids grow wild, and because they do, carnations – duller, but much rarer – are especially coveted. Some trees (like the *Angsana*) grow three or four feet a year; there are "Chewing Gum Trees" and on the slopes of Mount Kinabalu, pitcher plants the size of spittoons, which feed on insects; and importuning fig trees (*Ficus elasticus*), which attach themselves to other more docile trees and strangle the life out of them. My favourite Malaysian tree is called "The Midnight Horror" (*Oroxylum indicum*). Its leaves are so huge they look like branches, and its flowers – also quite large – begin to open at about ten pm and give off a stench which by midnight is unexampled. Though this tree is used by the Malays for making medicine, no Malay would admit to an affection for it. I admired it from a distance, but bats are devoted to it. They find the odor of The Midnight Horror irresistible; they hang by the claws on their wings to the corollas and poke their noses into the flower's throat. The Midnight Horror might have been designed by Algernon Blackwood or H. P. Lovecraft: it is one of half a dozen trees in the world that is actually pollinated by bats.

The best things to do in Malaysia are the simplest: taking a £1 boat ride to an island off the east coast; getting an hilarious massage in Kota Kinabalu or an inexpensive feast of chili crabs in a fishing village on scaffolding and stilts in Kukup; buying a carved bargain in Malacca; swimming at Batu Feringhi in Penang; spending a day at Trengganu watching thousands of sea-turtles hatch their eggs on the beach, or really, just observing snobberies at a polo match with an agreeable sultan.

Memories of Old Afghanistan

[1974]

Afghanistan is a nuisance. Formerly, it was cheap and barbarous, and people went there to buy lumps of hashish – they would spend weeks in the filthy hotels of Herat and Kabul, staying high. But there was a military *coup* in 1973, and the king (who was sunning himself in Italy) was deposed. Now Afghanistan is expensive and barbarous. Even the hippies have begun to find it intolerable. The food smells of cholera, travel there is always uncomfortable and sometimes dangerous, and the Afghans are lazy, idle and violent. I had not been there long before I regretted having changed my plans to take the southern route. True, there was a war on in Baluchistan, but Baluchistan was smaller. I was determined to deal with Afghanistan swiftly, putting that discomfort into parentheses. I had a train to catch in the Khyber Pass, at Landi-Kotal, for Peshawar in Pakistan. There is only one train a week there, a local called the "132-Down." It makes one stop; it leaves on Sunday.

But I have some memories of Afghanistan.

The Hotel in No-Man's Land

"Customs over there," said the motioning Afghan. But the Customs Office was closed for the night. We could not go back to the Iranian frontier at Tayebad, we could not proceed into Herat. So we remained on a strip of earth, neither Afghanistan nor Iran. It was the sort of bedraggled oasis that features in Foreign Legion films: a few square stucco buildings, several parched trees, a dusty road. It was getting dark. I said, "What do we do now?"

"There's the No-Man's Land Hotel," said the taller hippy, with the pajamas and bangles. His name was Lopez. "I stayed there once before. With a chick. The manager turned me on."

In fact the hotel was nameless, nor did it deserve a name. It was the only hotel in the place. The manager saw us and screamed, "Restaurant!" He herded us into a candlelit room with a long table on which there was a small dish of salt and a fork with twisted tines. The manager's name was

Abdul; he was clearly hysterical, suffering the effects of his Ramadhan fasting. He began to argue with Lopez, who called him "a scumbag".

There was no electricity in this hotel; there was only enough water for one cup of tea apiece. There was no toilet, there was no place to wash — neither was there any water. There was no food, and there seemed to be a shortage of candles. Bobby and Lopez grumbled about this, but then became frightfully happy when Abdul told them their beds would cost thirty-five cents each.

I had bought an egg in Tayebad, but it had smashed in my jacket pocket, leaked into the material and hardened in a stiff stain. I had drunk half my gin on the Night Mail to Meshed; I finished the bottle over a game of "Hearts" with Lopez, Bobby and a tribesman who was similarly stranded at the hotel.

As we were playing cards (and the chiefs played in an unnecessarily cut-throat fashion), Abdul wandered in and said, "Nice, clean. But no light. No water for wash. No water for tea."

"Turn us on then," said Lopez. "Hubble-bubble."

"Hash," said Bobby.

Abdul became friendly. He had eaten: his hysteria had passed. He got a piece of hashish, like a small mudpie, and presented it to Lopez, who burned a bit of it and sniffed the smoke.

"This is shit," said Lopez. "Third quality." He prepared a cigarette. "In Europe, sure, this is good shit. But you don't come all the way to Afghanistan to smoke third-quality shit like this."

"The first time I came here, in '68," said Bobby, "the passport officer said, 'You want nice hash?' I thought it was the biggest put-on I'd ever heard. I mean, a passport officer! I said, 'No, no — it gives me big headache.' 'You no want hash?' he says. I told him no. He looks at me and shakes his head: 'So why you come to Afghanistan?' "

"Far out," said Lopez.

"So I let him turn me on."

"It's a groovy country," said Lopez. "They're all crazy here." He looked at me. "You digging it?"

"Up to a point," I said.

"You freaking out?" Bobby sucked on the hashish cigarette and passed it to me. I took a puff and gulped it and felt a light twanging on the nerves behind my eyes.

"He is, look. I saw him on the train to Meshed," said Lopez. "His head was together, but I think he's loose now."

Lopez laughed at the egg stain on my pocket. The jacket was dirty, my shirt was dirty, and so were my hands; there was a film of dust on my face.

"He's loose," said Bobby.

"He's liquefying," said Lopez. "It's a goofy place."

"I could hang out here," said Bobby.

"I could too, but they won't let me," said Lopez. "That scumbag passport shit only gave me eight days. He didn't like my passport—I admit it's shitty. I got olive oil on it in Greece. I know what I should do — really goop it up with more olive oil and get another one."

"Yeah," said Bobby. He smoked the last of the joint and made another.

With the third joint the conversation moved quickly to a discussion of time, reality and the spiritual refuge ashrams provided. Both Lopez and Bobby had spent long periods in ashrams; once, as long as six months.

"Meditating?" I asked.

"Well, yeah, meditating and also hanging out."

"We were waiting for this chick to come back from the States."

What happened was this. They had gone to Mykonos that summer. Mykonos had its attractions: it was frequented by very wealthy people who enjoyed rubbing shoulders with hippies. There was no class barrier because on Mykonos both the wealthy people and the hippies went around in the nude. "Rich straights and scrounging freaks," Lopez said, "and all of them bare-ass." Lopez and Bobby sold silver Indian jewelry and hashish and salted away $2,000. They took the money to India and bought silk scarves and shirts. These they sent, with a reliable girl, to the States; then they went into an ashram. The girl sold the Indian silks in Chicago and returned with $7,000. They divided the money and then went to Katmandu to live the life of simple mountain folk.

Lopez was thirty-one. After graduation from a Brooklyn high school, he got a job as a salesman in a plastics firm. "Not really a salesman, I mean, I was the boss's right-hand man. I pick up a phone and say 'Danny's out of town,' I pick up another one and say, 'Danny'll meet you at three thirty.' That kind of job, you know?" He was earning a good salary; he had his own apartment, he was engaged to be married. Then one day he had a revelation: "I'm on my way to work. I get off the bus and I'm standing in front of the office. I get these flashes, a real anxiety trip: doing a job I hate, engaged to a plastic chick, all the traffic's pounding. Jesus. So I go to Hollywood. It was okay. Then I went to Mexico. Five years I was in Mexico. That's where I got the name Lopez. My name ain't Lopez, it's Morris. Mexico was good, then it turned me off. I went to Florida, Portugal, Morocco. One day I'm in Morocco. I meet a guy. He says, 'Katmandu is where it's happening.' So I take my things, my chick, and we start going. There was no train in those days. Twelve days it took me to get to Erzurum. I was sick. It was muddy and cold, and snow — snow in Turkey! I nearly died in Erzurum, and then again in Teheran. But I knew a guy. Anyway, I made it."

I asked him to try and imagine what he would be doing at the age of sixty.

"So I'm sixty, so what? I see myself, sure, I'm sitting right here – *right here* – and probably rolling a joint." Which seemed a rash prophecy, since we were in the no-man's land hotel, in a candle-lit room, without either food or water.

Somewhere at the front of the hotel a telephone rang.

"If it's for me," Lopez shouted, but he had already begun to cackle, "if it's for me, I'm not here!"

The Bus With A Hole in It

Lopez sat beside me. He said he liked me, "because freaks are so fucking boring and straights are sometimes a groove."

I dreaded the journey, not merely because we were traveling across a patch of stifling desert to the blighted town of Herat, but because I loathe buses. Most buses remind me of church summer-school outings to Nantasket Beach. This bus was on its last legs; it was filled with dust and gasoline fumes. We started out with eighteen people and picked up seven more along the way: a blind child, a very old woman, a man with a rifle, a family of four and their five chickens. No one got off. The men's turbans were loosely tied; one man hung out the window, and as he gawked at the desert his turban began to unravel, making a long flapping rag which reached nearly to the back of the bus. It was only when another man called his attention to it that he gathered it in.

We passed more of those sand castles, and after a while the black tents of nomads. Lopez called them "Coochies" (perhaps *Kutchis*) and said he had seen them all over India and Pakistan as well. He said they were fierce and unfriendly, but that he had always wanted to join them. The large black tents, ominously pitched in the Afghan desert, reminded me of that speech in *Tamburlaine* where one of the characters describes how Tamburlaine always pitches black tents when he is about to go to war. The historical Tamerlane actually traveled this same desert and captured the town of Herat.

We stopped again and again. The little bus was hot and crowded; all the windows, except the broken side one where the man had almost lost his turban, were closed and sealed, and a woman near me, who looked very ill, began quietly to puke. The children were crying, and the blind boy, squatting on the floor near the driver, was singing – that high, tuneless Muslim whining. Two hours passed in this way. Lopez said, "You digging it?"

Suddenly – I cannot describe my surprise at the speed of this occurrence – there was the loudest bang I've ever heard; I could not imagine what caused it. The whole interior filled up with blue smoke reeking of cordite. There was a moment of shock and confusion, total deafness – the driver swerved, nearly overturning the bus, and brought us to a halt.

When the smoke cleared, we saw a hole in the green formica ceiling; it was oval, about an inch and a half wide and edged with soot. Beneath this hole a trembling Afghan held a smoking shotgun. The gun belonged to another man who, wedged at the front of the bus, had no room for the gun. He had passed it to the man to hold, but had not warned him that it was loaded. The man might have pulled the trigger, or else the bumpy road might have set it off. There was a brief argument and then we went on our way.

"Didn't I tell you this was a goofy country?" said Lopez. "Ever see anything like that before?"

The frightening part came an hour later, when the man with the gun got out. There was a fierce argument between the driver and the man with the gun, and then the male passengers leaped out and they all stood in the desert beside the bus, shouting in the sunlight. It was complicated: the man who owned the gun hadn't been holding it when it went off; the man who was holding it hadn't known it was loaded. But there was a hole in the bus to pay for, and as everyone's belongings were tied to the top of the bus, the slug had penetrated suitcases and bundles. The argument became a fight, and three men rolled in the sand, shouting and kicking, as the shotgun changed hands.

Lopez said, "It's getting hairy."

The owner of the shotgun held the muzzle and swung it at his attackers, who dodged it and got him to the ground. They punched him; he shrieked and tried to get free. The other passengers hooted at him and kicked him when he rolled near.

"I think we should get out,". I said. I was for leaving the bus and hitching a ride. My fear was that someone would reload the shotgun and start shooting, and when that happened I wanted to be able to flatten myself against the ground.

"No, no, no," said Lopez. "You don't understand these goofs. They're not going to kill the guy. They just want to get some money out of him to fix the roof. He doesn't want to pay, see, because he wasn't holding the gun. But he'll pay – he's outnumbered."

"Meanwhile, we sit here –"

"Look, take it easy. In five minutes they'll all be back in here and we'll be going down the line. It'll be like nothing happened."

It took ten minutes, but Lopez was right: we were on our way. It was another hour to Herat. I spent it tremulously vowing that this would be my last bus ride.

It is hard to decide where Asia begins. The Russians say at the Urals, the Turks at Haydarpasa, but these are the kind of meaningless cultural perspectives of geography that produce such judgements as the one frequently heard in English pubs, "The wogs begin at Calais." Surprisingly, many faces one sees in eastern Turkey, in Iran and Afghanistan have a European cast, but they are darker and more deeply wrinkled. Perhaps Asia begins when the first dusky hand reaches out with obsequious arrogance for *baksheesh*. That's what I thought in Turkey. But now I knew. I had crossed the imaginary line between Europe and Asia. When that gun went off with such a crack, blasting a hole in the desert bus, Asia began.

A Bazaar, A Band, The Exchange Rate

To be in Herat, in the western corner of Afghanistan, is to be nowhere; and Herat is so far from Kabul there are still people in it who refuse to believe the king has been dethroned. News travels slowly; there are no newspapers in Herat. On the other hand, the bazaar is unexpectedly crammed with merchandise, dirt-cheap in all senses. Herat is a town of clumsy craftsmen, who have forgotten the fine points of their trade. They squat, biting on their tongues, making dangerously sharp jewelry and wooden objects, hacking at leather with dull scissors and making wolfpelts into valises much as one would make a sow's ear out of two or three silk purses. Between the shops – the tiny closets and cupboards where these crude results are displayed – are antique stalls, some selling genuine treasures, ancient Afghan flintlocks with mother-of-pearl inlay, braces of pistols, chunks of carvings pilfered from temples, old silver, carpets smuggled from Russia, brass samovars and rare coins. And further along, where the sidewalk ends, and bridging the open drain which is dammed to overflowing with the green excrement of donkeys, are the fruit stalls: grapes, figs and pomegranates, winged and humming because of the clusters of wasps on them. The stallholders do not shoo them away. They laze and watch the passers-by, mainly women, who in spooky pleated shrouds really do look ghostly as they peer through the thick lace at their eyes. These small draped figures move swiftly among the stalls, putting the wasps to flight when they unveil their skinny hands to choose their fruit.

Men stand idly in Herat's main street. You think they are jay-walkers until a horse cart approaches; then several men wave their arms – they are traffic policemen in Afghan robes and turbans; and several more scurry around with twig brooms and squares of cardboard – they are the Department of Sanitation. The driver reins his horse, obeying the frantic signals of the man with flapping robes, and the red pompoms and bells on the decorated cart sway as the vehicle proceeds. But the horse has been startled; he raises his tail and as he does so the men with brooms rush to the steaming pile, sweeping and scooping, and this they deposit at the side of the road, in the drains under the fruitstalls.

The bells of the horse carts tinkle throughout the night. It is a pleasing sound, but I got no sleep in Herat. Twice, once at midnight and once at about three in the morning, I was awakened by music – not eastern music, no stringed instruments or screeching voices, but trumpets, farting cornets and snare drums and the gulping sound of tambourines. It might have been a school band parading to a football game, except that this was the dead of night. I heard them coming when they were several streets away; it went on, distantly, for twenty minutes and then was raucous under my window. It was a band, men with lamps preceded it, their lights swinging, and I could hear but not see what I took to be children running in the street: their laughing voices and animated feet. The music was brassy, the drumming loud, though the tune was unfamiliar. It was the sort of bizarre nightmare old men have in German novels, and I watched with some apprehension the glint of the instruments, the nodding turbans and dancing lights.

It was typical of my baffling Afghanistan interlude that not only did I never discover who the musicians were, I also could not find a single person who had heard them playing. In such an atmosphere one could become paranoid in the twinkling of an eye, but the travelers had other things on their minds. They were certainly exercised about the exchange rate, and most of the conversations I overheard sounded like financiers' anxiety turned into slang.

The news was bad: the dollar was quoted at fifty Afghanis, but the first shock the hippies got was from a sleek robed man who beckoned to a chief and offered him forty-five Afghanis.

"So the black market rate is lower than the bank's. Right? Beautiful."

"I remember when you could get seventy to the dollar."

"Seventy! I remember when it was around ninety – and a bed was fifteen. You figure it out."

They stood in groups, cawing like brokers faced with a plunging market, the worst in years. And the amazing thing was that these youths, whose own description of themselves was "freaks" – the girl in the torn blouse, the bearded one with the cracked guitar, the boy who walked around in his bare feet during that very cold night in no-man's land, the ones in pajamas, pantaloons, dhotis; the men with ponytails, skullcaps, and sombreros, the girls with crew cuts and copies of Idries Shah, all of them fatigued after their flight across Turkey and Iran – the amazing thing, as I say, was that they talked with impressive caution about money. They were carrying French and Swiss francs, German marks, sterling and dollars; their money was in greasy canvas pouches and gaily colored purses and sequined bags with drawstrings.

At times, when the topic was drugs or religion, they were impossible to talk to. They struggled with the debased language of drug psychosis to express abstract concepts they had got third-hand from drop-out philosophy majors. But when the subject was money they never mocked: they were serious, cunning and shrewd by turns, because they knew — even better than their detractors — how much their life, so seemingly frivolous, was underpinned by cash.

"Listen, Bugsy got fifty at the bank."

"That's his fault for going to the bank."

"Yeah, fifty's not the official rate. Maybe here, but not in Kabul. I'm sure we can get fifty-eight."

"Fifty-eight is peanuts!"

"Anyway, we can't afford to get to Kabul at this rate."

"Bad scene, man," says a boy wandering over to the group. "I just changed some money."

Several eagerly importune him: "What'd you get?"

"Fifty-one."

"Hear that? So there's hope," says another. "I'm not changing mine for less than fifty-five."

The difference between fifty-one and fifty-five Afghanis is about seven cents.

"We've got English pounds," says a girl in a long grey skirt who has been listening with some intensity.

"You're fucked, baby."

A very thin boy with a scraggly beard considers this obscenity for a few moments, then says, "Yeah, you are. See, they're only buying dollars because the rate is low. They won't buy pounds but they'll sell you dollars for them — probably about two bucks for a pound. Then they'll buy the dollars from you. So you get ripped off twice."

The girl was dejected. She said, "I don't know what to do."

"Hang out. We don't know what the official rate is."

"Can't someone make a phone call?"

"This used to be a groovy place. What happened?"

"The cheapest country in the world," said a French boy. "Hah! It is not so!"

"Someone said he got fifty-two."

"You call *that* good?"

The conversation continues; it is circular, studded with rumors, and inconclusive. The oddest thing about it is that it is taking place in the wildest part of Afghanistan, where only thistles grow. Money is the unlikeliest subject here, but it is the only subject, because it seems as if the hippies are being priced out of the country, and like restless speculators in a time of crisis they find they are being driven to different places, to

Pakistan where the rate is fairer, and to India, where at the Mohan Singh Bazaar you still get (so one fellow remarks with a touch of confidence) eight and a half rupees for a dollar.

An Asylum in Kabul

On September 7, 1973, a Dutchman, an Englishman and a Canadian entered Afghanistan from Pakistan. They had come from India and were driving what might have been a stolen Volkswagen. Their knapsacks were in the back seat. Outside Kabul they picked up an Indian hitchhiker. They drove to Kandahar and then to Herat, where they dropped the Indian and found a hotel for themselves.

Herat is a good contact point: it is safe and changeless. When the hippy is confused he refers to Herat's Message Board: "Patrick it's behind the mirror", "*Je reste à l'hôtel Yaquin depuis Le 12 – Chambre No. 1, t'attends*", "Couldn't go Northern Route. Left for Kandahar Mon Sept. 24th. We'll be waiting . . .", "*Estoy en el Hotel Shaib*", "Dying to see you. Peace, Judy", "If we are not there on the second look for note at Mustapha Hotel", "Hope you don't look like this from your dysentery [postcard with skull on it]. Get well soon and contact me in London to hitchhike Scotland." And there is the occasional telegram, such as the following, which I eventually decided was a birth announcement: "TRUE HAS SOON BOTH WELL NUM."

Sometime on the evening of the 10th, the travelers looked for their knapsacks and discovered that the Canadian's was gone. Concluding that the Indian had stolen it for the money and passport, the three went to the Herat Police Station.

It is not clear what happened then. The police would not say later what exactly took place. What is certain is that when the police asked for identification none of the three could produce it. The Canadian, whose name was Peter, grew violent and attacked the policeman who told him he was under arrest. They were handcuffed, and because Peter was especially violent, he had leg-irons as well as manacles.

After being held for three days at Herat Police Station, they were taken in the back of a truck, handcuffed and lying on the floor, the bumpy six hundred miles to Kabul. This is at least a twenty-hour ride and must have taken two days. The Englishman and the Dutchman were released with a warning; Peter was held. "And we could hear him yelling," the Dutchman said.

About a week later the Dutchman was walking down a back road in Kabul and saw, quite by chance, Peter shambling in the sun, still in his handcuffs and manacles. He was being transferred from one prison to another, though at the time the Dutchman thought he was just being allowed some fresh air. He was surprised that Peter had not been released. He felt it had something to do with Peter's bad temper. He told the British Embassy.

The embassy official who saw Peter a few days later said that he was certain Peter was insane, either from the ordeal of the Afghan prison or else an imbalance of long-standing. Peter was raving, and he showed signs of having been badly beaten. The embassy official secured Peter's release on the understanding that he would be committed to the insane asylum in Kabul, Sanai Hospital, a crumbling wreck of what looks to have been a mission hospital; it is on the far side of Kabul, behind one of the rocky hills that ring the city. The British official cabled the Canadians in Islamabad.

It was from the Canadian Third Secretary, a man I shall call Albert, that I heard this story. We were in the Kabul Hotel, a marble mausoleum built by the Russians in the 1950s. Albert was nervous. The police had not given him any help, but had said Peter had assaulted them. And there was a further problem: assuming the legal tangle could be unraveled, how was it possible to get Peter out of the country if he was raving mad?

"I hate going up to that nut house," said Albert. "I get depressed."

"I'd like to have a look at it," I said.

"You'd have to be crazy to want to go there," said Albert. He realized he had made a joke and gave an embarrassed honk of laughter.

We parked in the shade of the asylum to keep the car out of the hot sun, and posted the driver nearby. Albert had been warned that patients sometimes tried to hijack visitors' cars. The building was a low one-storey affair with a corrugated iron roof and thick bars on the windows on which patients clung, staring out with large eyes. Their heads were shaven, their faces were grey, and some – clutching and balancing like monkeys – yelled to us as we passed by.

We were admitted by a fat sad-looking guard in a faded blue smock and skullcap. He shut the door after us, and secured it with two bolts and a padlock. I took one step and the stink hit me, a high stinging reek of putrescence, piss, dampness, mold and stale food. The chattering patients, all in dirty striped pajamas, flocked over to us. They were skinny, many were old, but although their eyes were wild and their teeth rotted to fangs, they did not appear to be violent. Then it was easy to see why: the guard, I noticed, was carrying a heavy truncheon. He paddled his palm with it as the lunatics frisked about us.

"Hello mister!"

"Goo' morning sir!"

They knew more English and used it with greater fluency than most Afghans I had met so far.

One put out his dirty hand, and so as not to offend him I shook it. The others were encouraged. They gathered, wagging their hands at me until the guard raised his truncheon, making them cower. I counted the men as we walked into the ward; there were twenty-six men, but only seventeen beds. It would have been impossible to fit more beds in the room – they were less than a foot apart – but I wondered where the others slept.

"What did I tell you?" asked Albert. "Ever see anything like it?"

Under a filthy blanket, in a bed jammed against the wall, Peter was sleeping. His feet protruded from the blanket, and I could see sores on his ankles from the leg-irons, some scabs the size of quarters. He was tall; even sleeping in a crouched position his head butted the top of the bed and his feet were against the bars at the bottom end. His skin was yellow-grey, his cheeks sunken and my first thought was that he was dead; he was covered with flies – on his face, on the blanket, on his open sores. Albert touched his shoulder and shook him slightly. He did not wake; briefly the flies left him, then returned.

"He sleep," said one of the lunatics. "No sleep at night – all talking and – " He made fluttering gestures with his hands to indicate excitement.

Albert said, "I think he's been up all night. We should let him sleep."

"What about the food?" I asked. Albert had brought a bag of bread, chocolate, cheese and ginger ale, because Peter had complained about the hospital food.

"If I leave it they'll steal it," he said.

We left, and returned in the afternoon about five o'clock. Peter was still sleeping, but he woke up and raised his head when Albert called his name.

"Hi," he said drowsily. "What have you got?"

"Some food," said Albert. "How're you feeling?"

"Okay. I want to go," he said. The blue-smocked guard was standing behind Albert. Peter said to him, "I'm going with my friends. Let's go."

"In a few days," said Albert. "Here." He opened the bag and took out a can of ginger ale.

"Freedom," said Peter when Albert popped the opener.

Albert took out a bar of Toblerone chocolate and tore off the wrapper.

"Freedom," said Peter, and he began to eat it. He had spoken the word languidly; he repeated it, chanting in a deadened voice.

"There's some bread in the bag, and cheese, and another can of ginger ale. You'll be okay."

"English." A lunatic stood several feet away, hugging himself. "English iss goot."

"Get me out of here, man," said Peter. "Let me come with you." He spoke softly, not moving his head, still eating the chocolate. His hands were large, and I could see the sores on his wrists. The manacles must have been huge: he wore a six-inch cuff of sores.

"You've been sleeping a lot," said Albert. "That's good."

"I love candy bars."

"Do you sleep at night?"

"No." Peter put his hands over his eyes. "The past three nights they tied me up."

The guard smiled and played with his truncheon. He didn't understand English. He was a big man. It was a lunatic asylum: he had been chosen for his size.

"I want to go. Get me out of here."

"We'll be sending you back to Canada pretty soon."

"No, I'd rather stay here."

I said, "In the hospital?"

"Afghanistan. I love Afghanistan." He saw I was looking at his sores. He lifted his hand and kissed the largest sore.

Most of the lunatics were gathered near the bed, watching the proceedings, scratching themselves and giggling at Peter. By comparison they were much healthier than Peter, more alert and attentive.

"They tied me up," said Peter, again in that low careless voice. "Is that fair? Is that right? No, man."

"Who tied you up?" asked Albert.

"Give me another candy bar."

"Hey, there's some cheese in the bag. Why don't you —"

"Hay is for horses." Peter raised his arms and punched the air. The blanket slipped down, and I could see his starved chest. "Oh, man, I can do it. I'm tough. Look, Muhammad Ali."

One lunatic heard. "Muhammad Ali iss boxer . . . boxer iss goot."

"Sophie — Sophie, where are you, man?"

"Still have diarrhoea?" Albert asked gently.

"Coming out," said Peter. "Pouring out! Sophie Tucker!" He started to rave. The lunatics were delighted. The guard muttered something and smacked the truncheon against his palm. The lunatics ran out of the room.

"We'll get you to Canada, don't worry," said Albert.

"Afghanistan!" howled Peter. He saw us leaving. "Don't go!"

"I'll be back tomorrow," said Albert.

Peter rolled onto his side and pulled the blanket over his head.

In the outer corridor, the rest of the lunatics crouched against the wall, squatting on their heels. It was such a show of obedience I was certain they were beaten often and hard. They were waiting for their supper. We saw the cauldron of stew being carried up the stony path by two men.

Albert said, "Want to hear something funny? There's a swimming pool on the compound at 'Pindi. I had this party. Everyone jumps in with his clothes on. I decided to have another party, a pool party – everyone in bathing suits. Guess what? No one goes into the pool. Funny."

The Pathan Camp

The center of Kabul is not the bazaar, but the river. It is black and seems bottomless, but it is only one-foot deep. Some people drink from it, others shit beside it or do their washing in it. Bathers can be seen soaping themselves not far from where two buses have been driven into it to be washed. Garbage, sewage and dirt go in; drinking water comes out. The Afghans don't mind dying this way; it's no trouble. Near the bus depot on the south bank bearded Afghans crouch at the side of a cart, three abreast, their faces against metal binoculars. This is a peep show. For about a penny they watch 8mm movies of Indian dancers.

Further up the Kabul River, in the rocky outskirts of the city, I found a Pathan camp. It was large, perhaps thirty ragged white tents, many goats and donkeys and a number of camels. Cooking fires were smoldering and children were running between the tents. I was eager to snap a picture of the place, and had raised my camera, when a stone thudded a few feet away. An old woman had thrown it. She made a threatening gesture and picked up another stone. But she did not throw it. She turned and looked behind her.

A great commotion had started in the center of the camp. A camel had collapsed; it was lying in the dust, kicking its legs and trying to raise its head. The children gave up their game, the women left their cooking pots, men crept out of tents, and all of them ran in the direction of the camel. The old woman ran, too, but when she saw I was following, she stopped and threw her stone at me.

There were shouts. A tall robed figure, brandishing a knife, ran into the crowd. The crowd made way for him and stood some distance from the camel, giving him room and allowing me to see the man raise his knife over the neck of the struggling camel and bring it down hard, making three slashes in the camel's neck. It was as if he had punctured a large toy. Immediately, the camel's head dropped to the ground, his legs ceased to kick and blood poured out, covering a large triangle of ground and flowing five or six feet from the body, draining into the sand.

I went closer. The old woman screamed, and half a dozen people ran towards her. They had knives and baskets. The old woman pointed at me, but I did not pause. I sprinted away in the direction of the road, and when I felt I was safe I looked back. No one had chased me. The people with the knives surrounded the camel – the whole camp had descended on it – and they had already started cutting and skinning the poor beast.

The Night Ferry to Paris

[1975]

The idea was that, after England had been crushed with German rockets and overrun by stormtroopers, Adolf Hitler would board his luxurious *Schlafwagen* in Paris and order the engineer to proceed to London. Then, with his mad staring eyes closed, and slumbering in his plush berth, he would make his triumphant entry into the conquered country, arriving at Victoria Station to find the surrendering British on their knees. It happened otherwise, but the plan was well-known: Hitler wanted to arrive in England on the Night Ferry via Dunkirk.

It is not surprising. The Night Ferry – a train, not a boat – is the best way from London to Paris, the cheapest luxury route, convenient, comfortable and great fun. It is preferred by ambassadors, royalty, heads of state and my whole family. The Queen of England used it for her state visit to Paris, and it has most recently been recommended by E. M. Frimbo, "the world's greatest railroad traveler", who says in *All Aboard*, "My favourite way of traveling between London and Paris is, need I say, the train known rather ambiguously as The Night Ferry." In one sense, it is the lazy man's route, moving from one great city to another in your pajamas. But it is dignified, too: you are hidden, you travel with your bed, and after dinner, while the train rolls through Kent, you can go to sleep and don't have to stir until the conductor rouses you. Snapping up the window shade you find you are yawning at Montmartre.

Since October, 1936, when it made its first trip, it has run almost continuously, interrupted only by the war. It leaves Victoria every night except Christmas Eve, on the dot of nine; it is very rarely canceled. Michael Barsley writes in his history of The Orient Express, "There is something solid and permanent and imperturbable about the Night Ferry." Solid in a British way, imperturbable in a French way: it is a combined effort – British Rail, French National Railways and the sonorously-named *Compagnie Internationale des Wagon-Lits et des Grands Express Européens*. "Bonsoir," says the French conductor in London, "Evening, sir," says the waiter in the dining car as Clapham flashes past, and the train continues through the southeast corner of England. At Dover the sleeping cars are loaded on the ferry – there is room for ten of them – and chained to the deck in its hollow interior; iron stanchions are put in place under the body of the carriage to prevent it from being derailed in a storm (there are tracks fixed to the deck like many parallel sidings). At Dunkirk the carriages are shunted off and recoupled, and, while the passengers sleep, the train is sped through the early morning darkness to Paris. What could be simpler?

Normally, the Night Ferry leaves from Victoria's Platform Two, an alley of polyglots, but I boarded at Platform Eight because the President of Tanzania was arriving on the Night Ferry the next morning at Platform Two. A special pavilion was being put up there so that the Queen could welcome this fervent socialist in the style to which he is accustomed. Immigration ("Is this your wife?") and Customs ("How much sterling are you taking out of the country?") are dealt with swiftly in a series of cubicles on the platform, and once on the train you hand your passport to the conductor, who will show it, on your behalf, to the French authorities at Dunkirk.

Railway travelers are not like other people. They are calm, and though they have lots of luggage, unburdened. They look wrinkle-proof and contented. The lady ahead of me in the line was reading a fashion magazine; next to her a porter wheeled her belongings – a huge trunk, a suitcase, a bulging bag and a hatbox. Leaving aside the question of whether anyone owns a hatbox any more, would any airline passenger risk bringing one onto a plane? And of course it would have cost the earth to fly that lady's trunk to Paris. There were others shuffling down the platform – businessmen with overnight bags and satchels crammed with figures, a conspicuous little patrol of hitch-hikers with rucksacks and lunchboxes, wintry-faced vacationers, and a sprinkling of adventurers, all sturdy and exportable.

I had bought a liter of Chablis at a liquor store near the station. My wife and I were settled in our compartment and had barely clinked glasses when the train was crossing the Thames and the lights on Albert Bridge a little way downriver gave a nice yellowy sparkle to my wine. A half hour later we were in the dining car, sipping Bourgogne Aligote with our meal, which was asparagus soup in Tonbridge, grilled halibut steak in Ashford and stilton and cream crackers in the outskirts of Folkestone. There is an unruffled club-like atmosphere in the dining car of the Night Ferry. The train makes no stops; you sit down and are served; there are no further intrusions, no late-comers, no one hurrying to get off. The businessmen leaf through their financial reports, the lady with the hatbox is alone with her novel and her sirloin. Diners reading: you never see that on a plane. When the coast appoaches and dinner is over, everyone retires to his compartment to be transferred to the boat in peace, horizontally.

But it was a wild night. A gale had been blowing all day and the canvas on the parked freight cars nearby was flapping noisily. By the lights of Dover I could see the Channel heaving and gulping. It was after eleven by the time we were loaded. I had a nightcap on the ferry's Veranda Bar, and there met Mr Herz Konopny, a tiny white-haired man, who made precise gestures and drank a whisky as he told me how he had been born in Minsk, moved to Warsaw before the Russian Revolution and then settled in Paris where, in 1939, he joined the Foreign Legion. He fought in Tunisia in a regiment composed of Italians, Poles, Greeks and Spaniards; indeed, this was the reason he'd just been in London – it was the annual meeting of Jewish War Veterans. I asked him how he liked the Night Ferry. He said it was going to be a rough crossing. "When I was young I could sleep anywhere – even on the bare ground – but now that I'm old I don't get much sleep."

Mr Konopny's whisky glass was sliding back and forth on the table. I said goodnight and went below to my sleeping car. Already the ship had begun to pitch; the waves were hitting the hull and the chains that held the cars stationary were rattling eerily; the iron stanchions creaked, and all night – it was such an unusual feeling – my railway berth tipped up and down, eventually rocking me to sleep to the sound of clanking chains and the shuddering hesitation of the ship's droning screws.

It was light when I awoke, a misty day in the north of France, drenched fields, corridors of slender trees, some with nests in their arms, and one wicked giraffe that became, as we drew near, a farm implement – a loader probably – with a long curved neck peering into a furrow. Through Picardy and Oise and the killing fields of two world wars, we drank coffee. Then I joined Mr Konopny at the window. He gave me his business card and invited me to come to his tailor shop – "We'll have a drink." Just as the French office workers were crowding out of the Metro to start the day we pulled in at the Gare du Nord – too soon. But then, all great trains arrive too soon.

Stranger on a Train: The Pleasures of Railways

[1976]

There are two sorts of people who like trains, and I am neither. The first is the railway buff, for whom trains are toys. With the mind of a child and the constitution of a night-watchman, he has been elderly in that pipe-stuffing British way since he started to smoke; he enjoys running his thumb along the coachwork and jotting down engine numbers on a greasy note-pad, and though he smiles bizarrely when the whistle blows, he doesn't climb aboard: he is going nowhere.

Put your feet up – get the bennyfit, say the second sort. Their knowledge of trains is non-technical. They like the space, the conveni-ence; they like fuddling and fussing from carriage to carriage, juggling cheese rolls and pale ale, or just sitting, dozing, darning socks, doing the crossword and gloating out the window at the traffic jams: "Another level-crossing, Doris. Look at the silly buggers!" Barrister and criminal, publisher and printer, all crammed elbow to elbow in the compartment with *Wankers* spray-gunned on its walls. They are going to work, or home for the weekend, or to the coast for a bit of fun. They aren't travelers – in a sense nothing alien is human to them; they are non-drivers and Season Ticket-holders – they love chatting: in the area of small talk they are the world's true miniaturists. They have, each of them, a destination.

I know I am not a railway buff, and I prefer not to travel with a destination in mind. Mine is the purest form of travel, a combination of flight and suspended animation. I enjoy getting on trains; I loathe getting off. For instance, last summer in Massachusetts my brother told me a hurricane was on its way. Even the tiredest and most mooching West Indian hurricane, when it reaches New England, causes floods, broken windows, power failures and a kind of fricassee on the television screen. I helped my brother secure his stables, bought a biography of the writer of weird tales, H P Lovecraft, and boarded the train for New York. In New York I caught "The Lake Shore Limited" for Chicago and en route my book proved an invaluable conversation piece, since most of my fellow passengers took the title, *Lovecraft*, to be that of a sex manual. I spent an afternoon in Chicago and at bedtime, instead of looking for a hotel, took

"The Panama Limited" to New Orleans: dawn in Winona, breakfast — ai-yugs and gri-yuts — in Jackson, mid-morning in the swamps of Louisiana, a vision of the Jurassic Age. My one regret, when I arrived, was that "The Southern Crescent" (New Orleans-New York) was fully booked. For a terrible minute, in the station at New Orleans, I contemplated a trip to Laredo, Texas, and "The Aztec Eagle" to Mexico City. The Laredo train was waiting. I could imagine the temptations in Mexico City: "El Mexicali" to Nogales, a sleeper on "El Jarocho" to Veracruz, or the three-day journey on Number 49, via Palenque, to Merida and thence to Guatemala, Nicaragua and who-knows-what *ferrocarril* in Costa Rica? I resisted, and walked to the French Quarter, ate five dollars' worth of oysters and a few days later was on my way back home through the deep south — perhaps Alabama? it was very dark — and the steward was moving through the Lounge Car shouting, "Last call for dinner! If you don't come now you ain't going to get no dinner, and you ain't going to hear this no more!"

The hurricane had passed.

That week was pure pleasure. I had wide berths, a good book, an afternoon in Indiana and a morning in Mississippi. Durant, Mississippi, is not Mandalay, which is a pleasant surprise, because Mandalay is unremittingly dull. And I had good company. To get an Indian on "The Howrah Mail" talking you have first to answer a number of his questions: nationality, occupation, marital status, destination, birth sign, and how much you paid for your wrist watch. They are prying questions, but they license you to be similarly inquisitive. No such preliminaries are required on American railways. To get an American talking it is only necessary to be within shouting distance and wearing a smile; your slightest encouragement is enough to provoke a non-stop rehearsal of the most intimate details of your fellow traveler's life. In one sense, this is the third degree turned upside-down: instead of being tortured with questions you are tortured with replies. This sounds like criticism; I mean it as praise, for conversationally I am a masochist, and there is nothing I like better than putting my feet up, tearing open a can of beer and auditing a railway bore in full cry.

It is well-known that the train is the last word in truth drugs. All the world's airlines have failed to inspire what one choo-choo train has: the dramas of "The Orient Express" and a whole library of railway masterpieces. A rail journey is virtually the only occasion in travel on which complete strangers bare their souls, because the rail passenger — the calmest of travelers — has absolutely nothing to lose. He has more choices than anyone else in motion: unlike the air-traveler strapped in his chair like a candidate for electrocution, he can stroll, enjoy the view and sleep in privacy in a horizontal position — he can travel, as the natives do, the six thousand miles from Nakhodka to Moscow, in his pajamas; unlike the person on ship-board, he can restore his eyes with landscape, eat whenever he chooses and never know the ghastly jollity of group games – and he can get off whenever he likes. He can remain anonymous, adopt a disguise, or spend the five days from Istanbul to Tehran canoodling in his couchette. The train offers the maximum of opportunity with the minimum of risk. A train journey is *travel*; everything else – planes especially – is *transfer*, your journey beginning when you arrive.

I am speaking of long journeys, good services, comfortable seats and berths. British Rail, in its characteristic frenzy of false economy, removes the dining car, abolishes coffee, foreshortens the train, and at the same time retains a brakeman on trains where no brakeman is needed and continues to ensure – on a simple journey from, say, Waterloo to Salisbury – that your ticket is examined no less than five times. For this thumb-twiddling and for braying, "I say that British Rail is second to none in the world!", the head of British Rail is handed a knighthood and enjoined to become part of the already grotesquely overmanned British Establishment. A long, fairly pleasant train journey is possible in Britain if one takes the sleeper to Glasgow and then, via Inverness and Wick, to Thurso, varying on the way back by heading for the Kyle of Lochalsh.

But they order these things better in India. You can leave Jaipur at midnight and, after changing to "The Grand Trunk Express" in Delhi, not arrive in Madras for four days – which can be extended to a six-day rail gala if you go on to Rameswaram at the tip of India's nose, or a full week if you make the short crossing of the Palk Straits and take "The Talaimannar Mail" in Sri Lanka for Colombo. And it's another day on a pretty train from there to Galle.

"The Orient Express" used to be a four-day affair, but why stop in Istanbul when six days and three trains later you can be in Meshed, close enough to Afghanistan to hear gunfire in Herat? Turkish trains have plush bedrooms, Iranian trains serve kebabs, "The Frontier Mail" out of Peshawar dishes up curry, everyone gets a banana with his morning tea on "The Golden Arrow" to Kuala Lumpur; Thai trains have shower rooms (a huge stone jar, a dipper and a well-drained floor), Russian trains have a samovar in every coach, and ones in Sri Lanka have special compartments for you if you're a Buddhist monk. There is a telephone booth on the Amtrak "Metroliner" between New York and Washington and a pop-group on "The Coast Starlight" (Los Angeles-Seattle). "The Vostok" (Nakhodka-Khabarovsk) serves caviar; you can buy roasted sparrows and grasshoppers on most Burmese railway platforms, and everyone in the dining car of "The Izmir Express' (Ankara-Izmir) is presented with a loaf of bread: tear off a hunk, attack your portion of stewed eggplant, *Imam Bayildi* ("The Imam Fainted"), and either examine the greenery of Anatolia or sip one of their dusty but *gamin* white wines and say to the lady at the next table, "I can't help admiring your hat —"

When people tell me nothing ever happens on trains I ask them what they mean by nothing. In December, 1964, on a long train journey from Bulawayo in Rhodesia to Lusaka, Zambia, I witnessed two strangers meeting. The man was an Afrikaner, the woman English, both middle-aged and sunburnt, both headed for the Copper Belt. Their courtship began in awkward formality and progressed archly to joshing; they clinked glasses, they exchanged reminiscences. When we crossed Victoria Falls they were holding hands, and that night the man confided to me that he was going to ask her to marry him: "If she'll have me," he added, as if daring me to laugh. He had not slept with her: the Africans on the train (and now, in Zambia, they had penetrated to the bar, wearing papooses and cowboy hats) made him self-conscious. But it was not really sexual reticence – it was part of the Bwana's Code. He said he'd have plenty of time for that once they got to Chingola. Their arrival in Lusaka was festive, their eyes were shining with gin: she had agreed to marry him.

The courtships on "The Orient Express" were brief. Within hours of meeting, the Italian cancer specialist and the Belgian girl were barricaded in a single compartment. On "The Van Gölü Express" hippies copulated standing up in the lavatories with the door ajar. On "The Tehran Express" a pair of Australians in the four-bunk cabin we shared, held a corroboree that ended with a ritual in the dark two feet from where I lay, unable to sleep.

And on "The Rossiya" of the Trans-Siberian Express there was a boy traveling with his father. The father was mortally ill, his face the color of clay, and throughout the trip to Sverdlovsk he remained in his berth under a thick wrapping of brown blankets. The boy sat opposite, drinking sweet Russian champagne. He invited me in, but after one drink I left. The compartment had a smell of death about it, the clammy decay of a tomb; and the combination of the champagne drinker looking out at the snowy forests of Central Russia and his father dying in a narrow berth were more than I could bear. Stretcher-bearers – men wearing harnesses – appeared on the platform at Sverdlovsk; the old man's face was waxen and the boy told me in German, "I think he is dead."

Courtship, copulation and death: it is all the proof I need that the most intense experiences we know are enacted on trains. I have never seen anyone give birth on a train (though a child was born on a steamship I took to Borneo, the M.V. *Keningau*: I didn't see the birth, but I did see the infant swinging in its bloodstained hammock in steerage) or had anything like the afternoon Philip Larkin records in his poem "The Whitsun Weddings".

My memory of trains does not go back very far, and yet – though it was only twenty-five years ago or so – it was another age, when the tracks were the frontier of every American town and there were tadpoles in the ditches beside them and the expression "to come from the other side of the tracks" was a warning of slums, tenements, children who picked fights, men with runny noses, "people," my mother said, "who'll molest you." My first solitary train journey was in 1949, when I was eight. My father put me in my seat and told me not to move. He gave me a book. Throughout the trip from Boston to Hartford – no distance at all, really – a huge black man in a railwayman's uniform appeared at intervals and said, "Not yet, sonny." It was summer, and soon there were tobacco fields out the window – large, still, spade-shaped leaves in rows that reached to Connecticut. I held my book, but I didn't read it; and I didn't stir until at one station my aunt appeared and knocked on the window, and the black man whom my father had tipped in Boston said, "Off you go." My uncle said I had shown I was a man for having gone all that distance alone, and – he had some connection with The Eagle Lock Company – gave me a brass padlock as a present. I have been catching trains ever since.

When travelers, old and young, get together and talk turns to their journeys, there is usually an argument put forward by the older ones that there was a time in the past – fifty or sixty years ago, though some say less – when this planet was ripe for travel. Then, the world was innocent, undiscovered and full of possibility. The argument runs: In that period the going was good. These older travelers look at the younger ones with real pity and seem to say, "Why bother to go?"

It is a ridiculous conceit to think that this enormous world has been exhausted of interest. There are still scarcely visited places and there are exhilarating ways of reaching them. You can fly to Merida in Yucatan from New York and spend an interesting week among the ruins, and come back to people saying, "It's not what it was," – every pre-war tourist acting like Quetzalcoatl, The Plumed Serpent. But there is a better way to go, as a stranger on a train, via Peachtree Station in Georgia and New Orleans to Nuevo Laredo and Mexico City. It is every traveler's wish to see his route as pure, unique, and impossible for anyone else to recover. The train is the answer; for the bold and even the not-so-bold (there has never been a time in history when the faint-hearted traveler could get so far) the going is still good.

I began by saying that there are two sorts of people who like trains – the railway buff and the joy-rider. There are also two sorts of travelers.

There are those whom we instantly recognize as clinging to the traditional virtues of travel, the people who endure a kind of alienation and panic in foreign parts for the after-taste of having sampled new scenes. On the whole travel at its best is rather comfortless, but travel is never easy: you get very tired, you get lost, you get your feet wet, you get little co-operation, and – if it is to have any value at all – you go alone. Homesickness is part of this kind of travel. In these circumstances, it is possible to make interesting discoveries about oneself and one's sur-roundings. Travel has less to do with distance than with insight; it is, very often, a way of seeing. The other day I was walking through London and saw an encampment of gypsies on a patch of waste ground – the caravans, the wrecked cars, the junked machines, the rubbish; and children wandering through this cityscape in metal. This little area had a "foreign" look to me. I was curious, but I didn't investigate – because, like many other people, I suppress the desire to travel in my own city. I think we do this because we don't want to risk dangerous or unpleasant or disappointing experiences in the place in which we live: we don't want to know too much. And we don't want to be exposed. As everyone knows, it is wrong to be too conspicuously curious – much better to leave this for foreign places. All these are the characteristics of a person with a traveling mind.

The second group of travelers has only appeared in numbers in the past twenty years. For these people travel, paradoxically, is an experience of familiar things; it is travel that carries with it the illusion of immobility. It is the going to a familiar airport and being strapped into a seat and held captive for a number of hours – immobile; then arriving at an almost identical airport, being whisked to a hotel so fast it is not like movement at all; and the hotel and the food here are identical to the hotel and the food in the city one has just left. Apart from the sunshine or the lack of, there is nothing new. This is all tremendously reassuring and effortless; indeed, it is possible to go from – say – London to Singapore and not experience the feeling of having traveled anywhere.

For many years, in the past, this was enjoyed by the rich. It is wrong to call it tourism, because businessmen also travel this way; and many people, who believe themselves to be travelers, who object to being called tourists. The luxury travelers of the past set an example for the package tourists of today: What was the Grand Tour but a gold-plated package tour, giving the illusion of gaining experience and seeing the world?

In this sort of travel, you take your society with you: your language, your food, your styles of hotel and service. It is of course the prerogative of rich nations – America, western Europe, and Japan.

It has had a profound effect on our view of the world. It has made real travel greatly sought-after and somewhat rare. And I think it has caused a resurgence in travel writing.

As everyone knows, travel is very unsettling, and it can be quite hazardous and worrying. One way of overcoming this anxiety is to travel packaged in style: luxury is a great remedy for the alienation of travel. What helps calm us is a reminder of stability and protection – and what the average package tourist looks for in foreign surroundings is familiar sights. This person goes to China or Peru and wants to feel at home. Is this a contradiction? I suppose it is, but we must remember that in the past the very rich went from castle to castle or court to court; from the court of George III in London to the court of The Son of Heaven in Peking. It is much the same among certain travelers today. I was once in Siberia, and I recall an Australian saying to me in a complaining way, "It's *cold* here!" In Peru an American woman said to me, "I hate these hills – they're too steep." We were in the Andes. And not long ago, in China, a woman said to me, "I've been all around the world – Madagascar, the Galapagos Islands, Arabia, everywhere – and I didn't walk. I never walk. I hate to walk. I never go to places where I have to walk. But I've been everywhere."

This is actually quite extraordinary. For that woman, travel is a sedentary activity. She has been carried across the world. She is the true armchair traveler.

It is easy to laugh at her, but her kind of traveling is very popular. Travel nowadays is seen to be a form of repose: most people you see in travel posters are lying down in the sunshine, or sleeping in a lounge chair, or just sitting. In a sense, Abroad is where you don't have to do anything but loaf. I realize that a great confusion has arisen because we regard *travel* and a *vacation* as interchangeable. But really there is no connection at all between being alone in upcountry Honduras and, on the other hand, eating fish and chips in Spain. For a person with two weeks' vacation, travel – in its traditional sense – would be unthinkable; which is why parts of Spain have become Blackpool with sunshine – it's more restful that way. I don't blame people for craving that, but I do object when it is regarded as travel.

The British-family-in-Majorca stereotype is often mocked. True, it may be described as a strange new sort of adventuring: travel as immobility. In this sort of travel you have an illusion of no movement at all and in a cultural sense (Watneys Red Barrel, the *Express*, chips, English food, English service, English-style hotels) no surprises at all. But the British are not the only people who do this. The Japanese now expect to find Japanese restaurants and Japanese courtesies in the countries they visit: it is comforting to go ten thousand miles and find that it is just like home –

which accounts for the proliferation of McDonald's restaurants and Holiday Inns and the identical (and easily exported) national paraphernalia of travel.

When a person says, in a foreign place, "I feel right at home here," he is making a statement about the nature of travel, not the texture of the place he's in. I found it extremely pleasant to have a cheeseburger and a beer at the Inter-Continental Hotel in Kabul, Afghanistan; but I would have been a fool for thinking that this in any way represented a kind of Afghan experience. A few hours later I was back in my own hotel seven miles distant, and it was a world away. I don't belittle this sort of travel, which I regard as Traveling As A Version Of Being At Home; but it is wrong to mistake it as the sort of travel that allows a person to make discoveries.

Many people travel in order to feel at home, or to have an idealized experience of home: Spain is Home-plus-Sunshine; India is Home-plus-Servants; Africa is Home-plus-Elephants-and-Lions; Ecuador is Home-plus-Volcanoes. It is not possible for people to travel in large numbers and have it any other way. In order to process and package travelers in great numbers a system has to be arrived at. This system, in an orderly way, defeats the traditional methods of travel and has made true travel almost obsolete. In order for large numbers of Americans to visit Bangkok, Bangkok must become somewhat like America. The change in China, since the arrival of foreign travelers, has been enormous; and the result has been some very un-Chinese-looking hotels, food, buses, and so forth. It seemed to me in China that these holiday-makers would, in the end, bring about a different sort of cultural revolution. Certainly, travelers in China constitute a new class of people in a society that had striven to be classless.

To a great extent, travel today is praised for its familiar, unshocking, homely and even immobile characteristics. But although you can get a bed on some airline flights to the Far East, and there is a toilet on long-distance buses, and bingo on Round-the-World cruises, it is the train that most gives the comforting illusion of Being Home.

A train offers protection, freedom, privacy, stability. It is possible, on a train, to entertain the notion that you are standing perfectly still – it is the world that is moving. The apotheosis of this notion is the Dining Car:

> Dinner in the diner,
> Nothing could be finer,
> Than to have your ham-and-eggs
> in Carolina!

In other words, why go all the way to Carolina if you can't enjoy the comforts of home? The French literary critic, Roland Barthes, wrote an essay in which he advanced the view that what Thomas Cook offered in the Wagon-Restaurant was "not so much food as a philosophy". The Dining Car offered a "mirage of solidity" – "starched linen, massive flatware", napkins, tablecloths, flowers, baskets – to convey the illusion that there are vast cupboards, gardens, washing facilities – everything associated with these props – somewhere on the train. The journey, Barthes says, is "sublimated". When it is not like eating at home it is like eating out, a special occasion; but it has the effect of removing from the traveler's mind any notion that he is on the move. Eating on a train, Barthes describes as a very orderly but strange experience:

> The traveller is subjected to a fatal rhythm of consumption whose unit is the *wave* . . . none (of the waves) can begin until the last is exhausted, the meal is merely a series of discontinuous takes: we ingest, we wait, like ruminants in their stalls, passively fed according to a series of mouthfuls which sweating keepers busily and fairly distribute down a long service corridor. There are thirteen waves: the aperitifs, the drink orders, the uncorking of the bottles, the five courses, the second bread . . . coffee, liqueurs, the bill, payment. The process is an inflexible one . . .

Barthes calls this the "décor of leisure". He is of course talking about a French dining car, with its five courses and wine, but a version of this – the "waves" of service – operates on most long-distance flights. What is impressive is the spectacle of service, and by eating "we participate in a transported immobility". The person who in China says, "*I never walk anywhere*" has managed a most modern triumph over the inconvenience of travel.

This strikes me as being a very ambitious kind of passivity: Eating-While-Traveling, Sleeping-While-Traveling, Making-Money (or Doing-Business)-While Traveling, and – as I said earlier – Traveling-to-China-or-Peru-Without-Leaving-America. This is a powerful simultaneity. (And you might also say that the train's future is assured precisely because it allows such passivity. It is totally sedentary travel at its most comfortable.)

I am not sneering at these odd forms of travel, or these homely recreations. I am calling attention to the phenomenon because it is so far from the traditional notion of travel as going away. And it is very important to understand what is happening to travel and tourism, and to all the present-day versions of the Grand Tour, because only by examining them can one see why people get on donkeys and ride across Ethiopia, or hitchhike to India, or go slowly down the Ganges, or simply disappear in Brazil. The interest in travel today, which is passionate, arises out of the fact that there is a form of travel prevalent that is now very easy – people want to find an antidote for the immobility that mass tourism has produced; people want to believe that somewhere, somehow, it is still very dangerous, bizarre, anxiety-making and exotic to travel, that one can still make discoveries in a glorious solitary way. Mock-travel has produced a huge interest in clumsy, old-fashioned travel, with its disgusting food and miseries and long nights. It has also given rise to a lively interest in travel literature, and the affirmation that the world is still large and strange and, thank God, full of empty places that are nothing like home.

An English Visitor

[1976]

Like Cock Jarvis in the novel he was unable to finish, Joyce Cary was for much of his life "A Conrad character, in a Kipling role". His instinct was wholly democratic, but he knew too much about Africa to chuck his job and dismiss the Empire as a racket. He had gone to Nigeria to work, and as a diligent DC he took his road-building, map-making and legal reform seriously. He had power, he had subjects. Quite different from the prowling journalist that Kipling was in India, or the ideological escapee that Orwell was in the Burmese police force, Cary had joined the Colonial Service to prove to his prospective father-in-law that he could take responsibility. Then he was inspired by a sense of mission. Africa provided him with the education he lacked; it was an impossible place – it made him a writer.

His formal education hadn't helped him much. After Clifton and early sorrows (the deaths of both his mother and stepmother), he had a spell in Paris in 1906 and finally a bumpy ride through Oxford, where he finished abysmally with a Fourth Class degree. Literary life for him at the time was his friendship with John Middleton Murry, whose own problems – a prostitute-mistress, poverty relieved by cadging Cary's money, gonorrhea – only intensified Cary's timidity. Meeting and falling in love with Gerty Ogilvie made him purposeful; a sojourn with the Red Cross in Montenegro encouraged in him a taste for adventure, which the dangers of the Cameroons Campaign intensified, but it was not until his home leave in 1916 and his marriage to Gerty that he began to write in earnest. Gerty became pregnant on the honeymoon, but Cary left her soon after for Nigeria, and from then until 1919 he remained in Africa, his occasional leaves enlarging his family and making Gerty more frantic. He was industriously occupied in the colony, with his people and his writing, and though life for Gerty (living with her parents in England, raising her children alone) could not have been more difficult, it is clear that Cary left Africa with reluctance and only after Gerty had issued an ultimatum.

Cary's characters are usually in impossible positions. They are innocents, life's misfits, who can't bear the betrayal of infidelity and yet force themselves to make allowances for it. Isn't love justifiable waywardness, not cheating? Cock Jarvis loves his wife as much as he loves Thompson, the man cuckolding him, but a million words of the novel did not lead Cary any closer to answering that question. Nina Nimmo, in *A Prisoner of Grace*, respects her husband Chester but feels a physical attraction for the muscular scoundrel Jim Latter. The disastrous liaison is concluded in *Not Honour More*, where Jim gives his version. As Cary's trilogies show, there are at least three sides to every story, and the wheedling wife-beating Gully Jimson of *Herself Surprised* is markedly unlike Jimson the painter in *The Horse's Mouth*, harassed by apocalypse and made a buffoon by fame. Sara Monday progresses from lover to lover, and though she has cooking on the brain (as Nina has "a brackety mind"), she becomes the victim of her own generous morality, trying to be all things to all men: wife, mistress, servant, punch-bag – and mother (she mentions her children so casually and infrequently one suspects the novelist of forgetting he'd lumbered her with them). The sympathetic colonial officer that Cary was – an Englishman in Nigeria, whose compassion could not be mistaken for weakness, writer and ruler – was in a cleft stick; the evacuee Charley Brown in *Charlie is My Darling* is as much among savages and suffering estrangement and social dislocation as Mr Johnson in Fada.

Cary began writing seriously in 1916; his writing sprawled, he started novels, abandoned them, wrote stories and developed a habit of writing what he called "a big scene" and then inventing a plot for it to make it a novel. It must have made writing difficult (and I would have thought robbed him of writing's chief pleasure: imaginative discovery); it makes some of his books lop-sided; and when Graham Greene described Cary's method to me he was chuckling rather sadly and shaking his head. On leaving Nigeria, Cary burnt most of his manuscripts. And he could: he had published a number of stories in the *Saturday Evening Post*, but that success (he was paid very well for them) did not sustain him for very long. The *Post* lost interest in his stories almost as soon as he took up residence in England. He continued to write, with very small reward, and it was not until 1932 that his first novel, *Aissa Saved* (begun in 1928), was published. M M Mahood's *Cary's Africa* (1964) is an illuminating guide to the African novels, but even her highly intelligent appraisal of *Aissa* does not persuade me that this book is anything but a muddle.

The greatly undervalued Cary novel, and certainly one of his best, is *An American Visitor*, which appeared the year after *Aissa*. Bewsher (Cary's names are always superb: Bonser, Preedy, the Clenches, the Beeders, Lepper, Mr Carrot) bears some resemblance to Cock Jarvis in his preoccupations with his people and the colonial routine; but in this novel Cary produces a likeable contradiction: a type of person that does not emerge convincingly in fiction with an African setting until thirty years later. American, female, an anarchist who enjoys whiffs of the pastoral, Marie Hasluck is the embodiment of the antagonistic vision that colonial officers hated. Cary shows how this woman's idealism is to be tested from the very first page: alluding to Marie, an old African says that whites "have set their hearts on the vanities of this world", and he is interrupted by another African "with a remark that everybody knew where Hasluck had placed her heart; and he added a suggestion so obscene and droll that even the old *mallam* laughed". By degrees, Marie sees herself to be naïve, a softie, and her distrust of Africans and her disappointment reconcile her to Bewsher, whom she eventually marries. She recognizes how wrong she's been:

> She gazed across the uneven floor, in waves of light and shadow which trembled in the flicker of the yellow lamp flames, and saw Obai and Uli walking hand in hand across the residency compound in Kunama, two of the most beautiful men she had ever seen, of the noblest carriage, the frankest look. They had been her Greeks of the fifth century, moving in friendship over the bright worn pavements of the Agora and discussing Plato's last discourse. But Obai and Uli had been talking about Bewsher (the first time she had heard his name) and probably they had been talking nonsense, like their Greek prototypes.

The reverie continues, the present corrects the past ("The golden age of Greece. Galleys full of agonised rowers bleeding under the whip – chained to battered leaking ships . . .") and then the whole folly of colonized Africa is revealed:

> But the voyage was over. They would soon reach harbour. No, of course, there weren't any harbours for the spirit, no rest. The slaves were chained, the captains, prisoners of the ship. And some day Bewsher would crack his whip for the last time. They would throw his old carcase into the sea, Gore would lie drowned among the rats, and she, if she did not die before, would toil on across the black waves – to nowhere – the ship itself, the ship of the whole earth, was rotting under their feet, at last it would open up in space like a burst basket.

Cary's understanding of Marie is profound; the novel is violent, but it is also one of his funniest, and violence and comedy are combined with insight in the chapter he gives to the Africans palavering about how to take power by killing Bewsher.

For many years Cary was praised quietly, but it was a long time before he made real money – it came, as it had in 1919, from America, when in 1944 the Book of the Month Club chose *The Horse's Mouth* as their Main Selection. He continued to work as he always had, writing several books at a time, trying to think of a superstructure for his big scenes. After the death of his wife in 1949 he worked even harder, began another trilogy (published posthumously as *The Captive and the Free*) and still puzzled over *Cock Jarvis*.

It was in these last years that he wrote most of the pieces which were published under the title *Selected Essays*. His name was made, and it is obvious that the ideas for the pieces arose from magazine editors who wanted him as a contributor. One can imagine the editorial requests ("Can you give us a few thousand words on your favourite sport?" – he chose polo; "How about someone for our Great Writers Rediscovered series?" – he chose Surtees). He did a workmanlike piece for *Holiday* on Westminster Abbey and a sensible piece on America – by now he was on the lecture circuit – for the *Saturday Review*. He wrote about writing and about novelists of the past whom he particularly liked – Tolstoy, Defoe, Anatole France. He gave interviews, his chatty *Paris Review* conversation, and a rather ghoulish one for what could only have been an intrusive reporter for *Coronet*: Cary was sixty-eight and very ill, and the interview, called "A Great Author Faces Up to Death," reads like an obituary. The best pieces are reminiscences of his childhood in "Barney Magonagel" and "Cromwell House," and of his years in Nigeria , "Africa Yesterday: One Ruler's Burden" and the poignant "Christmas in Africa". But Cary was no essayist. These are plain unsubtle responses to straightforward requests for copy and have little of the illustration, the imagery or the humor of his novels. He had practised novel-writing for too long to take the magazine market seriously.

"I have more unfinished novels than published ones," he wrote for a BBC broadcast. Two of the unfinished novels have now been published, but these frayed ends of his fiction have taught me more about writing than any number of masterpieces. It is the imperfect that is most instructive, and since Cary is never false it hardly matters that Preedy's sermon is interrupted, that Jimson is two people, Sara three and Jarvis a mass of fragments. Like *Edwin Drood*, *St Ives* and *Weir of Hermiston*, their fascination is inexhaustible because they are incomplete. Whenever I am idle I choose a Cary novel in the way I might seek a friend's company, and it is not long before I am encouraged, inspired to write. It is a relief to me that Michael Joseph has kept Cary's novels in print and, more, that I have half a dozen still to read.

Discovering Dingle

[1976]

The nearest thing to writing a novel is traveling in a strange country. Travel is a creative act – not simply loafing and inviting your soul, but feeding the imagination, accounting for each fresh wonder, memorizing and moving on. The discoveries the traveler makes in broad daylight – the curious problems of the eye he solves – resemble those that thrill and sustain a novelist in his solitude. It is fatal to know too much at the outset: boredom comes as quickly to the traveler who knows his route as to the novelist who is overcertain of his plot. And the best landscapes, apparently dense or featureless, hold surprises if they are studied patiently, in the kind of discomfort one can savor afterward. Only a fool blames his bad vacation on the rain.

A strange country – but how strange? One where the sun bursts through the clouds at ten in the evening and makes a sunset as full and promising as dawn. An island which on close inspection appears to be composed entirely of rabbit droppings. Gloomy gypsies camped in hilarious clutter. People who greet you with "Nice day" in a pelting storm. Miles of fuchsia hedges, seven feet tall, with purple hanging blossoms like Chinese lanterns. Ancient perfect castles that are not inhabited; hovels that are. And dangers: hills and beach-cliffs so steep you either hug them or fall off. Stone altars that were last visited by Druids, storms that break and pass in minutes, and a local language that sounds like Russian being whispered and so incomprehensible that the attentive traveler feels, in the words of a native writer, "like a dog listening to music".

It sounds as distant and bizarre as The Land Where the Jumblies Live, and yet it is the part of Europe that is closest in miles to America, the thirty mile sausage of land on the southwest coast of Ireland that is known as the Dingle Peninsula. Beyond it is Boston and New York, where many of its people have fled. The land is not particularly fertile. Fishing is dangerous and difficult. Food is expensive; and if the Irish Government did not offer financial inducements to the natives they would probably shrink inland, like the people of Great Blasket Island who simply dropped everything and went ashore to the Dingle, deserting their huts and fields and leaving them to the rabbits and the ravens.

It is easy for the casual traveler to prettify the place with romantic hyperbole, to see in Dingle's hard weather and exhausted ground the Celtic Twilight, and in its stubborn hopeful people a version of Irishness that is to be cherished. That is the patronage of pity – the metropolitan's contempt for the peasant. The Irish coast, so enchanting for the man with the camera, is murder for the fisherman. For five of the eight days I was there the fishing boats remained anchored in Dingle Harbor, because it was too wild to set sail. The dead seagulls, splayed out like old-fangled ladies' hats below Clogher Head, testify to the furious winds; and never have I seen so many sheep skulls bleaching on hillsides, so many cracked bones beneath bushes.

Farming is done in the most clumsily primitive way, with horses and donkeys, wagons and blunt plows. The methods are traditional by necessity – modernity is expensive, gas costs more than Guinness. The stereotype of the Irishman is a person who spends every night at the local pub, jigging and swilling; in the villages of this peninsula only Sunday night is festive and the rest are observed with tea and early supper.

"I don't blame anyone for leaving here," said a farmer in Dunquin. "There's nothing for young people. There's no work, and it's getting worse."

After the talk of the high deeds of Finn MacCool and the fairies and leprechauns, the conversation turns to the price of spare parts, the cost of grain, the value of the Irish pound which has sunk below the British one. Such an atmosphere of isolation is intensified and circumscribed by the language – there are many who speak only Gaelic. Such remoteness breeds political indifference. There is little talk of the guerrilla war in Northern Ireland, and the few people I tried to draw on the subject said simply that Ulster should become part of Eire.

Further east, in Cork and Killarney, I saw graffiti reading BRITS OUT or UP THE IRA. It is not only the shortage of walls or the cost of spray cans that keep the Irish in Dingle from scrawling slogans. I cannot remember any people so quickly hospitable or easier to meet. Passers-by nod in greeting, children wave at cars: it is all friendliness. At almost three thousand feet the shepherd salutes the climbers and then marches on with his dogs yapping ahead of him.

Either the people leave and go far – every Irishman I met had a relative in America – or they never stir at all. "I've lived here my whole life," said an old man in Curraheen on Tralee Bay; and he meant it – he had always sat in that chair and known that house and that tree and that pasture. But his friend hesitated. "Well, yes," this one said, "not here exactly. After I got married I moved further down the road." It is the outsider who sees Dingle whole; the Irish there live in solitary villages. And people who have only the vaguest notion of Dublin or London, and who have never left

Ballydavid or Inch, show an intimate knowledge of American cities, Boston, Springfield, Newark or San Diego. The old lady in Dunquin, sister of the famous "Kruger" Kavanagh – his bar remains, a friendly ramshackle place with a dark side of bacon suspended over one bar and selling peat bricks, ice cream, shampoo and corn flakes along with the Guinness and the rum – that old lady considered Ventry (her new homestead, four miles away) another world, and yet she used her stern charm on me to recommend a certain bar on Cape Cod.

I did not find, in the whole peninsula, an inspired meal or a great hotel; nor can the peninsula be recommended for its weather. We had two days of rain, two of mist, one almost tropical, and one which was all three, rain in the morning, mist in the afternoon, and sun that appeared in the evening and didn't sink until eleven at night – this was June. "Soft evening," says the fisherman; but that is only a habitual greeting – it might be raining like hell. In general, the sky is overcast, occasionally the weather is unspeakable: no one should go to that part of Ireland in search of sunny days. The bars, two or three to a village, are musty with rising damp and woodworm, and the pictures of President Kennedy – sometimes on yellowing newsprint, sometimes picked out daintily in needlepoint on framed tea-towels – do little to relieve the gloom. The English habit of giving bars fanciful names, like The Frog and Nightgown or The White Hart, is virtually unknown in Ireland. I did not see a bar in any village that was not called simply Mahoney's, or Crowley's, or Foley's or O'Flaherty's: a bar is a room, a keg, an Irish name over the door, and perhaps a cat asleep on the sandwiches.

The roads are empty but narrow, and one – the three miles across the Conair Pass – is, in low cloud, one of the most dangerous I have ever seen, bringing a lump to my throat that I had not tasted since traversing the Khyber. The landscape is utterly bleak, and sometimes there is no sound but the wind beating the gorse bushes or the cries of gulls which – shrill and frantic – mimic something tragic, like a busload of schoolgirls careering off a cliff. The day we arrived my wife and I went for a walk, down the meadow to the sea. It was gray. We walked fifty feet. It rained. The wind tore at the outcrops of rock. We started back, slipping on seaweed, and now we could no longer see the top of the road, where we had begun the walk. It was cold; both of us were wet, feebly congratulating ourselves that we had remembered to buy rubber boots in Killarney.

Then Anne hunched and said, "It's bloody cold. Let's make this a one-night stand."

But we waited. It rained the next day. And the next. The third was misty, but after so much rain the mist gave us the illusion of good weather: there was some promise in the shifting clouds. But, really, the weather had ceased to matter. It was too cold to swim and neither of us had imagined sunbathing in Ireland. We had started to discover the place on foot, in a high wind, fortified by stout and a picnic lunch of crab's claws (a dollar a pound) and cheese and soda bread. Pausing, we had begun to travel.

There is no detailed guidebook for these parts. Two choices are open: to buy Sheet 20 of the Ordnance Survey Map of Ireland, or climb Mount Brandon and look down. We did both, and it was odd how, standing in mist among ecclesiastical-looking cairns (the mountain was a place of pilgrimage for early Christian monks seeking the intercession of St Brendan the Navigator), we looked down and saw that Smerwick and Ballyferriter were enjoying a day of sunshine, Brandon Head was rainy, and Mount Eagle was in cloud. Climbing west of Dingle is deceptive, a succession of false summits, each windier than the last; but from the heights of Brandon the whole peninsula is spread out like a topographical map, path and road, cove and headland. Down there was the Gallarus Oratory, like a perfect boathouse in stone to which no one risks assigning a date (but probably 9th Cent.), and at a greater distance Great Blasket Island and the smaller ones with longer names around it. The views all over the peninsula are dramatic and unlikely, as anyone who has seen *Ryan's Daughter* knows – that bad dazzling movie was made in and around the fishing hamlet of Dunquin. The coastal cliffs are genuinely frightening, the coves echoic with waves that hit the black rocks and rise – foaming, perpendicular – at the fleeing gannets; and the long Slieve Mish Mountains and every valley – thirty miles of them – are, most weirdly, without trees.

We had spotted Mount Eagle. The following day we wandered from the sandy, and briefly sunny, beach at Ventry, through tiny farms to the dark sloping lake that is banked like a sink a thousand feet up the slope – more bones, more rabbits, and a mountain wall strafed by screeching gulls. We had begun to enjoy the wind and rough weather, and after a few days of it saw Dingle Town as too busy, exaggerated, almost large, without much interest, and full of those fairly grim Irish shops which display in the front window a can of beans, a fan belt, a pair of boots, two chocolate bars, yesterday's newspaper and a row of plastic crucifixes standing on fly-blown cookie boxes. And in one window – that of a shoe store – two bottles of "Guaranteed Pure Altar Wine" – the guarantee was lettered neatly on the label: "Certified by the Cardinal Archbishop of Lisbon and Approved by his Lordship the Most Reverend Dr Eamonn Casey, Bishop of Kerry."

But no one mentions religion. The only indication I had of the faith was the valediction of a lady in a bar in Ballyferriter, who shouted, "God bless ye!" when I emptied my pint of Guinness.

On the rainiest day we climbed down into the cove at Coumeenoole, where – because of its unusual shape, like a ruined cathedral – there was no rain. I sent the children off for driftwood and at the mouth of a dry cave built a fire. It is the bumpkin who sees travel in terms of dancing girls and candlelight dinners on the terrace; the city-slicker's triumphant holiday is finding the right mountain-top or building a fire in the rain or recognizing the wildflowers in Dingle: foxglove, heather, bluebells.

And it is the city-slicker's conceit to look for untrodden ground, the five miles of unpeopled beach at Stradbally Strand, the flat magnificence of Inch Strand, or the most distant frontier of Ireland, the island off Dunquin called Great Blasket.

Each day, she and her sister-islands looked different. We had seen them from the cliffside of Slea Head, and on that day they had the appearance of sea monsters – high backed creatures making for the open sea. Like all off-shore islands, seen from the mainland, their aspect changed with the light: they were lizard-like, then muscular, turned from gray to green, acquired highlights that might have been huts. At dawn they seemed small, but they grew all day into huge and fairly fierce-seeming mountains in the water, diminishing at dusk into pink beasts and finally only hindquarters disappearing in the mist. Some days they were not there at all; on other days they looked linked to the peninsula.

It became our ambition to visit them. We waited for a clear day, and it came – bright and cloudless. But the boat looked frail, a rubber dinghy with an outboard motor. The children were eager; I looked at the high waves that lay between us and Great Blasket and implored the boatman for reassurance. He said he had never overturned – but he was young. On an impulse I agreed and under a half-hour later we arrived at the foreshore on the east of the main island, soaking wet from the spray.

No ruin in Ireland prepared us for the ruins on Great Blasket. After many years of cozy habitation – described with good humor by Maurice O'Sullivan in *Twenty Years A-Growing* (1933) – the villagers were removed to the mainland in 1953. They could no longer support themselves: they surrendered their island to the sneaping wind. And their houses, none of them large, fell down. Where there had been parlors and kitchens and vegetable gardens and fowl-coops there was now bright green moss. The grass and moss and wildflowers combine to create a cemetery effect in the derelict village, the crumbled hut walls like old gravemarkers.

I think I have never seen an eerier or more beautiful island. Just beyond the village which has no name is a long sandy beach called White Strand, which is without a footprint; that day it shimmered like any in Bali. After our picnic we climbed to Sorrowful Cliff and discovered that the island which looked only steep from the shore was in fact precipitous. "Sure, it's a wonderful place to commit suicide," a man told me in Dunquin. A narrow path was cut into the slope on which we walked single file – a few feet to the right and straight down were gulls and the dull sparkle of the Atlantic. We were on the windward side, heading for Fatal Cliff; and for hundreds of feet straight up rabbits were defying gravity on the steepness. The island hill becomes such a sudden ridge and so sharp that when we got to the top of it and took a step we were in complete silence: no wind, no gulls, no surf, only a green-blue vista of the coast of Kerry, Valencia Island and the soft headlands. Here on the lee side the heather was three feet thick and easy as a mattress. I lay down, and within minutes my youngest child was asleep on his stomach, his face on a cushion of fragrant heather. And the rest of the family had wandered singly to other parts of the silent island, so that when I sat up I could see them prowling alone, in detached discovery, trying – because we could not possess this strangeness – to remember it.

The Exotic View

[1977]

Towards the end of a life he had spent largely in disguise – he was now sixty – Daniel Defoe sat down to write a book he hoped would clear him of debt. In his first novel, perhaps the first real novel in English, he gave shape to the oldest dream of Western man: he created a castaway Adam and marooned him in Eden. Although one must conclude that by the end of the novel Crusoe is a model colonist and has reduplicated in clumsy island artifacts the England he knew, it is also pretty certain that *Robinson Crusoe* contains most of the essential props of the exotic. The mild climate, the wild goats which provide food and clothing, the fruit trees, the fertile soil, and by happy accident a loyal servant willing to renounce cannibalism – it is a dream setting to which Crusoe brings homely skills (one of the triumphant chapters concerns his bread-making). Crusoe prospers in this island world. He ridicules money, he calls his hut his "castle", he has a tremendous sense of power, he is happy. It is the ultimate success story: he has regained Paradise.

The exotic dream, not always outlandish, is a dream of what we lack and so crave. It may be the plump odalisque squinting from her sofa with her hands behind her head, or else a glimpse of palm trees – the palm tree is the very emblem of the exotic: or else power, or riches, fine weather, good health, safety. It is the immediately recognizable charm of the unfamiliar, so the grizzled herdsman with his bullock in stony Kafiristan counts as much as the dancing girl. And something more: the exotic is elsewhere. The word itself implies distance, as far from the world of politics and scheming as Prospero's island is from Venice. It is the magic of travelers' tales, the record of enormous journeys of quest and discovery – the heroism of these returned travelers is the glorious note of enchantment in their stories. The legacy is both fictional (Odysseus and Othello) and historical (Marco Polo and Raleigh). But the notion is more than a bookish conceit. We would have a fairly clear idea of what the exotic means even without the occasions that art offers the imagination.

It seems as natural to dream of the exotic as to dream at all. We are born with the impulse to wonder and, eventually, to yearn for the world before the Fall in which we may be the solitary Crusoe (with his bad conscience he is rather more credible than Adam); and who has not dreamed of being a princeling with a jeweled sword marching across an eastern caliphate? In a sense, the literature comes later. Because the dream's perfection emphasizes that it is unattainable, man searches for proof that it is not. And whatever fantasy one has reveals one's peculiar hunger. It might be very simple: the island paradise. Or it might be complex: the oriental kingdom of silks and plumes.

And between Tahiti and Istanbul, the pretty island and the fabled city which are two of the exotic's frontiers, there is a middle zone that combines palm trees and riches, the exotic of India and China – *nautch* girls, *howdahs*, the pink palace, the court, and the sahib's pipe-dream of himself in stately repose. The frontiers are actual. It is possible with a model globe and a free afternoon to sketch the geography of the exotic. Isn't it a large rectangle on the other side of the earth, with lines running from Samarkand south to Africa and east through Peking to the Pacific? It is Persia and Egypt, Arabia and Burma, Central Asia and the tropics. Its capital – at its geographical center – is Shangri-La. The cruellest irony is that most of the lands comprise what is commonly known these days as The Third World, but nothing is more valuable than that irony in suggesting that the exotic is partly illusion.

It must be. How else could it contain so much of what we regard as ideal? And the exotic is not Christian – that is undoubtedly part of its appeal; it is not usually religious, it is never political in the harsh rigged-up sense (unless one regards the young chieftain in his silly hat as a political figure). With the Christian element removed, the concept of innocence is unnecessary – the word itself is meaningless. But gentleness is implied, for the exotic very often calls to mind a peaceable kingdom, an aristocracy in which every dream girl is a princess and every man a warrior. The contradiction is that the girls in the seraglio are seen to be virginal and the warriors rather comic and harmless – their antique weapons might be garden tools (it is a fact that in Africa, Asia and the Pacific, weapons – the long knife and the axe – *are* garden tools as well). The exotic image is not explicitly erotic but often subtly sensual, which is perhaps why we seldom associate elderliness with exoticism, and so often, in imagining this world, conceive a mental image of youth, of children and the child-like. Part of the formula which goes to make up this dream relates to time. In the world of the exotic, which is always an old world peopled by the young or the ageless, time stands still.

It goes almost without saying that the exotic notion is a Western dream, a hankering for the East. The ancient Chinese had the nautical skill of the Europeans, and they navigated as far as the East Africa coast. But the Chinese map of the world, in which China was – as it is called even now –

Chung Guo, "The Middle Kingdom", showed the oceans as filled with tiny islands of no significance, populated by devils and barbarians and hairy monsters. Lord Macartney's embassy to China was regarded by the Chinese as something of a joke; they laughed at Lord Amherst, they laugh still as Americans stumble along the Great Wall. Their dreams are inward. The search-stories, the travelers looking for fabled cities, the dream of a return to desert island simplicity, have a Western, Christian source: the European sought his opposite in imagining the exotic. He needed a word to express a refinement of the foreignness he found attractive; with the word "exotic" (which receives inadequate definition in the dictionary) he nailed it down.

The more I reflect on *Robinson Crusoe* the more convinced I become that it is confusing to deal with the exotic as a literary idea. It is all right to begin with a book – the concreteness of fiction is helpful to provoke thought; but after that the exotic asserts its ambiguity. I think its ambiguity ought to remain smoky and allusive: the image is half vapor anyway and cannot be fixed. And some of it is almost too unbearably detailed to be given fictional form. It seems quite appropriate that after dozing over *Purchas His Pilgrimes*, Coleridge woke and tried to describe his "Vision in a Dream", the city of Xanadu and Kubla Khan's Pleasure Dome. Similarly, his faltering is predictable, for he was stopped like a man dazzled by an overwhelming brilliance and on second thought put the blame on the person from Porlock (who had come to collect a debt: how much further could one be from the exotic than in confronting the plain fact of this intruder?). The exotic is really too beautiful or unlikely for words. It is worth mentioning that Samuel Purchas's book (1613) was partly based on Hakluyt's *Voyages* (also the source of some of Shakespeare's exoticism in *The Tempest*). But dreamers are not always readers, and they are seldom travelers.

No exotic dreams in fiction have ever compared with the visual dreams we see in paintings or photographs. Bosch in prose would be as unreadable as the most celebrated dream-fiction of all time, *Finnegans Wake*, a tumultuous obfuscation wherein Joyce's labors only demonstrate that the written word gives us little access to dreams. Language is a thicket: the unpronounceable merely confounds us and turns us away; the thwarted dream becomes nightmare. Defoe suggested a savage exotic, Coleridge wrote the prologue for a lush version, Elizabethan travelers reported on cities of gold and the dramatists they inspired made these cities idyllic; for Milton, the exotic was "the Golden Chersonese" of the Far East, for Kipling it was the stinks and stratagems of the bazaar. Some, like Pierre Loti, wrote about what they saw; others, like Robert Louis Stevenson, had a fantasy of the exotic long before they were able to witness it as travelers. Early in his life, Stevenson wrote:

I should like to rise and go
Where the golden apples grow;
Where below another sky
Parrot islands anchored lie.

"As an ailing youth in Heriot Row," James Pope Hennessy wrote of Stevenson in Edinburgh, "he had dreamed of an active life in exotic surroundings." It is like Fallen Man, marked with the sin of illness, yearning for a second chance to be Adam. For the last four years of his life, in Vailima, Samoa, Stevenson saw and understood what he had imagined so many years before. He had gone in search of the exotic. But some did not risk the journey. The vulgarity in the Tarzan books of Edgar Rice Burroughs (who never left the United States, but who fuelled his imagination on the work of Henry Morton Stanley) seems an accurate rendering of the jungly exotic because it is complete and, of course, because being wholly imaginary it confirms our stereotype of Africa. Yet the written word is somehow not enough. The exotic image is private and fantastic. It is so hard to share such a vision.

The challenge to fiction is an obvious truth: thought is pictorial. We don't dream gray pages of print; we see faces and landscapes, we are animated by the particularities of light, we think in pictures. And although the exotic is vivid in the reckonings of painters – the mental travelers like Blake, or else actual travelers who made careers for themselves by finding the exotic scenes they were to depict in their paintings, such as Zoffany and the Daniells – it was not until the invention of photography that it was possible to prove to the skeptics and reassure the dreamer that the travelers, the painters and poets had not been fancifully indulging themselves in a private vision.

Photography is alone among art forms in having a birthdate. After 1822, when the Frenchman Niepce made the first permanent photograph, the world was accessible to us in pictures. Almost from the first the exotic was considered an important subject for the camera. And no longer could the exotic be disputed as illusion or dismissed as fantasy.

Here was the evidence: from Samoa, the *matai*'s daughter, in her virgin's head-dress, bare-breasted and pigeon-toed before a hibiscus hedge, modestly clutching at her coconut leaf skirt; or from India, the *nautch* girls in stiff clothes and bangles and nose-jewels, very tiny and serious and young, not voluptuous but bearing a resemblance to painted and written reports; the *fakir* knotted on his mat, his legs twisted in two arches behind his head and his serene chalk-white face; the homely grandeur of the Zulu woman delousing her preoccupied husband with patient concentration; the pudgy Turkish girls in a vaguely vicious room; the Indians with flutes who seem wilfully to ignore the upright cobras they have charmed (and to the right, one supine snake – perhaps tone-deaf – making for the camera); a dwarf witch from Darjeeling with coins on her palms, the heavily bandaged corpse on a ghat awaiting combustion, a family group of head-hunters posed like picnickers, a donkey cart of shrouded women and children pausing in an Arabian street for their strangeness to be verified; camels and elephants, and landscapes – deserted beaches and steppes, the emblematic palms, water mirroring wilderness, flowers so strange they had yet to be named.

What is it that is so persuasive about these photographs? Like all photographs, however fudged or posed, they have the undiscriminating truthfulness which the human eye lacks; and where there are flaws the truth is even more emphatic. In some cases they are distortions of the exotic dream, rougher, bruised-looking or plainly dirty; but many are like the dream made flesh and have an uncanny exactitude. These are representations of a complete world that is utterly different from that inhabited by people in whose dreams this exoticism was prefigured. This is the world in a dew-drop, trembling on a very odd leaf. Look a bit closer: there is a demure girl waiting for you, petals crisply starched on branches, flower blobs on a bush, white sand and squirts of sunshine through cloud, cool damp hollows in hillocks, men in furry boots and snakes rising tamely out of baskets; it is not always sweet-scented, for there is a decrepit cliff, an overworked child, a loaf of buffalo dung or black hides stretched on a flyblown frame. We believe because, however bizarre the photographic subject, it is the bizarreness we require – it is the confirmation we need. These photographs of the exotic enlarge the meaning of the word and go on to furnish our dreams with a greater magnificence.

Each picture is an invitation to the exotic and seems to repeat in its strangeness that this is a world that awaits discovery. It holds out the promise – something the *Playboy* pin-up does in a crude posture – that you can enter this picture. Because it is a photograph, it is an affirmation of truth (even though we know that photographs are capable of cheating and trickery); and because it is exotic it beckons.

If the exotic is partly illusion, the illusion of what is not there is compensated by something that is there that we did not expect. Fifteen years ago, I went to Africa, where I was to remain for five years. The land of mud and smoke and low forest, of undersized people in rags, and odors of decay, was a surprise to me, but no less strange than the hot brightly-lit place I dreamed of years before I left home. Africa was cold. There was snow on the Equator: a further shock. I had not seen photographs that had prepared me for this. But very soon, frost was included in my notion of the exotic, and I cannot think of Africa now without smelling the wood smoke of a burning blue-gum log or seeing a humpy meadow covered with white frost and a darker solitary track of foot-marks – narrow as bird-prints, because the walker through that frosty meadow had no shoes. I was incapable of imaging the Giant Lobelia, the heights of the Ituri Forest, the Ngorogoro Crater; nor was I quite prepared for the Africans themselves. I wrote and wrote, disillusionment gave way to wonder. You had to see it to believe it.

Robert Louis Stevenson sailed the Pacific looking for the perfect island "where golden apples grow". He rejected Hawaii, he rejected Tahiti, he wasn't entranced by Australia. Then he happened upon Samoa and decided to stay. He did not live, as they say, *fa'asamoa*, "Samoa-style". He built a grand house with an enormous veranda. He extended the house and added servants. He emptied his Edinburgh house and shipped the contents – marble busts, ormolu clocks and all – to Samoa. He brought out his aged mother as well. He was one of the best, and best-known, writers of his time – his most popular writing was behind him (he had written *Treasure Island* in Braemar and Davos, "Dr Jekyll and Mr Hyde" in Bournemouth). He had a vast public, and people believed what he wrote. But in this house, which was almost Crusoe-like in the way it recreated an old bourgeois style of life on an exotic island, *Tusitala* ("The Writer of Tales", Stevenson's Samoan title) had one valued possession: a large square-headed plate camera on a gangling tripod. Stevenson even had a cameraman, Joe Strong, the husband of his stepdaughter. After Joe became burdensome as a drunkard and a spendthrift (and he had a Samoan mistress in Apia) and was expelled from Paradise, Stevenson took over the camera and supervised the rest of the picture-taking himself from then on.

Homage to Mrs Robinson

[1977]

She stood alone and completely calm on the empty railway platform, her long coat tugged by the train's draft. The first thing he noticed in the over-bright lights of the station were the lustrous bones in her face. Boarding the train she looked straight ahead and carried a small suitcase. Then she disappeared. Once the train pulled out on its journey to Ventimiglia he walked the length of it and didn't see her; he could only conclude that she was in one of the First-Class sleepers.

He saw her an hour later in the dining car and was stunned again by her composure, that odor of jasmine that reached him two tables away. Though she faced him – he could not help staring – she didn't appear to see him: she looked through him as she finished her meal and lit her cigarette and guillotined the flame with the lid of her lighter. Her eyes went to the window and watched with pitying interest the feebly lighted countryside. She crossed her legs and something ripped inside him.

She was forty, perhaps more, but make-up works – her lipstick was so neatly done, the highlights in her hair so convincing, and the languid glamor of her movements so studied she awoke in him his earliest sexual memory and she was ageless. More tempting even than her slender grace, her pretty mouth pursed on her cigarette and the movements of her breasts – with just a hint of weight they trembled over the table – more tempting than the hunger he saw in her bones was the fact that she had not looked him in the eye. She was perfect, private, impenetrable; she hadn't smiled, and yet she wasn't sad. She was a lioness in repose. She had lived in the world – he hadn't.

He considered offering her a drink, but hesitated. Being older, she had it in her power to make a fool of him. He decided to risk everything: the dining car emptied; he joined her, sitting next to her at her table. Then she smiled, unmistakably her victory, and before he could think of anything to say ("How far are you going?" he had ridiculously rehearsed), she said, "Where do you Americans get such splendid boots?"

"How did you know I was American?" he said. He had registered her British accent, the cool enthusiasm that was almost theatrical.

She ignored his question and went on, "I'd love to buy some for my son.

He's just started university."

Son eighteen; she got married at about twenty-four; a little arithmetic: she was about forty-two. He said, "You could probably get them here, but things in France are so expensive."

"France," she said, mimicking his accent. "You make it rhyme with pants."

"What's wrong with that?" he said. "I like pants."

She smiled and touched at her throat and said, "At least we have that in common."

It was then that he went for her with his hand, reaching under the table and placing it just above her knee where the hem emphasized the division between the heat of her leg and the coolness of her dress. If she had been younger it would have meant nothing, but she was old enough to understand that his hand there was both an appeal and an invitation. She did not react, she was still speaking about her son, and he moved his hand up her thigh and let it rest there, burning.

Without interrupting herself she gently lifted his hand from her leg and glanced around. The car was totally empty now, only one waiter lingered.

The boy wondered if he had made a blunder. He began to apologize.

"Listen," said the woman. "We haven't got much time. I'm only going as far as Cannes. I'm in the next coach, room fifty-two. Give me ten minutes." And she got up and left.

He did as he had been told, and when he knocked she opened the door a crack before letting him in. She wore a robe and when she kissed him and pressed herself against him it loosened and fell open. He caressed her, but she drew away and said, "Aren't you going to take those clothes off?"

The train rocked slowly southward; he was sprawled on the berth and could see the lights of passing stations in her hair – her head was against his stomach. *No, no,* she had said a moment ago, *let me do it,* and so he lay with his feet braced on the jolting wall while she knelt and worked on him with her feathery mouth and her hands. His orgasm trembled and teased him, rising and stopping, like fluid heating in a pipe; her tongue snaked and she became frantic with greed until at last and furiously the spurts came in five spasms that she controlled with her lips and he heard in the darkness the sound of her gulping it down.

Later – she hadn't spoken a word – she began again on him with her fingers and then mounted him. She moaned and cried out so acutely, finally uttering wild little shrieks that afterward his clearest memory was of having to stifle her sobs of pleasure and make love to her with his hand over her mouth.

This is of course fantasy: there was no woman, there was no dining car, there was only The Blue Train and the boy. But the encounter is plausible (more plausible now than when *Tea and Sympathy* was considered shocking), because you have seen that woman traveling alone and idly wished yourself upon her. If the woman had been younger she wouldn't be alone or would have asked for more, pretended to be sullen, demanded high spirits; her moves, from the beginning, would have been more obvious. The older woman makes no decisive moves except the last and she knows, if she is attractive, that you are hers for the taking. So she is seldom disappointed and never humiliated. She is not looking for flattery, and is certainly not husband-hunting; she has met you a hundred times before.

No apologies, no explanations. She knows the essential things about concealment and more than anyone in the world this woman has a heightened awareness of time: as the boy sees maturity in a sexual encounter – proof of his manhood, another statistic to relish – the older woman is granted a reprieve and in that encounter has outwitted her age. For her it is a private, a mutual compliment. In the classic situation she does not want to see you afterward. The preliminaries, the half-truths, the confidences – all these are dispensed with. There isn't time; she will come straight to the point.

And, unlike many of her younger counterparts, she does not want to be caught. She doesn't need witnesses. For someone younger, sex is not an end in itself but a means to another end – the image is intentional: job, money, marriage, power, domination. And so, if they never know this older woman and only deal with the twenty-year-old and her tough twinkle, most men grow up believing in sex as a favor they've been granted – sex as strategy or currency. Therefore, the act itself is a threat. The sexual power-seeker literally has you by the balls and can invent, in the only act of equality the human animal performs, a gross inequality. There is a dangerous bravado in the sexual publicity the younger woman seeks. If sex grants power she must be seen to be sexy – and involve you – before she can be acknowledged powerful. The older woman isn't really interested in power: her age has liberated her from that deception.

But this is all theory. There are better reasons for preferring an older woman, not the least of which is that a woman between the ages of thirty and fifty, sexually, is alight – her manner might be cool but her body blazes. At her age she could know every trick in the book and, if it weren't for her pride – which inspires respect and annoyance in the same degree – she could probably make a fortune as a hooker. One has to meet her in real life. Literature has very few older women who are convincingly seductive; within the conventions of the novel it is hard to establish such a character. Maybe Madame Bovary, possibly that woman in *Les Liaisons*

Dangereuses, perhaps Madame de Vionnet in James's *The Ambassadors*; but who else? One or two of Byron's ladies in *Don Juan*, no one in Dickens, Melville, Conrad or Dreiser. The older woman has not been well-served by fiction writers, though Stephen Vizinczey's *In Praise of Older Women* is a worthy contribution, and so is Brian Moore's recent *The Doctor's Wife*.

The movies and plays have succeeded where the novels have failed. The films that spring to mind are *Sunset Boulevard*, Bergman's *Frenzy* (1945), *This Sporting Life*, *Nothing But the Best*, *Sweet Bird of Youth*, *The Roman Spring of Mrs Stone* (also a novel, but better as a film), *A Cold Wind in August*, *The Last Picture Show*, *Room at the Top* and the brilliant Fassbinder film *Fear Eats the Soul* (1973). I think of Ann Bancroft in *The Graduate* or Deborah Kerr in *The Gypsy Moths*. Each is the older woman to perfection. Mrs Robinson is resourceful, responsive, independent, and a knock-out – was there anyone who saw that movie who did not regret the fact that the hero went off with the daughter and not with the mother? There is no doubt that masculine wisdom begins when a man prefers the mother to the daughter, though I suppose it is only normal to want them both. In *Lolita* Humbert Humbert marries the mother so that he can get the daughter; but that was many years ago, and he was a pedophile. Our pointless defloration mania or at least our fixation with a snug fit, has made many a misguided man a pedophile, inevitably a power-seeker (which is why Nabokov turns the tables and makes Lolita a pain in the neck).

The older woman is not trying to catch your eye – she is beyond that – but if you look she'll notice, and if she is interested she will make it simple for you, even protect you: you only have to co-operate. There is one chance in ten that she'll be hysterical or reckless, but the signs of that will become apparent long before the last move: and any hint of threat and you must fold your tent and steal away, for she is capable of destroying you.

She awoke in him his earliest sexual memory. I am not speaking of the Oedipus Complex, which is nonsense, and in any case enough of a taboo to make one suppress it. But that friend of your mother's, who visited and left an odor of perfume and cigarette smoke and an aphrodisiac smudge of lipstick on her gin glass; the first school-teacher you wanted – though you didn't know how it was done – to go to bed with; the first woman who gave you informed encouragement and knew what was happening to you even if you didn't – she was always older and always the ideal. We don't abandon that fantasy. The older woman gives us something that is very nearly incomparable, the chance to complete in adulthood what was impossible to complete as a child, a blameless gift of lechery that combines the best of youth, a maturity, romance and realism in equal parts.

My Extended Family

[1977]

Some years ago (I was about twenty-four) I was appointed Acting Director of an adult education institute. But this was in Uganda and my chief responsibility was okaying invoices and signing chits for the vast shipments of green bananas that were devoured by the residential students. Another task was counselling the students and helping them solve the ticklish problems that arose in their transfer from a mud hut to the barrack-like building in which they were housed on our Kampala compound. Most, if not all, were much older than I, and while some of the problems concerned merely bed-wetting or drunkenness or lighting fires in their rooms, other were more serious. Major Oyet, who attended our course in Current Affairs for Uganda Army Officers, kept a machine-gun in his trunk. What struck me as unsafe about his fondness for the gun was the tendency he shared with his fellow officers for drinking whisky at breakfast, and one Saturday night he threatened to shoot Mr Ofumbi, the cook. I need hardly add that but for the single Kakwa among them, all these officers have since been promoted to glory by Idi Amin.

On the surface of it, the simple request by a man from Kigezi, his desire to get to Wales as quickly as possible, was not unusual. Ugandan students were constantly pleading with me to help them leave the country – indeed (and this was long before Amin) most of the students saw education purely as a means to emigrate, to go on an overseas course and never come back. The man from Kigezi wanted to go on a course, any course – audio-visual, pesticides, agriculture, primary teaching, developing suitable materials for bush schools, mental health, it didn't matter. His desperation was apparent. He stated his reason: he was being forced to marry his sister-in-law.

He had, naturally, participated a few years before in the Urine Ceremony of the Bakiga. This ritual is a necessary part of the marriage vow. The groom and all his brothers place their hands on the seat of a stool, and the bride – who has been chosen for her obesity and the wide gaps in her teeth – lifts her skirt and jams her naked buttocks onto their hands. Finally, with a certain amount of encouraging hilarity, she urinates and in this way shows that she is symbolically wedded to each of the hands she taints, the brothers of her husband. The husband has the strongest claim, but if he happens to be out of town, any of the brothers may sleep with her. If the husband dies, one of the brothers must take charge of her, which is not the chore it might seem. Men in Kigezi do little more than spend the day drinking a kind of fermented porridge they call beer, while the women do all the farming and child-rearing.

The man in my office was muttering in what I first thought was his own language. I realized that he was saying "Coleg Harlech, Coleg Harlech", his destination, another adult education college in Wales. He wanted to leave Uganda; he did not wish to return to his village; he would not marry his sister-in-law.

I was deeply shocked. I told him so. I reminded him of his obligation, of the implications of the Urine Ceremony, and I advised him to go home. He became very fierce.

"You do not understand my life," he shouted. "African life is badness. Relatives always staying, cousins coming to Kampala to wear my shirts, brothers wanting money. I hate it! You do not know . . ."

His arguments were uninteresting and selfish, I thought. Yet as he was talking it occurred to me that while I saw only benefit in the kinship system called the Extended Family, he saw it as a burdensome invasion of his privacy. His answer – a diploma course in Wales – was evasive and provisional. But our discussion was futile. I believed in the Extended Family; he didn't.

Perhaps now he is convinced. In Uganda, there is no government, no law, and little paid employment. There is chaos. But beneath this chaos there is something orderly and protective, the old sowing, growing, beer drinking, hut-building superstructure of the extended family. Except for that, Uganda would be total jungle and cannibalism might prove a necessity.

It is a long way from the gorilla wilderness of Southwest Uganda to the prim suburbs of Boston, but the family pattern has similarities in both places. I didn't, thank God, have to endure a Urine Ceremony, and I would not jump at the chance to sleep with my sister-in-law, much less marry her. Yet there are dependencies I recognize, and virtues which have gone unremarked upon, and if life offers any greater pleasure than a secure place in a large family I do not know what that could possibly be.

It was part of my luck to have been born in a populous family of nine unexampled wits. But my father was one of eight, and so was my mother. Two fertile clans: and together they have produced the equivalent of a multi-national (French-Canadian-American-Italian) corporation of people – some, I admit, I barely know. Isn't that the way with all corporations? Only recently I learned that I have relatives in Piacenza and Guayaquil; it makes the thought of visits to Italy and Ecuador more attractive. The larger the family the more there is to do, but also there are more people to do it. In African societies, where women do all the farming, men take up polygamy and they prosper. In the fairer extended family there is a division of labor among the children which is unknown to the only child (inevitably made a bundle of nerves by the persistent attentions of his doting parents). The large family, splicing clan to clan, becomes more than a community – it becomes a nation. And nation speaks unto nation: no one wrote more passionately about Biafra, which was in every sense an Ibo family which had become a nation, than Auberon Waugh, himself a member of an extended family with the dimension and wholeness of a nation, being like-minded, self-sufficient and with its capital at Combe Florey. Because of this family's independence, Waugh writes from a position of strength.

Literature does not provide many examples of the extended family. It is a fiendishly difficult subject to deal with, for it is hard to do justice to it without writing a mammoth novel. The best of these is *A House for Mr Biswas* by V. S. Naipaul. It appears to be a chronicle of the inroads a huge family makes on the privacies and personal freedom of Mohun Biswas. Biswas's stated aim is to paddle his own canoe – "the paddler" his mockers call him. One could easily get the impression from reading *Mr Biswas* that Naipaul is describing an entire society. Well, he is; but Naipaul would call "society" a politician's word. He is describing a family, one of the largest in our literature. And though he deals with the persecution of one member of the family, he elaborates the plot in dynastic terms, for at the end of the novel Mohun Biswas has staked his own claim, and the "house" of the title becomes an extension of the Tulsi's "Monkey House". Naipaul's novel reads like a homage to family life. It is impossible to read this book and not be moved by the way the loyalties in Biswas's family resemble those of the Tulsis.

It is easier to describe the downfall of a family and its disintegration than to describe the complex ways a family grows and extends. Minor novelists have attempted it, but apart from the Russians I can think of very few writers who have managed to convey the complexity of the extended family. We get it in William Faulkner's "Snopes trilogy" – *The Hamlet, The Mansion* and *The Town*, in Galsworthy's *Forsyte Saga* and in the neglected novels of Wright Morris.

There is no shortage of family novels. But here one must make a distinction between the family – a group of blood-relations – and the extended family, a corporate group in which some members are related by loyalty and others by blood. We don't have very precise words for members of an extended family. Anthropologists become incomprehensible in trying to explain the subtleties of this sort of kinship. "Brother" is a fairly common designation, but "brother" is more affectionate than specific. A brother is just one of the bunch.

So it is in my own immediate family. The nucleus is recognizable: Father-Mother-First child. The addition of six more children was a complicating factor, various marriages added more family members, and the acquisition of property complicated things still further. The Tulsis, the Snopes, the Forsytes begin to make a little sense, and *Emma* no sense at all. No longer is it a question of a little family in a little house. With more children, more houses, more duties to perform, more skills to learn, I might have foundered. Quite early in life, I came to regard my eldest brother as nearly indistinguishable from my father; a good deal later, I found myself treating the youngest as I would my son. In small families authority rests with the parents, but I had to learn the chain of command. The eldest, having mastered a skill, passes this skill to the next in line. It begins with donkey-work, dishwashing and snow-shovelling, the eldest superintending; but it moves on to music appreciation, to reading, to learning to drive a car. I learned to drive from my second-oldest brother, who had been taught by the eldest, who himself had received instruction from my father. My sister blames her bad driving on me.

Careers were another matter. "Find your nitch," my father used to say. My parents seemed to believe that it was essential that none of our careers was duplicated, and (this might have been unconscious on their part) they had it mapped out. The idea was that eventually there would be a painter, a priest, a doctor, a nun, a teacher, and so forth. In the event, we did not pursue those particular vocations (I was supposed to be the doctor; I abandoned the study when I came to organic chemistry), but we followed the pattern: our careers are different and mutually useful. And there are priests and doctors and teachers elsewhere in the family – why put them out of business?

It amazes me just how complete the family was, and how it has grown. Many of us were delivered at birth by my uncle, the doctor, and he has remained medical adviser to the family. Every nation needs a free health service; in the land of the whopping medical bill (the average family of four forks out four thousand dollars a year to doctors) Uncle Jim was ours. Another uncle – I never know whether to call him Uncle Louis or Father Mario – has performed marriages for some of us and baptized others and administered the Last Rites to at least two. A doctor and a priest can take care of practically everything. But there is an engineer uncle, too, a father of – I think – ten children, and designer of a bridge in Brazil that appears on postcards. If one needed a summer job one could always find employment with his construction company. I didn't, though my two older brothers did and enjoyed the work, since several of their fellow workers were our cousins. One of my younger brothers chose a different option, working for a time in another relative's bakery. But I cannot imagine any of us doing this sort of work except for relatives: manual labor or bakery work is not drudgery when it is kept in the family, though I am sure we would have scoffed at the suggestion that we do it for perfect strangers.

In the same way, public issues could be kept within the family. When atomic testing was exercising people's minds in the 1960's it never occurred to us to write to the government, but rather to buttonhole our physicist uncle who worked for the Atomic Energy Commission in a nuclear reactor somewhere on Long Island. The question of faith was always put to our priest uncle and socialized medicine to our doctor uncle. My first girlfriend was my cousin, Susan – a harmless romance and because of that the memory is idyllic.

It sounds like perfection: examples of industry and ambition and achievement and romance. But there were unambitious ones as well, a few failures, some drop-outs and dolts. The beauty of the system is that, while the world finds it hard to be tolerant of the non-scorer, there is always room for him in the extended family. He is "a good scout", "loads of fun", the comedian at family get-togethers. To ridicule a member of the family for being bone-idle was considered heresy: if we wouldn't have him, who would? Indeed, being "a good scout" counted considerably more than splitting the atom, something I suppose our physicist uncle did every day.

But we had cousins who weren't cousins, aunts who weren't aunts. An extended family includes people who have been recruited because they are liked and might be useful. Growing up, I noticed how children from smaller families used to become attached to ours. They used my older brothers as I did – to find out how cars worked or to learn baseball. They ate with us and if we were going somewhere my father encouraged them to come along. He called each one "Jack" – he still calls most people "Jack". As time went on, they remained part of the family, acting as unpaid handymen or plumbers or lawyers or whatever. The system was subtle, but if an outsider was willing (and "a good scout") he could find himself the object of a recruitment campaign. Aunt Gert was not really an aunt. She had gone to college with my mother, her father had shot himself, she was unmarried. Aunt Gert took us to movies on Saturday afternoons and, after each movie, to confession. She frequently ate with us.

This made mealtimes something of an affair. "How are you, Jack?" my father would say to Eddie Flaherty at the end of the table. Eddie coveted my brother's shotgun. The next evening Eddie's seat might be taken by

John Brodie, who captured toads in our back yard and usually stuck around to eat, or by Kenny Hall, who taught me to make model planes, or by any of my brothers' friends. Perhaps as a reaction to my father's "Jack", my brother Alex gave all his friends bizarre nicknames: Pigga, Chicky, Dada, Pin. Ten years ago, when the family really began to sprawl, my parents decided to buy a house on Cape Cod. This proved too small. They bought another, then my brothers began to colonize the Cape, each buying a house within driving distance of my parents. And now I have one. So August is what every mealtime used to be, a sort of jamboree. Cooking, driving, outings to the beach and childminding are shared. No longer simply my parents and their children, but grandchildren, cousins and nieces and nephews, and the recruits. Meetings are arranged, meals planned, weenie roasts organized; but because it is a family of poor planners (the extended family, by its very nature, prevents one from being a good planner) things go wrong and there is usually twice as much food as is necessary.

Yet there is an advantage in the sheer numbers of people who gather on the Cape each August. One of my sisters had hesitated to introduce her new boyfriend to my parents. She couldn't face them and endure the silences, the awkward exploratory questions: he was divorced, he's from New York, a place my father regards as "full of fakers". But during one of these family parties – a soft-ball game here, my brother-in-law making hamburgers over there, some lost soul mowing the lawn, my father parked near a half-gallon of California sherry, seven oddly-assorted children playing Cowboys and Indians, my brother Alex doing his imitation of Sam Ervin, and Brother Gene countering with his Jimmy Carter impersonation, another group preparing to go to the beach, and Alex's girlfriend (her own parents about to arrive) wondering whether anyone is interested in a game of charades – it was during one of these parties, as I say, that my sister slipped her new boyfriend into the crowd. It was as good as his being introduced; he was tacitly accepted as one of the family, although many of us did not meet him, and there were some who were wholly unaware that he was present that day.

For a month, this family activity continues, from house to house, up and down Cape Cod. What makes it especially interesting is the fact that within the confines of the family there are dissenters from the manic day-to-day program. As the month wears on the imitations become personal: "Who's this?" someone says, and a cousin is imitated down to his tiniest mannerism; my brother Peter imitates my father putting on his trousers; Alex does his spectacular number about all of us going down in a plane – this requires his imitating each person's characteristic reaction, thirty seconds before the crash, in cruel mimicry; I hear a familiar echo and realize that someone is doing me on the porch, a know-it-all voice with strangulated vowels. By the end of the month the impersonations are affectionate, and we part friends, or more than friends.

There are many children. I am not sure of the exact number, but many. It is never a question of liking or disliking them, or of being protective towards one's own. I think that children are one of the pleasures of life, but that is a small-family satisfaction. In an extended family it becomes hard to distinguish between one's own and one's nephews and nieces. It is better to keep away; to separate them is to spoil their fun. They are tolerated and they play by themselves, creating what amounts to a subculture in the garden or the next room. The more there are the less supervision they need, and already it has been possible for me to see that they have formed a family of their own, two cousins leading, the rest following – skills, information, cant words and dirty stories circulating among them.

Watching these children I am reminded of my own upbringing, how much freedom I had, how little privacy, how well I was defended and protected. These came as ideas to me quite early in life, for with so much variety around me – such an ideal version of the world – I was able to see the difference between freedom and privacy. I had a keen sense of these concepts, yet never felt that I was being closely watched. My solitude was seldom loneliness. And the idea of success in a family in which many had been materially successful, was merely to win the admiration of my fellow members. In twenty years of writing I have felt that in order to write well I would only have to please the family. It has not always been easy; they are severer critics than anyone would face in the literary world and they can be devastating mockers. After my fifth novel had appeared, a book set in Malawi, my brother Alex felt I was getting a bit above myself and he lampooned me in his next book, *Three Wogs*: "Then, of some notoriety, was bespectacled Paul the Pseudoplutarch, American oligosyllabicist and poet laureate of rural Malawi, who scuttled around in his pants of beaten wool and round cap, waving copies of his own *Velocity: The Key to Writing* (o.p.), a vade-mecum for gerundmongers and the sourcebook of his widely cited, narrowly appreciated, long-held theory that one's literary output should cease only when one ran out of possible dedications – and that remained, not a family, but a world away." Students of such things will be interested to know that I put Alex together with his family-airplane-crash skit in my next novel, *Picture Palace*. This family is a little like having a country; it is, in every way, like having a culture: art, literature, common memories, a private language.

For the first fifteen years of my life, or more, all my needs were met, all the society I required was available to me; practically and intellectually I was provided for within the family: books, clothes, conversation, jobs, medical care, spiritual comfort, even a girlfriend – they were all part of the family paraphernalia. It seems like a recipe for insularity, an argument for never leaving home. But home was huge — not one house but a score of them in which one was always welcome. I was assured that the family was permanent and immoveable, that no matter what happened it would continue to exist and observe the informal rules. With this sense of membership, an identity more profound than nationality, it is not difficult to leave, for a year, or — in my own case — for sixteen years. Though I have returned nearly every summer and found the temper of the country a bit sourer on each visit, the family is bigger but otherwise unchanged. Great travelers seldom come from small unstable countries, and children who leave a house and two parents behind do not often return, since they seek to attach themselves to something greater or to find a new identity. One of the last things Alexander Selkirk (the model for Robinson Crusoe) did before leaving home was to kick his father down a flight of stairs. He was escaping; but the extended family is inescapable.

And living abroad I do not have to go through the contortions of adapting. My sense of familyhood — the Swahili word *ujamaa* is not easily translated — has kept me from any temptation to take out citizenship or to adopt that grotesque Anglophilia that is characteristic of loners in England (I would go further and say that Anglophilia is the hardest sentiment to sustain in England). Since I am, at every turn, reminded of my difference, I am content to live as a foreigner and expect no more than I would if I happened to be living in Costa Rica, treating my annual tax demand as something like a hotel bill. In any case, England operates like a small family, "a rather stuffy Victorian family," wrote Orwell in *England Your England*, "a family with the wrong members in control — that, perhaps, is as near as one can come to describing England in a phrase." Recruitment in Britain is selective and a man is considered a South African, or a Jamaican, or a Hungarian until he bats a century or knocks someone senseless in the ring or makes a million pounds selling mackintoshes. When a man is too rich or famous to ignore he is turned into an Englishman and given a place on the Honors List, but a "West Indian" here is like an "Asian" in Uganda — a poor slob who has lived for two or three generations in a country his color doesn't match. There is no real grudge in that sentence. I know I do not belong here, and when my bill gets too large I will go home. But if I were not a part of an extended family I think it would have been impossible for me to travel or stay away for any length of time.

My own tendency is to extend the limits of my family even further, partly for my own purposes — it seems more worthwhile and it is certainly much easier to write if one enjoys the affection of a large family — and partly to graft this branch onto the family tree. I would like my children to understand that they can expect little from the state; that they will be swindled by politics and short-changed by every authority except the family. It is even more important for my children than it was for me. My children, born in Singapore and Uganda, living in a country in which they are officially aliens, must feel that they are part of an extended family which is settled and which will never disown them.

If my notions of the extended family are exaggerated, it might be because no one in three generations of the family has cared a damn for status in America, where only status matters – not family esteem but public esteem. One can't dismiss public esteem without supplanting it with another system of values, and if a family has decided to go it alone it needs genuine love and loyalty. Numbers help, so does property – there has to be space. If we all lived in one house we would get on each other's nerves; even a village would not contain us – but who would want to live in that sort of village? The pleasure of the extended family is the knowledge that one is not alone, the visible proof of love, the faith in this happy nation – it is like a believer's satisfaction in religion.

In less settled places there are alternatives, but they are short-lived. The extended families of the hippies can only last one generation, though they are more complete in any definition of "family" than the inadequate nests that produced them, the small over-tidy households that were answered with communes. Still, I am not in favor of communal living. Life is easy if sentiments are shared; it is intolerable if one is expected to share one's radio – it was an incursion of just this sort that a very good friend of mine gave as his reason for fleeing a kibbutz. And few books get written or paintings get painted in communes, which seem little more to me than occasions for gardening or arguing or displacing natives. The separate households in my own extended family are not an example of joint ownership, though anyone in need of a car or a house will find it his for the asking. The item will be returned and the favor remembered, but it is a favor, not a right. When an extended family falters, or alienates a member, it does so because that member is carrying an unfair share of responsibility. Usually, if the sat-upon man does not make for another country (America was populated by these escapees from the extended families of Europe, some of whom resurrected the practise in order to establish themselves or defy their cultural enemies) he finds himself in a house bursting with sponging relatives.

So I was surprised last summer when my mother, announcing that she had bought a new plot of land, said that she wanted us to meet together to discuss it. She described its features. It was large, she said, a corner plot away from the road, a very choice piece of land. In my mind I saw a house, the kind of communal dwelling I have always loathed: the bathrooms never free, dishes in the sink, the family garden in need of a good hoeing, nowhere to write, no peace, the clatter on the stairs, the washing machine continually sudsing, "Let me borrow your radio."

I had arrived a bit late and caught only her description of the site, the southerly view and ". . . room for all of us." I raised an objection. I said I didn't see why it was necessary for us to live on top of each other, or why, since we were all content in our own houses and with everything running smoothly, we needed another plot.

Someone guffawed, but my mother silenced him with a glance and my father said, "Hold on, Jack."

"Not a house, Paul," my mother said. "This is a burial plot, and we're very lucky to get it. The graveyards around here are filling up fast, and it's very unusual for something this size to come on to the market. They say it's designed for eight, but look at the plans" – she unrolled the map – "we could easily fit in more if we were buried a bit closer together."

A Circuit of Corsica

[1977]

Corsica is France, but it is not French. It is a mountain range moored like a great ship with a cargo of crags a hundred miles off the Riviera. In its three climates it combines the high Alps, the ruggedness of North Africa and the choicest landscapes of Italy, but most dramatic are the peaks which are never out of view and show in the upheaval of rock a culture that is violent and heroic. The landscape, which furnished some of the imagery for Dante's *Inferno*, has known heroes. The Latin playwright Seneca was exiled there, Napoleon was born there, and so – if local history is to be believed – was Christopher Columbus (there is a plaque in Calvi); part of the *Odyssey* takes place there – Ulysses lost most of his crew to the cannibalistic Laestrygonians in Bonifacio – and two hundred years ago, the lecherous Scot (and biographer of Dr Johnson) James Boswell visited and reported, "I had got upon a rock in Corsica and jumped into the middle of life."

The landscape is just weird enough to be beautiful and too large to be pretty. On the west are cliffs which drop straight and red into the sea; on the south there is a true fjord, on the east a long flat and formerly malarial coast with the island's only straight road, on the north a populous cape, and in the center the gothic steeples of mountains, fringed by forests where wild boar are hunted. There are sandy beaches, pebbly beaches, boulder-strewn beaches; beaches with enormous waves breaking over them, and beaches that are little more than mud flats, beaches with hotels and beaches that have never known the pressure of a tourist's footprint. There are five-star hotels and hotels that are unfit for human habitation. All the roads are dangerous, many are simply the last mile to an early grave. "There are no bad drivers in Corsica," a Corsican told me. "All the bad drivers die very quickly." But he was wrong – I saw many and I still have damp palms to prove it.

On one of those terrible coast roads – bumper-scraping ruts, bottomless puddles, rocks in the middle as threatening and significant as Marxist statuary – I saw a hitch-hiker. She was about eighteen, very dark and lovely, in a loose gown, barefoot and carrying a basket. She might have been modeling the gown and awaiting the approach of a *Vogue* photographer. My car seemed to stop of its own accord, and I heard myself urging the girl to get in, which she did, thanking me first in French and then, sizing me up, in halting English. Was I going to Chiappa? I wasn't, but I agreed to take her part of the way: "And what are you going to do in Chiappa?"

"I am a *naturiste*," she said, and smiled.

"A nudist?"

She nodded and answered the rest of my questions. She had been a nudist for about five years. Her mother had been running around naked for eleven years. And Papa? No, he wasn't a nudist; he'd left home – clothed – about six years ago. She liked the nudist camp (there are nine hundred nudists at Chiappa); it was a pleasant healthy pastime, though of course when the weather got chilly they put some clothes on. Sooner than I wished, she told me we had arrived, and she bounded towards the camp to fling her clothes off.

At Palombaggia, the tourist beach a few miles away, I hid behind a pine tree and put on my bathing trunks. I need hardly have bothered – the beach was nearly deserted. Rocks had tumbled into the sea, making natural jetties, and I decided to tramp over a dune and a rocky headland to get a view of the whole bay. There were, as far as the eye could see, groups of bathers, families, couples, children, people putting up windbreaks, strollers, rock collectors, sand-castle-makers – and all of them naked. Naked mummy, naked daddy, naked kiddies, naked grandparents. Aside from the usual beach equipment, it was a happy little scene from idealized prehistory, naked Europeans amusing themselves, Cro-Magnon man at play. It was not a nudist camp. These were Germans, as bare as noodles, and apart from the absence of swimming togs, the beach resembled many I have seen on Cape Cod, even to the discarded Coke cans and candy wrappers. I stayed until rain clouds gathered and the sun was obscured. This drove the Germans behind their windbreaks and one woman put on a short jersey – no more than that – and paced the beach, squinting at the clouds and then leering at me. I suppose it was my fancy bathing trunks.

I had decided to make a circuit of Corsica, to rent a car and drive slowly around the edge of the island, then pause and make my way over the mountains, from Moriani-Plage via Corte to Ile-Rousse, arriving where I had begun, in Ajaccio. The trains are too small and tram-like to be anything but practical for the Corsican and vaguely amusing to the visitor; the three and a half hours by rail from Ajaccio to Bastia are not my idea of a railway trip. Besides, the best parts of Corsica are unreachable by train.

The first twenty miles south of Ajaccio, through the Col St Georges to the handsome port of Propriano were gorgeous — a fatal distraction because the road was so narrow and winding. Once out of the capital it is clear how underpopulated Corsica is, an emptiness of eucalyptus trees and deep blue hills, stubbly fields, and vineyards, and forests of cork oak and sweet chestnut. Ambitious Corsicans flee the island as soon as they can scrape the fare together, and the ones who stay rather despise the menial servicing jobs in hotels. Two decades ago the island was dying economically, but the arrival of ex-colonials from Algeria brought mechanized wine-making methods and the growing of mandarin oranges to Corsica. And now there is a degree of prosperity in Corsica's agriculture, with the export of cheap wine. The good wine — and it is not the plonk the mainlanders say it is — is drunk locally. I can vouch for the Torraccio, Patrimonio, Sartene, Domaine Vico and the resinous Clos de Bernadi. The Corsican table wine that is exported is little more than red ink.

Propriano has many good restaurants, specializing in the seafood that is caught offshore — the *langouste* and the ingredients for *bouillabaisse*. It has three excellent hotels and, like many other Corsican towns, a number of pizza joints. It is the sort of place you expect Antibes or Juan Les Pins to be, small, uncrowded, sunny and decked with oleanders and geraniums — geraniums so healthy they have become bush-like, three or four feet high. The climb by car to the fastness of the steep mountain town, Sartene, is not rewarded by anything other than a glimpse of one of the most forbidding (Prosper Mérimée called it "the most Corsican") towns I've ever seen. It is a town like a citadel, built on the summit of a rocky hill, with a dark main street and a reputation for the vendetta.

Beyond Sartene, still moving south, I saw two remarkable sights: the great granite mountain of white oblong boulders, called Montagne de Cagna; and, as I neared the coast, the splendid sight of a lion in stone crouched on Cap de Roccapina. The strange features along this road are preparation for something even stranger at the end of it, the sheer limestone cliffs which plunge past the fortified town of Bonifacio, the settlement on the fjord. It is a natural harbor, and the town one of the oldest in Corsica, but although it is spectacularly beautiful, it has no good hotel. For that I drove up the coast to Porto-Vecchio, Corsica's newest resort town. Porto-Vecchio, for all its sandy beaches (Palombaggia is the best of these), has a blowsy look of gimcrack modernism unrelated to the ancient town above it that shares its name.

From this point in the southeast to Bastia in the northeast are sixty or more miles of empty glittering beaches, rising to extensive vineyards which disappear at the foothills of tremendous mountains. Because this is Corsica's straightest road, it is also the island's most dangerous — the only stretch, really, where you can get out of second gear. The seaside towns here are small likeable places, some looking as if they have been put up within the past year, others (such as Aleria) were resorts at the time of the Roman Empire. Further north, at Moriani-Plage, a seedy half-abandoned resort with one overpriced hotel flanking a stagnant swimming pool, it is hard to make out whether the town is in the process of being built or destroyed. I had no sooner concluded that I would never return to Moriani-Plage than the waiter, who was also the cook, said he had a plump pheasant in the kitchen which was mine for the asking.

I had been apprehensive – as who would not be? – by the thought of crossing the spine of Corsica's mountain range. I took what I later realized to be one of the worst roads on the island. But if one proceeds slowly along these mountain tracks (the road to Corte follows the course of the Tavignano River – Edward Lear went this way in the 1860's purely for its scenic beauty) one can get from the east coast to the northwest via Corte, in less than a day's drive. Corte is a bright windblown town on a crag, with at least one fine restaurant (in the Place Paoli). It is the heart of the island's political and cultural identity, and was the capital of the brief republic declared by Pascal Paoli in 1755. At Corte, if one seeks a destination, one has many choices: a short drive to the hunting lodges at Venaco, or the longer drives to Bastia, the quiet promontory of Ile-Rousse, the noisier resorts of Calvi or Porto. I struck out for Ile-Rousse and ended up at the two hundred-year-old Grand Hotel Napoleon Bonaparte, a bizarrely ramshackle château with a billiard room and a porter who tells you to go to bed when the clock strikes eleven. Ile-Rousse is a neglected town, a bit geriatric in tone, with a great deal of charm. Some of this charm still lingers in the narrow streets of Calvi, but in the oversettled gorge which is Porto – a harrowing four-hour drive away – the charm is gone. It is as if, having accepted that German tourists were inevitable, the Corsicans decided to dump them wholesale in this almost inaccessible notch to bellow away their vacation.

Because it is purely for vacationers, I think Porto is a place for vacationers to avoid. The fact that it is probably the most beautiful corner of the island is a bit sad, for what is inescapable is that it is overcrowded, overdeveloped and irredeemably Teutonic. The pseudo-luxury is similarly a feature of the newer resorts at Sagone and Tiuccia, but none of these west coast watering-holes have the down-to-earth hospitality and comfort that I found elsewhere in Corsica.

A car seems a necessity, but cars are easy to hire and, driving, one discovers how small Corsica is, how much can be seen in a week. There is no need to be stuck anywhere on the island, and the Corsicans speak French badly enough so that no visitor need feel self-conscious. I spoke nothing but Italian for a week and managed very well. The only Corsican

I met who spoke English was the girl nudist near Chiappa, but I guessed that she came into contact with all sorts of people.

The Corsicans have a reputation for being unfriendly. They certainly look gloomy, and their character is incontestably dour; but they are not smug or critical, they can be helpful and they seem genuinely interested in strangers. "Simple in manner and thoroughly obliging," wrote Edward Lear; "anxious to please the traveler, yet free from compliment and servility." One old woman in the market at Ile-Rousse told me in pidgin Italian that she thought Americans were "sweet". It is not a sentiment I have heard expressed anywhere else in Europe.

Nixon's Neighborhood

[1977]

The San Clemente "City Song" was written in 1970 by Marjorie and Walter Botts before, as one San Clemente surfer put it, "they caught the crook." When a local group such as the Elks or the Junior Woman's Club meet they often sing *San Clemente by the Sea*:

> There's a spot so breathtaking
> Where waves are softly breaking
> And the sands are like a golden shawl.

> There I take my troubles
> And just like bubbles
> They disappear into nothing at all.

The last verse is about the Nixons ("The native folk are joyful that they picked this lovely town"). These days that verse is not usually sung.

There I take my troubles. Having seen an aerial photograph of it, the Nixons moved there in 1969 and dubbed the Spanish-style, twenties house ("Damas" on the Ladies, "Caballeros" on the Gents) the Western White House. After his resignation he fled there and he has been pretty much in residence ever since. Yet he is not at all a ghost figure: he plays golf regularly at a local club and his servant Manolo Sanchez makes a weekly trip to the nearby Alpha-Beta Supermarket to buy food; Pat has been spotted strolling on the old rum-runners' path to the beach (the town was founded by smugglers and bootleggers) and Mr Nixon often waves to the townsfolk from his limousine. Some people wave back. Opinion in town is about equally divided on the man. Last year the San Clemente *Sun-Post* asked three hundred and fifty local residents, "Are you still interested in reading news about Richard Nixon?" 47% said yes, 53% said no. Nearly everyone I spoke to said it was a real shame he had to resign. So what if he was crooked? They say: all politicians are crooked. But it was still a blow to civic pride that their leading citizen was just like the rest.

The surfers are the exception. They are delighted that he was forced to resign, because the best surfing waves on that part of the coast rise in frothy peaks below "La Casa Pacifica." While Nixon was President, the Secret

Service declared the beach a security area. "It was a problem," says Dave, a surfer who looks — as surfers do — like John the Baptist. "We still surfed there, but if we got near the beach they grabbed our boards and confiscated them."

Now the beach is open again to surfers, morning joggers, pot-smokers ("Are you a pig?" one surfer asked me), beer-drinkers (a six-pack at sundown on Nixon's beach is an especially favored recreation), dog-lovers, time-killers, strollers — the town is full of people old and young who, like Mr Nixon, are in retreat from the world. "But it isn't what you might think — a sleepy small town," a lady told me. "A lot of wealthy people live here. Real important people with character, like bank presidents. And there's no smog."

Under clear skies, the town (pop. 28,000) of bleeding pastels and dusty palmettos and hamburger joints seems to tumble down a hillside of biscuity cliffs, pausing in clumps on the main street, El Camino Real ("The Royal Road"), and continuing to the lizard-haunted shore where a cosy wooden pier puts one in mind of Herne Bay. Its most bizarre feature is never mentioned: the town is sliced in half by the ten lane San Diego Freeway, Interstate 5. Mr Nixon lives on the posh, ocean side of the freeway in a house on a five-acre corner plot of the Cyprus Shore Estate. Many of those hundred Cyprus Shore families are millionaires, who have chosen San Clemente for the reason its planner Ole Hanson chose it in 1925: "This will be a place where a man can breathe." Hanson was a nimble real estate speculator. He bought two thousand acres; he decreed that all the houses would have red-tiled roofs and be white, and no blacks would live in them. Hanson went broke, but remains a local hero. He was in character and career remarkably like Mr Nixon, a busted operator. "And to this day," says Warren Estes, editor of the *Sun-Post*, "you won't see many blacks in San Clemente."

Cyprus Shore Estate is so closely guarded even the police stay out ("We have real neat parties," the son of a resident told me), and Nixon's house, a fortress within that fortress, is impenetrable to anyone who hasn't got a contract with Mr Nixon. It is secured by a system of walls, hidden mikes, tv cameras, and chain-link fences that make it seem like Gulag-by-the-Sea. It is amazing that a house on such high ground is so hidden. It can't be seen from the hills or the freeway or the drive; it is invisible to surfers and yachtsmen, and though it is smack on the Amtrak railway line to San Diego, all the train-traveler sees is a board fence and beyond it an eight-foot wall; and beyond that the dense trees and green closed-circuit tv cameras on Nixon's bluffs. You can walk a mile and a half along its perimeter from El Presidente Road down to the shore and see nothing more than cypresses and the out-buildings of the Coast Guard Station, which are Nixon's sentry-boxes. It can only be seen from a helicopter. If the helicopter comes in too low, the guards say, "We'll deal with you as if you came over the wall" – they'll shoot.

"You look over the wall from Nixon's garden," says the film-maker Peter Bogdanovich, and he laughed as he remembered the party he went to at the house a few years ago. "You expect to see the ocean or the beach. But no – there's a huge chain-link fence and a *railway track*! About ten times a day the train goes by, clackedy-clack, whistle blowing. That's his idea of privacy."

"Who said Nixon was a hermit?" said Warren Estes. "You call a regular golfer a hermit? No, he doesn't address the Elks now, but he didn't before he was dumped. He's interested in the South Coast Boys' Club. They're building a gym – he throws a few bucks their way. Sure, if things had been different he would have shown up at a Rams football game, but he's no Howard Hughes. Go up to the golf course – you'll probably see him."

I had been turned away by the telephone operator ("President's office," she'd said) and by the polite security guard, Mr Richard Phillips, at the Cyprus Shore gate. ("What Nixon did was awful dumb," he said. "But I still think he's a smart man and I wave to him when he goes by in his car – that man pays my salary.") I had been rebuffed by the Coast Guard and Nixon's publisher, Warner Books; I had been flummoxed by the fences and the screens of trees. A bad week for me because it had been a bad week for Mr Nixon: his golf pro had received more than the usual hate-mail and the day before I arrived a lady had shown up at Cyprus Shore waving a pair of scissors in the direction of La Casa Pacifica. "It wasn't funny," said Mr Phillips. "She was going to kill him with them scissors."

Shore Cliffs Golf Club does not seem a natural choice for either a golfer or even an ordinary paranoiac. It is on a slide area. Because it is in the process of being sold it is in a state of scruffy neglect. The club house is uncared for. The restaurant has been closed for months, the bar is empty, the fairways are brown and pitted. The entire place is bisected by Interstate Five – nine holes on this side, nine holes on the other and a narrow tunnel under the freeway connects them. There is a housing estate along the margins of the course and the boxy yellow bungalows are so close their windows sometimes get broken. "I shanked one through a glass sliding-door a few weeks back," said Jack Wright, a leathery old member in a birdbill cap. Ground squirrels frolic on the course; and the club is only semi-private: anyone who can afford the $3.50 daily membership plus $8 for a self-drive golf-cart (there are no caddies) can play at Shore Cliffs.

Mr Nixon plays three or four times a week. Why? For one thing they made him an Honorary Member, so he plays free and gets three self-drive carts – secret servicemen in the front and rear carts, Nixon and his partner in the middle one. "He likes it here a whole lot," said Homer Welborne, a senior member. "They'd pick on him at the municipal course. Hell, early on, they picked on him here – heckled him – 'Did you cheat on the course?' That kind of thing."

"He's got to play golf. He's writing a book," says Tom Perrin the Club's pro, who gets the hate-mail (*How can a liar and a cheat play free at your club? No wonder the country's sick*, etc.) "He told one of the members 'Writing's driving me crazy.' He's got to whack a golf-ball around, for his sanity. But, man, he gets around the course like lightning. Twenty-seven holes in two and a half hours, that's twice as fast as anyone else. He still gets good scores. The course is a par seventy-one and Nixon shoots in the eighties – eighty-four, eighty-five."

But a year ago, Homer Welborne's partner, Dick Hulbert, found a score card blowing down one of the fairways. He showed me this interesting item. One player's name was pencilled in as "Jack," the other as "The President" – odd, since he had been out of office for months. "Jack" (Col John Brennan, Nixon's aide) had shot a respectable eighty-three, "The President" a duffer's one hundred and three. Hulbert said, "Maybe he's improved since then," and he grinned in disbelief. "Aw, he's a good guy!"

Homer said, "Oh, sure. He's very plebeian. Always says hello, poses for pictures, gives autographs. We've all had our picture taken with him. Stick around, he might be over today. Anyone can get his picture taken with him."

I stuck around. It was bright and cool, the sea twinkling, Freeway traffic roared past the ninth hole.

"You waiting for the President?" asked Roland Bennett ("the only black assistant pro this side of Watts").

"The former President," I said.

"Yeah, well, he might be up today. But we haven't had a call. We always get a call beforehand. 'The President is coming in half an hour,' they say. Then six FBI guys and Nixon and Brennan hop out of their cars and the next thing you know they're teeing off. They don't waste no time. He says hi to me. Once or twice he asked me if I wanted to play with him."

"That's quite an honor, isn't it?"

"Quite an honor for *him* to play with a pro! But I'm too busy."

Unlike the surfers, none of the golfers had an unkind word for Mr Nixon. "We're so used to seeing him we don't pay too much attention to him," said John Perrin. "But there is one strange thing about him. He only plays with Brennan. If Brennan's out of town Nixon doesn't play golf. Now that's a bit unusual."

"You mean abnormal?" I asked.

"Let's say kind of peculiar," said Perrin. "He'll only play with one certain guy. Most golfers will play with anyone. I'm not saying he's not a wonderful person, but he's funny in some ways. Like the time he almost got a hole-in-one. Up to then he hadn't joined the Hole-in-One Club. It's like insurance. You pay a dollar and if you get a hole-in-one you win a jackpot, about seventy bucks, which you spend buying everyone a drink. He didn't join, then one day he almost got a hole-in-one, then he paid his dollar. It's peculiar."

The "Hole-in-One Club" board on the back of the bar listed a newly-printed name among the others, *Richard Nixon*.

"You're out of luck. I don't think he's coming today. Brennan must be out of town." Perrin squinted across town. "Probably working on his book."

The book was mentioned by many people I met in San Clemente. In Southern California, a book is considered a mysterious thing, even by the college students who gather on Nixon's beach to turn on. One of these, Martin Nelsen ("I think Nixon's a real neat guy. If you could see his house you'd know it was a prime place"), majors in Ornamental Horticulture at Pasadena. He hopes to get a MA and possibly a PhD in Ornamental Horticulture and become America's answer to Capability Brown. He spoke with awe of Nixon's book, so did Mr Phillips, the security guard, and Brian Sardoz, the scuba diver, and Mrs Dorothy Symms of San Clemente Secretarial Services, publisher of *Fishcarts to Fiestas, the Story of San Clemente*.

"I met the man who's writing Mr Nixon's book," said Mrs Symms.

I said, "Isn't Mr Nixon writing the book?"

"No. There's a man doing it for him. He writes all the movie stars' books. He's a very famous writer. You say you're from England? Oh, this man wrote Winston Churchill's memoirs, too."

Mrs Symms thinks Nixon is "just great," but seemed defensive, almost embarrassed when I mentioned his name. It is a common reaction in San Clemente. The name is spoken. They sigh and sort of smack their lips. *Oh gosh* and then: Look, all politicians are crooked. But it is clear they have been down in the dumps since Watergate. After all, the Kennedys started a real estate boom in Hyannisport. It might have happened there.

There are no Nixon pictures in town and apart from the ten cent postcards ("The Richard M Nixon Home") nothing to indicate that he lives there. "Did you see the museum?" people ask. But it is hardly that. It is a collection of Nixoniana in the lobby of the San Clemente Inn, called the "A Little Bit of History Museum." No mention of Watergate or the resignation, though one framed Nixon letter refers to "these difficult times." On display are Nixon's golf-balls and spare golf-bag, some expensive bicentennial junk, mementos (menus, fans) from the China visit, election buttons ("Lithuanians for President Nixon"), a copy of Mao's poems open to "The PLA Captures Nanking, April 1949" and thirty-two "thank you" letters, addressed to the former manager of the San Clemente Inn, Mr Paul Presley. The museum was Presley's idea. He seems to have been an inexhaustible gift-giver: thank you for the patriotic scroll, thank you for the nice letter, thank you for the banquet, thank you for the hospitality, thanks for finding Henry Kissinger a house at Cyprus Shore, thank you for your congratulatory telegram, thanks for the birthday cake – and all ending with the wild oversized signature, Richard Nixon. The wobbly handwriting ("P.S. Thanks also for the beautiful flowers!") speaks volumes, but the museum is uninspiring, even a bit of a joke. Mr Presley, who retired last year, is known as a "Nixon freak." There are not many in San Clemente. They are decent folk. If asked, most people will say they have nothing against him, but you get the impression that they'd prefer not to be asked.

Nixon's Memoirs

[1978]

The artichoke John Ehrlichman was defoliating with big brown fingers seemed an apt metaphor for the Nixon years – somewhere beneath the goop and scales of this thistle was a misshapen heart. Quite by coincidence, Mr Ehrlichman and I were having lunch together on the day Mr Nixon's memoirs were released to reviewers. He had recently been released from prison. Although we had never met before, we had corresponded – he had helped me penetrate the mysteries of San Clemente, I had offered him (unsolicited) literary advice. Radiating good health – he played tennis every day and ran the prison's power station every night – an attentive listener twice my size, he could have passed for my parole officer. Yet it was Mr Ehrlichman who had been the model prisoner for two years: he wrote two novels, a dissertation on alternative sentencing, and compiled a dossier on the Mexican illegal immigrants and drug-smugglers who were his fellow convicts. He took up painting, he learned Spanish. He did not become a "Born Again" Christian like Mr Colson, or a fink like John Dean, or a cantankerous old fat-head like Mr Mitchell. And unlike his former employer, he has not written a White House memoir.

I wondered whether he could give me a litmus test for the veracity of the *Memoirs*. How does one know when Mr Nixon is not telling the truth?

"I doubt if he knows himself when he's not telling the truth," said Mr Ehrlichman. "But read that description of his family. They're all perfect, right? But what man can say his family's perfect? Those people are human – they sweat, they get upset, they get sore feet. He makes them into waxwork dummies. It's a serious injustice – and if he doesn't come clean about them, how could he come clean about anything else?"

I told him that I had read some of the book and that it struck me as nothing short of amazing that so far Mr Nixon's career had been entirely triumphant – even his defeats were victories. Mr Ehrlichman smiled broadly, "Ah, that's Vintage Nixon."

And I suppose it is, which is why this enormous doorstop of a book, 1,200 pages of self-justification, is such a soulless uncontrite document. Vintage Nixon is Election Poster Nixon, the beaky face, the empty rhetoric, the fighting gesture, the neatly selected memories. "College football at Whittier gave me a chance to get to know the coach, Wallace 'Chief' Newman. I think that I admired him more and learned more from him than from any man I have ever known aside from my father." This is a piece of "Chief" Newman's wisdom: "Show me a good loser, and I'll show you a loser."

No one ever accused Mr Nixon of being a good loser, but he seldom loses in this book. You will say: But he lost the Presidential campaign of 1960 to John Kennedy! Mr Nixon says: Not really. The votes were not counted correctly, "many Republican leaders were ... urging me to contest the results and demand recounts," the Chicago results were plainly cooked, and "There is no doubt that there was substantial vote fraud ..." In a farrago of poisonous innuendo, Mr Nixon implies that he actually beat Kennedy.

"This fellow has a silver tongue," said one of Mr Nixon's early political opponents. Mr Nixon makes no such claims, though he alludes more than once to "my rocking socking style" and he is constantly pushing other people's praise into his narrative. The Indian leader, Rajagopalachari, said to him, "Younger men must be found to conduct the fight. Younger men like you." ("Infinitely wise," Mr Nixon remarks of Rajaji.) "This is one of the young men I have been telling you about and I want you to get acquainted with him," said Eisenhower to Churchill, when introducing the fidgetting Vice-President in 1954. "You are the man to lead the country!" screams his maid, Fina, summoned ("after dinner") to hear his decision to run: "This was determined before you were born!" A few years later a girl in a crowd cries, "I love and respect you so much!" ("Even though we were leaving, I danced with her for a few minutes.") And a glowing testimonial from Harold Wilson – the scribble is reproduced on a full page: "You can't guarantee being born a lord. It is possible – you've shown it – to be born a gentleman." Put that in your pipe and puff on it!

The proportions of the *Memoirs* are interesting. The first thirty pages concern the first thirty-three years of Mr Nixon's life; the next few hundred are a blow-by-blow about Congressman Nixon and Vice-President Nixon, and the last seven hundred pages are a detailed but disingenuous account of the last four years of his presidency. Out-of-office Nixon is a legal partner with a heavy mortgage, warming up TV-dinners, and in spite of his protests he gives no clear explanation as to how, a mere decade after his bleak TV-dinner period in 1961, he emerged a millionaire. Mr Nixon was keel-hauled and marooned. It follows that his book ought to have the loony fascination of a castaway's chronicle, but not even his Friday-like butler Manolo or his vulgar righteousness can lift him to the level of Crusoe. Mr Nixon – to quote Palmerston on

Commissioner Yeh Ming Ch'en – is truly "an uninteresting monster" and his memoirs a self-serving monstrosity.

One of the themes that runs through it is his strong identification with Kennedy, but having grown up poor, Mr Nixon implies that he was the more honest, the more temperate in speech (Mr Nixon presents Kennedy as incredibly foul-mouthed). He is Irish like Kennedy and makes much of his Irish pedigree; as junior senators they swop letters and share railway compartments; their wives buttress them (and later Jackie writes passionate thank-yous to Mr Nixon), their ages almost match, their fathers are similar (bad tempered, "combative"), and so are their mothers (peace-loving, "saintly"); the two men confer on important issues.

But John Kennedy was assassinated, you will say. Of course, but the bullet was intended for Mr Nixon, who was in Dallas on Pepsi-Cola business (this was the TV-dinner period) the day before Kennedy was shot. "Months later Hoover told me that Oswald's wife had disclosed that Oswald had been planning to kill me when I visited Dallas and that only with great difficulty had she managed to keep him in the house to prevent him from doing so." If Mr Nixon has a literary counterpart who can match him in *chutzpah* it is Charles Kinbote, the lugubriously vain character in Nabokov's *Pale Fire* ("I was the shadow of the waxwing slain . . .").

He was not just poor, but poverty stricken – the most important splinter in any hunk of American Presidential timber. As late as 1934 he was eating candy bars for breakfast to save money (I would have thought an egg cheaper, but let that pass: this was before the chickens had come home to roost). Times were hard, Mr Nixon was unattractive, his feet were enormous (size 11E) and he had little to sustain him but the prayers of his mother who "went into a closet to say her prayers at night" because St Matthew exhorts us to pray "behind closed doors." Using the Republican slogan "Had Enough?" (the answer was "Yes!"), Mr Nixon entered politics to clean up "that mess in Washington." The mess in Washington is referred to again and again for the next thousand pages, but never once does Mr Nixon claim an iota of responsibility for it.

His first great chance, and it was the making of him, was the Alger Hiss case. Here, as elsewhere in the book, Mr Nixon rehashes his *Six Crises*. Nixon pursued Hiss for a number of years and it paid off: Hiss was ruined, Nixon in the ascendant. He says his motive was not political, and yet it was virtually the only reason Eisenhower chose him as his running-mate, saying, "the Hiss case was the text from which I could preach". It seems odd that a man with the moral sense of Daffy Duck and the political enlightenment of a 25-watt bulb could build a career purely out of anti-communist spite and partisan infighting, but that is exactly what happened. It is also useful to remember throughout this book how very young Mr Nixon was: just thirty-nine when he was Vice-President, President at fifty-five, disgraced at sixty-one. In a party of geriatrics, Mr Nixon looked like one of the Beach Boys, and he always surrounded himself by men who had ruthless political savvy. "We made him President," Mr Ehrlichman told me. "He couldn't lose. But we could have made you President much quicker. For one thing, you're better looking."

Mr Nixon's loathing for Truman is undisguised. He professes to admire Eisenhower, but slips in numerous allusions to Eisenhower's fickleness, laziness, authoritarianism and untrusting spirit – Eisenhower certainly did not trust Mr Nixon, but Mr Nixon was an untypically active and ambitious Vice-President, taking every opportunity to hog the limelight. Besieged by screaming Venezuelans, Mr Nixon returned to the United States a hero (the scars were evident on his Cadillac); heckled by Khrushchev, Mr Nixon wagged a finger at the camera and became known as someone who didn't stand for back-talk – politically, these scarcely significant encounters did him a world of good.

Don't give up! groans his mother on her deathbed. She is dying, but the crisis is Mr Nixon's: he resolves to fight. When Eisenhower has a heart-attack, it is again Mr Nixon's crisis. It does not seem to matter that Ike has one foot in the grave: Mr Nixon has the solemn duties of President thrust on his shoulders. Mr Nixon has nerves of iron. If something untoward happens, it is the people around him who suffer: when Eisenhower wanted to dump him, it was Pat who fell ill and "The stress was so great that she had developed a painfully stiff neck and had to stay in bed"; after the so-called "Checkers Speech," "I found out that my proud and combative father had been reduced to bouts of weeping as each new smear surfaced." There are many more instances of this projected anguish; one wonders what a psychiatrist would make of it.

The plumpest part of this book begins in 1970. This is the year that the microphones were installed in the Oval Office. One expects a bit of candor here, but when we arrive at the burglary of Ellsberg's psychiatrist all we get is waffle: "I do not believe I was told about the break-in at the time . . . I cannot say that I had been informed of it beforehand . . . I do not recall this . . ." Quite a lapse of memory for someone who can remember the brand of candy bar he ate in North Carolina in 1934 – a Milky Way. Cambodia is bombed and Mr Nixon's reasoning becomes even more wobbly; his description of the war in Bangladesh is almost wholly muddle; and if anyone wonders why Mr Nixon's African policy was – to put it mildly – uninformed, one needs only read a Diary Entry of 1971: "Pat was obviously elated by her trip. She was particularly impressed by the President of the Ivory Coast. She pointed out that he did not believe in using force against South Africa, and I realized that this is the reason that many in the State Department don't like him . . ." How can he have been so ignorant of French influence, of Ivory Coast trade relations, or the diplomatic hand-holding that existed between Vorster and Houphouet-Boigny?

"It certainly is a great wall," Mr Nixon said on his China visit ("This was the week that changed the world"), but no wall in this book is greater than the one he builds around the Watergate episode and its aftermath. One reads it and one is no wiser. He knew nothing about it; he knew nothing about the erased tape. He paces the floor throughout the final four hundred pages of the book, back and forth on huge flapping feet, urging his henchmen to give him information. Who was involved? he asks. Why did they do it? He had two major objections: it was handled stupidly (the men were caught); and "I could see no reason whatever for trying to bug the national committee." He persists in his bafflement until the very end, when, threatened with impeachment and over a mammoth barrel, he resigned. His last speech was full of fobbed-off anguish, this time his mother was the victim: how she suffered, how no books would ever be written about her, how she was a saint. What a terrible thing it must have been, after that humiliation, to have to appear a good loser. Well, this book puts that right: it is a bitter piece of self-promotion.

Where are they now, those scores of White House people? That's easy. They're nearly all in jail or looking for work. In America Mr Nixon is still a hated man. He is hated not because he proved his enemies right, but because he let down the millions of people who had given him a landslide victory. Mr Ford, who pardoned him, lost miserably against Mr Carter for that reason and was forced to abandon his political career. Meanwhile, what is the truth? It is not in this flatulent book – that is obvious. It might be in the tapes which Mr Nixon clings to and is fighting a court action to keep. At our lunch, Mr Ehrlichman said he thought they would eventually be released and then, picking up his fork, he grinned and rolled his eyes and said, "Murder will out!" It might have been hyperbole, but he did not strike me as a man who was given to gratuitous literary allusion.

The Orient Express

[1978]

It began with George Mortimer Pullman, whose sleeping car – scoffed at until it was used to transport the corpse of Abraham Lincoln from Chicago to Springfield – left a lasting impression on a Belgian engine-maker. The Belgian was Georges Nagelmackers, and his idea was to start a company in Europe operating Pullman-like cars to the Riviera, the Danube, and the Black Sea. In 1876, Nagelmackers founded the sonorously named *Compagnie Internationale des Wagon-Lits* and by 1882 his "Grand Express" – all Wagon-Lits – had reached Vienna. The following year, on October 4, 1883, the highly publicized *Express D'Orient* made its inaugural run to Constantinople, its two sleeping cars full of distinguished journalists, diplomats and railway officials, and its dining car stocked with the vintage wine and gourmet food which, long after it had been removed from the menu, people would associate with the great train.

Though its route, 1,800 miles, was much shorter than the Trans-Siberian's 6,000, its romance remained undiminished until the Second War. With the exception of James Bond's trip in *From Russia With Love*, all Orient Express fiction is set in the 'twenties and 'thirties, beginning with Maurice Dekobra's *The Madonna of the Sleeping Cars* (1924) and including Graham Greene's *Stamboul Train*, Agatha Christie's *Murder on the Orient Express*, part of Eric Ambler's *A Coffin for Dimitrios*, and Ethel Lina White's *The Wheel Spins* – this last became the Hitchcock film, *The Lady Vanishes*. The atmosphere is familiar, a blend of the cozy, the glamorous and the sinister: so many national frontiers are crossed, the possibilities for sexual stratagems and the occasions for disappearance, deception and surprise are practically limitless. Every feature of the train had a novelistic dimension; its route had a plot-like structure; its atmosphere was well-known. It was made for the novel and it matched fiction exactly. It could also have been the setting for a wonderful farce, since farce is so often a mockery of romance – very nearly a definition of The Orient Express's last days.

The war disrupted service and there was still rationing in 1947 when Irving Wallace took it and reported his findings to the readers of the *Saturday Evening Post*. His was the first of many post-war pieces which, harking back to the good old days – Wallace dusts off the cliché and uses it to prop up one of his paragraphs – have the latecomer's resentment and the slightly fraudulent and elegiac tone of an obituary. Fifteen years later, when the by-now moth-eaten *Grand Express Européen* was scrapped, *Time* magazine (taking its metaphor from the Hitchcock film) said, "The only things that ever really vanished were the good service and the passengers." Joseph Wechsberg wrote in the *Saturday Review* in 1962, "Long before its last run it had become an anachronism." The "Simplon-Orient" ended in 1962, and the slower "Direct-Orient" took its place and has been visibly deteriorating since then. When the *Compagnie Internationale des Wagon-Lits* announced last September that the service was to be discontinued there was no sense of shock in anyone who had ever traveled on it; indeed, only a justified sigh of relief and regret, as when a geriatric distant acquaintance is overtaken by a lingering illness and the inevitable happens.

The Orient Express had been fuelled by that most profitless of emotions, sentimentality, and like the *Queen Mary*, London Bridge, and Scollay Square, it had outlived its usefulness and lapsed into obsolescence. A different train was needed, to serve different needs, but the *Wagon-Lits* company did not even have the resourcefulness of Amtrak to understand what these needs might be. The only quaintness that is supportable is the quaintness that pays; and the idea of the Orient Express was always more enlivening to the imagination than a trip in one of its drab compartments. Latterly, the dining car – its last claim to fame – was abolished. It became a remote abstraction, a symbol of an age that was itself a symbol, and though travel-writers, eager for a whiff of romance, have chosen it as an occasion to empurple their prose style, even the most enthusiastic could not suppress his disappointment. The dullest and most dispiriting chapter of *The Orient Express*, "The Story of the World's Most Fabulous Train" (N.Y., 1967), by Michael Barsley, is the last, in which the author actually boards the train and goes to Istanbul. The thrilling pedigree, lovingly elaborated in the preceding chapters, does not quite prepare us for the spavined old war-horse that carries Mr Barsley eastward. But he is quick to point out, in indignation and apology, that for all its defects the train retains a certain charm.

Charm is in the heart of the beholder. I took the train myself all the way to Sirkeci Station in Istanbul about three years ago, and I remarked in my own history of the event that it really was murder on the Orient Express. Poor Mr Duffill was left behind in Domodossola, the efficient salute of the Italian conductors had degenerated into a discouraging shrug, a pair of Bulgarians were frog-marched off the train at Dragoman for not holding a medical certificate, and mealtime was a hand-to-mouth affair, bringing back memories of school outings on rainy afternoons in the suburban trains of Boston. In spite of that, I liked the trip well enough to write about it, and I could report that the Orient Express had more than its share of friendly and mysterious passengers, because all long train journeys – no matter what the service – attract the adventurous and the affable – seekers after the unexpected: romance is part of their luggage. Still, the food is better on "The Van Gölü Express" (Istanbul – Lake Van), the proportions of "The Trans-Siberian" are much greater, there is a more bizarre assortment of travelers on "The Panama Limited" (Chicago – New Orleans); Japanese trains are more prompt, Indian ones a better bargain, and the features of Thai and Malaysian trains more convivial.

Instead of lamenting the inevitable, we would do well to recognize the example of Pullman and Nagelmackers. A combination of poor service, the cheapness of air-travel and the short-sighted bickering of little countries in full cry killed the Orient Express. The great international train requires vision, diplomacy and cash; in a world fragmented by nationalism, a simple but brilliant scheme like the cross-Channel railway tunnel from England to France (started in 1872) becomes merely a series of false starts. Post-war bureaucracy has turned travelers into refugees: if you want to go to Istanbul from Paris now you will have to change trains in Venice and Belgrade. But we can't feel self-righteous about this until we can travel from, say, New Orleans to Mexico City without changing trains in Laredo.

So the Orient Express is gone. It was for many years little more than a bewitching name. But the tracks are still in position and so is the rolling stock. As Mr Barsley says, in describing the many changes that have taken place on the route to Istanbul, "*Le train est mort: vive le train.*"

Traveling Home: High School Reunion

[1979]

When a childhood friend calls me now, it all comes back. I see a freckly boy or a pot-bellied girl in the disc of the telephone receiver – the cowlick, the bubble-gum breath, the squint in the smeared glasses. The night before my high school reunion – Medford High's Class of '59 – the telephone rang. It was Geoffrey Howe – or, more properly, "Humphrey". He had changed his name to that of a comic book character he liked and resembled, Humphrey Pennyworth. At the age of seven, we had both been in Miss Purcell's class at the Washington school and had sung "John Peel" to the parents. We had remained close friends until the high school graduation, and were still friends, though I had not seen much of him over the past twenty years. But he sounded unchanged – fat-faced, funny, wheezing with mockery. He would go to the reunion, he said, if I went. That was very Medford High, the timid adolescent dare: *I will if you will.*

I said it was my sole reason for being in Massachusetts this October night, away from work, family and my London household. I did not tell him that I had spent the afternoon reading our year-book, *The Blue and White*, and rediscovering what a poor student I had been – not in the National Honor Society, not even in The Slide-Rule Club; no awards, no sports. What had I done? Humphrey had been on the football team, "The Mustangs."

"Guess who won't be there?" Humphrey said, and quickly added, "Gagliardi. Guess why?"

"No idea."

"He's dead. Killed in the slammer, by another prisoner. The amazing thing is that about a year or two before he died, *he* killed someone in the slammer. Guess who? Albert DeSalvo!"

"The name rings a bell. Was he at Medford High, too?"

"You were probably in Fuckawiland – you usually are. Listen, Albert DeSalvo was the Boston Strangler."

So a Medford boy, a murderer from the Class of '59, had killed the Boston Strangler. And I remember Gag – a sallow-faced Italian who, even at the age of fourteen, had a vicious scar over his eye. He was a merciless bully at the Milton Fuller Roberts Junior High, affecting the tough style of

1955; low-slung pegged pants, suede "spade" shoes, shirt collar up, a flick-knife in his pocket. He sneaked smokes in the boys' john, exhaling the smoke through the ventilator, so no one would know. He was halitotic with meatballs and nicotine. Once – we were both in the seventh grade – I walked past the gym and saw Gagliardi beating up another boy and hitting him so hard the boy was being stuffed into an open locker. Gagliardi turned from the boy's bloody nose and smiled at me. "Theroux," he said. "You don't see nothing, do you?"

I said no, and walked away. I could have reported him to the principal, George F. Weston, who was known to everyone as "Poopy". Poopy had written a book, *Boston Ways: High, By and Folk* ("Copiously Illustrated"). He was an intelligent and learned Yankee and had made a study of the Chinese community in downtown Boston. What was a sensitive soul like this doing at such a foul school as the Roberts? He would have suspended Gag for fighting and, nipped in the bud, Gag's homicidal tendencies might have been curbed. I didn't report Gag, and I have never told this story before. But then, Gagliardi is dead.

Humphrey said, "I'll see you at the reunion. But if you think I'm wearing a suit, forget it. I haven't owned one for fifteen years. By the way, I'm not married. I've got a good mind to pick up a huge blonde bimbo in the Combat Zone and take her. They'd shit!"

The reunion was held at the Hilton Inn, a preposterously over-sized motel on that part of Route 128 in Massachusetts which is thick with topless bars, country-and-western lounges, massage parlors and discount stores – in Lynnfield, the suburb's suburb. Humphrey was at the reception table, sticking a name-label (*Hump*) on his lapel. There was no blonde with him, but even so he looked fairly spectacular, in a fawn suede jacket and black silk shirt with a chrome chain around his neck. By way of greeting he said, "You asshole – I saw you on television!"

But this was pure affection. We had grown up together, built huts in our backyards out of old lumber, gone "coasting" in the snow down Water Hill and, one summer, constructed a large raft on which we had poled down the Assabet River in Hudson, Mass. Humphrey had the largest collection of comic books I had ever seen ("Yogi Berra reads nothing but comic books," he once said). I swapped him my "Classic Comics" (*Lorna Doone, Moby Dick*) for his horror comics – *Tales from the Crypt*, they were called, about ghouls and cannibalism in towns much like Medford.

Humphrey said, "Look, there's Goose!" and went to hug him.

Oscar ("Goose") Goings was black. He wore a powder-blue jumpsuit and carried a sheaf of papers. Throughout high school Goose said, "I'm going to be a Leatherneck when I get out of here," and for twenty years, whenever I heard the word "Leatherneck" I thought of Goose. But Goose took me aside and said that in the end he had decided against the Marines. "I've been writing poetry," he said. "Let me know what you think of this one." He pushed a folded sheet of paper into my pocket.

The room was jammed. Humphrey and Goose squirmed towards the bar and left me buying coupons for drinks. Fishing for my money I pulled out Goose's poem. *What's wrong with being black?* it said. *I'll tell you — nothing!* There was more, but in the crush of people I could not read further. There had been five hundred and seventy-four in the class of '59; there were close to three hundred people in the room, mostly graduates, a scattering of spouses — the non-Medford spouses were the stunned, disbelieving ones wearing rigid smiles. With my coupons in my hand I headed for the bar. A girl I knew as Jeanne Ventresco said to me, "Buy me a drink, you fruit" and "Why are you talking funny like that?" And here was Chris Cunha. He had just flown in from Hawaii, where he was in the service. He said he was retiring. *Retiring? At the age of thirty-eight?* He said, "I've done twenty years."

Richard Travers was retiring, too. He was in Army Intelligence and had, he said, been on missions throughout Southeast Asia. "Tank" we called him in high school, but the name was far more apt now: he must have weighed close to three hundred pounds. He was retiring to start a detective agency. My memory of Travers was an early one. After school — this was the Swan School: we were ten years old — we used to cut through the railway yard near Riverside Avenue and hop the trains while they shunted. Travers asked me if I had seen John Brodie. But I hadn't — not for twenty years.

"Remember the toads?" he said.

Brodie, Travers and I spent the fifth and sixth grade catching toads along the railway line, where they lived in the ditches. We lugged them away in buckets to carry out obscure dissections. Travers said Brodie had become a teacher. They were all teachers, he said.

A familiar figure appeared. He crunched my hand and said, "Your father always told me I'd make a good cop." This was Paul Agostino, the wild man of Fulton Heights. True to my father's prediction, he had become a policeman; but he had retired early, with a disability.

"Stick any frogs lately?" he said.

I said no, but remembered. It was Augie who had shown me how to spear a frog with a sharpened stick. We did it after dark on summer nights at Wright's Pond, on the feeble pretext of earning a merit badge. We were Boy Scouts.

Augie was elbowed aside by a man unmistakably Pete Thompson, as cherubic in adulthood as he had been in childhood. But his innocent look was misleading: he was a crack shot and owned an arsenal of guns.

"You still got that old Mossberg repeater?"

"I sold it," I said.

Thompson was now speaking to another classmate. "We had these 22's. We used to go to Paul's house and shoot out of his bedroom window. Squirrels, pigeons, anything that moved – *bam! bam!*"

Besides Thompson and Travers, there was Trotta, Terranova, Tartachny, Trebino. They were more vivid to me now than the others, because they had been in my home-room, at the end of the alphabet.

There is a bad dream which everyone suffers. It takes place in a large overbright room, filled with people going, "Quack! Quack!" You know every person in the room, and it seems incredible, because there are so many, big and small. Your whole populous past has assembled for a long night to torment you. I often get these dreams in distant places. I had them in Africa and Singapore, the Medford dreams in the tropical early-morning.

The years fall away. The smallest figure in the corner has a name; one person's posture, another's ears, buck teeth, crewcut – it is all familiar. Face after face appears, most of them laughing and perspiring and poking fun. You wonder: What's the occasion? They know you better than anyone, and though you have only been subtly scrutinized you wake up feeling naked, because you have been judged. You have been reminded of what you are.

We like to think we have secrets. Childhood and early youth are full of them. Time passes, and the secrets are lost to us. But the high school reunion disinters the past and rehashes it, like that dream. Decades are pressed into a few hours. If it were not so brief it would be a nightmare. But it happens so quickly it is painless, and yet a shock, for no one changes so much that he becomes unrecognizable to his childhood friends. What shocked me there at the Hilton Inn, among the Class of '59, was the fact that I had kept my secrets so well they had become practically undiscoverable to me, and if I had not gone to the reunion I would never have known how I had made my childhood and high school days into a fiction.

It was not only the guns, the frog-sticking, or Humphrey's raft. Here was Patrick Shea reminding me of the time we made a canvas canoe, pushed it over a high steel fence at Spot Pond and paddled like mad to an island in the centre. This was illegal: it was a reservoir – drinking water! There were mounted police patrolling the bridle paths, but we escaped getting caught, and even pissed contemptuously into the reservoir before we made off with our canoe. Was this a youthful lark? No, not so youthful. I was about sixteen and should have known better. My older brothers said I ought to take up basketball.

For twenty years, until the reunion, these high school days had receded and become distorted in a haze that made retrospection bearable. I saw myself as bespectacled and bookish, a bit of a shut-in, boning up for the Science Fair. As the years passed I concocted a version of high school which was an intellectual preparation for becoming a writer. The version continued to elude me: I could never quite pin down how it had happened. I had done very little writing in high school, apart from the required essays about *Julius Caesar* and my "project" on Piltdown Man (the Piltdown Hoax went on hoaxing Medford, long after it was debunked in academic circles). I did not edit the school magazine (the boy who did took up television production), and contributed only cartoons to the yearbook. And – weirdest revelation of all – I never threw a ball or swung a bat. In twelve years of school, I never joined a single team, wore an athlete's uniform, or competed in a sport. Even now, sports bore me stiff, with their bogus drama, their ill-will and their yelling. I have never sat through an entire baseball game.

Medford custom paired the cheer-leader with the athlete in romance: they fell in love, they married. At the reunion I could see that these marriages worked, apparently. Paul King had married Judy Wallace, Joe Raffin had married Pat Gawlinski, Sonny Rossi had married Maureen Hurford, Wes Foote had married my first-grade girl-friend, Linda Rice. The hockey-player Dom DeVincenzo had married Jean Bordonaro, the quarterback Angelo Marotta had married Louise Carpenito. Every wife a cheerleader! Every husband a jock! The girls had been trained from a very early age to root for boys. I searched the yearbook in vain for pictures of girls' sports teams – twenty years on, their absence seemed the cruellest anomaly. But at Medford High, girls cheered, boys played – and I had done neither. The only thing worse than not being a jock was agreeing to be a water-boy. Well, at least I had escaped that.

Your intellectual upbringing – the pompous but kindly-meant phrase has been used in questions put to me by people interested in how I became a writer. For twenty years I tried to account for my choice of this profession. I mentioned books I had read in high school. But the books I read in high school had not made me a writer (and if they had, they would have made me a bad writer). I read Perelman and J. D. Salinger for laughs, John O'Hara for its sex, and pored much more seriously over the L. L. Bean catalog which advertised tents, hand-warmers and snow-shoes. So: what intellectual upbringing? Television, radio, comic books, camping manuals and *The American Rifleman*? I didn't play baseball and wasn't interested in electronics. That ought to have left me with plenty of time for the library, but in fact I chose guns, bombs and fires.

At least three men at this high school reunion reminded me of how we had made bombs. The bombs were simple and powerful – powdered zinc and sulphur sealed in a tube – but the detonators required ingenuity, a number of different wires of varying thicknesses and a transformer adapted from a set of model trains. The bombs were buried in my back yard: each one blew three cubic feet of Medford sky-high. It was very satisfying, thrilling even, and I still have scars on my right hand from one – it was my last one – which went off prematurely. Some fool had left the juice on. What else was there? Yes, Richie Collins said, once we had skinned a tom-cat and boiled the corpse, hoping to reassemble the bones. But the stink of the stewing cat was so godawful we had abandoned the project.

Other people's memories were fresher than mine. I prowled the ballroom button-holing my old pals, and I was told how we had gone swimming bollocky – it was the Medford word for skinnydipping – at Pickerel Rock, set grassfires at the Sheepfold, and fished through the ice at Wright's Pond. In those days, my heroes were sharpshooters and pool-sharks, and I had a sneaking admiration for Willie Sutton, "the man with a thousand faces," who was a bank robber.

School was a tedious punishment. It seemed slow and pointless and inescapable. The subjects were surprisingly easy, the discipline hard and humorless. I was amazed then – I am amazed now – that I did not do well. Perhaps I was afraid of the enemies that kind of excellence would have made me. Good, conscientious students were somewhat despised by us. They were collaborators, future Rotarians; they weren't interested in beating the system.

"There's Vic Garo," Humphrey said at the reunion. He sounded sourly triumphant. "He never missed a day of school. They mentioned it at graduation. Remember? He still looks like a pisser."

Everyone in the room was thirty-eight years old. The effect was odd and improbable; we were like obscure cultists, or members of a secret society. Some of the men had gone grey, a few were totally bald. Physically, the men had changed most. A girl of seventeen or eighteen has reached her full growth, so these women were roughly the same size as they had been in high school, and many were still pretty, even glamorous. Nearly all the men were bigger than they had been when I had last seen them, in June, 1959. They were fuller-faced, bearded, mustached, lined – older-looking than the women – and most of all they were taller. Some were enormously fat; no woman was. Each conversation was penetrated by unspoken self- scrutiny, the nagging thought: *Do I look like you?*

The few hundred who were missing, someone said, must have stayed away because they thought they were physically repulsive: men and women who could not bear to face their old friends who remembered them as handsome and agile, and who didn't want to disappoint them. There is a kind of distress that changes people, more than time or bad food does — a slight agony, a hint of despair, the abrasion of grief. No one here looked desperate. And there is snobbery. Six members of the Class of '59 had gone to Harvard; only one turned up at the reunion. He said to me, "I didn't expect to see you here," and he spoke to me in a faintly conspiratorial way, as if we did not belong in this mob. His impertinence was in talking about the present. It was bad form. We were here to toast the past and to celebrate the fact that we were still alive.

Many I had met at the age of seven, in the first grade. Not only Humphrey and Travers, but Tom Drohan, who remembered beating me in a spelling bee at the Washington School, and Linda Rice, my first girl-friend. What a land of lost content; but there was a new contentment now, and at last I could say to the girl I had taken to the Prom, "Do you know how badly I wanted to go to bed with you?"

Twenty years ago we had all been innocent — or most of us. Kissing was the most that any of us had done. I did not sleep with a girl until I was nineteen, and when I mentioned this at the reunion it turned out that this was the age when most of the others had begun. Sex, unlike most other sins, was inconvenient for the urban high school student in the fifties: you needed a car, you needed money, you needed a place to go, and most of all you needed a willing partner. *She fucks*, we used to whisper, but we regarded such girls as priestesses, and we were implausible and timid. For this generation, sex was a harrowing bargain, implying penalties and vows. It was not shameful, but it was horribly serious. Most of us went without, and suffered, and now feel an envious admiration for the young, who have been spared all this longing. The great difference on this reunion night was a new look of experience on the faces of these old friends. The look of experience is slightly weary, a wince that is both sheepish and knowing, and it is practically indistinguishable from a look of disappointment.

We were now, in the best sense, shameless. We could not kid anyone, but also — now — sex between us was as unthinkable as incest. We knew each other too well to be able to play the sexual game with any spirit of conviction. We had grown up in post-war dreariness and repression, expecting a cataclysm. The cataclysm came: after high school everything happened — Vietnam, Ban-the-Bomb, drugs, race riots, casual sex, Black Panthers, the John Birch Society, draft-card burning, Nixon, political assassinations and junk food. No wonder we looked weary. In twelve years of school the only world event that impressed me was Sputnik: nothing else mattered. It had been a busy two decades since, but now things were much as before — indeed, the rock-and-roll we had listened to in 1959 was back in vogue, Buddy Holly, Elvis, Chuck Berry, Little Richard and Bo Diddly.

There was a banquet, but that was no more than a hectic interval of yammering and face-searching; and then prizes — Cunha and I got bottles of wine for having traveled so far. Someone — no one was quite sure of his name — got a bottle of wine for having fathered eight children. Walter Buckley said it ought to be a bottle of Geritol.

The class members we had spotted as future Rotarians had become Rotarians. Most, it seemed, had been on course from the start: Paul Chalmers, the class president, was a businessman in Seattle; Marotta was the mayor of Medford, Paul Donato was deputy mayor. Kaloostian, a bagger in his father's grocery store, now owned a string of super-markets ("Ever go to Armenia?" he asked me. "If you do, let me know what it's like"). Position had come naturally to most: the saloon, the Dunkin Donuts franchise, the Toyata dealership — they had been preordained. Jean MacSweeney, one of the more literate among us (lovely handwriting, a good speller), said she owned "a bunch of newspapers." Peter Thompson, whose father was a truckdriver, now ran a fleet of trucks, and Pat Shea, my fishing friend and fellow canoe-builder, owned a bait shop. Many had become teachers. It was perhaps the last high school generation which went willy-nilly into high school teaching: it was respectable, it was a familiar routine, and the jobs were still available.

What about our own teachers? Few people mentioned them, because this was not a night for churlishness (the mood of a high school reunion is hilarious or nostalgic; it is not stuffy, it is seldom sour — it is too late to settle old scores). Our school had been run in an authoritarian way — no back-talk, no sass, no dungarees. The teachers were peevishly elderly — at least they seemed that way to us — and they kept discipline but imparted little wisdom. They were not readers. They were too busy for books. They were certainly underpaid. Some moonlighted in other jobs — Mr Orpen worked at the race track, but we regarded this as stylish. Mr Finnegan sometimes acted in Boston plays — he was Hickey in *The Iceman Cometh* — but by the time we graduated he was a failed actor and had taken to drink. Mr Flynn (who swore to us that Sacco and Vanzetti were guilty) carried a hip-flask. I can't remember the name of the teacher who had the wooden leg, but I recall that at the end of the afternoon he used to lean back in his swivel chair and rest it on his desk: I can see the yellow polished wood, and the bolts in his hip. Miss Dole, the guidance counseller, shrieked at me once (I was seventeen), "You'll never go to college – you'll never get in! You're not going anywhere!" And another teacher said to me sorrowfully, "Why do you run around with Berkowitz – why do you always pick up the lame and the halt?" These teachers had lived in another age; the two qualities they valued in education were silence and order. They were willfully uninspiring.

None of us at the reunion had had a poor high school education, but for all of us it had been mediocre – non-intellectual rather than anti-intellectual. It had been decent, social, sporty, strict, but that bookworm image I had had of myself had been inaccurate. Meeting these people, all of whom were pushing forty, reminded me of all those idly-spent years – no goals scored, no girls slept with, no books read, nothing achieved but a prize at the Science Fair – the toad-hunting and frog-sticking had paid off in a small way. Who had I been all those years ago? The answer was easy, and at last I could find it bearable: I had been a punk.

I think I am an optimistic person, but that night, traveling home to my house on the Cape, I had a dreadfully hollow feeling. Things had not seemed so black since high school. *What is going to happen to me?* I used to think. I had wanted to write. I did not have the courage to say I was going to be a writer. A doctor, a teacher, a forest ranger – it did not seem to matter what I said, because it would never happen. I knew only one thing for sure. It was this: Nothing will happen to me in Medford – worse, I will fail here. High school was proof of that. Was my brain teeming with schemes and fantasies? I think it was. I had a riotous imagination, but even that worried me into secrecy, for I had done nothing, and I certainly had not used it. Going home now was like going home from high school, and it provoked the same reflection: *We are all riding into the dark, alone.*

An October mist hung over the Cape. It was late. We had stayed up drinking and talking until three am. Now I passed a watching raccoon at the roadside. Twenty years ago I would have wanted to put a bullet between his bright yellow eyes. Dead leaves lay thick on the road; there was no other car here to scatter them. I was lonelier than I had been for years. But that was how I had felt in high school – impatient and a bit lost and mournfully horny. In high school I was still ungrown, with my home-made bombs and my gun and a horror of adulthood. The reunion was a celebration of the youth and violent innocence that had been in me. I had been right to be fearful in 1959, for everything was about to happen. I had not known – how could I? – that my education was about to begin. I had good friends, but I was nagged by one thought: the world was elsewhere. I left Medford the first chance I had, and Medford became part of the dark beyond, as I converted my memories into fiction. But I was lucky in this brief reunion. It didn't damn me the way dreams do. It was worthwhile and funny and a relief, and I was reassured. Now I knew I could go back. Such, such were the joys.

Rudyard Kipling: The White Man's Burden

[1979]

One of the more grotesque falsifications of taste, and it is usually propounded in schools, is the pious belief that a work of literature must be morally pure and right-minded before it can wholly satisfy us. No villain can enthrall us, the argument runs; no sinful passion can make us happy or inspire us. And yet if this were so, half of literature would be lost to us in our self-denying refusal to see, as Angus Wilson puts it in *The Strange Ride of Rudyard Kipling*, "the difficult truth that aesthetic satisfaction is not one with ethical satisfaction." There are morally disgusting stories that one reads with absolute enchantment, and from the Jacobeans onward villains who are truer and vastly more enjoyable than saintly heroes who never put a foot wrong.

Kipling embarrasses critics, and even his biographers have felt the necessity to suppress stories they have found morally untidy or politically dubious. We have had to endure the preposterous suggestions that Kipling wasn't really an imperialist, or vindictive in his fictions, or that he didn't scoff at some races and hate others. But he did believe in the salvation of imperialism, and any number of his stories and poems indicate his hatred for certain races or groups of people. No, not Indians, though he made Kim's companion a Buddhist rather than a Hindu; but apart from his approval of "Fuzzy Wuzzy" in his home in the Sudan he never referred to Africans as other than "Hubshis" (a neat Hindi evasion derived from "Abyssinians") and he believed that the Germans were satanic. These views in fine and subtle works have caused confusion and have made Kipling one of the most misunderstood writers in the language.

Long before he died (he died comparatively recently, in 1936) he was praised, mocked and hounded in about equal measure. After his death he was ignored for a decade, then pounced upon – so vigorously that a book published in 1945, Hilton Brown's *Rudyard Kipling*, proclaims that its intention is for Kipling "to be restored to his throne." Orwell's defensive and indignant essay was mainly a response to Eliot's saying (in his selection of Kipling's poems) that Kipling was "a versifier." In America, Randall Jarrell tried with a certain amount of success to make sure that "the Kipling that nobody read" (the title of Edmund Wilson's essay) reached a wide public. In England, Somerset Maugham edited a companion piece to Eliot's, a selection of stories he prefaced with the view that Kipling was the greatest short story writer in English. More recently, V. S. Naipaul has discussed – but not dismissed – Kipling as "a club writer," and Philip Mason in an enormous book of critical chat (*Kipling: The Glass, the Shadow and the Fire*) has directed our interest to the later stories. Charles Carrington's official biography (it appeared in 1955, but has been reissued with corrections) started a new Kipling boom; it is a politely factual book, plodding and reverential, that goes its earnest way, buffing up the slightly tarnished halo. Both J. I. M. Stewart and Angus Wilson have improved our understanding – Mr Wilson in particular – but some bafflements have persisted.

And no wonder, for Kipling himself was no help. In his lifetime Kipling actively discouraged anyone from invading his privacy. He had a mighty distrust of journalists, and in his poem "The Appeal" he wrote,

> And for the little, little span
> The dead are borne in mind,
> Seek not to question other than
> The books I leave behind.

Fine, you say, and you pause at the Kipling shelf. Here it is, nearly as long as The Grand Trunk Road and with much the same motley traffic: kiddies' stories and "Mary Postgate" (one of the nastiest stories ever written), poems about Puck and poems about whores and sergeants, fables about immortality and one disagreeable ode about the Kaiser dying of throat cancer; a great knowingness about adultery and divorce and spooks in cupboards, written when he was in his twenties, and some later stories that are positively boyish. There is the precise technical detail of railway engines and radios, and the hilarious photographic gaffe in "The End of the Passage" where a character snaps a picture of the bogeyman printed on a dead man's retina. He never saw Mandalay, and yet it is the title of his best-known poem; he suffered in America, but wrote remarkably little about it. His India, which has become our India (and even many Indians' India – the scholar Nirad Chaudhuri ranks *Kim* as far greater than Forster's *Passage to India*), he imagined from just seven years of working on colonial newspapers and mooching in Simla and the bazaar. From year to year he is reassessed. He has never, I think, gone unread; but a wilder combination of traits – philistinism and fine-feeling, vulgarity and clear-sightedness, militarism and mercy, public serenity and private sorrow, fierceness and gentleness – is hard to imagine. Could there be a better subject for a novel or play?

I wrote a play about Kipling in 1979, calling it "The White Man's Burden." This play seems to me (but I hope to no one else) like the sort of Chinese pot I have seen reassembled in a museum case. A dozen or so fragments of porcelain, big and small, are dug up; they do not make a whole pot, but a careful person studying the breaks and curves in the pieces begins to fathom the design. With new clay and old fragments he makes his vessel, the plain biscuit-colored clay holding the opaline fragments in place. It is the right shape, but a strange mixture of styles and tones, a work of collaboration, the past informing the present. Sometimes, if it is done well, you hardly notice the patches. In a sense, most writing is like this; the writer is usually working with vivid splinters and trying to make their shine indistinguishable in his creation.

I was lucky in the fragments I found.

The story began in London, in 1889. Kipling was then twenty-four and living in several small rooms on Villiers Street, next to Charing Cross Station. He had made his reputation with his book of short stories, *Plain Tales from the Hills*, and he was regarded as a prodigy. He had recently returned from India; he was hard at work. Not very far away, in Dean's Yard, Westminster, there was an American about Kipling's age, who had just arrived and was energetically writing, signing up authors for a new publishing venture, and moving in society. This was Wolcott Balestier. He was all bustle – charming, impatient, clever, imaginative, businesslike. He had already written two novels, but now he had a new scheme.

The American copyright laws allowed any foreign book to be pirates' loot – Dickens had complained about this some years earlier. The only way an English author could secure copyright in the United States was in collaboration with an author who was an American citizen. Soon after he set up his office in Dean's Yard, Wolcott hired Arthur Waugh (Evelyn's father) as his assistant – it was Arthur Waugh's first job. In his autobiography, *One Man's Road* (1931), Waugh wrote that Wolcott had "conceived the idea of crossing to England, and setting up a collaboration with some established English writer, say, Mrs Humphry Ward – which would secure that writer the protection of American copyright."

Waugh was impressed by his young boss. The American was tremendously hard-working and deeply respected. He was, said Waugh, "an inspired leader, and made everybody, or almost everybody, believe in him." Wolcott's motto was that nothing was impossible: you could do anything, meet anyone, go anywhere, change the copyright laws, make a fortune or effect any conquest. "He was not merely one of our conquerors," Edmund Gosse wrote, "but the most successful of them all."

It was almost inevitable that Wolcott should meet Rudyard Kipling, although the first time he heard of him he said, "Rudyard Kipling – is it a man or a woman? What's its real name?" Very soon Wolcott was discussing the possibility of publishing Kipling in America and – odd for the reclusive and single-minded Englishman – collaborating with him on a novel, to be called *The Naulahka* (the word was misspelled: Kipling never corrected it). Kipling began visiting Wolcott; he met Wolcott's mother and two sisters, who were very proud of the way Wolcott had made inroads on English society. At the same time, Wolcott was cultivating the friendship of Henry James, and to his occupations of publisher, novelist, collaborator, and party-goer he added one more – he became Henry James's literary agent. "The precious Balestier," James called him, and in a letter to a friend he wrote, "He will probably strike you, as he strikes me, as the perfection of an 'agent'." James was then fifty. He treated Wolcott as his son, and they made trips together – once, they planned to spend a weekend on the Isle of Wight, but it was more than a week before the pair returned to London. "He became in a manner part of my life," James wrote. There can be no doubt that James loved him in the helplessly idealizing way that he did attractive and talented young men.

Henry James also met Wolcott's sisters. Josephine was very pretty, and perhaps as a consequence of her unapproachable beauty we know almost nothing about her. Caroline, known to everyone as "Carrie", was "a little person of extraordinary capacity," James said. She was small and genial, and capable to the point where a number of people compared her to a man. Kipling's parents were slightly alarmed by her. His father remarked obliquely that she was "a good man spoiled," and his over-protective mother said, "That woman is going to marry our Ruddy."

It is not known what sort of courtship, if any, went on between Carrie and Kipling. The focus of attention was Wolcott, who was now doing business in Europe. He had joined forces with the English firm of Heinemann in the hope of producing cheap pocket editions of novels, to rival those of Tauchnitz. Kipling meanwhile set off alone, in a state of mental exhaustion brought on by overwork, for a round-the-world cruise. He visited South Africa and New Zealand, and he had given Henry James the impression that he was on his way to Samoa to visit Robert Louis Stevenson. Indeed, Stevenson expected him: "R. K. is planning to visit us," he wrote to James in September, 1891. But Kipling abandoned the Samoa trip and sailed to Australia and Ceylon. In Colombo he had news that Wolcott was dangerously ill; just before Christmas in Lahore he learned that Wolcott had died in early December, in Dresden.

Henry James had been summoned to Dresden. He dreaded the errand, but managed to play a fatherly role at the bleak funeral ceremony. James was desolated by Wolcott's death, but full of admiration for Carrie's fortitude, "the intense – and almost manly – nature of her emotion." The Balestier women and James returned to England, and they were astonished to see Kipling on the 10th of January – it had taken him just fourteen days to travel from Bombay to London. A week later, Kipling and Carrie were married, at All Souls, Langham Place. Henry James gave the bride away – "a queer office for *me* to perform – but it's done – and an odd little marriage."

A month after their marriage, in the middle of February, 1892, the Kiplings were in America. They stopped at Brattleboro, Vermont, where some of Carrie's relatives lived, and Kipling was overwhelmed by the snow and the isolation. With the haste that characterized his decisions during this first hectic part of his life, Kipling determined to buy some land, build a house and live in Vermont. All this he managed quickly, and then the honeymoon couple crossed America to Vancouver, sailed to Japan (where Carrie's maternal grandfather had been an adviser, twenty years earlier, to the Mikado) and discovered, one afternoon in Yokohama, that their bank had gone bust. Penniless, they returned to Brattleboro. That story is in Kipling's somewhat evasive autobiography, *Something of Myself*, written when he was seventy.

No reader of this autobiography can have much idea of what Kipling's American years were like. You get the impression that he has a grievance, but it is impossible to say how it came about. The book is short on particulars – unusual for a writer who could describe down to the last valve and piston ring the workings of a steam engine. But perhaps that was the problem. James described Kipling's writing as a steady diminishing, moving from "the less simple in subject to the more simple – from the Anglo-Indians to the natives, from the natives to the Tommies, from the Tommies to the quadrupeds, from the quadrupeds to the fish and from the fish to the engines and screws." There is no mention in Kipling's autobiography of the vast amount of work he did in Brattleboro (he doesn't even name the town), but the four years after his marriage – Kipling was filled with optimism and settled for the first time in his life – were the most productive of his literary career. He wrote most of the poems in *The Seven Seas*, both *Jungle Books*, all the stories in *The Day's Work*, the second series of *Barrack Room Ballads*, worked at *Mother Maturin* (he was never happy with this novel and finally ditched it), started *Kim* and wrote most of *Captains Courageous* – this last was his only strictly American book. He also wrote a number of poems which were subsequently collected. His output was enormous and profitable and within a few years the Yokohama bankruptcy became no more than a funny incident, part of the colorful past.

Kipling loved the American landscape; he was uncertain of the people. He hated the drinking, the talking, the spitting, the greed, the noise, the illiterate immigrants, the xenophobia – specifically a hurtful anti-Brtish feeling which prevailed in the 1890's. "So far as I was concerned," he wrote in *Something of Myself*, "I felt the atmosphere was to some extent hostile. The idea seemed to be that I was 'making money' out of America – witness the new house and the horses – and was not sufficiently grateful for my privileges."

There is no reference in his autobiography to his brother-in-law, Beatty Balestier, or to the Venezuela-British Guiana boundary dispute which brought America and Britain to the brink of war. The Beatty memory must have been horrible – no human being could have been less like Kipling in character than Beatty. It is not surprising that the two men fought. I am inclined to think that Kipling identified in Beatty all the weaknesses and evils he saw in the United States: Beatty, for him, was the very embodiment of the boasting, irresponsible American. And it is quite likely that Beatty saw in Kipling a young John Bull, imperious, aloof, dedicated to work, unfunny and not particularly friendly. We know Beatty from his shouts of pain and pleasure; he was not immoral, only extravagant, coarsely expressive and loud, with the harum-scarum attitude of Huck Finn. He had Wolcott's energetic presumption, but none of Wolcott's tact or grace. Beatty was popular in town; Kipling was not and, what was worse, Kipling did not give a damn. But when Kipling decided to take on Beatty – breaking all his own rules about settling arguments in a judiciously wolf-like way – he did not know how it would expose and humiliate him, and how it would drive him out of his first real home.

Kipling placed much of the blame for the anti-British feeling in America on the national press. From his first visit to the States he was appalled by the state of American newspapers, and it was not long before he was pestered by journalists. He was usually successful at keeping them at bay, but his evasions only convinced them that he would make good copy. They hounded him as he disembarked from ships, they sneaked onto his property, interviewed neighbors and generally made a nuisance of themselves. Kipling never changed his view that the journalists were bums and their papers foolish, trivial and jingoistic. In doing research for my play, I read many American newspapers published in 1895 and 1896 and, with some sadness – the *Boston Post* was one of the most scabrous of the bunch – I began to see Kipling's point. The front pages were filled with reports of murders, muggings, suicides, gossip, hearsay, "society" rubbish and tub-thumping over Cuba and Venezuela. Kipling saw these same papers. He could have ignored them; he could have dismissed Beatty's ravings as wild talk – it wasn't much more than that. But in the end he brought the journalists to his doorstep and the scorn of the press upon his head. Rashly, in May, 1896, he had Beatty arrested.

I think he was striking the blow he believed Lord Salisbury should have struck a few months before. Britain had been taunted over the boundary between Venezuela and British Guiana – Venezuela making the ridiculous claim that well over half the British colony was rightfully her own. This issue had been in the air for about fifty years, but in 1895 the Venezuelans jumped a part of the disputed territory, captured an outpost and fired on a British schooner. When Lord Salisbury demanded their withdrawal, the United States asserted the Monroe Doctrine. Secretary of State Olney provided a clumsy gloss on the Monroe Doctrine by telling Lord Salisbury that "Distance and three thousand miles of intervening ocean make any permanent political union between a European and an American state unnatural and inexpedient." (Some years later, Olney explained his sharp tone by saying that "in English eyes the United States was then so completely a negligible quantity that it was believed only words the equivalent of blows would be really effective.") Olney's message was delivered in July; it was not until November that Lord Salisbury replied. To Olney's charge that union between Britain and British Guiana was "unnatural and inexpedient," Lord Salisbury said, "Her Majesty's Government are prepared emphatically to deny it on behalf of both British and American people who are subject to her Crown." He went on,

> Great Britain is imposing no "system" upon Venezuela ... It is a controversy with which the United States have no apparent concern ... It is not a question of the imposition upon the communities of South America of any system of government devised in Europe. It is simply the determination of the frontier of a British possession which belonged to the Throne of England long before the Republic of Venezuela came into existence.

Lord Salisbury called the Monroe Doctrine "a novelty" and said it was not recognized as any part of international law. He implied that he would deal with the Venezuelans in his own way.

This was fierce, but the American response to it was so threatening that it produced panic on Wall Street and an uprush of reckless patriotism that was given voice in anti-British sentiment. The American reply was President Cleveland's Message to Congress of 17 December, 1895. He said that, as Britain had refused to submit the boundary question to arbitration, he would request that Congress set up a commission to determine the true Venezuela-British Guiana frontier. In closing, he said,

> When such report is made and accepted it will in my opinion be the duty of the United States to resist by every means in its power as a willful aggression upon its rights and interests the appropriation of

Great Britain of any lands or the exercise of governmental jurisdiction over any territory which after investigation we have determined of right belongs to Venezuela.

In making these recommendations I am fully alive to the responsibility incurred and keenly realize all the consequences that may follow.

I am nevertheless firm in my conviction that while it is a grievous thing to contemplate the two great English-speaking peoples of the world as being otherwise than friendly competitors in the onward march of civilization, and strenuous and worthy rivals in all the arts of peace, there is no calamity which a great nation can invite which equals that which follows a supine submission to wrong and injustice and the consequent loss of national self-respect and honor beneath which are shielded and defended a people's safety and greatness.

Even gracelessly under-punctuated, Cleveland's message was clear: We will fight you if you don't accept our commission's decision.

In his *Oxford History of the United States*, Samuel Eliot Morison interprets the provocative language as growing out of a suspicion that the British government was procrastinating and that Venezuela, "if further put off, would declare a war, in which the United States must participate." It is true, as Lord Salisbury's biographer said of him, that he could be masterfully inactive, but Morison's is a charitable assessment, a historian's retrospective look at a bewildering piece of intransigence by two great powers over a precinct of South American jungle. Still, it gladdened Americans and it encouraged Latin Americans – the dictator, Porfirio Díaz, crowed his approval in Mexico City (but it was not long before he would be fleeing to safety in Europe). Seeing that the atmosphere had become hostile, Kipling wondered whether he might not be better off in Canada. He wrote hysterically to his friends, with his hopeless reading of the situation. He and his coachman were the only Englishmen in Brattleboro: the "little wooden town, white-cloaked and dumb" had become enemy territory.

For Henry James, still gloomy over the failure of his disastrous stage play, *Guy Domville*, the American belligerence was cause for greater gloom. He compared Cleveland's outburst of militarism to something Bismarck might utter in Germany. He expressed his fears in a letter to his brother, William:

One must hope that sanity and civilization, in both countries, will prevail. But the lurid light the American newspapers seem to project on the quantity of resident Anglophobia in the U.S. – the absolute war-hunger as against this country – is a thing to darken one's meditations. When, why does it, today, explode in such immense volume – in such apparent preponderance, and whither does it tend? It stupefies me –

seems to me horribly inferior and vulgar – and I shall never go with it . . . I had rather my bones were ground into British powder!

Henry James was ashamed and angry in London. In Brattleboro Kipling was frenzied, and he saw that it might be impossible for him to continue living in this small provincial town.

When the British government finally capitulated, in a face-saving gesture of agreeing to a treaty with Venezuela for submission of the dispute to arbitration, they did so because they were afraid of Germany, rather than out of any apprehension over an American attack. In the early winter of 1896, the German Kaiser had sent a telegram of congratulation to President Kruger of the Transvaal after the Boers frustrated the Jameson raid. It was clear to the British that a war in South Africa was imminent. This also had the effect of chastening what Joseph Pulitzer called the "jingo bugaboo" of President Cleveland. But none of this was any comfort to Kipling, who saw his leonine government provoked from another part of the globe.

It was at this time, from the first rumblings over Venezuela, to a British defeat (with German applause) in South Africa, that Kipling quarrelled with Beatty Balestier, had him arrested on a charge of "threatening murder and assault with opprobrious language," participated in the Brattleboro hearing, and made his decision to leave the United States for good. These unusual events – unusual for Kipling, at any rate – were the subject of my play.

A Grand Jury trial was set for September, but the day after the May hearing the newspapers – which had made a meal of it – carried headlines to the effect that Kipling was leaving. *Goodbye, Green Mountains!* and *The Author, After a Day as Witness, Says He's "Sick of the Whole Business"* were the headlines in the *New York Herald*; and the *New York Times*'s was *Kipling Talks of Leaving the Country to Protect Himself*. The local Brattleboro paper, *The Phoenix*, carried no mention of Kipling's plan to leave, and indeed reported the hearing with dignity and impartiality. In an editorial published three days after the hearing, the paper gave Kipling's knuckles a gentle rap: "For reasons which Mr Kipling doubtless knows very well, the reporters have seen here a chance to get even with him." The editorial went on to summarize his behavior:

He has chosen to live his life in his own way, and the Brattleboro community have respected his reserve. Whatever rebuffs ambitious interviewers from the city press may have invited, Mr Kipling's townsfolk have given themselves no occasion for grievance in this respect. He has undertaken no social responsibilities and has made few personal friends, but these few have found him the most genial and delightful of men. What seems to us his unfortunate way of meeting the

well-meant advances of newspaper men and would-be friends of the
literary guild when he first came to this country won him a reputation
for exceeding brusqueness, and, in the public mind this covered and
sunk out of sight the sensitive, appreciative and intense temperament
which intimate friends know him to possess, and the mark of which is
found on all his best work.

It was blame and praise. It ended with a cordial invitation for Kipling to
stay, and the hope that Brattleboro would "long be his home". Kipling
did not reply to this; if he commented privately no record survives.

The next newspaper report of Kipling is an item from *The Boston
Journal* (22 May, 1896) about another visit by him to Gloucester "to
afford him material for the story of New England life upon which he is
now at work." Two months later, *The Phoenix* reported that *Captains
Courageous* was nearly done and that the serial rights had been sold to
McClure's magazine. At the end of July there was a tiny paragraph in *The
Phoenix* about Kipling planning to build "an additional farm barn" (and
under this, "Austin Miller has placed a pop corn and peanut roaster in
front of his store"). On the evidence of these newspaper stories it seemed
as if Kipling was planning to stay in town for the September trial, and
perhaps much longer. The trial was now only a month away.

But the *New York Times* of September 2nd carried a small report on an
inside page which settled the question. The headline was *Rudyard Kipling
Goes Abroad*:

> Rudyard Kipling, the novelist, accompanied by his wife and children,
> sailed yesterday on the North German Lloyd Steamship *Lahn* for
> Southampton. Mr Kipling will be gone for several years. He goes direct
> to Torquay, a small fishing village situated in the south of England.
> Although he has removed all his furniture from his home in Naulakha,
> Vt., he did not take it with him, but stored it in Rutland, Vt.

Apparently, Kipling told the New York reporters, "I expect to come back
when I get ready. I haven't the least idea when that will be."

Three years later, in 1899, Kipling returned to New York, intending to
make a visit to Brattleboro. But he fell ill with pneumonia and for many
days he was near to death. His small daughter Josephine was also
dangerously ill. The papers reported that Beatty Balestier had hurried to
New York to bring a court action against Kipling, demanding $50,000
damages for "malicious persecution, false arrest and defamation of
character." Within days, little Josephine died; this terrible news was kept
from Kipling until he recovered. Sick with grief, he took the remainder of
his family away from the United States – without making the one-day
journey to Vermont – and he never returned. Thirty-seven years later,

Beatty was still talking about his old enemy. "He never has come back to Vermont," he said to one writer. "He never will, while I'm alive."

So Kipling stayed in England. After a few years he found a large isolated house in Sussex. He was just thirty-seven, but already he seemed to the world, and to his family, an old man. The American experience – the shock in Brattleboro, the death of his daughter in New York – had aged and saddened him. He said he had "discovered England" and "at last, I'm one of the gentry." He lived in this house for the rest of his life, and he did not write about America until, at the age of seventy, he described it in his autobiography. He seemed embittered, and people wondered why. An American friend wrote to inquire. Kipling replied, "Remember that I lived in that land for four years as a householder . . . As the nigger said in Court: 'If I didn't like de woman, how come I take de trouble to hit her on de haid?' "

John McEnroe, Jr.

[1979]

Most of the linespeople were nervous wrecks, one linesperson had "Not you again!" screamed at him, the referee – so rattled he was gibbering – retired in the middle of a match the previous night and had to be replaced. Even the spokesperson was a bit puzzled. "It doesn't cost anything to be friendly" said the spokesperson (a clue to this spokesperson's sex was the pair of bulges under the spokesperson's official *$50,000 Smythe Tennis Grand Prix* tee-shirt – the words *Smythe* and *Prix* were levitated and trembling hugely). Another person said, "See, he's real sort of edgy during a match, and sometimes afterwards, too. Last night for example he told all the reporters to go take a flying jump and they had to go home without quotes."

Ten feet away, an off-duty linesperson was saying, "I says to him, 'Here's where I explain the ropes to you.' He says, 'Forget it.' I says, 'I'm supposed to explain the ropes.' He says, 'I know the ropes.' 'But this is the rules,' I says, 'that I'm supposed to explain the ropes.' 'What rules?' he says, so I say to him, 'Look, kid, pretend I'm your father, okay? Give me a break'!"

Over this monologue, the first spokesperson said, "And the most incredible thing is the silence when he serves. Like they know he'll have a tantrum if there's a hiccup or anything. When the other players serve, people are relaxed. But when he serves you can hear, like, a pin drop. It's fantastic. I'm sitting there with a cup of Coke. There's ice-cubes in the cup and I know if I wiggle it the ice-cubes will make a noise and maybe he'll go crazy and shout at me. I've never seen anything like it. It's a kind of fear."

The cause of this funk might well have been Caligula, but was in fact John McEnroe – "Junior" as he is known to his fellow players, "The Kid" to his fans, and "Johnny" to his doting parents. Minutes later, he was prowling the baseline, pawing the "textured" plastic mat of the indoor court, somewhat graceless and podgy, and with a red head-band around his lopsided hairdo, looking like a slightly swollen Shirley Temple playing Hiawatha on the war-path. There was a shudder of pique in his shoulders and then the three thousand people in the Civic Auditorium in San José, California, went dead quiet in apprehension. His body changed from a pudding to a meteorite, became airborne, and he served – a fault. His features tightened at the error and he turned immediately to the spectators. *"Who's talking right there!"* He stared at a wedge of spectators, and there was horror in the silence now. Would he howl, as he had last night? Would he throw down his racket, or perhaps bean someone with a ball? No: he shook his frizzy peruke in dismay, strutted to the baseline again, and aced his second service.

"The Kid's behaving himself tonight," giggled a man in front of me, as a reluctant cheer went up.

And he was. He only threw his racket once (McEnroe seems to have developed a technique for throwing his racket without damaging it, though earlier this year he snapped one in half playing a particularly vicious smash); he threatened the floor with a woodchopper's motion, and he hollered obscurely into his cupped hand numerous times. But not once did he whine, "Oh, no, man! That was out, man! I ain't playing, man!" as he had in London some months before. There were no tantrums tonight. He stamped his feet, pouted, stared spectators down, and made faces – he has a different but equally twisted face for each call, like separate chunks of malevolent putty. Often he tied and retied his sneakers, and it seems as if he does this for no other reason than to aim his defiant posterior at his opponent, the way the Chinese attempt the ultimate curse on an enemy.

He was playing the lithe but hapless "Butch" Walts, ranked thirty-eighth. Butch was grim, and at no point did Junior smile. There was nothing good-humored about this. It was stern and serious; a piece of inventive destruction on McEnroe's part, punctuated by baboon-like cries from McEnroe when the ball went haywire. No doubt someone like the Maharishi would have a remedy for his colicky temperament, but the fits and the contortions seem to work in his favor and make his play all the more surprising, the leaps more agile, the silences more silent, as he unknots himself and becomes balletic. The audience was not really on his side – probably because they suspected that McEnroe would reward their cheers by yelling abuse at them. They acknowledge his skill, but McEnroe has a reputation for making everyone who watches him and plays him feel victimised: he has to prove himself with every shot. Nonetheless, he demolished Walts, and afterwards, Walts said sadly, "I didn't expect to win."

What did Walts think of McEnroe's gamesmanship?

"He's got a right to question a point," said Walts. "Everyone does. He just does it a bit louder than everyone else."

I had told the chief spokesperson that I was rather hoping that McEnroe would grant me an interview. After all, that was my sole reason for being here in San-Jose-on-the-Freeway.

"Funny thing," said the spokesperson, who as Barry MacKay had been on the Davis Cup team twenty years ago, "when I was playing tennis we used to hunt around for someone to talk to. But no one cared. These days – forget it. Last night was a fiasco – he wouldn't open his mouth. And the night before, a photographer asked him to pose in front of that picture of Tilden" – there was a blow-up of William ("Big Bill") Tilden, the American tennis star of the 'thirties, on the wall – "and all he said was, 'No thanks' and walked out of the room. But I'll try to talk to him – I'll quarterback it for you."

After the singles match, McEnroe, partnered by his friend Peter Fleming, played doubles. In his white samurai headband, and noticeably more relaxed in the buffoonery that is a convention of doubles, McEnroe chaffed Fleming and they gave Bengtson and Menon a pasting. I wondered, after his exhausting five hours, whether McEnroe would keep his appointment with me. His non-appearance would have been a blow; but I did not relish the thought of being savaged by a cantankerous twenty-year-old.

I felt mingled anxiety and relief when McEnroe appeared in the room. What now? But he looked quite different. His hair dripped, he seemed apologetic and ill-at-ease, he sounded youthfully adenoidal. "His interviews are disjointed and thin," one reporter wrote in a recent profile. McEnroe is in fact rather shy, but his shyness is so obvious – unfeigned and unexpected – it amounts to charm. His suspiciousness makes him appear slow-witted: he squints at questions and tugs his hair and studies his shoes. An athlete can easily deceive an onlooker into thinking that physical grace implies verbal eloquence. How can such a nimble person be so flat-footed in conversation? How can one so violent in play be so meek in an interview? I had been worried that I would end up writing yet another version of Beauty and the Beast, or else be reduced to screaming impotently, "Look, Junior, show some respect – I'm old enough to be your father!"

It surprised me, therefore, that McEnroe, who is regarded as America's answer to Nasty, The Howling Rumanian (and even Nasty has said, "He's worse than Connors and me put together"), can be quite nice, and when he does not have a tennis racket in his hand, loses his demonic sense of malignancy and becomes the sort of sweet freckled-faced chap a lady might like to take on her lap – that is, if he didn't weigh so much.

Off the court he looks another person altogether, a bit callow and dreamy, lugging a valise full of sweaty tennis clothes, and carrying six wooden rackets and a plastic racket-cover which, when unzipped, is revealed to contain wads of paper, tickets, coins, a large wrist-watch and a number of crumpled $20 bills. I had had a brief glimpse of this side of his personality. Just after his match finished, I watched him signing autographs for a group of adoring ten-year-olds. McEnroe signed without a qualm, exchanged a few words, and left them happy. He did not, as I suppose some of the tots had been led to expect, bite their noses off. It seems a small thing, this favor to tiny sports fans performed with a kindly grace, but I believe it is the key to his character. He is at ease with anyone his own age or younger; he is suspicious and almost resentful – and certainly disbelieving – of anyone older. He does not travel with his mother, as Connors did for so long; he has no coach on hand to guide him through the tournaments. "I don't need a guy traveling with me to buy tickets and do my laundry," he says. He is, in asserting this lonesome independence, rather unprotected; he feels exposed, and consequently, when a match finishes, he slopes off into the night and disappears. His view of older people, whom he sees as ignorant gawpers, or mockers, or snipers, has given him a sense of distrust. He is not unusual among tennis players in finding court officials myopic, but is rare in seeing them as treacherous. "There are some umpires who deliberately try to make me look bad," he told me, speaking softly, eyes down. "And a lot of people come to watch me lose. And there are some players – hey, I'm not mentioning any names – some players who try to get the crowd against me. See, I don't have the greatest reputation, do I? People expect me to behave bad."

I said that at Wimbledon two years ago the crowd was rooting for him when he played against Connors.

"They didn't know me then," said McEnroe, with a wan smile. "Now they do."

I could not understand his combative attitude towards spectators. Wasn't it better if they cheered you?

"Sure, it's better if the crowd is on your side. I want them on my side, but I don't know how to do it. I play Borg and the crowd goes bananas for him. Why? Because he doesn't change his expression? I don't know. The crowd's funny – they want you to talk to them, I guess. But I don't make jokes. So they yell things at me, they say stupid things, pop flashbulbs, clap at the wrong time, walk around, make noise."

I had got nowhere in discussing *The Deerhunter* with him (he had seen it in Rotterdam the previous week; the film had shocked him, but "I couldn't really relate to the war – I was too young"), but he became animated on the subject of spectators. He described a fantasy he sometimes has where an unruly crowd is concerned. As soon as the match is over, McEnroe sees himself stepping forward. "Stay where you are," he says in this imagining, as the crowd begins to rise. "I'd like to talk to you about some of the things you've just done. You were too noisy. You were laughing in the wrong places. You clapped at a double fault. That's rude!"

"But not all spectators are rude," I said. "They say the Wimbledon spectators are the most knowledgeable in the world."

"Who says?" demanded McEnroe, hunching his shoulders and assuming that I would say Fred Perry. "Who told you that?"

"My wife," I said.

"Your wife!" he cried, then quietly conceded that this might be true. "But they don't have too many sports over there, do they? Only tennis and soccer and, whats-it – cricket."

Soccer is one of McEnroe's passions. He played it all the way through school ("It was considered a sissy sport, but it gave me a lot of satisfaction to play on the team"). More revealing is his plain love for the way the British play football. "The England team really knows how to do it," he said, speaking of his admiration for the aggressive attacking style which is a counterpart of his own in tennis. "The Dutch and the Germans just kick the ball to each other – it's so dull it's like chess."

Because he regards dullness in sport as the greatest vice, he despises the poker-faced play of someone like Stan Smith. "If every guy were like Smith tennis would stink – it'd be boring. People criticise Nastase, but Nasty's done more for the game than any one man. He's made it lively and now more people are interested in it."

I suggested that losing one's temper destroyed one's concentration – it certainly seemed so in the case of Nastase who, after blowing his top, usually went on to lose the match. McEnroe denied this was so: "Anger doesn't necessarily affect your concentration." He went on to say that if there was a bad call a player was obliged to make a fuss; but he admitted that it seldom did much good to complain, since officials were so stubborn and unwilling to admit their mistakes. (A man who knows McEnroe's game well told me, "He's almost always right when he questions a call – he's got sharp eyes.") He loathes opponents who accept disputed points. This happened while he was playing Peter Fleming in Jamaica, and he swore at him throughout the match until finally Fleming screamed back, "What do you think I am, Junior, the Salvation Army?"

But it wasn't right, said McEnroe. His innocent sense of fair play is not confined to tennis. "These people who recognise me – I go into a restaurant and they give me the best table, or they do things for me that they wouldn't do for anyone else – that's not fair." This struck me as an honorable attitude in one so young, but his youth has something to do with it. It surprises him, he says, that he has found so much deceit and dishonesty since he started to play tennis professionally; he is only calm and talkative when the atmosphere is sympathetic, and he cannot bear to be scrutinised or judged.

In this sense he could not be more American. He insists he plays for pleasure, but he is intensely competitive (and withdraws and falls silent when the talk is of anything but sports or rock music), obsessed with winning, more tenacious in play than any tennis player I have ever seen – he throws himself on impossible shots, often risking a fracture as he somersaults into the scoreboard, knocking numbers all over the floor. He has been playing tennis in a serious way since he was twelve and beating older opponents at the Douglaston Club in New York. Little else matters to him.

Challenged on this, he says, "I've learned more about life in a year of pro tennis than I would have in four years of college. Now I can see through people a lot quicker" – and he goes on to describe the phonies he's met and their dreary deceptions.

His father has been quoted as saying that his famous son ("but I don't feel famous – I get nervous when I meet real sports stars") is living in an unreal world. McEnroe laughed at this. "My father's in an unreal world. He's my manager! He's learned a lot, too – suddenly I'm earning more than he is. He figures I was going to earn maybe a hundred thousand or so – was he surprised! There's about six people in his law firm working on my accounts – taxes, all that stuff. He says, 'Hey, this is getting serious' or 'I'm concerned that you're playing too much.'

"But I take time off – weeks sometimes, when I'm tired and can't stand the sight of a racket. There are lots of players who practise more than me – six hours a day. That's not my style. Or those long flights – one day in Tokyo, the next day in Stockholm or Miami, playing on two or three hours' sleep. I hate that. Gullikson won Jo'burg and then for about two months he was walking around like a Zombie. Not me, man. If I'm playing in London on Monday I try to arrive on Saturday."

The next day in San Jose he had two matches, the singles and doubles finals, both of which he won. A night in San Francisco and then he went to Las Vegas to compete in an exhibition tournament at Caesar's Palace. On his way to Las Vegas he passed through San Francisco Airport. I happened to be there, waiting for my own flight. I did not recognise his face, but identified him because he was carrying six tennis rackets under one arm and an enormous radio-cassette player in the other. He loped through the lobby alone, and no one else saw the mild, anonymous-looking youth anymore than, in another dimension, anyone had assumed that Jekyll could be anything but a nice-natured doctor who was away most evenings.

Christmas Ghosts

[1979]

The tradition in England of ghost stories at Christmas is much older than Dickens. "It is evident enough that no one who writes now can use the Pagan deities and mythology," Dr. Johnson said in 1780. "The only machinery, therefore, seems that of ministering spirits, the ghosts of the departed, witches and fairies." Although Dickens is the most celebrated exponent of the machinery of ministering spirits and ghostly epiphanies at Christmas, there was no better practitioner of the English ghost story than Montague Rhodes James. His stories are more eerie than Dickens's, dustier than L. P. Hartley's, less harshly suburban than Elizabeth Bowen's, and though lacking the narrative gracility of his namesake Henry's, are much scarier for their persuasive antiquarian detail.

People die horribly in M. R. James's stories; their bones are found in marshy woods, finely spun with cobwebs or in ghoulish coitus – two skeletons embracing; their hearts are knifed out and diabolically used; they are murdered and burnt and visited by dark creatures from the distant past. Perhaps this is not so odd. Mr James was himself an antiquary, a translator of the New Testament Apocrypha, passionately interested in paleography and for many years Provost of Eton, where he had any number of pupils and colleagues to sit at his feet. The lovable and learned old bachelor is a natural teller of ghost stories. But the curious thing is that, nearly always, M. R. James used Christmas as the occasion for giving his devotees the creeps with these strong tales. Indeed, he called the most hair-raising of them his "Christmas productions."

The fireside, the indoor life which winter demands, the somberness and good cheer which combine to become something like hysteria – these matter. So does the dark, the penetrating blackness that makes the English December a month almost without daylight, filling the afternoon with a clammy graveyard gloom – everyone hurrying through the wet streets with his head down, and homeward-bound schoolchildren looking blank-faced and lost. In the countryside, the trees drip like leaking wounds in the darkness, and owls squeeze out hoots from where they creepily roost; in the city, the housefronts stare through the trachoma of torn curtains across deserted parks, and moisture blackens every brick with a look of decay, giving the once-solid city some of the atmosphere of a hugely haunted ruin. It is the perfect weather, the perfect setting, for ghost stories, and it does not seem unusual to me that it has produced so many in England.

But why such stories as "Oh, Whistle, and I'll Come to You, My Lad" – or, for that matter, the one that begins with the ghost of Jacob Marley – at *Christmas*? I think, to understand this, one has to understand the English dislike of piety and church ceremony, the distrust of Catholic liturgy and the low esteem in which most English hold Catholicism. I say "dislike" and "distrust", but uneasiness is its true source, and I should say that in the English character is a kind of protesting residue of paganism. It is a revolt against sanctimony – Christmas pulls one way, pagan skepticism the other, and the result is frequently a blend of the pious and the supernatural, a species of half-belief that is persuasive because it is frightening: fear is the oldest excuse for reverence. And so the Christmas catharsis of the ghost story, that half-belief made into fiction, God in the shape of a bogeyman with a face of crumpled linen, making his annual visitation to an imperfect world. And because Christmas celebrates birth, we are nagged by its opposite, that things end; the ghost story celebrates the experience of death. In Dickens, the haunted man gets a reprieve; in M. R. James, he gets the chop. But Christmas is the only holiday that is specifically associated with a fictional genre, and though the English have contrived a characteristic way of expressing it, the tradition has a shadowy charm, and it is, ultimately, easy to see why it has caught on in other places.

Two Christmases ago, I decided to write such a story for my children. Their requirements were fairly undemanding. They wanted to appear in the story themselves; it had to have snow in it, and a ghost. I wrote it easily, but afterward they suggested with a certain diffidence that it wasn't right – the ending was sad. The old man disappeared – where was he? What happened to him? Was he all right? They said, in so many words, that the lugubrious inconclusiveness of it would keep them awake. So I cobbled together a new ending, and the next night they were satisfied. This I published last year as "A Christmas Card." Interested readers may notice in it a piece of plot I cannibalized from M. R. James's story, "The Mezzotint."

It was a happy experience, this Christmas ghost story. My children are now too young to read any of my other books, and they have only the vaguest notion of what I do all day. They are proud and pleased when they see my name on a new book, but beyond an acquaintance with the titles they have no idea of what is between the covers. (And I wonder, sometimes with a sense of dread, what they will think at the age of twenty or so, when they chance upon a novel of mine; will it arouse pity, or admiration, or cause embarrassment?) It struck me that they would not read anything of mine that was not written specifically for them. So, in the spirit of Edward Lear, who gladly turned from one of his Indian watercolors to sketch a cartoon for a young friend, I made another attempt last Christmas.

Their requirements: a London setting; snow; suspense; a happy ending; and "please put a cat in it." I had the setting immediately. There is a church near where we live in which William Blake was married. It is a Georgian church, St. Mary's in Battersea, sited directly on the south bank of the Thames. One of the windows in the church is dedicated to the memory of Benedict Arnold, a useful reminder that one country's traitor is another's patriot-hero. Arnold's bones lie somewhere in the muddy churchyard, and there is also a boat and mooring at the edge of that churchyard. From this dingy precinct of South London you can see clearly the prim pink brick and iron balconies of Chelsea.

"London Snow" – the title, but nothing else, is from a Robert Bridges' poem – was a hit with my children, and reading it to them on the three nights preceding Christmas, leaving the hammerstroke for Christmas Eve, was an intense pleasure for me. It was in a way like a rehearsal of the oldest form of fiction, telling this long story on successive nights in the close seclusion of my children's room; it was also an excuse to be alone with them, an invitation to see what my work is and a homemade groping toward an enchantment in producing some of my own ghosts. I felt lucky in being able to share it with them, and I promised that I would do it every year – a new story – for as long as they could stand it.

Purely for my own amusement, I hired the wood-engraver, John Lawrence, to illustrate the text, and decided to print a small edition myself, with the best paper I could lay my hands on, the best printing and binding. It is a limited edition: I will sell enough copies to pay for the publication, and I'll give the rest away as Christmas presents. That is for this year, and the whole enterprise has been immensely satisfying, the result a more grandly produced book than I have ever seen commercially published. Really, a book can be a beautiful thing, given patience, the collaboration of a gifted artist, a little money and a lot of time.

And I suppose the appeal of a Christmas story should not be a riddle. It is the imaginative and civilized celebration of a time of year that is full of mystery – part joy, part fear. It is expressed as an ambiguous epiphany in the last sentence of the best Christmas story ever written, James Joyce's "The Dead": "His soul swooned slowly as he heard the snow falling faintly through the universe and faintly falling, like the descent of their last end, upon all the living and the dead."

Henry Miller 1891–1980

[1980]

There is a poem entitled "Shitty" by Kingsley Amis in D. J. Enright's *Oxford Book of Contemporary Verse*. Reading it, I was instantly put in mind of Henry Miller, because it is not shocking but bright and funny, less a tone of voice than a startling gesture, the respectable writer clearing his throat and going *ptooey* while you watch. I think we are shockproof as far as coarse language is concerned; now, what alarms us, and rightly, is squalid action, the aristocrat and the boy scout, the traitorous don, the cabinet ministers wheeling and dealing in slag-heaps and ennobling shifty little asset-strippers. Next to these men's deeds, what is Miller's grunting? Anyway, he made it possible – he among others – for us to say exactly what we mean in our own words, and it is enjoyable to hear Mr Amis, grumpily profane, expressing common sentiments in direct language.

When Henry Miller stopped shocking people with his gonadal glow he was no longer taken seriously. But that was a long time coming. *Tropic of Cancer* was published in France in 1934, yet it was almost another thirty years before it was freely available in America and England. The illicitness contributed to his legend and he was forgiven his flatulence. A loophole in French law meant that books in English were not subject to censorship, and Miller's books could be regularly published under the Obelisk Press imprint alongside epics of coprophilia by "Akbar del Piombo."

Miller was a late bloomer – forty-two when his first book appeared – though he claimed that in the 1920s he hawked his prose-poems like Fuller brushes from door to door in his Brooklyn neighborhood. He loved this starving-artist image of himself, the romance of penury and neglect, writing against the odds, whistling in the dark, with his flat cap yanked over his eyes and (he says) muttering "Fuck you, Jack" to curious bystanders.

Anyone who has read Orwell's essay "Inside the Whale" knows how profoundly Miller affected and liberated at least one English temper. He was Orwell's opposite – reckless, amoral, loud, boastful, mendacious, and wholly contemptuous of politics. Orwell praised Miller's vigor and imagination, Miller returned the compliment by saying (in *The Paris Review*), "Though he was a wonderful chap . . . in the end I thought him stupid . . . a foolish idealist. A man of principle, as we say. Men of principle bore me . . ." What was Miller's philosophy? "One has to be a lowbrow," he said, "a bit of a murderer . . . ready and willing to see people sacrificed, slaughtered for the sake of an idea, whether a good one or bad one."

Typically, he talked through his hat, and apart from the most dubious generalities, didn't have an idea in his head. He claimed to be on the side of joy, freedom, criminality, insanity, ecstasy; he wasn't particular, but neither was Whitman, whom he much resembled. His writing was wild talk, scatological rather than sexual ("I am for obscenity and against pornography"). He was a shouter – a boomer, as they say Down South – and there are not many of those who achieve much in literature. His look, that of a Chinese sage, was misleading. Underneath was a hobo, the sort who sits stinking and dozing in public libraries, who screams abuse (some of it quite original) when he is told to move on, and who cherishes views such as "Civilization is the arteriosclerosis of culture."

He is the only hero in his books. Gore Vidal remarked (in a review of *Black Spring*) on how people are constantly saying, "You're wonderful, Henry!" and "How do you do it, Henry?" and never once does someone say, "Did anyone ever tell you you're full of shit, Henry?" Rumbustious-ness was his watchword and his ego was all that mattered. From *Tropic of Cancer* to the *Rosy Crucifixion* trilogy it is all Henry Miller, calling attention to himself. He attempted to write about Greece in *The Colossus of Maroussi*, but his cacophonous meditation obscures the ruins. His unfinished book on D. H. Lawrence was crowded with Miller on Life and Sex. In the early forties he applied for a Guggenheim fellowship to write a book about America. He was turned down for the fellowship but wrote the book all the same – *The Air-Conditioned Nightmare*, cross-country in a purring old car: Miller at large. By then he had just about stopped writing sentences such as "O glabrous world, O glab and glairy – under what moon do you lie cold and gleaming" and turned his attention to American bread, which he found disgusting and full of chemicals.

At the end of that trip he settled in what is certainly one of the most beautiful parts of America, the California promontory known as Big Sur, and wrote *Remember to Remember*, *The Books in my Life*, and his memoirs of the 'twenties, *Sexus*, *Plexus* and *Nexus*.

In his later years he moved to Los Angeles and found fulfillment playing table tennis with naked Japanese girls, which was one of his versions of paradise. I suspected he was gaga when he championed Erica Jong as a great writer. His judgement had not always been so bad. His literary friendships – Lawrence Durrell, Alfred Perles – were wide-ranging and generous; he was besieged by would-be writers hoping for his bear hug.

I first read him in school, the smuggled *Tropics* and then *The Henry*

Miller Reader. I was shocked and uplifted by what seemed to me great comedy and the rough and tumble of exuberant language. I had never read anything so deflating to pompousness, so manic or irreverent. It loosened something in my adolescent soul and helped me begin to write. I did not know that it was mostly fakery, using words for their sound alone, posturing and booming. It was a tonic, and it was only later that I discovered its ingredients to be piss and vinegar.

Earlier this year, a biography of Miller described that wonderful, hilarious life he claimed he had led to be totally imaginary. His life had been rather dull, he had been hen-pecked, he always did the washing-up. But this makes him, for me, a better writer – perhaps one of our more imaginative novelists instead of a noisy memoirist.

We are lucky to live in an age when books are seldom suppressed or banned – I speak of Britain and America, not Singapore or Paraguay or Iran. For this alone, our debt to Henry Miller is considerable. Walt Whitman wrote, "Unscrew the locks from the doors. Unscrew the doors themselves from their jambs!" Miller was not a very subtle carpenter. He kicked that door down, and allowed many writers to pass through.

V. S. Pritchett

[1980]

We live in an age when a book called *Modern Men of Letters* would be as thin as *Great Chinese Comedians* or *Famous Women Composers*; and yet there are exceptions. The finished copies of his biography of Turgenev had just arrived; his essay on Gabriel Garcia Marquez was in the current issue of the *New Statesman*; the previous night the usually punctual *Ten O'Clock News* started fifteen minutes late to allow extra time for the TV adaptation of his story "Blind Love," and that morning the London *Times* had described the author in a review as "truly venerable."

He entered the restaurant in his Russian-style fur hat and was intercepted by waiters and diners – handshakes and salutes, "So good to see you," "Wonderful play" – and as he sat down, a man at a nearby table whispered admiringly to his companions, "Why there's Victor Pritchett!" It was the sort of entrance Chesterton might have stage-managed, but Sir Victor Pritchett takes it in his stride. He doesn't like to be made a fuss of, he writes every day ("it excites me to work hard") and he loathes being called venerable: "It makes one feel rather like a dean, someone who expects to be bowed to – with my hands clasped behind my back and walking very slowly, muttering and moralizing."

At the age of seventy-seven he has a hiker's obvious health, a downright manner, an exuberant curiosity and the sort of twinkle that puts one in mind of a country doctor – that spirit-boosting responsiveness that works cures on malingerers. He looks lovable, he writes with a vigorous flair, bringing insight to appreciation; and he has done so for fifty years – his first book, *Marching Spain*, appeared in 1928. The broadcast of "Blind Love" was a satisfaction. The first time he saw it he wept he was so moved by it. The second time he winced and concluded that the adaptation – not his – wasn't much good. The story, which is almost certainly a masterpiece, was rejected by an American magazine editor who said, "When I see a swimming pool at the beginning of a story I know someone's going to throw himself into it."

Although he has written six novels, four books of literary criticism, six of travel, two volumes of autobiography and two major biographies, the short story is his real love, as he has demonstrated in eight collections. In his prize-winning memoir, *Midnight Oil*, he described his first attempts to write. Apart from a few years at Alleyn's School he had no formal education. "Out of an old-fashioned conviction about wanting to be a writer," he told me, "I went to Paris in the 'twenties. I didn't know of other writers, though I met Man Ray and I chatted a number of times with him and his mistress. It wasn't until I went to Spain and Ireland that I met writers and serious intellects, and of course by going abroad I completely by-passed the English class system. In Ireland I wasn't bound by any code. You must know the saying – 'Nothing is lower than an Irish aristocrat'. I never missed not having an English education. I used to feel sorry for the Eton-Oxford chap – business, friends, golf, the grind. 'God, what a life,' I used to think. 'I suppose he's not going to be a writer – that's hard luck on him.' "

Pritchett is, to my mind, not only the complete man of letters but also the ultimate Londoner, as familiar with club life as with the routine in the outer suburbs of Peckham and Herne Hill. He has seen Yeats and Wells rolling penny pieces down the ballroom bannister of the Savile Club and launching them into the hall outside the snooker room, and schoolchildren in South London in 1910, confronted by their first motorcar, rushing into the street and chanting,

> Old iron never rusts!
> Solid tires never bust!

In his most famous novel, *Mr Beluncle*, he satirized the émigré lower-middle-class Londoner, and in many of his stories, most notably in the volumes *Blind Love* and *The Camberwell Beauty* – depicted minutely the people of the city, antique dealer, interior decorator, barrow-boy. "Every story causes me agony – trying to find out how to write it," he says. "I can't think. That's the real trouble. I need a piece of paper." His writing, like his reading, is vast: "I read for the pleasure of learning how to write." At the age of sixteen he admired Belloc ("Don't read Conrad, I was told. He writes very bad English and he's a hopeless romantic. Yeats thought very poorly of Shaw and they said Proust was on the way out"), Anatole France, and later Liam O'Flaherty, the Spaniard Pio Baroja ("I liked his terse style") and Chekhov, "though I identified myself unavailingly."

Here are two openings:

> The leaves fly down, the rain spits and the clouds flow like a dirty thaw before the wind, which whines and mews in the window cracks and swings the wireless aerial with a dull tap against the sill; the House of Usher is falling, and between now and Hogmanay, as the draughts lift the carpets, as slates shift on the roof and mice patter behind the

wainscot, the ghosts, the wronged suitors of our lives, gather in the anterooms of the mind.

A cloud of dust travels down the flinty road and chokes the glossy Kentish greenery. From the middle of the moving cloud come the ejaculations of an unhandy driver; the clopper of horses' hooves, the rumble of a wagonette or trap. One catches the flash of a top-hat or a boater. One smells horse manure and beer. And one hears that peculiar English spoken by the lower middle class . . . the accent is despairing, narrow-voweled yet truculent, with something of the cheap-jack and Sunday League in it, and it is broken by a voice, not quite so common, which says things like 'We're not the finished thing. We're jest one of Nature's experiments, see. We're jest the beginning.' And then – I don't quite know why – there is a crash. Over goes the wagonette . . . Most surprisingly a nearby house catches fire . . .

You might mistake these for stories. They are, in fact, the openings of essays, the first on the Irish ghost-story writer, Sheridan LeFanu, the second on the scientific romances of H. G. Wells. Both are from Pritchett's *The Living Novel* (1946). I asked him about his style of writing, which brought the vividness of fiction to literary criticism. It is almost inconceivable that any critic today – apart from Pritchett himself – would take this trouble in an essay review; Pritchett was knocking off one of these a week throughout the Second World War for the *New Statesman*. "It never occurred to anyone at the time to write in an academic way," he said. "Now practically all reviewers have academic aspirations. The people from the universities are used to a captive audience, but the literary journalist has to please his audience."

I wondered what Pritchett thought of the American literary character. It is common enough knowledge that we do not have a Pritchett, and since the death of Edmund Wilson have not had a literary critic of any real eminence. We have ambitious academics, either using the review as a means of gaining tenure, or else thirty-grand-a-year men who crave the doubtful glamor of a by-line; we have a handful of curmudgeons, who cross the year's books with a heavy tread, and habitual odd-jobbers.

"In America, the writer's ego is allowed to expand," says Pritchett. "In any other country he would be forced to know his own literature. And circumstances would impel him to review. I don't think I could have made my living otherwise. I do it out of interest, duty – and there is the temptation of taste. It has always been a tradition in England. In the nineteenth century, most writers did it for nothing. This wore off in the Gissing period – when Gissing was a literary hack. I don't know whether Hardy ever reviewed books. Meredith did his whole life. Bennett of course, and Belloc, and Chesterton. T. S. Eliot turned it down as a waste of time – an interesting decision – very American."

Pritchett has experienced American life – hiking across Tennessee and lecturing at Princeton, Smith and Berkeley. "It's no disgrace not to have money in England. It's hopeless in America. If you go broke you're not supposed to appear at parties, and American writers expect to make an enormous amount of money. If they teach at universities they are paid handsomely. But job status is so important in your country – the title on the door, the something on the floor – how does it go?

"American life is so much more serious than English life. Your seriousness is always a way of gaining status, too. I gave a lecture at Princeton and someone stood up in the audience and said, 'Surely that contradicts something Aristotle said.' I told him I hadn't read Aristotle – although I had – and I thought, 'Good God!'

"I felt terribly lonely in American academic society. The first time in my life I was in a university building was in Princeton (in 1953). They were so busy! It was like a monastery."

"Aren't monasteries quiet contemplative places?" I said.

"No, no," said Pritchett. "Very busy. These academics were at prayer constantly – one praying about 'The Esthetics of Conrad,' another doing 'The Rhythms of Proust'. But the students at Berkeley were very enjoyable, and at Smith I had only one class. I had a lot of leisure, and I got over my initial loneliness by writing. I started my autobiography while I was at Smith."

"Americans are so gregarious," he said a moment later. "In and out of each others' houses. They say the English are reserved. I don't think we are reserved, but we value our privacy. Americans are remorseless. They invite you to a party. You can't say, 'I've got a splitting headache' – they'll send the doctor around."

So, in spite of his travels to Spain and South America, New York and Ireland – all of which he has written about – Pritchett has always returned to London, moving from the dim precincts south of the river to Regent's Park, where he now lives. His work is there, his books, his sources of inspiration. And just as he had earlier written a masterful essay about Balzac and returned to write a biography of him, he did the same with Turgenev. The essay on Turgenev's *Rudin* is in *In My Good Books* (1942), the biography is just appearing.

"I would like to have done Chekhov," he said. "But he's been done well, and anyway there is no life you can seize. It's all in his writing. As a biographical subject he's rather shallow. With Turgenev I was on firmer ground – there has been no definitive biography. And Turgenev is an attractive figure – he was the first to introduce the Russians to Europe or America. At the time, they saw him as the perfect gentleman – he lived on an estate and shot birds. He had a rapport with English literature. And he had a curious position in Russian society. His situation vis-à-vis the Russian problems was similar to our own upper middle class to reform. He is now in-date as opposed to out-of-date. We are dealing with the kind of revolutionaries he knew – that was his situation. When the Russian craze began in England in 1900 all they cared about was the Russian soul, but Turgenev has entirely come back to us as a man of the moment."

I asked whether he felt any identification with his biographical subject.

"I feel strongly on the side of his detachment. He was cultivated and greatly influenced by literature. He was much more civilized than Tolstoy, for example, and probably the most westernized Russian writer."

The restaurant had emptied. It was time to go. I chanced a question about Orwell. Pritchett said, "Orwell had an ecstatic side. If he was in this room he'd come over and sit down, order a lot of brandy, start out by being mildly insulting to us and then he'd get terribly friendly."

On went the overcoat, the Russian hat, and we walked down Charlotte Street. Fifty years earlier Pritchett had a room on this street, over a tailor shop. He was writing then, he is writing today – three reviews to do, a story he has worked on for several months, some traveling to plan. He continued chatting all the way to the corner, about the country ("Wiltshire's full of delinquent peers"), his knighthood ("I have no power, no influence. I'm the freak there, I tell them they're all right"), and just before we parted I mentioned that I might be off to South America soon. "Try the Dutch parts of Brazil, Peru is wonderful, and Ecuador – well, Ecuador is nice in its tiny way."

"A man my age is a social problem," Sir Victor Pritchett said three years later, and then he laughed. He has a rich, resonant pipe-smoker's laugh, and the lively curiosity of a man who has traveled in fifty countries. He had rambled in and written about both New York City and the hinterland of peckerwood Tennessee – in fact, he has just returned to Tennessee, to lecture at Vanderbilt. He is small, soft-spoken and sees everything.

He is not indifferent to his achievement, but neither is he vain. Vanity is the egotism of the idle, the self-regarding, the lingerer at mirrors. But Pritchett says in baffled tones, "One of the great surprises to me – and I mean this – is that people think I am eminent. Is it that everyone else has died, and I am the last one left?"

His bafflement has something to do with the fact that he associates eminence with leisure – the pontificating oldster in a country house, making trenchant or scandalous remarks, boasting about his impotence and – deaf to any reply – dropping off to sleep by the fireside, while a whole seminar of Guggenheim Fellows genuflect in his study and fish card indexes out of their phylacteries. Pritchett has no leisure. He works alone. He gives flatterers and foot-in-the-door biographers the kindly inattention he extends to Jehovah's Witnesses. "I am one of the non-striking self-employed," he says.

In 1980, he wrote, "Today I still go fast up the four flights of steep stairs to my study in our tall late-Nash house, every day of the week, at nine o'clock in the morning, Saturdays and Sundays included, cursing the Inland Revenue and inflation, groaning at the work I have to do, crying out dishonestly for leisure . . . complaining that surely at my age I should be able to get some time off." But he was smiling when he wrote that. He has no wish to move ("Moving would betray our furniture and new drafts often kill old men") and he is delighted that, at his age, he still has work to do. He believes himself to be a very lucky man.

Luck shines in his face like good health. The first time I met him he seemed to me like an English country doctor, the sort of man who rides a bike and eschews antibiotics, who smiles if you claim you have 'flu and orders you outside for some fresh air. Was it his healthy complexion and his talk of having spent time in really pestilential places? More likely it was his handwriting. It is certainly a medical man's script. It looks like Sanskrit, and one of the few persons who can read it is Dorothy Pritchett, who types everything he writes (usually four or five times: he is a perfectionist) and who is the complete writer's wife – lover, amanuensis and boon companion.

Now I have come to see Sir Victor as the magician that all great writers are. It is not such an extravagant idea – Thomas Mann's family called him a magician, and he signed his letters to them with a "Z" – *Zauberer*. The magician conjures wonders out of thin air and makes you believe in him. You try to repeat the trick privately, and fail. Sir Victor's writing has enchanted millions of people, and his stories go on being reprinted. He is not only the finest living short-story writer, but the greatest literary critic of our day. He has been at it a long time. Decades ago, he gave Graham Greene his first good review, and Greene felt, with Pritchett's praise, that he was at last a writer.

Pritchett denies his magic quality, but he is emphatic about his luck. His mother was a Cockney, his father a salesman from Yorkshire – neither was educated. But Pritchett says that it was his good luck to have grown up among "non-intellectual people, all in trades" and "better luck to have a vocation fixed in my mind – so few boys have . . . Good luck to escape, by going abroad, the perpetual British 'no' to the new boy; good luck to meet the American 'yes' to my first bits of writing. France, Ireland, Spain were my first universities. I grew up in the time of great British power and influence. The French were Frogs, the Spanish something else. The dominant feeling was British. But by being uneducated I did not have this conceit. I recognized the cultures and inherited differences."

But how does a man begin to write, and live by writing alone, and earn the accolade of a knighthood? Pritchett is somewhat self-mocking about his knighthood, but he is definite about his first yearnings to write: he conceived the ambition at the age of ten, when he was a schoolboy in south London. And his grandfather was an influence. "My grandfather started as a bricklayer, but later went to a theological college. I was impressed with his air of learning. I felt a sort of kinship with him – books and words. And he impressed me because he had been poor as a boy. Learning mattered to me. I was well-taught at school and I thought, 'Why shouldn't I be Tennyson or Scott?' But that was vanity! And I was always plagued by doubts. It takes a long time to discover one's ability. Until I was twenty-five I had no certainty that I could make it as a writer."

France liberated him and taught him. "I found I could speak French well. I was an accent snob! I was passionately interested in language – language is not only useful, but enchanting. And it's awfully good to get away from one's family."

He was now able to tackle any French book. He read omnivorously, and he began to write stories and sketches. His writer's sensibilities were bound up with an urgency to discover the differences in places. He went to Spain, learned Spanish and studied the work of Pio Baroja, a writer he feels has deeply influenced his style. In time, he was writing the lead fiction review – a weekly essay – to finance the writing of his short stories. It was not easy. During the Second World War, when very few new books were being published, he concentrated on French, British and Russian classics and reminded his readers that literature had prevailed over other wars. Those essays are masterpieces, but Pritchett explains, "If you're seriously interested in writing fiction, you take too much time over your criticism."

But how else was he to proceed? "I got five pounds for most stories – I remember I got three pounds for 'The Sailor'. I had to write many reviews to be able to go on writing stories. The novel is discursive and ruminative – it takes time. The form of a story is like the form of a ballad. I'm still fond of some of my early stories – 'When My Girl Comes Home' – I wish I could write like that now. I think it's rather well-done."

We were in his house, talking, as the twilight faded and turned the large lovely windows into mirrors. Suddenly Pritchett laughed. "I ought to have written a best-seller," he said. "That's the maddening thing! I may write a play – I've always wanted to. I was raking leaves yesterday, and I thought, 'When I finish raking these leaves and burn them, I'll start writing again.' "

I wondered if, at the age of eighty, he looked back and saw himself taking any other path; or was writing truly inevitable from the age of ten? His answer was surprising. "I might have been a painter," he said. "I have a small talent. I love pictures. In a daydream, I see myself at an easel and thinking, 'I could be Pissaro' – that would be satisfying." He leaned forward and laughed again. Not everyone in Britain is as fulfilled and fully employed as Sir Victor Pritchett; there are two and a quarter million people out of work, and all the talk is of retraining people for new jobs. Pritchett said, "Perhaps Mrs Thatcher would retrain me in an art school!"

Sir Victor Pritchett has been writing short stories for almost sixty years. Each of his books displays vitality, humor, and tremendous imaginative strength. He has a gift for the unexpected word or phrase. His writing is both passionate and serene. There is no hatred in it at all. Can that be said of any other writers today? The short story, Pritchett has said, "is the glancing form of fiction that seems to be right for the nervousness and restlessness of contemporary life." And in his Introduction to *The Oxford Book of Short Stories* (1981) he describes the form in a wonderful way: "The novel tends to tell us everything whereas the short story tells us only one thing, and that, intensely." Pritchett's literary achievement is enormous, but his short stories are his greatest triumph. And one can say with perfect confidence that there is nothing like them in the language, because every short story writer of brilliance makes the form his own.

The astonishing thing about his *Collected Stories* is that although it is twice the size of his *Selected Stories* (1978), it is still incomplete. These thirty magnificent stories are only part of Pritchett's output. For example, five from his most recent collection *On the Edge of the Cliff* (1979) were omitted; and five from *Blind Love* (1969) were also left out. So *Collected Stories* does not include "The Spanish Bed", "The Vice-Consul", "The Honeymoon", or "The Chainsmoker". Going back even farther, two of the stories in which Noisy Brackett figures are not here – though "The Key to My Heart" is. There are a dozen more that could have been included. The point is that Pritchett has left out as many stories as he has collected – presumably for reasons of space. It is a pity he didn't have room for them all, but it is excellent to have the expectation of a further volume.

What we have here is masterful. They seem to have no echoes or influences; they are whole, bright moods – never false-sounding, never mannered – always fresh. Anyone of intelligence can spot Chekhov's luminous shadow here, but it is not a configuration of style or language; it is a quality of wisdom compounded of clearsightedness, impartiality, gentleness, an absence of malice and real love.

There are of course certain conventions in the form, but as I said earlier the greatest practitioners invented their own kind of short story. Kipling did so in *Plain Tales from the Hills*, and Joyce in *Dubliners*, and James, Hemingway, Faulkner and Katherine Mansfield in collections which proclaimed the uniqueness of their vision. This necessity for each writer to reinvent the form is as evident in Saki's *The Chronicles of Clovis* as it is in M. R. James's *Ghost Stories of an Antiquary* or Borges's *Ficciones*.

It is also true of Pritchett's stories, which could not possibly be anyone else's. Typically, the Pritchett story is unhurried and somewhat rural; and there is a salesman or a cyclist or someone a little cabin crazy – a sharp-tongued spinster; nearly always, someone is distinctly out of his element, in love, or moving house, or stuck with strangers. The Pritchett story is full of interesting weather and sweet smells; and everyone has a different face. Here is Mrs Coram in "Handsome Is As Handsome Does":

> . . . She was a short, thin woman, ugly yet attractive. Her hair was going grey, her face was clay-coloured, her nose was big and long, and she had long yellowish eyes. In this beach suit she looked rat-like, with that peculiar busyness, inquisitiveness, intelligence, and even charm of rats. People . . . were startled by her ugly face and her shabbiness, but they liked her lazy voice, and her quick mind, her graceful good manners, the look of experience and good sense in her eyes.

The description is full of paradox, but so is the story, which is one of Pritchett's most powerful ones, a drama of opposites. Pritchett never lapses into stereotypes. He always scruples to differentiate between characters, and shows us what individuality means. This is not merely a literary exercise or a skillful use of language: it is a belief in human variation. Pritchett is among other things a great appreciator.

He is able to tell a great deal about someone in one sentence, as in the story "The Saint" – a serious comedy about a religion somewhat like Christian Science – where the visiting preacher Mr Timberlake is summed up: "He had a pink square head with very small ears and one of those torpid, enameled smiles which were said by our enemies to be too common in our sect." Or another perfect sentence from an almost surrealistic story, "The Fall": "Peacock felt a smile coming over his body from the feet upwards."

"He had been a bland little dark-haired pastry-fed fellow from the North," begins another portrait in "A Debt of Honour". "He was a printer but had given that up, a man full of spit when he talked and his black eyebrows going up like a pair of swallows." These are never random descriptions, word-floods through which a face appears in the turbulence. They are lightly done and so enjoyable – making the reader's task so effortless – that it is not until the story is over that one realizes that the spell has been cast, a face has been glimpsed, a friend made. There is no moralizing, there are few symbols: these people are flesh and blood. The stories do not demand to be studied, they offer themselves as pleasures and they are absolutely unforgettable.

Pritchett himself has outlined the difficulties facing the short story writer. He has done so with fine intelligence. In fact, I cannot think of another writer, aside from Henry James, who both writes short stories, and writes about them, with equal brilliance. The novelist is expected to be discursive, Pritchett says, and he can sustain his narrative in this sprawling fashion, but "the writer of short stories has to catch our attention at once not only by the novelty of his people and scene but by the distinctiveness of his voice, and to hold us by the ingenuity of his design."

It doesn't sound particularly difficult, does it? But in practice these are hard requirements. The best illustrations of them, of course, are in Pritchett's own openings. The first paragraph of the chirpy antique dealer in "The Camberwell Beauty" is superb but too long to quote. Here is the opening of "Sense of Humor":

> It started one Saturday. I was working new ground and I decided I'd stay at the hotel the weekend and put in an appearance at church.
>
> "All alone?" asked the girl at the cash desk.
>
> It had been raining since ten o'clock.
>
> "Mr Good has gone," she said. "And Mr Straker. He usually stays with us but he's gone."
>
> "That's where they make their mistake," I said. "They think they know everything because they've been on the road all their lives."
>
> "You're a stranger here, aren't you?" she said.
>
> "I am," I said. "And so are you."
>
> "How do you know that?"
>
> "Obvious," I said. "Way you speak."
>
> "Let's have a light," she said.
>
> "So's I can see you," I said.
>
> That was how it started. The rain was pouring down on the glass roof of the office.

As a reader and critic, Pritchett is the most open-minded of men; this same attitude characterizes his writing – it is not complacency but compassion. The attitude is as rare today as his kind of prose – the light touch, the suggestion of sparkle, the underlying seriousness. Reading these stories, I began to think how profitable it would be for any aspiring writer to look closely at them. I wish someone had put a Pritchett story in my hand twenty years ago to remind me that you have to be a whole person and tell the truth to write well; and you have to read everything and experience love and enjoy some happiness, for your stories to be as full of life as Pritchett's.

The Past Recaptured

[1980]

Memory often simplifies past events: the mind can be merciful. There is probably no greater burden than a capacity for total recall, but few of us are burdened this way. We tend to be content with fragments of the past – the anecdote highly polished in retelling, the once-painful vision given the soft focus (if not complete revision) of tranquil recollection – and we may smile when we are corrected and reminded that we have been betrayed by memory. It is certainly easier to reflect on experience as a monochrome or something prettified and made manageable by repetition. We might deliberately seek to uncover a complex image in our memory and find that time has turned it into a piffling snapshot. All we can do, if so much has been lost to us – so much discarded or altered – is turn our back on the past and flee it, setting our face at the abstraction of a dimly-perceived future. So we are spared reality.

History can seem as simple as our personal past, and the memory's mechanism for simplifying can mislead us into believing history to be no more than anonymous leaders and featureless emblems, and historical change having something to do with the algebra of dates or the inevitability of armies. We think of armies and we see ants. Even portraiture has been simplified into shapes, rather than the particularities in faces and clothes. Stalin is a fierce mustache and Lincoln a kindly beard and the Tsaritsa's face is squeezed between diamonds; the peasant is barefoot, the African is naked. The war-bonnet, the pigtail, the soldier wrapped in bandoliers – emblems. We may read biographies and histories and trek through museums, and still be convinced that "human history" is a bloodless phrase for an unreadable epoch.

We are left, then, with the anonymity of history – the faceless soldiers in the ant-like armies, the nameless shapes tilling the land, the politicians and millionaires distorted in glorifying busts or memoirs. Compressed and robbed of subtlety, those who acted out the past are seen illustrating the most basic emotions – fear, triumph, hope, or greed – and nothing as fragile as fatigue, boredom or compassion. Ultimately, because the past seems ungraspable, we may cease to care. Pornography is like this. It may suggest an emotion, but it cannot engage us for long, because it does not inspire anything like thought or feeling. The paradox of pornography is not only that it is unfeeling but often unphysical, an abstraction of emblems exhibiting anonymous pleasure. It gives us nothing but a reminder of our own solitude.

Photography did not kill painting ("From now on, painting is dead," the early photographers declared), but it caused its derangement into abstraction and – what seems much worse – made us unsure of realism. It made us regard realism as inartistic. What we have seen lately is photography hurrying to compete with painting's abstraction, mimicking its postures and geometry. Many painters have succeeded in conveying a sense of power with color and line, even randomly – indeed, painting has never been able to be realistic in a photographic way. But photographers, huffing and puffing after painterly effects – I am thinking of the cubism of the New York photographer or the mess his European counterpart makes of photographic impressionism or the Japanese passion for dead branches – nearly always fail. Why should the exact science of optics be turned into an instrument for examining merely a blank wall, or a girder's rivets, or a banana? The pity of it is that almost since its inception photography has been able to give history a human face by supplying us with a crystal image.

The eye is selective, the camera lens is not; which is why photography, when it is masterful, is both an art and a science, the triumph of technology creating a luminous and symmetrical artifact. And it seems to me (though not to everyone) that what photography does best, when successful, is suggest imagination by dealing with the actual. Its subtlety is its exactitude, for in photography light is everything, and in light is its capacity for utter clarity. It is not necessary for the photographer to hedge or deal in shadows or to fudge a plain image in an attempt at poetry. Because we know how untruthful a photograph can be, the photographer's integrity is crucial (and I may say that the famous picture of the flag-raising at Iwo-Jima has always struck me as something of a phoney, a sop to jingoism – it did not surprise me to learn that it was posed). Nothing is more bogus-looking than a bogus photograph; we might linger over a mediocre painting, but no one pauses more than a few seconds after summing up a photograph as faked.

Of course, a photographer may take liberties. When Julia Margaret Cameron did her portrait of Herschel, she rumpled his crown of white hair beforehand to make him seem Jovian and astronomer-like. But her greatest photographs are those in which she practised the keenest fidelity to her subject. It was not for nothing that Tennyson called the portrait she did of him, "The Dirty Monk," but there does not exist a painting of the poet which has the smell and feel of that photograph, the grubby cape, the unkempt hair, the ragged beard. It does not diminish the poetry – on the contrary, we begin to see that Tennyson's orotund verse was written by a hand with a human smell.

We have become accustomed to photographs of photographs, pictures of pictures, overlaid with dust and dead air. In the reprinting they have become coarsened and blurred, coarsening our own vision. Technically, it is often impossible to make photographs from original negatives, and the crystal image clouds in successive reproduction. We have even made the mistake of thinking of early photography as imperfect, slightly astigmatic, a primitive craft improved and modernized only recently. This is more than merely unfair – it belittles the skill of the nineteenth century photographers and, in consequence, does violence to our idea of history.

It ought to have been apparent to us in reviewing the history of the past century that we were dealing with men and not gods, with dead soldiers and not casualty statistics. But to a large degree, we were cheated, given a foreground, or a full face, and denied the background, the periphery, the detail that tells more than the man at the focal point. "Focal point" itself is meaningless here, since the large plate-camera and the long exposure allowed everything within its frame to be picked out. And it is details, particularities, that shock us, touch us, make us laugh, invite us to look closer – or, at any rate, make us understand what in the world we have lost.

I think we may have been in danger of forgetting how clear a photograph can be or how much paraphernalia it can contain. The picture of Booker T. Washington at Tuskegee is a fine family portrait – four faces with a lively intensity of gaze, but notice the wooden steps in the picture. We know at a glance they have been swept, that someone has climbed them and tracked dust on them; that they will be swept again. The dust is palpable. The Chinese and Japanese photographs are chiefly remarkable for the way they let us see the weave in the cloth – velvet and silk in the case of the noblewomen, rough wool or thin cotton loosely draping the servants. The noblemen do not always look healthy or contented. In other portraits we have our share of statesmen and rulers with unreliable-looking expressions or wild staring eyes, or the symptoms of illness. The panoply, the diamonds and costumes are never anything but grand – and yet see: Those are very human animals who, until now, we have regarded as larger than life. Queen Victoria is pint-sized and pouting, and as she sits it seems that her feet do not reach to the ground.

In the schoolroom and factory and in the long dark line of coalminers waiting to be paid, the faces stare out helplessly, trapped by circumstances, and we feel judged, because we have never been gazed at in quite that way, so immediately, across time. Moments before many of these pictures were taken, the last words spoken were "Hold still!" We can see the effect of that command in the small boy's shoulders or the man's grip on the chairback. Everyone here is holding his breath, as if for a hundred-year leap to the present. And you want to weep after seeing some of these faces, or the conditions that are so obviously suffered. We have seen bare feet before – bare feet, as I said earlier, are the cliché emblem of the peasant. But look at the Russian peasants and much more than that is revealed, for we can almost be indifferent to bare feet, but cannot but be moved by those feet in the mud of a wet mushy road. They are deeply physical, and this is the beginning of understanding, for they not only arouse simple concern, but compassion as well. We know, from this perspective, what happened to these people, why they revolted, how they fought or submitted, and how they died.

Photographic archives are full of pictures of beheadings. They were as sought-after and widely-prized as movies or stills of modern executions. When a prisoner is electrocuted or shot today the first frantic rapping on the door of the execution chamber is sure to be that of photographers or men with TV cameras. I have seen a number of photographs taken in the last century, usually in China, of beheadings. Invariably the sword is shown poised over the neck (sometimes the head has been struck off and it lies severed on the ground).

But this beheading in China is electrifying. We see more than the sword and the head. The man has been hit with the blade several times, and the executioner is tensed to take another stroke. The condemned man, clearly bleeding – that is blood, not hair, coursing from his twisted face – is a goner. But look at the faces of the men who are holding his ropes and supporting his gibbet. This is hardly the routine event we have been taught took place in Imperial China. These men are as close as we are (and we are seeing something the witnesses in the background are missing) and they wear expressions of terror and disbelief. The whole affair is as shocking to them as it is – one hopes – to us. This is the opposite of anonymity, and after the experience of this photograph one cannot think of such an execution as something taken for granted, a ritual which we can regard as conventional and commonplace. It is almost cathartic, for those wincing men are expressing our own shock.

Some of these photographs are fixed in time – the Panama Canal, Mark Twain at his billiard table, George Bernard Shaw hugely enjoying a cruise – but others are much older than their dates suggest. They give us access to the past. The Ainus, the Bedouin, the Irish peat-carriers, the Wa-Kikuyu and American Indians – these might have been taken in the 'eighties or 'nineties of the last century, or even more recently, but we may be assured that for the preceding century, and perhaps for many centuries before, the people looked exactly like this. Our glimpse is not of people caught on a given year, but of an image carried away from a much remoter past, and a few decades before they were to change out of all recognition. And the photographic method, the revealing glass negative and the bulky efficient camera let us see something of their surroundings, too, the hut, the foliage, the pioneer woman in the poke bonnet, the whole of the Grand Canyon.

The art in some of these photographs is indisputable, and this is appropriate, because by the time we turn the last page we believe we have recaptured the past, and in a distinctly Proustian way. In Proust's masterpiece, photographs are repeatedly used to verify an event or nail down a memory. Proust mentions stereoscopes as well, in speaking of how a passionate memory can be re-examined clearly much later, "as though one had placed it behind the glasses of a stereoscope."

That perception occurs in *The Guermantes Way*. A bit later in that same volume, and in one of his most powerful pieces of hyperbole, Proust speaks of kissing Albertine. This embrace takes several lushly written pages. The kiss is practically incomparable, but he risks one comparison. A kiss evokes so many things in such a new dimension, he says, that there is almost nothing to liken it to, "apart from the most recent applications of the art of photography". Photography like a kiss: it is a pretty conceit.

Railways of the Raj

[1980]

The Raj had no shortage of symbols, but the railway was the greatest of them (even today that spinninng wheel on India's flag could be the wheel of a locomotive and mean as much). It was the imperial vision on a grand scale; it tested the ideas and inventions of engineers. India was the proving ground for the Victorian imagination: the railway builders sewed together the entire subcontinent with a stitching of track.

It was self-serving, of course; it was, from the beginning, a commercial enterprise, and after the Mutiny the railway with its fortified stations and tunnels was part of the military might of the Raj – the long march and the relief column were supplanted by the troop train. But it had a humane side. It was not, as in East Africa, only an expedient for moving minerals and farm produce to market. The railway was the blood-stream of the Raj, and it affected nearly everyone. It linked the centers of population; and the cities, which until then had been identified with their temples and forts, became identified with their railway stations, Howrah with Calcutta, Victoria with Bombay, Egmore and Madras Central with Madras. It involved millions of people, it required immense paperwork, the clipboard, the manifests in triplicate, the endless chain-of-command from Director to Sweeper – so it suited the complexity of Indian life, and it was an institution of limitless subtlety. Aesthetically, it was pleasing.

Very quickly, the railway became part of Indian legend and a source of romance. Here is an opening paragraph from one of the greatest tales of the Raj:

> The beginning of everything was in a railway train upon the road to Mhow from Ajmir. There had been a deficit in the Budget, which necessitated travelling, not Second-class, which is only half as dear as First-class, but by Intermediate, which is very awful indeed. There are no cushions in the Intermediate class, and the population are either Intermediate, which is Eurasian, or native, which for a long night journey is nasty, or Loafer, which is amusing though intoxicated. Intermediates do not patronize refreshment-rooms. They carry their food in bundles and pots, and buy sweets from the native sweetmeat-

sellers, and drink the roadside water. That is why in the hot weather Intermediates are taken out of the carriages dead, and in all weathers are most properly looked down upon.

This is vintage Kipling, in *The Man Who Would Be King*, and it is interesting not merely because it describes the conditions in which the narrator is about to meet two men who will conquer Kafiristan, but because its seedy effects were patiently collected by the author a year before on the railway, in the Rajput states of the Indian desert. And when it was printed in 1888, it appeared as the fifth volume in Wheeler's Railway Series. These pamphlet-sized books with line drawings on their covers were sold at railway bookstalls all over the Raj. This adventure story, researched on a railway, describing a fateful railway journey, and sold on railway platforms, helped to make Kipling's reputation and create the first Kipling boom. Where, one wonders, would Kipling have been without the train?

Eight years after Rudyard Kipling toured the dusty provinces with his notebook on his lap, avowedly in search of material for stories for *The Week's News* and the *Pioneer Mail*, another traveler boarded the Raj railways and, characteristically, introduced a note of comedy. This was Sam Clemens, looking for something to fill Mark Twain's cracker barrel. He had had a success with *Innocents Abroad* and *Roughing It*; he was between books, and he needed money to go on financing the development of the type-setting machine which very nearly bankrupted him. He had also started a publishing company. He needed a selling title. His idea was to circle the globe, giving lectures on the way, and to write a book about it. The book became *Following the Equator*, a bright sprawling travelogue of Hawaii, South Africa, Australia, Ceylon and India. It is very funny, casually learned, and extremely intrepid. It is hard to say why this book has never been reissued. But there is nothing in it for the English Department, no fodder for the graduate student; perhaps that is the reason.

In *A Little Town in India* (1913), R. Palmer reported: "Every train (except mails) stops at every station a quarter of an hour for purposes of gossip, and at all large stations half an hour or an hour." Sam Clemens, on various branch lines from Calcutta to Lucknow, wrote about this peculiarly neighborly use of the railway, but typically he was more expansive:

This train stopped at every village; for no purpose connected with business apparently. We put out nothing, we took nothing aboard. The train hands stepped ashore and gossiped with friends a quarter of an hour, then pulled out and repeated this at succeeding villages. We had thirty-five miles to go and six hours to do it in, but it was plain that we were not going to make it. It was then that the English officers said it was now necessary to turn this gravel train into an express. So they gave the engine driver a rupee and told him to fly. It was a simple remedy. After that we made ninety miles an hour.

Clemens was full of praise for Indian railways, and he was impressed by the fact that they were exclusively manned by Indians of an especially solicitous nature. One day, on his way to Allahabad, he got down at a platform and was so transfixed by the whirl of activity on the platform ("that perennially ravishing show") he did not notice the train starting. But an Indian with a green flag in his hand saw him about to sit down to wait for another train; he approached the American.

"Don't you belong in the train, sir?"
"Yes," I said.
He waved his flag and the train came back! And he put me aboard with as much ceremony as if I had been the General Superintendent.

Nothing escaped Mr Clemens' notice as he travelled throughout India on the trains, and it was clear to him that the Indians had made the railways their own. They had a knack for inhabiting the stations, washing and sleeping on the platforms, cooking near the shunting engines, arriving days early for a journey and setting up camp in the booking hall. He devotes pages to the crowds and he describes how Hindu caste and railway class produce excruciating ironies: "Yes, a Brahmin who didn't own a rupee and couldn't borrow one, might have to touch elbows with a rich hereditary lord of inferior caste, inheritor of an ancient title a couple of yards long, and he would just have to stand for it; for if either of the two was allowed to go in the cars where the sacred white people were, it probably wouldn't be the august poor Brahmin." As for the carriages, "No car in any country is quite its equal for comfort (and privacy) I think." Best of all, he said, the most notable feature on the railways of the Raj was their cosiness.

Once they were established, the railways of India blended with the country; they seemed as ancient and everlasting, and the stations as grand and as foolish-seeming and marvelously vain, as any maharajah's palace. In South America and in Africa, you look at the railway and see how it has been imposed on the landscape: it sticks out, it doesn't belong, it is a rusty, linear interruption of snoozing greenery, and where are the passengers?

But in India the railway seems to have grown out of the culture, accommodating everyone and everything. There were no obstacles that were not surmounted – the widest river was bridged, the steepest mountainside climbed, the harshest desert crossed. The railway possessed India and made her hugeness graspable. Now, any Bengali with the fare could make his *yatra* from Calcutta to the Kali shrine in distant Simla, the pilgrim could visit the remote and holy hamlet of Rameswaram. The trader could trade, the salesman could sell, and workers on the railway soon numbered in the millions. Indians were no longer marooned by work: they could go home.

There is a seclusion about railway carriages. For an English civil servant who suffered an intense conspicuousness in his post, this seclusion was a relief. We have the word of George Orwell on this. In an unlikely place for such a reminiscence, *The Road to Wigan Pier*, he says,

> I remember a night I spent on the train with a man in the Educational Service, a stranger to myself whose name I never discovered. It was too hot to sleep and we spent the night in talking. Half an hour's cautious questioning decided each of us that the other was 'safe'; and then for hours, while the train jolted slowly through the pitch-black night, sitting up in our bunks with bottles of beer handy, we damned the British Empire – damned it from the inside, intelligently and intimately. It did us both good. But we had been speaking forbidden things, and in the haggard morning light when the train crawled into Mandalay, we parted as guiltily as any adulterous couple.

It is hard to imagine this episode taking place anywhere but in a railway carriage. It is ironic, though, too. Orwell (who was a policeman at the time) and the stranger did not realize that if it had not been for the Empire they would not have had the safe solitude of the railway in which to damn it.

The railway had few detractors, and it has endured – not as a feeble relic, but as a vital institution. Indeed, it has grown. India is still building locomotives and coaches, and extending the lines.

Today, the flavor of the Raj is less in the rolling-stock than in the timetables, with their complex rules and prohibitions and their curious locutions. Under its twenty-one "Rules for Passengers," Pakistan Western Railway includes "Awakening Passengers at Night," "Ladies Travelling Alone at Night," "Servants' Tickets" and "Servants in sole charge of children." *Notes for the Guidance of Public* describes in detail the uniforms of the catering staff ("Refreshment-room contractors: Plain white chapkan and white pyjamas, with green kamarband, 4 inches wide, green turban band 2 inches wide and badges" – and so on, six uniforms). There are pages of "Catering Arrangements" in today's Indian Railway timetable, and these too have that formal exhaustiveness one associates with the Raj, together with some of the Victorian phraseology: "On prior intimation Chota hazari and evening tiffin will be served in trains at stations where Vegetarian Refreshment Rooms are working . . ."

In an important sense, the railways of the Raj still exist. The great viaduct still spans the Gokteik Gorge in Upper Burma, Victoria Terminus has not been pulled down to make room for a dual-carriageway, the train from Kalka is still the best way to Simla, and there are steam locomotives huffing and puffing all over India. This artifact of the past is carrying India into the future. I have had the luck to travel the subcontinent on these same rails. "With typical Victorian loyalty," Satow and Desmond remark, "streets were named according to the custom of the age: Church Road, King's Road, Queen's Road . . . Steam Road . . ." I was once in Lucknow and was talking idly with an Indian man. Where did he live? I asked. "Just down the road," he said, "in Railway Bazaar." I made a note of that, and I remember thinking what a marvelous title that would make for a travel book.

Subterranean Gothic

[1981]

New Yorkers say some terrible things about the subway – that they hate it, or are scared stiff of it, or that it deserves to go broke. For tourists it seems just another dangerous aspect of New York, though most don't know it exists. "I haven't been down there in years," is a common enough remark from a city dweller. Even people who ride it seem to agree that there is more Original Sin among subway passengers. And more desperation, too, making you think of choruses of "O dark dark dark. They all go into the dark . . ."

"Subway" is not its name, because strictly-speaking more than half of it is elevated. But which person who has ridden it lately is going to call it by its right name, "The Rapid Transit"? You can wait a long time for some trains and, as in the section of T. S. Eliot's "East Coker" I quoted above, often

> . . . an underground train, in the tube, stops too long between stations
> And the conversation rises and slowly fades into silence
> And you see behind every face the mental emptiness deepen
> Leaving only the growing terror of nothing to think about . . .

It is also frightful-looking. It has paint and signatures all over its aged face. People who don't take it, who never ride the subway and have no use for it, say that these junky pictures are folk-art, a protest against the metropolitan grayness, and what a wonderful sense of color these scribblers have – which is complete nonsense. The graffiti are bad, violent and destructive, and the people who praise them are either malicious or lazy-minded. The graffiti are so extensive and so dreadful it is hard to believe that the perpetrators are not the recipients of some enormous foundation grant. The subway has been vandalized from end to end. It smells so hideous you want to put a clothespin on your nose, and it is so noisy the sound actually hurts. Is it dangerous? Ask anyone and he will tell you there are about two murders a day on the subway. It really is the pits, people say.

You have to ride it for a while to find out what it is and who takes it and who gets killed on it.

It is full of surprises. Three and a half million fares a day pass through it, and in 1981 the total number of murder victims on the subway amounted to thirteen. This baker's dozen does not include suicides (one a week), "Man-Under" incidents (one a day), or "Space-Cases" – people who quite often get themselves jammed between the train and the platform. Certainly the subway is very ugly and extremely noisy, but it only *looks* like a death-trap. People ride it looking stunned and holding their breath. It's not at all like the BART system in San Francisco, where people are constantly chattering, saying, "I'm going to my father's wedding" or "I'm looking after my Mom's children" or "I've got a date with my fiancée's boyfriend." In New York, the subway is a serious matter – the racketty train, the silent passengers, the occasional scream.

We were at Flushing Avenue, on the GG line, talking about rules for riding the subway. You need rules: the subway is like a complex – and diseased – circulatory system. Some people liken it to a sewer and others hunch their shoulders and mutter about being in the bowels of the earth. It is full of suspicious-looking people.

I said, "Keep away from isolated cars, I suppose," and my friend, a police officer, said, "Never display jewelry."

Just then, a man walked by, and he had Chinese coins – the old ones with a hole through the middle – woven somehow into his hair. There were enough coins in that man's hair for a swell night out in old Shanghai, but robbing him would have involved scalping him. There was a woman at the station, too. She was clearly crazy, and she lived in the subway the way people live in railway stations in India, with stacks of dirty bags. The police in New York call such people "skells" and are seldom harsh with them. "Wolfman Jack" is a skell, living underground at Hoyt-Schermerhorn, also on the GG line; the police in that station give him food and clothes, and if you ask him how he is, he says, "I'm getting some calls." Call them colorful characters and they don't look so dangerous or pathetic.

This crazy old lady at Flushing Avenue was saying, "I'm a member of the medical profession." She had no teeth, and plastic bags were taped around her feet. I glanced at her and made sure she kept her distance. The previous day, a crazy old lady just like her, came at me and shrieked, "Ahm goon cut you up!" This was at Pelham Parkway, on the IRT-2 line in the Bronx. I left the car at the next stop, Bronx Park East, where the zoo is, though who could be blamed for thinking that, in New York City, the zoo is everywhere?

Then a Muslim unflapped his prayer mat – while we were at Flushing

Avenue, talking about Rules – and spread it on the platform and knelt on it, just like that, and was soon on all fours, beseeching Allah and praising the Prophet Mohammed. This is not remarkable. You see people praying, or reading the Bible, or selling religion on the subway all the time. "Hallelujah, brothers and sisters," the man with the leaflets says on the BMT-RR line at Prospect Avenue in Brooklyn. "I love Jesus! I used to be a wino!" And Muslims beg and push their green plastic cups at passengers, and try to sell them copies of something called *Arabic Religious Classics*. It is December and Brooklyn, and the men are dressed for the Great Nafud Desert, or Jiddah or Medina – skullcap, gallabieh, sandals.

"And don't sit next to the door," the second police officer said. We were still talking about Rules. "A lot of these snatchers like to play the doors."

The first officer said, "It's a good idea to keep near the conductor. He's got a telephone. So does the man in the token booth. At night, stick around the token booth until the train comes in."

"Although, token booths," the second officer said. "A few years ago, some kids filled a fire extinguisher with gasoline and pumped it into a token booth at Broad Channel. There were two ladies inside, but before they could get out the kids set the gas on fire. The booth just exploded like a bomb, and the ladies died. It was a revenge thing. One of the kids had gotten a summons for Theft of Service – not paying his fare."

Just below us, at Flushing Avenue, there was a stream running between the tracks. It gurgled and glugged down the whole length of the long platform. It gave the station the atmosphere of a sewer – dampness and a powerful smell. The water was flowing towards Myrtle and Willoughby. And there was a rat. It was only my third rat in a week of riding the subway, but this one was twice the size of rats I've seen elsewhere. I thought, *Rats as big as cats*.

"Stay with the crowds. Keep away from quiet stairways. The stairways at 41st and 43rd are usually quiet, but 42nd is always busy – that's the one to use."

So many rules! It's not like taking a subway at all; it's like walking through the woods – through dangerous jungle, rather: Do this, Don't do that . . .

"It reminds me," the first officer said. "The burning of that token booth at Broad Channel. Last May, six guys attempted to murder someone at Forest Parkway, on the 'J' line. It was a whole gang against this one guy. Then they tried to burn the station down with molotov cocktails. We stopped that, too."

The man who said this was six-feet four, two hundred and eighty-one pounds. He carried a .38 in a shoulder holster and wore a bullet-proof vest. He had a radio, a can of Mace and a blackjack. He was a plainclothesman.

The funny thing is that, one day, a boy – five feet six, one hundred and thirty-five pounds – tried to mug him. The boy slapped him across the face while the plainclothesman was seated on a train. The boy said, "Give me your money," and then threatened the man in a vulgar way. The boy still punched at the man when the man stood up; he still said, "Give me all your money!" The plainclothesman then took out his badge and his pistol and said, "I'm a police officer and you're under arrest." "I was just kidding!" the boy said, but it was too late.

I laughed at the thought of someone trying to mug this well-armed giant.

"Rule one for the subway," he said. "Want to know what it is?" He looked up and down the Flushing Avenue platform, at the old lady and the Muslim and the running water and the vandalized signs. "Rule one is – don't ride the subway if you don't have to."

A lot of people say that. I did not believe it when he said it, and after a week of riding the trains I still didn't. The subway is New York City's best hope. The streets are impossible, the highways are a failure, there is nowhere to park. The private automobile has no future in this city. This is plainest of all to the people who own and use cars in the city; they know, better than anyone, that the car is the last desperate old-fangled fling of a badly-planned transport system. What is amazing is that back in 1904 a group of businessmen solved New York's transport problems for centuries to come. What vision! What enterprise! What an engineering marvel they created in this underground railway! And how amazed they would be to see what it has become, how foul-seeming to the public mind.

The subway is a gift to any connoisseur of superlatives. It has the longest rides of any subway in the world, the biggest stations, the fastest trains, the most track, the most passengers, the most police officers. It also has the filthiest trains, the most bizarre graffiti, the noisiest wheels, the craziest passengers, the wildest crimes. Some New Yorkers have never set foot in the subway, other New Yorkers actually live there, moving from station to station, whining for money and eating yesterday's bagels and sleeping on benches. These "skells" are not merely down-and-out. Many are insane, chucked out of New York hospitals in the early 1970's when it was decided that long-term care was doing them little good. "They were resettled in rooms or hotels," Ruth Cohen, a psychiatric social-worker at Bellevue Hospital, told me. "But many of them can't follow through. They get lost, they wander the streets. They're not violent, suicidal or dangerous enough for Bellevue – this is an acute-care hospital. But these people who wander the subway, once they're on their own they begin to de-compensate –"

Ahm goon cut you up: that woman who threatened to slash me was decompensating. Here are a few more de-compensating – one is weeping on a wooden bench at Canal Street, another has wild hair and is spitting into a Coke can. One man who is de-compensating in a useful way, has a bundle of brooms and is setting forth to sweep the whole change area at Grand Central; another is scrubbing the stairs with scraps of paper at 14th Street. They drink, they scream, they gibber like monkeys. They sit on subway benches with their knees drawn up, just as they do in mental hospitals. A police officer told me, "There are more serious things than people screaming on trains." This is so, and yet the deranged person who sits next to you and begins howling at you seems at the time very serious indeed.

The subway, which is many things, is also a madhouse.

When people say the subway frightens them they are not being silly or irrational. The subway is frightening. It is no good saying how cheap or how fast it is, because it looks disgusting and it stinks. It is also very easy to get lost on the subway, and the person who is lost in New York City has a serious problem.

New Yorkers make it their business to avoid getting lost. It is the stranger who sees people hurrying into the stairwell: subway entrances are just dark holes in the sidewalk – the stations are below-ground. There is nearly always a bus-stop near the subway entrance. People waiting at a bus-stop have a special pitying gaze for people entering the subway. It is sometimes not pity, but fear, bewilderment, curiosity, or fatalism; often they look like miners' wives watching their menfolk going down the pit.

The stranger's sense of disorientation down below is immediate. The station is all tile and iron and dampness; it has bars and turnstiles and steel grates. It has the look of an old prison or a monkey cage. Buying a token the stranger may ask directions, but the token booth – reinforced, burglarproof, bulletproof – renders the reply incoherent. And subway directions are a special language.

"A-train . . . Downtown . . . Express to the Shuttle . . . Change at Ninety-sixth for the two . . . Uptown . . . The Lex . . . CC . . . LL . . . The Local . . ."

Most New Yorkers refer to the subway by the now obsolete forms "IND," "IRT," "BMT." No one intentionally tries to confuse the stranger; it is just that, where the subway is concerned, precise directions are very hard to convey.

Verbal directions are incomprehensible, written ones are defaced. The signboards and subway maps are indiscernible beneath layers of graffiti. That Andy Warhol, the stylish philistine, has said, "I love graffiti" is almost reason enough to hate them. One is warier still of Norman Mailer who naively encouraged this public scrawling in his book *The Faith of Graffiti*.

Graffiti are destructive; they are anti-art; they are an act of violence, and they can be deeply menacing. They have displaced the subway signs and maps, blacked-out the windows of the trains, and obliterated the instructions. *In case of emergency* – is cross-hatched with a felt-tip; *These seats are for the elderly and disabled* – a yard-long signature obscures it; *The subway tracks are very dangerous. If the train should stop, do not* – the rest is black and unreadable. The stranger cannot rely on printed instructions or warnings, and there are few cars out of the six thousand on the system in which the maps have not been torn out. Assuming the stranger has boarded the train, he can only feel panic when, searching for a clue to his route, he sees in the map-frame the message, *Guzmán – Ladrón, Maricón y Asesino*.

Panic: and so he gets off the train, and then his troubles really begin.

He may be in the South Bronx or the upper reaches of Broadway on the Number One line, or on any one of a dozen lines that traverse Brooklyn. He gets off the train, which is covered in graffiti, and steps onto a station platform which is covered in graffiti. It is possible (this is true of many stations) that none of the signs will be legible. Not only will the stranger not know where he is, but the stairways will be splotched and stinking – no *Uptown*, no *Downtown*, no *Exit*. It is also possible that not a single soul will be around, and the most dangerous stations – ask any police officer – are the emptiest. Of course, the passenger might just want to sit on a broken bench and, taking Mailer's word for it, contemplate the *macho* qualities of the graffiti; on the other hand, he is more likely to want to get the hell out of there.

This is the story that most people tell of subway fear – the predicament of having boarded the wrong train and gotten off at a distant station; of being on an empty platform, waiting for a train which shows no sign of coming. Then the vandalized station signs, the crazy semiliterate messages, the monkey scratches on the walls, the dampness, the neglect, the visible evidence of destruction and violence – they all combine to produce a sense of disgust and horror.

In every detail it is like a nightmare, complete with rats and mice and a tunnel and a low ceiling. It is manifest suffocation straight out of Poe. And some of these stations have long platforms – you have to squint to see what is at the far end. These distances intensify a person's fear, and so do all the pillars behind which any ghoul could be lurking. Is it any wonder that, having once strayed into this area of subterranean gothic, people decide that the subway is not for them?

But those who tell this story seldom have a crime to report. They have experienced shock, and fear, and have gone weak at the knees. It is completely understandable – what is worse than being trapped underground? – but it has been a private little horror. In most cases the person will have come to no harm. But he will remember his fear on that empty station for the rest of his life.

When New Yorkers recount an experience like this they are invariably speaking of something that happened on another line, not their usual route. Their own line is fairly safe, they'll say; it's cleaner than the others, it's got a little charm, it's kind of dependable, they've been taking it for years. Your line has crazy people on it, but my line has "characters." This sense of loyalty to a regularly-used line is the most remarkable thing about the subway passenger in New York. It is, in fact, a jungle attitude.

"New York is a jungle," the tourist says, and he believes he has made a withering criticism. But all very large cities are jungles, which is to say that they are dense and dark and full of surprises and strange growths; they are hard to read, hard to penetrate; strange people live in them; and they contain mazy areas of great danger. The jungle aspect of cities (and of New York City in particular) is the most interesting thing about them – the way people behave in this jungle, and adapt to it; the way they change it or are changed by it.

In any jungle, the pathway is a priority. People move around New York in various ways, but the complexities of the subway have allowed the New Yorker to think of his own route as something personal, even *original*. No one uses maps on the subway – you seldom see any. Most subway passengers were shown how to ride it by parents or friends. Then habit turns it into instinct, just like a trot down a jungle path. The passenger knows where he is going because he never diverges from his usual route. But that is also why, unless you are getting off at precisely his stop, he cannot tell you how to get where you're going.

The only other way of learning how to use the subway is by maps and charts – teaching yourself. This very hard work requires imagination and intelligence. It means navigating in four dimensions. No one can do it idly, and I doubt that many people take up subway riding in their middle years.

In general, people have a sense of pride in their personal route; they may be superstitious about it and even a bit secretive. Vaguely fearful of other routes, they may fantasize about them – these "dangerous" lines that run through unknown districts. This provokes them to assign a specific character to the other lines. The IRT is the oldest line; for some people it is dependable, with patches of elegance (those beaver mosaics at

Astor Place commemorating John Jacob Astor's fur business), and for
others it is dangerous and dirty. One person praises the IND, another
person damns it. "I've got a soft spot for the BMT," a woman told me,
but found it hard to explain why. "Take the 'A' train," I was told.
"That's the best one, like the song." But some of the worst stations are
on the (very long) 'A' line. The 'CC', 8th Avenue local, was described to
me as "scuzz" – disreputable – but this train, running from Bedford
Park Boulevard, The Bronx, via Manhattan and Brooklyn, to Rockaway
Park, Queens, covers a distance of 32.39 miles. The fact is that for some
of these miles it is pleasant and for others it is not. There is part of one
line that is indisputably bad; that is, the stretch of the '2' line (IRT) from
Nostrand to New Lots Avenue. It is dangerous and ugly and when you
get to New Lots Avenue you cannot imagine why you went. The police
call this line "The Beast."

But people in the know – the police, the Transit Authority, the people
who travel throughout the system – say that one line is pretty much like
another.

"Is this line bad?" I asked Robert Huber of the Transit Authority, and
pointed to the map in his office.

"The whole system is bad," he said. "From 1904 until just a few years
ago it went unnoticed. People took it for granted. In 1975, the first year
of the fiscal crisis, Mayor Beame ordered cutbacks. They started a
program of deferred maintenance – postponed servicing and just
attended to the most serious deficiencies. After four or five years of
deferred maintenance, the bottom fell out. In January-February, 1981,
twenty-five per cent of the trains were out of service, and things got
worse – soon a thirty minute trip was taking an hour and a half. No one
was putting any money into it. But of course they never had. It was
under-capitalized from the beginning. Now there is decay everywhere,
but there is also a real determination to reverse that trend and get it
going right."

No train is entirely good or bad, crime-ridden or crime-free. The
trains carry crime with them, picking it up in one area and bringing it to
another. They pass through a district and take on the characteristics of
that place. The South Bronx is regarded as a High Risk area, but seven
lines pass through it, taking vandals and thieves all over the system.
There is a species of vandalism that was once peculiar to the South
Bronx: boys would swing on the stanchions – those chrome poles in the
center of the car – and raising themselves sideways until they were
parallel with the floor they would kick hard against a window and burst
it. Now this South Bronx window-breaking technique is universal
throughout the system. Except for the people who have the misfortune
to travel on "The Beast" no one can claim that his train is much better

or worse than any other. This business about one line being dependable and another being charming and a third being dangerous is just jungle talk.

The whiff of criminality, the atmosphere of viciousness, is so strong in the stations and trains that it does little good to say that, relatively speaking, crime is not that serious on the subway. Of course, many crimes go unreported on the subway, but this is also true outside the transit system. In one precinct they might have seventy-seven murders in a year, which makes the thirteen on the subway in 1981 look mild by comparison. In the same year there were thirty-five rapes and rape attempts (an attempt is classified as rape), which again, while nothing to crow about, is not as bad as is widely believed ("I'll bet they have at least one rape a day," a girl told me, and for that reason she never took the subway). The majority of subway crime is theft – bag-snatching; this is followed by robbery – the robber using a gun or knife. There are about thirty-two robberies or snatches a day in the system, and one or two cases of aggravated assault a day. This takes care of all "Part I Offenses" – the serious ones.

It is the obvious vandalism on the subways that conveys the feeling of lawlessness. Indeed, the first perception of subway crime came with the appearance of widespread graffiti in 1970. It was then that passengers took fright and ridership, which had been declining slowly since the 'fifties, dropped rapidly. Passengers felt threatened, and newspapers gave prominence to subway crime. Although the 'CC' line is over thirty-two miles long a passenger will be alarmed to hear that a crime has been committed on it, because this is *his* line, and the proprietorial feeling of a rider for his line is as strong as a jungle dweller's for his regular path. Subway passengers are also very close physically to one another, but this is a city in which people are accustomed to quite a lot of space. On the subway you can hear the breathing of the person next to you – that is, when the train is at the station. The rest of the time it is impossible to hear anything except the thundering of the train, which is equally frightening.

"Violence underground attracts more coverage in the papers, but it is foolish to imagine the subway is some sort of death trap." This statement was not made by anyone in the New York Transit Authority, but by Nadine Joly, the twenty-eight-year-old head of the Special Paris Metro Security Squad. She was speaking about the Paris Metro, but her sentiments are quite similar to those of Edward Silberfarb of the Transit Authority Police.

"The interest in subway crime is much greater than in street crime," Mr Silberfarb said. "Crime actually went down six per cent in September, but the paper reversed the statistic and reported it as having gone up. Maybe they're looking for headlines."

The most frequent complaint of subway passengers is not about crime. It is, by a wide margin, about delayed trains and slow service. The second largest category of complaint is about the discourtesy of conductors or token-sellers; and the third concerns unclean stations. "Mainly the smell of urine – it's really horrible at some stations," said Mr Huber of the Transit Authority.

The perception of crime is widespread, and yet statistically the experience of it is quite small.

"But what do those statistics matter to someone who is in a car and a gang of six guys starts teasing and then threatening the passengers?" the New York lawyer Arthur S. Penn remarked to me. "Or that other familiar instance – you get into a car and there's one guy way down at the end sitting all by himself, and the rest of the people are crowded up this end of the car. You know from experience that the man who's sitting alone is crazy, and then, when the train pulls out, he starts screaming . . ."

Discomfort, anxiety, fear – these are the responses of most passengers. No wonder people complain that the trains are too slow: when one is fearful, every trip takes too long. In fact, these are among the fastest subway trains in the world. Stan Fischler, in his enthusiastic history of the system, *Uptown, Downtown* (1976), gives fifty-five mph as the top speed of an average express, such as the Harlem-Bronx 'D'. The train going by sounds as if it is full of coal, but when one is inside, it can feel like a trip on "The Wild Mouse."

People's fears can be at odds with reality. It is interesting that the two most famous movies with New York subway settings, *The Incident* (about a gang terrorizing a group of passengers on an express), and *The Taking of Pelham 1-2-3* (about the hijacking of an IRT train), are both preposterous. But as fantasies they give expression to widely-held fears of subway violence. (The famous chase in *The French Connection* starts at Bay 50th on the B-line and finishes deep in Bensonhurst on the West End line.)

Some people do get mugged – about twelve thousand a year. I asked a uniformed police officer what reaction he got upon entering a car. "A big sigh of relief," he said. "You can actually hear it. People smile at me. They're relieved! But the ones who are the most pleased to see me are the handicapped people and the old people. They're the ones who get mugged mostly."

That is the disgraceful part: the victims of subway crime are most often the old, the mentally retarded, the crippled, the blind, the weak. The majority of victims are women. Minorities comprise the next largest category of victim: a black person in a white area, an hispanic in a black area, a white in an hispanic area, and all the other grotesque permutations of race. Of course, the old and handicapped are also minorities, regarded as easy targets and defenseless. But cities can turn people into members of a minority group quite easily. What makes the New Yorker so instinctively wary is perhaps the thought that anyone who boards the wrong train, or gets off at the wrong stop, or walks one block too many, is capable of being in the minority.

The most-mugged man in New York must be the white-haired creaky-looking fellow in Bedford-Stuyvesant who has had as many as thirty mugging attempts made on him in a single year. And he still rides the subway trains. He's not as crazy as he looks: he's a cop in the Transit Police, a plainclothesman who works with the Mobile Task Force in the district designated "Brooklyn North." This man is frequently a decoy. In the weeks before Christmas he rode the "J" and the "GG" and the "2" lines looking like a pathetic Senior Citizen, with two gaily wrapped parcels in his shopping bag. He was repeatedly ambushed by unsuspecting muggers, and then he pulled out his badge and handcuffs and arrested his attackers.

Muggers are not always compliant. Then the Transit Police Officer unholsters his pistol, but not before jamming a colored headband over his head to alert any nearby uniformed officer. Before the advent of headbands many plainclothesmen were shot by their colleagues in uniform.

"And then we rush in," says Sergeant Donnery of the Mobile Task Force. "Ninety per cent of the guys out there can kick my ass, one on one. You've got to come on yelling and screaming. 'You so-and-so! You so-and-so! I'm going to kill you!' Unless the suspect is deranged and has a knife or something. In that case you might have to talk quietly. But if the guy's tough and you go in meek you get sized up very fast."

The Transit Police have three thousand officers and thirteen dogs. It is one of the biggest police forces in the United States and is separate altogether from the New York City Police, though the pay and training are exactly the same. It is so separate the men cannot speak to each other on their radios, which many Transit Police find inconvenient when chasing a suspect up the subway stairs into the street.

What about the dogs? "Dogs command respect," I was told at Transit Police Headquarters. "Think of them as a tool, like a gun or a nightstick. At the moment it's just a test program for high-crime stations, late night hours, that kind of thing."

I wondered aloud whether it would work, and the reply was, "A crime is unlikely to be committed anywhere near one of these dogs."

The Canine Squad, doing its part towards taking a bite out of crime, is housed with a branch of the Mobile Task Force at the underground junction of the LL and GG lines—Metropolitan Avenue. The bulletin board on the plainclothesmen's side is plastered with Unit Citations and Merit Awards, and Sgt Donnery of the Task Force was recently made "Cop of the Month" for a particularly courageous set of arrests. Sgt Donnery is in charge of thirty-two plainclothesmen and two detectives. Their motto is "Soar With the Eagles". A sheaf of admiring newspaper clippings testifies to their effectiveness. As we talked, the second shift was preparing to set out for the day.

"Morale seems very high," I said. The men were joking, watching the old-man decoy spraying his hair and beard white.

"Sure, morale is high," Sgt Donnery said. "We feel we're getting something accomplished. It isn't easy. Sometimes you have to hide in a porter's room with a mop for four days before you get your man. We dress up as porters, conductors, motormen, track-workers. The idea is to give the appearance of being workers. If there are a lot of robberies and track-workers in the same station we dress up as track-workers. We've got all the uniforms."

"Plainclothesmen" is something of a misnomer for the Task Force that has enough of a theatrical wardrobe to mount a production of *Subways Are For Sleeping*.

And yet, looking at Howard Haag and Joseph Minucci standing on the platform at Nassau Avenue on the GG line you would probably take them for a pair of physical education teachers on the way to the school gym. They look tough, but not aggressively so; they are healthy and well-built – but some of that is padding: they both wear bullet-proof vests. Underneath the ordinary clothes the men are well-armed. Each man carries a .38, a blackjack and a can of Mace. Minucci has a two-way radio.

Haag has been on the force for seventeen years, Minucci for almost seven. Neither has in that time ever fired his gun, though each has an excellent arrest-record and a pride in detection. They are funny, alert and indefatigable, and together they make most television cops look like hysterical cream-puffs. Their job is also much harder than any City cop's. I had been told repeatedly that the average City cop would refuse to work in the conditions that the Transit Police endure every day. At Nassau Avenue, Minucci told me why.

"Look at the stations! They're dirty, they're cold, they're noisy. If you fire your gun you'll kill about ten innocent people – you're trapped here. You stand here some days and the cold and the dampness creeps into your bones and you start shivering. And that smell – smell it? – it's like that all the time, and you've got to stand there and breathe it in. Bergen Street Station – the snow comes through the bars and you freeze. They call it 'The Ice-Box'. Then some days, kids recognize you – they've seen you make a collar – and they swear at you, call you names, try to get you to react, smoke pot right under your nose. 'Here come the DT's' – that's what they call us. It's the conditions. They're awful. You have to take so much crap from these schoolkids. And your feet are killing you. So you sit down, read a newspaper, drink coffee, and then you get a rip from a shoe-fly –"

Minucci wasn't angry; he said all this in a smiling ironical way. Like Howie Haag, he enjoys his work and takes it seriously. A "shoe-fly", he explained, is a police-inspector who rides the subway looking for officers who are goldbricking – though having a coffee on a cold day hardly seemed to me like goldbricking. "We're not supposed to drink coffee," Minucci said, and he went on to define other words of the Transit Police vocabulary: "lushworker" (a person who robs drunks or sleeping passengers); "Flop Squad" (decoys who pretend to be asleep, in order to attract lushworkers); and "skell" (an unwashed person who lives in the subway).

Just then, as we were talking at Nassau, the station filled with shouting boys – big ones, anywhere from fifteen to eighteen. There were hundreds of them and, with them, came the unmistakable odor of smoldering marijuana. They were boys from Automotive High School, heading south on the GG. They stood on the platform howling and screaming and sucking smoke out of their fingers, and when the train pulled in they began fighting towards the doors.

"You might see one of these kids being a pain in the neck, writing graffiti or smoking dope or something," Howie Haag said. "And you might wonder why we don't do anything. The reason is we're looking for something serious – robbers, snatchers, assault, stuff like that."

Minucci said, "The Vandalism Squad deals with window-kickers and graffiti. Normally we don't."

Once on the train the crowd of yelling boys thinned out. I had seen this sort of activity before: boys get on the subway train and immediately begin walking – they leave the car immediately, bang through the connecting doors and walk from car to car. I asked Minucci why this was so.

"They're marking the people. See them? They're looking for an old lady near a door or something they can snatch, or a pocket they can pick. They're sizing up the situation. They're also heading for the last car. That's where they hang out on this train."

Howie said, "They want to see if we'll follow them. If we do, they'll mark us as cops."

Minucci and Haag did not follow, though at each stop they took cautious looks out of the train, using the reflections in mirrors and windows and seldom looking directly at the rowdy students from Automotive High.

"They play the doors when it's crowded," Minucci said.

Howie said, "Schoolkids can take over a train."

"Look at that old lady," Minucci said. "She's doing everything wrong."

The woman, in her late sixties, was sitting next to the door. Her wristwatch was exposed and her handbag dangled from the arm closest to the door. Minucci explained that one of the commonest subway crimes was inspired by this posture. The snatcher reached through the door from the platform and, just before the doors shut, he grabbed the bag or watch, or both; and then he was off, and the train was pulling out with the victim trapped on board.

I wondered whether the plainclothesmen would warn her. They didn't. But they watched her closely, and when she got off they escorted her in an anonymous way. The old woman never knew how well-protected she was and how any person making a move to rob her would have been hammered flat to the platform by the combined weight of Officers Minucci and Haag.

There were men on the train, drinking wine out of bottles sheathed in paper bags. Such men are everywhere in New York, propped against walls, with bottle and bag. A few hours earlier, at Myrtle-Willoughby, I had counted forty-six men hanging around outside a housing project, drinking this way. I had found their idleness and their stares and their drunken slouching a little sinister.

Minucci said, "The winos don't cause much trouble. It's the kids coming home from school. They're the majority of snatchers and robbers."

Subway crime to a large extent is schoolboy crime. So much for the Mafia. But some New York schoolboys are the very embodiment of menace.

Minucci went on, "On the LL line, on Grant Street, there's much more crime than before, because Eastern District High School relocated there. It's mostly larceny and bag snatches."

It is worth pointing out that what is called larceny in the subway might be called something else in the street. Necklace-yanking, which was very popular in the summer of 1981 (because of the high price of gold and the low necklines), was called "Robbery" in the street but "Grand Larceny" in the subway. If a so-called lushworker robs a sleeping drunk of his watch, the Transit Police have a choice not only between "Robbery" or "Grand Larceny", but if they want to bring down the crime statistics they can call it "Lost Property" – after all, the drunk did not see the thief and might well have lost it.

It was a salutary experience for me, riding through Brooklyn with Officers Minucci and Haag. Who except a man flanked by two armed plainclothesmen would travel from one end of Brooklyn to the other, walking through housing projects and derelict areas, and waiting for hours at subway stations? It was a perverse hope of mine that we would happen upon a crime, or even be the victims of mugging-attempt. We were left alone, things were quiet, there were no arrests; but for the first time in my life I was traveling the hinterland of New York City with my head up, looking people in the eye with curiosity and lingering scrutiny and no fear. It is a shocking experience. I felt at first, with bodyguards, like Haile Selassie; and then I seemed to be looking at an alien land – I had never had the courage to gaze at it so steadily. It was a land impossible to glamorize and hard to describe. I had the feeling I was looking at the future.

Some day all cities will look like this, the way they appear from the windows of the el or the tunnels of the subway. You can see in New York how parts have become more dangerous and fiercer and other parts have softened or become richer. A large section of the Bronx has been levelled. There is no crime in that bare place. Some sections of Queens are very pretty, and blocks of Manhattan on the upper west side have become trendy. In most of Brooklyn the situation is different – haunted and awful – and you can well believe that there are people, not evil people but hopeless ones, who live and die on the dole and never know a day's work. In this patchy pattern the city will go on changing, one district breeding savages and another breeding bankers, until it is ten cities in one, some fortified, and others neutral and still others totally wild.

Propped up by the plainclothesmen, unafraid, and sticking near the subway, I saw New York in a way I had never seen it before. What surprised me most, after seeing the housing projects and the desperate idleness and the rather fierce and drugged-looking people on these derelict frontiers, was that they had not wrecked more of the subway or perhaps even destroyed it utterly.

"It's not the train that's dangerous – it's the area it passes through."

The speaker was a uniformed Transit Police Officer named John Burgois. He was in his mid-thirties and described himself as "of Hispanic origin." He had four citations. Normally he worked with the Strike Force out of Midtown Manhattan in areas considered difficult – 34th and 7th, 34th and 8th, and Times Square. Officer Burgois told me that the job of the uniformed cop is to reassure people by being an obvious presence that someone in trouble can turn to. The Transit cop in uniform also deals with loiterers and fare evaders, assists injured people and lost souls, keeps a watch on public toilets ("toilets attract a lot of crime") and as for drunks, "We ask drunks to remove themselves."

I asked Officer Burgois whether he considered his job dangerous.

"Once or twice a year I get bitten," he said. "Bites are bad. You always need a tetanus shot for human bites."

One of the largest and busiest change-areas on the subway is at Times Square. It is the junction of four lines, including the Shuttle, which operates with wonderful efficiency between Times Square and Grand Central. This, for the Christmas season, was John Burgois's beat. I followed him and for an hour I made notes, keeping track of how he was working.

4:21 – Smoker warned (smoking is forbidden in the subway, even on ramps and stairs).

4:24 – Panicky shout from another cop. There's a woman with a gun downstairs on the platform. Officer Burgois gives chase, finds the woman. She is drunk and has a toy pistol. Woman warned.

4:26 – "Which way to the Flushing Line?"

4:29 – "How do I transfer here?"

4:30 – "Is this the way to 23rd street?"

4:37 – *"Donde es Quins Plaza?"*

4:43 – "Where is the 'A' train?"
    As Officer Burgois answers this question, a group of people gather around him. There are four more requests for directions. It occurs to me that, as all maps have been vandalized, the lost souls need very detailed directions.

4:59 – *Radio Call*: There is an injured passenger at a certain token booth – a gash on her ankle. Officer Burgois lets another cop attend to it.

5:02 – "Where ees the Shuffle?" asks a boy carrying an open can of beer. "Over there," Officer Burgois says, "And dispose of that can. I'm watching you."

5:10 – *Radio Call*: A man whose wallet has been stolen is at the Transit Police Cubicle on the Times Square concourse. Officer Burgois steps in to observe.
    Man: What am I going to do?
    Officer: The Officer-in-charge will take down the information.
    Man: Are you going to catch him?
    Officer: We'll prosecute if you can identify him.
    Man: I only saw his back.
    Officer: That's too bad.
    Man: He was tall, thin, and black. I had twenty-two dollars in that wallet.

Officer: You can kiss your money goodbye. Even if we caught him he'd say, 'This is my money.'

Man: This is the first time anything like this has ever happened to me.

5:17 — Seeing Officer Burgois, a member of the public says, "There's two kids on the train downstairs snatching bags — go get them!" Officer Burgois runs and finds the boys hanging over the gate between the trains, the favorite spot for snatching bags from passengers on the platform. Officer Burgois apprehends them. The boys, named Troy and Sam, are from the Bronx. They can't remember when they were born; they seem to be about fourteen or fifteen. They deny they were snatching bags. Each boy has about $35 in his pocket. They are sullen but not at all afraid. Officer Burgois gives them a Y.D. form and says, "If I catch you again, your mother's going to pick you up from the station . . ."

5:28 — "Hey, officer, how do I get to . . .?"

At this point I stopped writing. I could see that it would be repetitious — and so it was, dreary questions, petty crime and obstinate sneaks. But no one bit Officer Burgois. He has been doing this every hour of every working day for twelve and a half years, and will go on doing it, or something very much like it, for the rest of his working life.

It costs $25 or more to go by taxi from Midtown to Kennedy Airport. For $5 it is possible to go by subway, on "The JFK Express" and the forty minutes is the same or less than a taxi. But it is rumored that this service will soon be withdrawn, because so few people use it. If that happens, there is another option — the express on the "A" line to Howard Beach, which takes under an hour and costs seventy-five cents.

There are ducks at Howard Beach, and herons farther on at Jamaica Bay, and odd watery vistas all the way from Broad Channel to Far Rockaway. The train travels on a causeway past sleepy fishing villages and woodframe houses, and it's all ducks and geese until the train reaches the far side of the bay, where the dingier bungalows and the housing projects begin. Then, roughly at Frank Avenue station, the Atlantic Ocean pounds past jetties of black rocks, not far from the tracks; and at Mott Avenue is the sprawling two-storey town of Far Rockaway, with its main street and its slap-happy architecture and its ruins. It looks like its sister-cities in Ohio and Rhode Island, with just enough trees to hide its dullness, and though part of it is in a state of decay it looks small enough to save.

That was a pleasant afternoon, when I took the train to the Rockaways. I spent this freezing week in December doing little else except riding the subway. Each morning I decided on a general direction, and then I set off, sometimes sprinting to the end of the line and making my way back slowly; or else stopping along the way and varying my route back. I went from Midtown to Jamaica Estates in Queens, and returned via Coney Island. There are white Beluga whales at the Aquarium at Coney Island, and Amazonian electric eels that produce six hundred and fifty volts (the Congo River electric catfish is punier at three hundred and fifty volts), and the African lungfish which drowns if held underwater but can live four years out of water. There are drunks and transvestites and troglodytes in the rest of out-of-season Coney, and the whole place looks as if it has been insured and burned. Though it is on Rockaway Inlet, it is a world away from Rockaway Park. It is also the terminus for six lines.

Never mind the dirt, ignore the graffiti – you can get anywhere you want in New York this way. There are two hundred and thirty route miles on the system – twice as many as the Paris Metro. The trains run all night – in London they shut down at quarter to midnight. New York's one-price token-system is the fairest and most sensible in the world; London's multi-fare structure is clumsy, ridiculous and a wasteful sop to the unions; Japan's, while just as complicated, is run by computers which spit tickets at you and then belch out your change. The Moscow Metro has grandiose chandeliers to light some stations, but the New York subway has hopeful signs, like the one at 96th and 7th Ave: "New Tunnel lighting is being installed at this area as part of a Major Rehabilitation Program. Completion is expected in the summer of 1980." They were over a year late in finishing, but at least they recognized the problem. In most of the world's subway trains, the driver's cab occupies the whole of the front of the first car. But on the New York system you can stand at the front of the train and watch the rats hurrying aside as the train careers towards the black tilting tunnel and the gleaming tracks.

The trains are always the same, but the stations differ, usually reflecting what is above-ground: Spring Street is raffish, Forest Hills smacks of refinement, Livonia Avenue on the LL looks bombed. People aspire to Bay Ridge and say they wouldn't be caught dead in East Harlem – though others are. Fort Hamilton turns into the amazing Verrazano Bridge and the "One" into a ferry landing. By the time I had reached 241st Street on the "2" I thought I had gotten to somewhere near Buffalo, but returning on the "5" and dropping slowly through the Bronx to Lexington Avenue and then to Lower Manhattan and across on the "4" to Flatbush, I had a sense of unrelieved desolation.

No one speaks on the subway except to the person on his immediate right or left, and only then if they are very old friends or else married. Avoiding the stranger's gaze is what the subway passenger does best: there is not much eye-contact below-ground. Most passengers sit bolt upright, with fixed expressions, ready for anything. A look of alertness prevails. As a New York City subway passenger you are J. Alfred Prufrock – you "prepare a face to meet the faces that you meet." Few people look relaxed or off-guard. Those new to the subway have the strangest expressions, like my English friend, who told me there was only one way to survive the subway: "You have to look as if you're the one with the meat cleaver. You have to go in with your eyes flashing."

In order to appear inconspicuous on the subway, many people read. Usually they read the *Daily News* – and a few read *Nowy Dziennik* which is the same thing; the *Times* is less popular, because it takes two hands to read it. But the Bible is very popular, along with religious tracts and the Holy Koran and Spanish copies of *The Watchtower*; lots of boys study for their Bar-Mitzvah on the "F" line in Queens. I saw *The Bragg Toxicless Diet* on the "B" and *La Pratique du Français Parlé* on the "RR". All over the system, riders read lawbooks – *The Interpretation of Contracts*, *The Law of Torts*, *Maritime Law*. The study of law is a subway preoccupation, and it is especially odd to see all these lawbooks in this lawless atmosphere – the law student sitting on the vandalized train. The police officers on the vandalized train create the same impression of incongruity. When I first saw the police they looked mournful to me, but after I got to know them I realized that most of them are not mournful at all, just dead-tired and overworked and doing a thankless job.

Not long ago, the *Daily News* ran a series about the subway called "The Doomsday Express". It was about all the spectacular catastrophes that are possible on the New York system – crashes and nuclear disasters and floods with heavy casualties. "Doomsday" has a curious appeal to a proud and vaguely religious ego. One of the conceits of modern man is his thinking that the world will end with a big bang. It is a kind of hopeful boast, really, the idea that it will take destruction on a vast scale for us to be wiped out.

It is easy to frighten people with catastrophes – much harder to convince them that decay and trivial-seeming deterioration can be inexorable. The New York subway system is wearing out, and parts of it are worn out; all of it looks threadbare. No city can survive without people to run it, and the class divisions which have distinct geographical centers in New York make the subway all the more necessary.

There is a strong political commitment to the subway, particularly among down-market Democrats. But only money can save it. To this end there is a plan afoot called "The Five-Year Capital Program" of $7.2

billion. It is the largest amount of money ever spent in a non-federal program and will involve fixing cars and buses, retiling and cleaning and lighting stations, restoring maps, windows and signs, repairing tracks and bridges – all the day-to-day things which, because they have been ignored, have given the subway a bad case of arteriosclerosis. It remains to be seen whether this program is instituted. If it isn't, New York will come even closer to looking like dear old Calcutta. There will be no big bang.

Anyway, I am a supporter of the Whimper Theory – the more so after my experience of the subway. "I pity you," people said when I told them what I was going to do. But I ended up admiring the handiwork of the system and hating the people who misused it, the way you hate kids who tear the branches off saplings. Most people who live in New York act as if they own it – it makes some people respectful and others it turns into slobs; and that is how they treat the subway.

The subway is buried and unspectacular-looking. Its worst aspects are not its crime or its dangers, but the cloudy fears it inspires, and its dirt and delay. It ought to be fixed, and very soon, because its slow death has made New York uglier and more inconvenient, and if it is not restored to health the future will be much nastier for us all.

Easy Money: Patronage

[1981]

When I was asked to speak at the Library of Congress, I was told that my "honorarium" would come from the Gertrude Clarke Whittal Fund. At once, I knew what my subject must be.

In some of my short stories, and in several novels – *The Family Arsenal* and *Picture Palace*, in particular – I dealt directly with patrons and recipients. The idea of patronage has always fascinated me, perhaps the more because I have never received a grant or won a fellowship. (I realize that in saying this I risk sounding patronizing about patronage.) Of course, I have benefited from other kinds of patronage – it would be hard to find anyone on earth who can claim that he has not been touched in some way by the busy attentions of a philanthropoid. Were you going to except the farmers in rural Mozambique? But they owe their political independence to the Frelimo guerrilla movement, which was aided by the Mozambique Institute, which was partially funded by the Ford Foundation. This is to say nothing of the poor peasants of Puno in Peru, patronized by the Frente Departmental de Campesinos de Puno, whose bank balance was entirely the generosity of the International Development Foundation, the Rabb Charitable Foundation and, ultimately, those inexhaustible patrons, the gentlemen of the Central Intelligence Agency, whose inscribed motto (it is on the building in Langley, Virginia) states, "And ye shall know the truth, and the truth shall make you free" (*St John, 8:32*).

(Biblical quotations are commonplace among patrons and their critics. Professor Robert Merton of Columbia University described what he called "The Matthew Syndrome" in philanthropy. His text was Matthew, 25:29 – "For unto everyone that hath shall be given, and he shall have abundance: but from him that hath not shall be taken away even that he hath." If I had to choose a text from the Bible, I would choose *Amos 3:3* – "Can two walk together except they be agreed?")

Art and money, artist and patron, are wonderfully seen, hand in hand, in the story about Charles Sackville, the Sixth Earl of Dorset. Sackville was a great patron, a great host at his house, Knole, and a friend of Dryden, Pope, Prior, and even our own William Penn. He was in other ways a typically rakish figure of the Restoration court of Charles II, which is to say another lover of Nell Gwyn. He was very rich. Lord Rochester said that Sackville could get away with anything – and that was praise indeed, since we have no record of Rochester having been caught with his pants down, and as his biographer mentions in surpassing detail, they were often down.

Alexander Pope wrote Sackville's epitaph:

> Dorset, the grace of courts, the Muse's pride,
> Patron of the arts, and judge of Nature, died.
> The scourge of pride, though sanctified or great,
> Of fops in learning, and of knaves in state, etc.

One evening, Sackville was with a group of illustrious friends at Knole House. To entertain them in front of the fire, Sackville suggested that they all write "impromptus" – a few brilliant lines apiece – and that John Dryden, who had probably ceased to be Poet Laureate at this point, should act as judge. The guests took pens and paper and put their minds to the task, each hoping to win with his own piece. The papers were collected and given to Dryden, who carefully examined each entry. He then announced Sackville as the winner. This was not so surprising – Sackville, as well as being a patron, was also a considerable poet.

Dryden read out Sackville's winning impromptu. It was not a poem. It went as follows: "*I promise to pay Mr John Dryden five hundred pounds on demand. Signed, Dorset.*"

Patrons usually have the last word. Is there a better example of this than Washington D.C.? The visible art and sculpture in the city are almost completely the result of patronage. The patronage from the beginning was intended to create culture. We were sensitive about being a new nation, and Europe was not kind to our feelings. In 1820, the *Edinburgh Review* commented, "In the four quarters of the globe, who reads an American book? or goes to an American play? or looks at an American picture or statue?" That quotation is given in Lillian Miller's *Patrons and Patriotism; The Encouragement of the Fine Arts in the United States, 1790–1860*. Prof. Miller describes how our economic nationalists were often at the same time cultural nationalists – we had a country, and money, and commerce, but no art. So nationalism, and money, produced patrons. Of course, art had its detractors. John Adams held the view that "the arts had been from the dawn of history the product of despotism and superstition and so should be avoided in the new republic". And Ben Franklin wrote that all things had their season: "To America, one schoolmaster is worth a dozen poets, and the invention of a machine or the improvement of an implement is of more importance than a masterpiece of Raphael."

Within thirty years of his saying that, Franklin's portrait was painted for all to see, by Constantino Brumidi, an exiled Italian artist who received patronage for twenty-five years in Washington, and whose fat cherubs were ridiculed by the downright tastes of Washingtonians from the moment the paint was dry. Franklin was enshrined by Brumidi with Columbus, Amerigo Vespucci and William Brewster, as representing "The Four Forces of Civilization". Franklin was History. Brewster, the Pilgrim Father, was Religion. These are in the President's Room of the Capitol Extension. Brumidi received $8 a day for his painting in the 1850's and towards the end of the decade this was raised to $10.

His patron was the United States government, but the man responsible for hiring him was Captain Montgomery C. Meigs, a professional soldier and engineer. Meigs was pleased with Brumidi's work. Prof. Miller wrote, "As an investment, the captain believed it was in the long run a cheaper substitute for wallpaper or whitewash." But Brumidi had many critics, notably the American artists who had been overlooked when the Italian was hired. And was this Italianate farrago of garlands and flying cherubs really *American* art? That it was the result of patronage there is no doubt.

Thomas Crawford's fresco on the Senate Pediment of the Capitol Building was similarly contentious. He was American – he also had been hired by Meigs, as a free-lance sculptor. His fresco was Grecian, and ponderously – and even racially – symbolic. It represented (this was his commission, the patron's order) "The advancement of the white race and the decadence of the Indians." It was later retitled as "The Progress of American Civilization". Now, I suppose, it is simply, "That pediment up there." Crawford had been asked to submit designs and to avoid any obscure symbolism – the prerogative of the patron. In the center of the group is "a majestic goddess," America; on her left is "the march of civilization" from the Indian to the pioneer; on the right are figures symbolizing activities of successful Americans ("the triumphant white race," Prof. Miller says) – mechanic, merchant, soldier, and so forth.

Crawford's work was generally unpopular. It was seen as unrealistic, offensive to the Indian character, it falsified history; and Senator Sam Houston ridiculed it as stiff, badly observed and untruthful. The figure of Liberty on the Capital Dome was also ridiculed by Crawford's patrons, who hated the un-Indian shoes and the Liberty Cap. Houston was a senator. He could do no more than make his fellow senators laugh as he jeered. But Jefferson Davis was Secretary of War, one of the higher patrons. He actually redesigned the headgear and gave Liberty (or "Armed Freedom" as it was first called) a plumed helmet. Crawford obeyed his patrons' command.

Like Hiram Powers, who did the statues of Jefferson and Franklin,

Thomas Crawford was already at the time of his commission an
accomplished sculptor. His work may have been news to Sam Houston,
but his reputation was established. The most withering critic of patronage, Samuel Johnson, would not have been surprised by Washington's
treatment of her hired artists. As Johnson wrote to the Earl of
Chesterfield, "Is not a Patron, my Lord, one who looks with unconcern
on a man struggling for life in the water, and when he has reached ground,
encumbers him with help?" (In his *Dictionary* he defined *patron* thus:
"Commonly a wretch who supports with insolence and is repaid with
flattery.")

During the period that these sculptors and painters were being heavily
patronized in Washington, no one was encumbering American writers
with much help. Just before Captain Meigs began hiring artists and
commissioning busts and pictures, Edgar Allan Poe died (1849) – his
work was done; and Brumidi was still cleaning his brushes and preparing
his palette when *Moby Dick* appeared in 1851; *Uncle Tom's Cabin* came
out the next year, *The Scarlet Letter* in 1850, *Walden* in 1854 and
Emerson's *English Traits* in 1856. Sam Clemens in 1857 had just become
a riverboat pilot and was saying "Mark Twain" for the first time, as a
command.

Perhaps these American writers had heeded Emerson's call ten years
earlier to be self-reliant. None I have mentioned had patrons, though in
1852 Hawthorne wrote the campaign biography of Franklin Pierce,
idealizing his old friend and Bowdoin College classmate. For this,
Hawthorne was on the receiving end of a piece of political patronage. As
soon as he was elected president, Pierce made Hawthorne American
Consul in Liverpool. In a sense, they proved what Dr Johnson had told
Boswell about merit. "I never knew a man of merit neglected," he said. "It
was generally by his own fault that he failed of success. A man may hide
his head in a hole: he may go into the country, and publish a book now
and then, which nobody reads, and then complain he is neglected. There
is no reason why any person should exert himself for a man who has
written a good book: he has not written it for any individual. I may as well
make a present to the postman who brings me a letter. When patronage
was limited, an author expected to find a Maecenas, and complained if he
did not find one. Why should he complain? This Maecenas has others as
good as he, or others who have got the start of him."

It would have been ironic if Harriet Beecher Stowe had received a
government grant to write *Uncle Tom's Cabin*. Jefferson Davis became
Pierce's Secretary of War the year after it appeared, and the novel did
much to hasten his new appointment in the Confederacy. He might have
remarked, as the generous French statesman did in the Dr Johnson story,
"*J'ai fait dix mécontents et un ingrat,*" which can be roughly translated in

Henry Ford's dictum, "Give the average man something, and you make an enemy of him."

Patrons are by no means a recent growth in America, and they have not always been so concerned with the arts. Ben Whitaker argues in his study *The Foundations* that the first Foundation in the United States was probably the Magdalen Society, which was started in Philadelphia in 1800, "to ameliorate the distressed condition of those unhappy females who have been seduced from the paths of virtue, and are desirous of returning to a life of rectitude." Apparently, there was a shortage of candidates; it was eventually reorganized into a foundation to assist schoolchildren.

Whitaker is comprehensive in his treatment of foundations and lists among others, "the Robbins Fund of Chicago with its assets of $8. The James Dean Fund . . . to provide for the 'delivery to the Boston Light Vessel of one copy of each of the principal Sunday newspapers published in Boston'. A Horses' Christmas Dinner Trust" – in Kansas – "The Benefit Shoe Foundation provides for people with one foot. A foundation in Latin America is devoted to the deportation of foreign bull-fighters. A Science Fiction Foundation has recently been started in Britain, where the Scientology Foundation is already active, and the Osborne Foundation now offers to pray for you for £2 a month . . . not long ago a United States Flag Foundation brought a lawsuit against a New York artist whom it accused of showing a lack of respect for the Stars and Stripes" – though the artist may well have had a Guggenheim to do it – "Recently" – this was in 1974 – "in the Philippines, President Marcos announced that he is donating all his worldly possessions to the Marcos Foundation as an example of self-sacrifice to his people; and the Search Foundation dispatched its seventh expedition to find Noah's Ark." We also have a Lollipop Foundation and two foundations to preserve prairie chickens. But prairie chickens are no laughing matter, nor is other desert fauna. In 1980, the Guggenheim Foundation awarded one of its Fellowships to a man in order to assist his study, "The social ecology of free-ranging coyotes."

This is a far cry from Brumidi's per diem of $8, and even farther from Dr Johnson's having to find subscribers to his dictionary, and so cross about Lord Chesterfield's cold shoulder that he rewrote his imitation of Juvenal,

> Yet think what ills the scholar's life assail,
> Toil, envy, want, the *Patron*, and the jail.

Mr Whitaker is very good on the paradoxes of philanthropy, and on the numerous motives that impel the philanthropoid to give his money away. There is the religious emphasis – alms-giving, which may have evolved from the tradition "of making a sacrifice to propitiate fate or hostile spirits, together with a more material fear of the malevolence of the poor." There is tax deduction, but this is recent – no deduction was allowed for charitable gifts prior to 1917. There is simple kindness; and complicated kindness, motivated by a mixture of idealism, pride, and the wish to be loved. "At least ninety per cent of all existing foundations today," Mr Whitaker remarks, "perpetuate the donor's name" – not only Ford, Carnegie and Kennedy, but also, as we have seen, Gertrude Clarke Whittal, and not only all recent presidents but members of their cabinets – the John Volpe and Maurice Stans Foundations are but two of very many. There is the selfish motive, to which Will Kellogg, the cereal tycoon, admitted: "I get a kick out of it (giving to children). Therefore I am a selfish person and no philanthropist." There is real malice. Mr Whitaker cites the case of the American who "established the fund to help French peasants to dress up as matadors or hula dancers, to prove his thesis that there is no degradation to which French people will not stoop for money." There is also the straightforwardness of James Buchanan Duke, who founded the Duke Endowment. He said, "People ought to be healthy. If they ain't healthy they can't work, and if they don't work they ain't healthy. And if they can't work there ain't no profit in them." From such down-to-earth sentiments came the great institution we know as Duke Medical School and pioneering scholarship in the field of extra-sensory perception and parapsychology, and what we laymen call ghosts.

One of the subtlest and most paradoxical points Mr Whitaker makes in *The Foundations* regards patronage between enemies, or gift-giving out of suspicion. It is the hectoring of one group upon another's uneasy conscience, the sort of eleemosynary blackmail that frequently creates an even greater suspicion between the races in the United States. In this connection, Mr Whitaker quotes Lévi-Strauss's *Elementary Structures of Kinship*. Small nomadic groups of Nambikwara Indians in the Brazilian jungle

> are in constant fear of each other and avoid each other. But at the same time they desire contact . . . and from being arrayed against each other they pass immediately to gifts; gifts are given, but silently, without bargaining, without any expression of satisfaction or complaint, and without any apparent connexion between what is offered and what is obtained.

That "constant fear" and wary, circumspect behavior, that sense of mutual suspicion, puts me in mind of an escaped convict suddenly confronting a child in a foggy, marshy graveyard, and the following dialogue:

"You know what a file is?"

"Yes, sir."

"And you know what wittles is?"

"Yes, sir."

After each question he tilted me over a little more, so as to give me a greater sense of helplessness and danger.

"You get me a file." He tilted me again. "And you get me wittles." He tilted me again. "You bring 'em both to me." He tilted me again. "Or I'll have your heart and liver out." He tilted me again.

And so begins the relationship between patron and recipient in what is certainly the greatest novel about patronage, Dickens's *Great Expectations*. The complex motives of both giver and receiver have never been more cunningly delineated than in the surprises and plot-shifts of this novel. George Orwell called it "an attack on patronage," but if it were as simple as that one would only need to list its abuses. Dickens was at pains to demonstrate the paradoxes.

After one has read the novel, one quickly sees how, like Pip, one has misapprehended the source of his funds, and it is possible to feel a sympathetic sense of victimization. Certainly, Pip is a snob, but we have seen his humble origins, and we understand how glad he is to receive the grant of money that liberates him from the blacksmith shop apprenticeship and the pretensions of his provincial town. The story is of Pip's rise and fall, and his rise again. As a child, he is summoned to the house of Miss Havisham and commanded to play with the girl, Estella. Miss Havisham urges Estella to break his heart; Miss Havisham is reputedly wealthy. Pip longs to be rich himself and he believes that his ambiguous welcome at Miss Havisham's will ultimately make his fortune. He also longs to be a gentleman, as he tells the kindly Biddy – Biddy is also an orphan, "Mr Wopsle's great-aunt's granddaughter"; Pip is not sure of the relationship to Wopsle, but very early in the novel he notices that she is rather unkempt, unwashed and even slovenly. He unburdens himself in this way:

"Biddy," said I, after binding her to secrecy, "I want to be a gentleman." . . .

"You know best, Pip; but don't you think you are happier as you are?"

"Biddy," I exclaimed, impatiently, "I am not at all happy as I am. I am disgusted with my calling and my life. I have never taken to either since I was bound. Don't be absurd."

And he goes on to say:

. . . understand once for all that I never shall or can be comfortable –
or anything but miserable . . . unless I can lead a very different sort of
life from the life I lead now.

He confesses that his wish to be a gentleman has something to do with
Estella, and Biddy wonders whether this aspiration is meant to spite the
girl, or to win her over. She observes, "Because, if it is to spite her, I should
think – but you know best – that might be better and more independently
done by caring nothing for her words. And if it is to gain her over, I should
think – but you know best – she was not worth gaining over."

Shortly after this seemingly fruitless plea for patronage, Pip is visited by
the lawyer Jaggers, who informs him that his expectations have been
fulfilled: someone wishes to give him a great deal of money, clothes, a
tutor, a new life – in short, wishes to make him a gentleman. Pip is
delighted; within a few pages he is a raging snob; a few pages more and he
is dreaming of becoming a philanthropist. His reflection is like a
paraphrase of Andrew Carnegie's *The Advantages of Poverty*. Pip feels a
"sublime compassion" for the church-goers in his village, for their low
state and their mean lives. But he is rich now and "I promised myself that I
would do something for them one of these days, and formed a plan in
outline for bestowing a dinner of roast-beef and plum-pudding, a pint of
ale, and a gallon of condescension, upon everybody in the village."

One advantage of charity, Carnegie said, was that it allowed the rich to
"find refuge from self-questioning."

Pip assumes that Miss Havisham is his benefactress, and in that reverie
of philanthropy that I quoted, he remembers the convict he met, the brief
friendship, and he concludes that his comfort is that the felon has been
transported and is probably dead. Pip is consoled by the thought that this
foul creature is out of the way and that he, Pip, is in no danger of further
contamination.

It would take too long to show how Pip squanders his money in
London, preens himself, dispenses charity and is jilted by Estella. Suffice
to say, he is in for a shock, for his patron turns up. It is, much to Pip's
embarrassment, the convict Magwitch.

Magwitch is a fascinating character. He is the unwelcome aspect, the
unacceptable face of patronage. And he is like many patrons, many
starters of foundations. Like Carnegie, he made his pile far from his native
land; like Guggenheim and others, he is a bit vague about his methods;
like Joe Kennedy, he is rather sanctimonious; and like James Buchanan
Duke, his syntax is somewhat twisted. He is also the soul of generosity; he
has not forgotten the kindness that was done to him so many years ago by
the boy who gave him "wittles" and a file to free him of his manacles. It is
another characteristic he shares with philanthropoids – he has a very long

memory. Lastly, he passionately craves respectability. You might easily mistake him for the show business comedian and buffoon who solemnly reveals himself as a patron of the fund to combat muscular dystrophy, or that other unlikely combination, the tobacco man and the sportsman who seem anxious to associate smoking and money with tennis-playing and health (in the Virginia Slims Tournament there is the added factor of Triumphant Woman, a sort of chain-smoking world-beater). Magwitch's victory is that he has turned Pip into a gentleman, through patronage – funnelling the funds through the lawyer, Jaggers – without the young man knowing. Pip is appalled and ashamed. There is something about his shame that cannot fail to remind us of the combined outrage and embarrassment evinced by writers and scholars, when they learned that the distinguished magazines *Encounter* and *Preuves* were funded by that other Magwitch-like patron, the CIA.

Magwitch has been living in Australia and denying himself luxuries in order that Pip might prosper. If there is something pitiful in his self-denial, there is also something quite horrible in his gloating over what he has achieved.

> "Look'ee here!" he [Magwitch] went on, taking my watch out of his pocket, and turning towards him a ring on my finger, while I recoiled from his touch as if he had been a snake, "a gold 'un and a beauty: *that's* a gentleman's, I hope! A diamond all set round with rubies; *that's* a gentleman's, I hope! Look at your linen; fine and beautiful! Look at your clothes; better ain't to be got! And your books too," turning his eyes round the room, "mounting up, on their shelves, by hundreds! And you read 'em, don't you? I see you'd been a reading of them when I come in. Ha, ha, ha! You shall read 'em to me, dear boy! And if they're in foreign languages wot I don't understand, I shall be just as proud as if I did."

And then the convict, the "warmint" as he calls himself, takes Pip's hands and kisses them, and Pip's blood runs cold. Pip's perplexity arises not from any scruple that he has been unworthy, or that he is a spendthrift and a snob; but rather that his patron is unworthy, an ex-con, a spendthrift and a vicarious snob. Magwitch, in Pip's eyes, has "a savage air that no dress could tame", he sits like a lout, he eats with a jack-knife and wipes it on his leg to clean it. Pip's main objection is that he does not want to be the vindication of Magwitch's obsessive sacrifice. The patron has dirty hands. He has no right to be proud of Pip:

> What would alone have set a division between that man and us . . . was his triumph in my story . . . he had no perception of the possibility of my finding any fault with my good fortune. His boast that he had made

me a gentleman, and that he had come to see me support the character
on his ample resources, was made for me quite as much as for himself.
And that it was a highly agreeable boast to both of us, and that we must
both be very proud of it, was a conclusion quite established in his own
mind.

Pip tells his friend, Herbert Pocket, that Magwitch must be stopped in his
giving. Herbert says, "You mean that you can't accept —" And Pip replies,
"How can I? . . . Think of him! Look at him!"

It is the moment in literature that most accurately mirrors that moment
in history when, for many writers, the CIA's clumsy figure (savage air,
jack-knife, dirty hands) appeared behind the dignified façade of The
Congress for Cultural Freedom.

Pip disengages himself from Magwitch after a time and takes a humble
job with Herbert Pocket. Pip would not have minded receiving the money
from the pathetic, crazy, vindictive Miss Havisham; she, after all, is a kind
of pillar of the community, the sort of crank who would not miss a few
thousand. Pip is penitent, but the irony is that it was Pip's patronage – an
anonymous handout – that allowed Herbert to start the firm that redeems
Pip and makes him his second fortune. In one ending of the novel he loses
Estella, in another upbeat ending suggested by Bulwer-Lytton, he gains
Estella.

There are not many novels which deal with patronage.

The Member, by John Galt, published in 1832, is a brisk, Scottish
fictional memoir about political patronage, in which the pious note is
struck on the first page, as Archibald Jobbry finagles to get into
parliament:

> . . . I began to take shares in divers public concerns, and to busy myself
> in the management thereof, slipping in a young friend now and then as
> a clerk. I will not, however, say, that in this I was altogether actuated by
> affection; for public spirit had quite as much to say with me as a regard
> for my kindred: indeed, it is a thing expected of every man, when he
> retires from business, that he will do his endeavour to serve his country,
> and make himself a name in the community.

Galt's hero buys his way into parliament and finds that he can only stay
there by continuing to dispense patronage, though he occasionally allows
himself a kickback.

Patronage is conspicuously absent in George Gissing's *New Grub
Street*, the best novel ever written about the life of hard-pressed writers,
literary journalists, and outright hacks. There is one patroness in
Conrad's *The Secret Agent*, and another in James's *The Princess
Casamassima* – indeed, it is the princess herself (formerly plain old

Christina Light from his earlier novel, *Roderick Hudson*). The career of Hyacinth Robinson is well worth studying by anyone interested in the ups and downs in the relationship between patron and recipient, for the Princess Casamassima is quite determined that only money stands between Hyacinth and refinement. (Incidentally, it is Hyacinth who says that he would never marry a girl who would have him for a husband – predating by some fifty years Groucho Marx's "I'd never join a club that would have me as a member".)

And no one, as Pip's experience shows, can truly enjoy patronage unless it boosts his self-esteem. Pip's self-esteem is in for a knock as soon as it is revealed that his money is from an ex-convict. Patronage always works best when both patron and recipient are held in mutual esteem; and each has what the other lacks. So often, it is the uneducated millionaire who founds a university; the scarcely-literate one who starts a library; the artless tycoon who patronizes the artist. Here, the philistine and the publican are happily paired. It is not merely that the patron wishes to become respectable and artistic through his gift; the recipient, too, gains respectability by association with his patron. If the patron is distinguished enough, the actual money may be regarded as no more than a detail. The Guggenheim Memorial Foundation claimed in its *Annual Report* 1965–66 that, since its awards, "year after year were seen to be based on rigorous professional standards, the informed public came to realize, in the words of one observer, that a Guggenheim Fellowship constitutes a sort of 'intellectual knighthood'. Thus the Foundation has gradually assumed a role in the validation of intellectual excellence that is quite as significant as its role in the provision of material assistance." Prestige matters. Charles Sackville's patronage may have been no more than a spirited evening at Knole House, but Sackville's friendship was an affirmation that you were of the élite, and if you were a poet, a great poet.

It sometimes works the other way. There are instances where patron and recipient disappoint each other. In 1932, Diego Rivera was hired, for $21,000, to paint a mural on the RCA building in Rockefeller Center. His patrons were of course the Rockefellers, who assigned him the theme, "Man at the Crossroads Looking with Hope and High Vision to the Choosing of a New and Better Future." Assisted by Ben Shahn, Diego set to work, but before the mural was finished, Nelson Rockefeller walked by and saw that one of the faces in the mural was that of the first premier of the USSR, V. I. Lenin. Nelson Rockefeller had the painful task of informing Diego that this would not do. He complimented the painter on his work, but added, "As much as I dislike to do so I am afraid we must ask you to substitute the face of some unknown man where Lenin's now appears." Diego refused; work stopped; the mural was destroyed by the Rockefellers, in spite of their prior assurances to the contrary; and Diego painted a similar mural in Mexico City, enhancing it with a portrait of John D. Rockefeller.

On the whole such failures in patronage as this are not widely publicized, and it is the "intellectual knighthood" conferred on recipients that is stressed, or as the current (1981) report of the Guggenheim Foundation has it, "The Fellowships are awarded to men and women of high intellectual and personal qualifications who have already demonstrated unusual creative ability in the arts." It makes it seem like an award for achievement, rather than a sum of money intended to help start or complete a project. It signals arrival and is, for many, the beginning of self-esteem. And where once appeared in books sycophantic expressions of gratitude to patrons, phrased as fulsome dedications, we have "Thanks to my intrepid editors . . . And thanks to the National Endowment for the Arts for a grant which helped" (*Fear of Flying*, by Erica Jong) or "Thanks are due to the J. S. Guggenheim Memorial Foundation." These are not always boasts, but it is difficult not to read in them a smug satisfaction, and even a suggestion of *Imprimatur* in their formula.

And there are more candid assessments. Consider these three:

1. "Receipt of the fellowship gave me new confidence in my work and in my choice of writing as a profession."
2. "This was the first time my work had been given credibility by an outstanding outside source. The results were that my family, my colleagues within the local community, the region and the state accepted that I was a serious writer – and that it was all right to be that."
3. "Often the result of such a grant is intangible – it has more to do with your own psychological attitude, toward your work and toward the society in which you're living."

These comments are from the report circulated by the National Endowment for the Arts, their "Literature Program Follow-Up on Creative Writing Fellowships," 1972–1976. The report states, "A large number of writers specifically commented on the added 'prestige' and 'recognition' brought to them and their work by the award." These fellowships were not given on the basis of need; the only considerations were "the talent of the writer and the quality of the manuscript submitted." The greatest boast in this report is that, after having received a National Endowment fellowship, nearly half of them (129 out of 293 surveyed) went on to secure other fellowships or grants – twenty-two Guggenheims, four Rockefellers, four Fulbrights, and so forth. It is almost as if the National Endowment for the Arts is a means by which a writer may attract further patrons, the first rung on the ladder of patronage. Critics may say that this smacks of the kind of acceptance accorded to approved writers in the

Soviet Union. It is true that Soviet authors who toe the line are elected to the Writers Union, but this carries no stipend. On the other hand, if you are in the Writers Union you get published; and if you're not, you don't. How could you? You're not a writer.

So, what about those American writers whose applications were turned down by the National Endowment for the Arts? We have no way of telling, because the report did not cover unsuccessful applicants. But wouldn't it be interesting to know if the refusal of a grant was such a blow to an aspiring writer's self-esteem and so damaging to his prestige that he abandoned writing? And what if it made no difference at all? To say that half your respondents have become patronage-pensioners after receiving their first grant does not impress me, but only confirms my view that grantsmanship is often a game that is played at the peripheries of art. There *is* a Grantsmanship Center in Los Angeles, which conducts "grantsmanship classes" and publishes, among other titles, *The Guide to Corporate Giving* and *Ten Steps to a Million-Dollar Fund Raiser*. Unsuccessful applicants for the National Endowment might well consider one of these classes or gold-digging textbooks.

The British equivalent of the National Endowment for the Arts is the Arts Council of Great Britain. Until 1980, the Literature Panel felt it was (in the words of one director) "ungentlemanly" to ask how the money had been spent by the writers who received Arts Council patronage. For about fifteen years, no one knew; and then in 1980 a report was commissioned. But for this, unsuccessful applicants were questioned. The Chairman of the Literature Panel, as a result of the report's findings, concluded that it made little difference whether a writer received a grant or not. That is, patronage was not crucial to any of the writers – unsuccessful and successful applicants for patronage seemed indistinguishable in their final results; though having read the report I must confess that the unpatronized ones sounded very aggrieved. The Arts Council decided to abandon grants to writers, except for (I quote) "Two or three writers of outstanding ability in exceptional circumstances."

"The books we were subsidizing seemed very dull," the Chairman told me. "And we have come close to producing a breed of poets who can't write poetry without a grant." The Arts Council is happier subsidizing magazines and small publishers, and the Chairman of the Literature Panel confided that what he would like to see is a very large state publishing house, something like the National Theatre or the Royal Opera House. In any case, individual patronage to writers is more or less at an end in Britain, and this is largely due to a report which asked unsuccessful applicants whether patronage mattered to them.

"We couldn't point to a *Ulysses* having been written," the Chairman of the Literature Panel said glumly, suggesting that a masterpiece might have vindicated his bursaries. It is a wonderful example, because the writing of *Ulysses* – in fact, the life of James Joyce – superbly shows how patronage can work, providing the patron is very rich and the recipient is a genius. But Joyce was also a great spender. His biographer, Richard Ellmann, wrote that Harriet Weaver's "benefaction did not make Joyce rich; no amount of money could have done that; but it made it possible for him to be poor only through determined extravagance." Miss Weaver provided Joyce with a stipend in 1918. This continued for the next twenty-three years. He had dozens of other patrons, and a Civil List grant, and a sort of bloodhound in Ezra Pound frantically sniffing out new patrons. Joyce's biography (written with the help of a Guggenheim Fellowship) is filled with anecdotes of handouts, grants and stipends, and with sorely-pressed patrons and patronesses. Joyce was not only a master of English fictional prose – he could also write an effective letter beseeching a potential patron for funds.

Mrs. Harold McCormick, *née* Edith Rockefeller, was his patroness for a time. She was also Jung's patron, and what seems to have ended her relationship with Joyce was her insistence that the Irish novelist be psychoanalyzed by Jung – at her expense. Joyce refused, and got no more money from Mrs. McCormick. It might have happened anyway, since Jung's treatment of another of Mrs. McCormick's artists (the composer, Wolf-Ferrari) was in advising the patroness to withdraw her subsidy. Cut off without a penny, the composer "pulled himself out of dissipation and inertia" and began again to compose music. Even after Mrs. McCormick stopped paying Joyce's bills, Joyce wrote her asking if she would reconsider and take him aboard – she was reputedly the richest woman in Zurich. But silence was her stern reply. Joyce secured other patrons, and his revenge on Mrs. McCormick was in putting her in the brothel scene in the "Circe" episode of *Ulysses*; she is The Honourable Mrs. Mervyn Talboys who appears as a rich sadistic horsewoman, "In amazon costume, hard hat, jackboots cockspurred, vermilion waistcoat, fawn musketeer gauntlets with braided drums, long train held up and hunting crop with which she strikes her welt constantly" – she threatens to bestride the cringing Leopold Bloom and flay him alive.

Joyce did well out of his patrons; and his patrons had the satisfaction of knowing their man was a genius, even though they hardly understood what he wrote. And yet in the world of patronage there are few real success stories. The writer doesn't want a patron half so badly as he wants a paying public. In his lifetime, Joyce's public was not large – his royalties were lamentably thin, and like Stephen Dedalus he owed money to everyone.

Here is Joyce on publication day, 1939. *Finnegans Wake* has just appeared. He has published his poems, *Dubliners*, *Exiles*, *Portait of the Artist*, *Ulysses* and his essays. He is fifty-seven. His life's work is done. At his publication party today, his wife says, "Well, Jim, I haven't read any of your books but I'll have to some day because they must be good, considering how well they sell." Joyce is not consoled. His financial situation is terrible. He considers returning to teaching, and his secretary Samuel Beckett reveals that there is a job open as lecturer in Italian at the University of Capetown, South Africa.

For a few days, Joyce toyed with the idea. But he gave it up. He heard there were often thunderstorms in Capetown. He was afraid of thunder. He died two years later and his funeral was paid for by his patroness, Harriet Weaver.

Would James Joyce have secured a Guggenheim Fellowship? It is idle to speculate, but it is certain that a one-year fellowship would have done him little good: his talent was too vast, his working method too slow, his tastes too extravagant for a one-year fellowship. He did not require prestige, and it is fair to say that literary patronage is always limited – a garbage collector earns more than any recipient of a literary grant; and there is the limitation of time – what is a year to someone writing *Ulysses*? It seems almost as if latter-day patrons are determined to encourage the small book, the small talent, the slight ambition. Nationality aside, Joyce would probably not have applied for any grant. It was his inheritors – his biographers and critics and masters of the footnote – who made a living from foundations, in his name, and put one in mind of barnacles on the *Titanic*.

Nathanael West applied for a Guggenheim, and was turned down. Henry Miller had the same experience and was so embittered by it that in a note to what would have been his Guggenheim project, *The Air-Conditioned Nightmare*, he listed in that book the loony-sounding projects of the successful applicants. And notice: he wrote his book all the same. So did West. So would Joyce have done. It is possible to feel, when reading a mediocre novel by an author who has received patronage, that instead of a check through the door, the cause of literature would have been better served by a visit from The Person from Porlock.*

Even so, we are dealing with very small sums. For the period 1977-1978, ten per cent of the money awarded by major foundations was

---

*see Coleridge's preface to "Kubla Khan" or the Robert Graves poem, which ends:

> O Porlock person, habitual scapegoat,
> Should any masterpiece be marred or scotched,
> I wish your burly fist on the front door
> Had banged yet oftener on literature!

earmarked for the humanities, and of this only two per cent was used in activities classified as language and literature. Of the 272 Guggenheim Fellowships awarded in 1981, only eight were given to writers of fiction. The National Endowment of the Arts fellowships are currently $12,500 for "creative writers," and state art agencies' grants are much less.

But this is not the whole story. It is impossible to calculate the numbers, but I would venture to guess that the greatest amount of patronage extended to writers is that of colleges and universities; that is, the Creative Writing Program of the English Department in whose precincts we find the writer-in-residence, the visiting writer, the professor who writes when the spirit moves him, and the scribbling students. The post-war phenomenon of Creative Writing as a subject, which allowed a graduate student not to study the *Bildungsroman*, but to write one of his own, gave rise to a system of continuous patronage that will be with us for some time. It is, in fact, self-perpetuating. It began in Iowa and Stanford, and it worked this way. A person who wished to write a novel, registered for a post-graduate degree. He had a teaching fellowship or a scholarship to help him along. Like other MA and PhD candidates, he had a supervisor – probably a novelist. He wrote his novel. The novel was submitted to the usual committee and if it was approved, the candidate earned his degree. In time, a blurb-like plot-summary of the novel appeared in the leaden pages of the publication, *Dissertation Abstracts*. And the successful candidate, now a Doctor of Fiction Writing with a dissertation/novel under his belt, developed that schizophrenia that afflicts anyone who is heavily patronized: half-academic, half-novelist – Doctor Jekyll in the classroom, Mr. Hyde at the typewriter. Yes, I do believe the potion of patronage is that strong.

Although many such graduates have gone on to become professional writers, many more have joined universities and done all the things that academics do – taught classes, graded papers and demanded tenure. Their novels may never have been published, but academically at least they have passed muster by earning the person a post-graduate degree. George Gissing's novel, *New Grub Street*, was never like this; moreover, the very situation of the Creative Writing Program caused a particular kind of novel to be written, something quite different from what had been written before – that is, the university novel. The 1930's and '40's had given us the "Hollywood novel" for precisely the same reasons – Hollywood offered a kind of patronage to practically every major American novelist of those decades, except Hemingway, and William Faulkner continued to write movie-scripts into the 'fifties. In fact, Faulkner wrote the script for *Land of the Pharoahs* (1953) after he had received the 1950 Nobel Prize for Literature. The main distinction between the teacher-novelist and the script-writer-novelist is the nature of the patron. The university is Maecenas; Hollywood is Magwitch.

The effect of this creative writing on the profession of letters in the United States has been profound. It has changed the profession out of all recognition. It has made it narrower, more rarified, more neurotic; it has altered the way literature is taught and it has diminished our pleasure in reading – books must be worthy (goodbye *Treasure Island*), books must be seminar-fodder (have a nice day, *Kim*), books must be symbolic (farewell, *Diary of a Nobody*); and hello to every pompous piece of fiction that makes literature-like noises.

Most of all, university patronage has spelled the decline of book-reviewing in the United States. After the foundations delivered novelists into the arms of universities, there was no need for anyone to engage in the habitual tasks associated with the profession of letters. A campus of creative writers does not mean that the local newspaper will be lively with literary journalism; it means its opposite. Book-reviewing, the literary essay, the *feuilleton* – all of these went out the window when university patronage came in the door; and a sharp, and I think unfair, distinction came to be drawn between the literary man and the literary journalist. We have a handful of reliable book reviewers in America, which is a pity; but it is a far greater pity that reviewing is seen to be so despicable a labor that it is done – when it is done at all – by nonentities on the Entertainment Page. Most newspapers get by on syndicated reviews, "notices", and mentions cobbled together from the plot-summary on the book jacket. The writer-in-residence is perhaps right in refusing to review a book; why should he bother, on his salary? And yet, when such a person's own book appears, he may object to its thin treatment, and with some justification. Patronage is odd that way; it prevents a person from doing the very thing that may free him from patronage; it is nearly always at odds with the kind of commercial considerations that make patronage unnecessary. In a world of patrons, who needs large advances? Who needs literary journalism? Who needs to be professional? When patronage is extensive, who indeed needs readers?

There is a sort of Malthusian effect in literary patronage; it has altered the nature of readership, the way books get written, and has changed the notion of the literary profession – in fact, taken away so many of the writer's duties, that writing has almost ceased to be a profession. In my reading around this subject, the strongest feeling I have had is that anyone in America who aspires to authorship finds it very hard to admit this except on an application. It has less to do with prevailing philistinism than the plain truth that in our society you are measured by how much money you make. Writers do not make very much, on the whole, and have to look to patronage for justification and the respectability that is money's equivalent. I should add that it is possible to be so respectable as a novelist in America that the act of writing a book review or anything else

begins to appear somewhat distasteful, and literary journalism is
regarded as a blow to one's prestige.

I have moved from the general to the particular. I cannot speak about
theaters, opera companies, or orchestras. I think there are arts that can
only survive with a great deal of patronage. The sculptor, the painter, the
composer will always need patrons of one sort or another; but one can
often see the patron's taste reflected in their work. The performing arts
prosper under patronage, but there is a Malthusian dimension to this as
well. In the ten years prior to 1978, with the assistance of the National
Endowment for the Arts, opera companies grew from twenty-seven to
forty-five; professional symphony orchestras from fifty-eight to one
hundred and ten; professional dance companies from ten to seventy, and
legitimate theater companies from twelve to fifty. The patronage that
makes them multiply, has to keep them alive, which makes the patron a
bit like a rabbit breeder.

These figures were given in an article in the *New York Times* (26 Oct.,
1980) by Waldemar A. Neilsen, author of *The Big Foundations*. The
article was titled "Where Have All the Patrons Gone?" and argues that
organized philanthropy "has become Calvinist, conscience-ridden, tech-
nocratic and bureaucratized. Most of all it has become painfully infected
with social scientism. It has contracted a bad case of what could be called
sociologist's foot."

I have tried to limit my remarks to patrons of fiction writers, but it is
worth mentioning what Neilsen calls the "new patrons". They are three:
the consumer public; large business corporations; and government. The
National Endowment for the Arts funds have already been reduced by the
Reagan administration, but as Neilsen points out, there are worse things
than indifference. There is, for example, meddlesome interest and
political opportunism – "the destruction of the WPA's Federal Theater
Project in New Deal days by a witch-hunting House Committee; the
successful demand by Senator Joseph McCarthy in the 1950's for a
purging of the U.S. Information Service's libraries overseas of 'subversive
literature,' and the powerful effort by the Nixon White House to
politicize the programming of the Corporation for Public Broadcasting."

And Neilsen warns also of a subtler effect, "the creeping advent of
'official culture' . . . as a consequence of supporting the arts with
Government money. By an insidious process, bland traditionalism and
conformist official standards gradually penetrate the cultural atmosphere."

That is what a stockbroker would call the "downside risk." I prefer to
think of Doctor Johnson saying, "I never knew a man of merit neglected,"
and reflect on Diego Rivera repainting his Rockefeller mural in Mexico;
and Joyce outspending the bottomless purses of his patrons; and go on

believing that a reduction of patronage would mean fewer mediocre novelists but a richer literary life, and perhaps signal the return of the man of letters. And remember, patronage does have its opposite in the totalitarian denial of cultural freedom, the determination to silence and squash the artist. Art is not such a frail thing as it has often been made out to be, or so badly in need of moneyed well-wishers. It flourishes in the most unlikely places, even in complete adversity, in Siberian labor camps. There are many ways of encouraging it – patronage is one, and patronage has its ambiguities – but no one, not the rankest philistine, the silliest know-nothing, the most paranoid senator, preacher, commissar or jailer, has figured out a way to kill it.

Mapping the World

[1981]

Cartography, the most aesthetically pleasing of the sciences, draws its power from the greatest of man's gifts – courage, the spirit of inquiry, artistic skill, man's sense of order and design, his understanding of natural laws, and his capacity for singular journeys to the most distant places. They are the brightest attributes and they have made maps one of the most luminous of man's creations.

But map-making also requires the ability to judge the truth of travelers' tales. Although Marco Polo's *Travels* allowed early European cartographers to give place-names and continental configurations to their maps, the book itself contained only a tiny sketch map and had many odd omissions (no Great Wall, no mention of tea). Columbus had the Latin version of 1483 among his belongings on his voyages westward – which was why, in Cuba in 1493, he sent a party of men searching the Cuban hinterland for the Great Khan, and on later voyages believed he was coasting past Indochina (it was Honduras) and about three weeks away from the Ganges. Columbus was not unique in his misapprehension: cartographic ignorance has been universal. There are the many maps of the Abyssinian kingdom of Prester John, and the maps which show California to be an island (this belief persisted throughout the seventeenth century). And it was only seventy or eighty years ago that the Chinese were finally satisfied that the world was round.

"It would seem as though cartography were an instinct implanted in every nation with any claim to civilization," the geographer Sir Alexander Hosie wrote. He had in mind a map of China, carved in stone, and discovered in the Forest of Tablets at Hsian, the capital of Shensi province. That stone map is dated in the year called *Fou Ch'ang*, 1137, but the Chinese had been making maps for centuries on wood, silk and paper. The Chinese and the Romans were making maps of their respective known worlds at roughly the same time. In 128 BC, Chang Ch'ien, China's first historic traveler, returned home after having covered the immense distance to the Oxus (we know it as the Amu Darya) in Central Asia. Chang reported to the Emperor Wu on what he had seen, and the emperor named the mountains K'un-lun, where the Yellow River rose.

For the next thousand years, China was active – a nation of travelers, warriors, conquerers, traders and, inevitably, map-makers. What was the point of conquering if the subject lands were not then given a shape, and their rivers and households described on maps? The Chinese word for map, *t'u*, also means "plan," "chart" and "drawing." (Our own word *map* has Latin cousins meaning "napkin" and "sheet.") Chinese cartography could be ambitious. P'ei Hsiu (224-271), sometimes called The Father of Chinese Cartography, did a magnificent map of China in eighteen panels ("The Map of the Territory of the Tribute of Yu"), and codified map-making in Six Principles. His First Principle, an enormous contribution to the art, was *fen lu*, the grid system.

P'ei's successor was Chia Tan, whose masterpiece in 801 was "The Map of China and Barbarian Countries Within the Seas." Chia was working in the T'ang Dynasty (618-907), one of the most renowned in Chinese history. It was very much a map-making dynasty – it had imperial ambitions, pursuing a policy of conquest in the west and south. Chia was commissioned to make maps of the conquered territories. Subsequent maps of China for the following few hundred years were based on Chia's ninth century work.

China also exemplifies the way cartography can go into decline. As a nation craves silence and becomes xenophobic and inward-looking, demanding tribute instead of initiating trade, it loses the will to communicate with the world and begins to wither of its own egotism. The Chinese still continued to regard the world as flat and four-square (though they believed the sky to be round). One cannot attribute this to stubborn ignorance; after all, it took Europe a thousand years to accept the notion that the world was round.

Yet all of China's naive geocentricity can be seen in the outrage of the Imperial Court's scrutiny of a Jesuit map in which China was situated in the eastern corner. What was the Middle Kingdom doing on the far right? Father Matteo Ricci cleverly redrew his map by spinning his globe, so to speak, and placing the Celestial empire smack in the middle, with Europe in the distant west. That was in 1602. The Chinese accepted the priest's version of the world – it somewhat resembled their own – but they rejected his spherical projection.

When China lost interest in foreign countries her maps became inaccurate, not to say bizarre. These maps showed European countries and the United States and Africa as tiny islands and sandbars off the Middle Kingdom coast. Even in the mid-nineteenth century Chinese maps depicted the natives of these little islands as monstrous and one-eyed, and some were shown with holes through their stomachs for their convenient carrying on poles. Around the turn of the nineteenth century, the Chinese accepted that the world was round. It is possible, I think, to read in this acceptance of a new map a profound understanding of their place in the world.

Cartography has always required utter truthfulness – it is one of its most appealing features: crooked maps are worse than useless, and nothing dates more quickly than the political map ("German East Africa," "French Indochina," "The Central African Empire," "Jones-town"). But until the recent past, maps have been more than scientific; they have depended on a high level of pictorial art – vivid imagery and lettering – and a style of labeling and a conciseness in description that is literary in the best sense.

Blaeu is the Rembrandt of geography. Most maps, even modern ones, are beautiful – beautiful in colour and contour, and often breathtaking in their completeness. They can tell us everything, and the best ones, from the great periods of trade and exploration – our own is one such period – have always attempted to do this. In 500 BC Anaximander's successor, Hecataeus, made a disc-shaped map – it was a startling illumination. But maps specialize in such surprises.

Consider the Ortelius map of China of 1573 – "Regnum Chinae." It is full of fictitious lakes, but it accurately places rivers, mountains, and cities – enough to guide any explorer or trader to his destination. It also includes the westernmost portion of America ("America Pars") at 180° longitude, and it shows what we know as the Bering Sea. In vivid marginal pictures it tells us about the Far East – the Great Wall is drawn, a Chinese junk is rendered in perfect detail, a man is shown being crucified in Japan for being a Christian and keeping the faith (there is a warning in Latin). In a corner is a Chinese four-wheeled cart, powered by a sail, and this cart (so the inscription tells us) can also be used as a boat. The map is a masterpiece of practicality and imagination.

Cartography has the capacity to open up countries to world trade. For example, throughout most of the nineteenth century it was recognized that a canal was needed in Central America to join the two great oceans. Mexico and most of the Central American countries were exhaustively mapped, and a dozen canals were proposed. These maps expressed hopes, promises and fantasies. On a map by F. Bianconi in 1891, Honduras – which could not have been emptier – is shown as a teeming go-ahead republic. "Railways under construction," it says and you see hundreds and hundreds of miles of track, two lines from coast to coast. Who needs a canal with such trains! In the Mosquito jungle you have the impression of intense cultivation, and mining, and cattle-grazing. Honduras looks blessed – full of sarsparilla and sugar-cane, and iron, zinc, silver and gold. The word "gold" appears on this map sixty-five times, in each spot where it apparently lies in the ground.

There were similar maps of Panama, and of course Panama won out.

But a modern map of Honduras shows most of the cartographic detail in this hundred-year-old map to be unfulfilled promises. Anyone who looks at a lot of maps becomes highly suspicious of the designations "Proposed railway," "Road under construction," "Projected highway" – with dotted lines; or that other heart-sinker, "Site of proposed Hydro-electric Dam." These are not features which are found only on maps of Third World Countries. "The M25 Ring-Road" is shown on some maps of Outer London, though the road has yet to be finished. The most ominous line on a map is the one labelled "Disputed boundary," and it makes one think that there are perhaps fifty versions of the world map, depending on your nationality. Israel has about four different shapes, and on some modern Arab maps it does not exist at all.

The map of the London Underground is by almost any standard a work of art – a squint turns it into late-Mondrian – but it also has great practical value. After ten years of residence in London I still have to consult this map every time I travel by tube: the underground system is too complex for me to hold in my head. The same goes for the New York subway, which is a problem for cartographers – at least three recent attempts have been made to map it so that it can be understood and used by a stranger. None has succeeded. It remains an intimidating map.

The map predates the book (even a fairly ordinary map may contain several books' worth of information). It is the oldest means of information storage, and can present the most subtle facts with great clarity. It is a masterly form of compression, a way of miniaturizing a country or society. Most hill-climbers and perhaps all mountaineers know the thrill at a certain altitude of looking down and recognizing the landscape that is indistinguishable from a map. The only pleasure I take in flying in a jet plane is the experience of matching a coastline or the contour of a river to the corresponding map in my memory. A map can do many things, but I think its chief use is in lessening our fear of foreign parts and helping us anticipate the problems of dislocation. Maps give the world coherence. It seems to me one of man's supreme achievements that he knew the precise shape of every continent and practically every river-vein on earth long before he was able to gaze at them whole from the window of a rocket-ship.

This sense of map-shapes is so strong it amounts almost to iconography. The cartographer gives features to surfaces, and sometimes these features are resonant. It is easy to see a dependency in the way Sri Lanka seems to linger at the tip of India; Africa looks like one of its own paleolithic skulls; and some countries are, visibly, appendages. Who has looked upon Chile and not seen in it an austere narrowness, or smiled at Delaware, or wondered what Greenland is *for*? The shape of a country may condition our initial attitude towards it, though I don't think any conclusion can be drawn from the fact that Great Britain looks like a boy riding on a pig. And position matters, too. It does not surprise me that the Chinese called their country the Middle Kingdom. It is human to be geocentric. Every country, to its people, is a middle kingdom – zero longitude, where East and West begin. And what a shock it must be for the Pacific islander looking for his country for the first time on a world map, and not finding it, and having to be told that his great island is this tiny dot. The opposite is also remarkable. We have the word of many British people who have spoken of their pride at seeing the Empire verified in pink on a globe.

Maps have also given life to fiction. From *Gulliver's Travels* to *The Lord of the Rings*, novels have contained maps of their mythical lands. Thomas Hardy carefully drew a map so that his readers could understand his Wessex novels, and so did Norman Mailer when he published *The Naked and the Dead*. In these books the map came later, but there is an example of a fantasy map preceding a work of literature. Robert Louis Stevenson wrote,

> ... I made the map of an island; it was elaborately and (I thought) beautifully coloured: the shape of it took my fancy beyond expression; it contained harbours that pleased me like sonnets; and with the unconsciousness of the pre-destined, I ticketted my performance *Treasure Island* ... as I pored over my map of Treasure Island, the future characters in the book began to appear there visibly among imaginary woods; and their brown faces and bright weapons peeped out upon me from unexpected quarters, or they passed to and fro, fighting and hunting treasure. The next thing I knew I had some paper before me and was writing out a list of chapters ...

I was delighted to find this example for Stevenson's cartographic inspiration, because for two years I worked on a novel – *The Mosquito Coast* – with a map of Central America next to my desk. When I was stuck for an idea, or when I wanted to reassure myself that my fictional settlements really existed, I studied this map.

Most novelists are map conscious, and all great novelists are carto-graphers. So are all true explorers, and the most intrepid travelers and traders. The real explorer is not the man who is following a map, but the man who is making one.

I do not think that it is profit alone, the desire for financial gain or celebrity, that animates such men. But it is a fact that the most commercial-minded countries have also been the most outward-looking. In the past, there were no trading nations that were not also the dedicated patrons of cartographers. Today, the proudest boast of any commercial enterprise is its illustration, with a map, of its influence and success. All maps are records of discovery; without fresh discoveries no new maps are possible. Our fastidious curiosity and our passionate business sense and even our anxieties have made ours a cartographic age.

Maps reflect the face of the land. They tell us most things but not everything. Long ago, they were shorelines; and then they were riverbanks; and at last they were territories with a million features. But they have always been surfaces figured with routes and suggestions. To the most courageous and imaginative of us, these surfaces are eloquent, showing the way to new discoveries. In a sense, the world was once blank. And the reason cartography made it visible and glowing with detail was because man believed, and rightly, that maps are a legacy that allows other men and future generations to communicate and trade.

A good map is better than a guidebook: it is the ultimate tool of the man who wishes to understand a distant country. It can be merciless in its factuality. It can also tell us things that are unobtainable anywhere else.

About ten and a half years ago, in Singapore, I rented a house – sight-unseen – in the English county of Dorsetshire. I had been to England twice, but never to Dorset. The village, South Bowood, was not mentioned in any guidebook. What descriptions I came across were general and unhelpful. After a great deal of reading I still knew absolutely nothing of the place in which I was now committed to spend six months with my wife and two small children. I began to wonder if the place existed.

It was then that I found some Ordnance Survey Maps. The whole of Britain is scrupulously mapped. I had the correct sheet. I located South Bowood: it was a hamlet of about eight houses. Letters and symbols told me there was a public house down the road, and a mailbox, and a public telephone. The post office and school were a mile distant, and the nearest church was at Netherbury; but we would be on a hill, and there were meadows all around us, and footpaths, and not far from us the ruins of an Iron-Age hill fort. The houses were small black squares, and at last, sitting there in the Singapore Library studying the map, I worked out which house would be ours. So I knew exactly where I was going, and all my fears vanished. With this map, I was prepared: without it, I would have been in darkness.

The Last Laugh

[1981]

Humorists are often unhappy men and satirists downright miserable, but S. J. Perelman was a cheery soul who, when he flew into one of his exalted rages, seemed to have the gift of tongues. He gave his mockery a bewitching style. In his stories, or *feuilletons* as he liked to call them, he represented himself as a victimized clown. He was "button-cute, wafer-thin" and reared turkeys ("which he occasionally exhibits on Broadway"); or Doctor Perelman, "small bore in Africa"; or a mixture of Sad Sack and Pierre Loti, haplessly sampling the pleasures of out-of-the-way places; or finally as a sort of boulevardier and roué who, at the moment of sexual conquest, is defeated by a wayward bedspring.

When I first began reading him in the 1950's – I was in junior high school – I was excited by his malicious humor, his huge vocabulary and what I took to be his lunatic fantasy. I sensed a spirit of rebellion in him that stirred the anarchy in my schoolboy soul. After I started to travel, it struck me that much of what he wrote was true: Perelman's Africa was the Africa no one else had noticed. His stories were bizarre because he sought out the bizarre. He cherished oddity and, being truly adventurous, was willing to put himself to a lot of trouble to find it (he strolled around Shanghai, in 1947, looking for it). Then I met him. He *was* button-cute, and also a bit of a roué, and accident-prone. If he had been writing fantasies, we would think of him as a humorist, a writer of gags, whose object was merely to entertain. But he wrote about the world, and his intensity and his anger made him into a satirist.

A satirist seems a sour and forbidding figure – a mocker, a pessimist, a grudge-bearer, a smirker, something of a curmudgeon, perhaps with a streak of cruelty who, in inviting the reader to jeer at his victim, never misses a trick or withholds a nudge. How does one suggest that such a man may also have a great deal of charm? Perelman's friends liked him very much. He was generous, he was funny, he was enormously social, he didn't boast. Travel has the effect of turning most people into monologuists; it made Perelman an accomplished watcher and an appreciative listener. When he talked in his croaky drawl he did so in the elaborate way he wrote, with unlikely locutions and slang and precise descriptions diverted into strings of subordinate clauses. He was small and neatly made; he wore very handsome clothes, usually of an English cut, and in his pockets he carried clippings he tore from the newspapers — one he showed me was about the movie *The Texas Chain-Saw Massacre*, which he eventually worked into a story. He read the London *Times* every day (he had an air-mail subscription) — more, I think, for the unusual names than for anything else. In today's *Times*, Sir Ranulph Twisleton-Wykeham-Fiennes has just reached the South Pole; Captain Sir Weldon Dalrymple-Champneys has just died; and both Miss C. Inch and Miss E. L. F. I. Lunkenheimer have just got married. Perelman welcomed news of this kind.

In his way, he was a man of the world. A man of the world, almost by definition, is never content anywhere. Perelman was a bit like that. He had a great capacity for pleasure, but he was restless, always active, game for anything; he fed himself on change. He began writing at Brown University, where a fellow classmate was Nathanael West (Perelman married West's sister Laura in 1929), and at the age of twenty-five, with the success of his first book, *Dawn Ginsbergh's Revenge*, he was invited to Hollywood to write jokes for the Marx Brothers. He went, and he liked to say that Hollywood reminded him of a novel he had read in Providence as a boy, *In The Sargasso Sea*, by Thomas Janvier (anyone who has the luck to find this 1899 story of marooning and murder in the nightmare swamp will immediately see the connection). From time to time throughout his life, Perelman returned to Hollywood, struggled with scripts and then fought free. At the age of seventy-four, fresh from the travels he recounted in *Eastward Ha!*, he tried to drive his vintage 1949 MG from Paris to Peking, commemorating the trip of Count Something-or-other. It was not such a crazy scheme. He had been around the world a dozen times. He was in good health, his car had recently had a tune-up, he had a generous sponsor and many well-wishers, and he liked to say (though joshing himself with his chain-smoker's chuckle) that he knew Malaysia and Hong Kong like the back of his hand.

In a Thai restaurant, in London, on Christmas Eve, he told me about his drive to Peking. He had just flown in from China. The trip, he said, was a total disaster. The glamor girl he had chosen for navigator had been fired at the outset for selling her story to a magazine. He had quarreled with his fellow drivers all the way through India. There had been kerfuffles with customs men in Turkey. The car was not allowed through Burma and, as there was no room on a ship to Malaysia, the car had been air-freighted to Hong Kong. There were more scenes in Hong Kong. "The others freaked out," Perelman said, but with the old car now parked in Kowloon, he flew to Peking and spent two weeks in a Chinese hospital with a severe case of bronchitis, aggravated by double pneumonia.

"Now I have to write about it," he said. "It'll be horrible."

Frankly, I thought the subject was made for him. Nothing is more Perelmanesque than a marathon drive across the world, interlarded with set-backs, blown gaskets, howling Turks and long delays in flea-ridden Indian hotels. And pneumonia in Peking was the perfect ending for someone who always racked his brain for grand finales. (His editor at the *New Yorker*, William Shawn, told me, "He always had trouble with endings.") But the last collection of Perelman pieces contains nothing about that Paris to Peking trip. This is odd, because he had made his reputation by describing the complicated orchestration of fiascos.

A month before he died, he wrote me a letter in which he said, "I myself have spent altogether too much time this year breaking my nails on the account of the Paris–Peking trip I made . . . and after a lot of bleeding cuticle, I decided to abandon it. I guess there are certain subjects – or maybe one's subjective reactions to them – that in spite of the most manful attempts are totally unproductive. The one I picked certainly was, and it took a lot of *Sturm und Drang* to make me realize that my Sisyphean labors were getting me nowhere."

This was the only gloomy paragraph in an otherwise chirpy letter. His letters were long, frequent, and sensationally funny – indeed, so funny that, after receiving a few, Raymond Chandler (always a hoarder and procrastinator where writing was concerned) replied worriedly warning Perelman against squandering his wit: "You shouldn't give the stuff away like that when you can sell it, unless of course your letters are just rough notes for articles."

But they weren't "just rough notes for articles." They were generous and intelligent expressions of friendship and most of them far too scandalous to be retailed. Here is the opening paragraph of a letter Perelman wrote me on Christmas Eve, 1976:

"Between the constant repetition of 'White Christmas' and 'Jingle Bells' on Station WPAT and the increasing frenzy of Saks' and Gimbel's newspaper ads as these fucking holidays draw near, I have been in a zombie-like state for weeks, totally incapable of rational thought or action. I must have arrived at near-paralysis yesterday afternoon when I was in the 4th-floor lingerie section ('Intimate Apparel') in Saks 5th Avenue. I had just purchased two such intimate garments for gifties to a couple of ladies of my acquaintance, a tall blonde and a somewhat shorter brunette. For the former, I had chosen a black lace chemise in the style known as a teddy back in the 'twenties (familiar to you as the scanty garment worn by Rita Hayworth in the war-time pin-up). For the shorter brunette, a similar peach-colored job. Both of these real silk, parenthetically, and as I signed the charge slip, I knew that when the bill comes in after January 1st, I would kick myself for my prodigality. Anyway, while the hard-featured saleslady was wrapping them up with appropriate mash-notes to each bimbo, I went upstairs to the men's dept. to buy myself a cheap tie-tack. When I returned for the feminine frillies, I found (a) that the saleslady had forgotten to identify which box was which, and (b) that she had switched the notes. In other words, the blonde Amazon would find herself with the brunette's undershirt and some steamy sentiment addressed to the latter, and vice-versa. I broke out into a perspiration – it's tropically hot in those department stores anyway – and insisted on the saleslady clawing open the boxes, which meant destroying all the fake holly berries, silver cord, and mish-mash they were entwined in. This of course put her in a foul temper, and meanwhile a waiting queue of customers became incensed. The upshot was a group shot of seven or eight people leering and cackling obscenely as I stood there holding the two chemises and the notes appropriate to the recipients. Given the savoir-faire of Cary Grant I might have risen above it, but the only savoir-faire I possess is Oliver Hardy's, and little enough of that . . ."

When Perelman's letters are collected, as they surely deserve to be, they will comprise the autobiography he promised and began, but never got around to finishing. The three chapters printed here are all we have of *The Hindsight Saga* – anyway, with a title that good you hardly need a book; or did its promise of disclosures intimidate him? He was always more personal and ruminative and risqué in his letters than he was in his stories, and he heartily disliked people who boasted by reminiscing about the past. "I see Scott Fitzgerald's gossip-columnist mistress has been cleaning out the contents of a thimble," he wrote me when Sheilah Graham's *The Real Scott Fitzgerald* appeared.

Perelman knew Fitzgerald as a sober, hard-working script-writer, who had gone to Hollywood for the money, much as today's writers accept tenure at universities. Fitzgerald believed himself a failure, but Perelman was one man (Faulkner was another) who used Hollywood to fuel his other projects; his script-writing career coincided with his first appearance in the pages of the *New Yorker*. It seems extraordinary that he was able to keep his enthusiasms separate, but to California and New York he added the world. From the 'thirties onward he traveled widely, first in the Pacific and then in Africa, Europe and Asia. I cannot think of another writer who was so adept as Perelman in prevailing over such vast cultural incongruities and whose appreciations included B-movies, pulp magazines, Joyce's *Ulysses*, Hollywood dives, the societal norms in Bucks County, Manhattan and Nairobi, detective fiction, English country-house weekends, vintage cars, dogs (he once, on a whim, bought a bloodhound), cantankerous producers and pretty women. He talked with passionate energy about Fellini's *Satyricon* and Alfred Russel Wallace's *The Malay Archipelago*. He knew Dorothy Parker well and had a close friendship with Eric Ambler. He was the only person I have ever known who dropped in on J. D. Salinger, whom he called "Jerry."

His greatest passion was language. In "Listen to the Mockingbird" he wrote, "As recently as 1918, it was possible for a housewife in Providence, where I grew up, to march into a store with a five cent piece, purchase a firkin of cocoa butter, a good second-hand copy of Bowditch, a hundredweight of quahogs, a shagreen spectacle case and sufficient nainsook for a corset cover and emerge with enough left over to buy a balcony admission to 'The Masquerader' with Guy Bates Post, and a box of maxixe cherries." He was parodying inflation, but it is impossible to read "cocoa butter," "Bowditch," "quahogs," "shagreen," "nainsook," and the rest without a sense of mounting hilarity. He worked hard for a kind of insane exactitude in his prose and would not settle for "sad" if he could use "chopfallen." I think his travels were bound up for his quest to find odd words or possible puns. They were more than mere souvenirs of travel: they were the object of his arduous jaunts. The uniqueness of his writing depends for its effects on linguistic virtuosity, finding room for "oppidan" or the verb "swan" or the weirder lingo he abstracted in India and Africa. E. B. White once wrote about how Perelman, after crashing his car in Florida, savored the phrase, "We totalled it!" and his pleasure in being able to use it took the sting out of the accident.

His interests and his travels swelled his vocabulary and gave him his style. But none of this would have been accessible without his memory, which was faultless. That too is a distinguishing feature in his fiction. A good memory is one of the most valuable assets a writer has, and Perelman's memory amounted to genius. One day, years ago, he was passing through Shropshire, and a glimpse of that green countryside stayed with him. He plotted to return to Shropshire and rent a house and live there like a squire; but, though he visited England often, he always became restive. Apart from the precincts of *Punch*, where he was fêted, he found England tight and dry and a little dull. And the house rents in Shropshire were too high. He was too much of an Anglophile to like England greatly.

He died on October 17, 1979, in New York City, where he was born.

Graham Greene's Traveling Companion

[1981]

"I hadn't even realized that she was making notes," Graham Greene wrote in his 1978 Introduction to *Journey Without Maps*, "I was so busy on my own." And the reader looks in vain for a portrait of Barbara Greene in that book. She is named once, and mentioned ("My cousin . . .") eleven times in three hundred pages. She is not important to his narrative; she hardly exists. Once, on the way to Bamakama, the cousins are separated. In Graham Greene's telling this is an incidental anxiety in a couple of paragraphs; in Barbara's it is six pages, something approaching adventure, before – in what is a sheer coincidence – the cousins bump into each other in the thick bush. We never see Barbara Greene's face in *Journey Without Maps*, we never hear her voice. This was deliberate. Graham Greene wanted to avoid "the triviality of a personal travel diary" by making it profoundly personal, filling it with "memories, dreams, word-associations", and so allowing it to become metaphorical and akin to fiction. "We share our dreams," he wrote, and it is true that our most powerful dreams are of wild places; the land of dreams – or nightmares – is pretty much unmapped.

It was for both a brave trip. They were young enough not to be intimidated by the risk they were taking. Graham was thirty-one, Barbara was twenty-three. The year was 1935, but the most detailed book on Liberia – Sir Harry Johnston's – had appeared thirty years earlier. The map of Liberia was blank – some rivers indicated, a few coastal towns, and the interior marked *Cannibals*. What was the appeal, then, of an exhausting journey along jungle tracks? Graham listed the attractions in his own book: it was a black republic, pledged to liberty and progress, which was brutal, disease-ridden and almost unknown to Europe; it was dark; it was the past. The lingo of Liberian politics was grandiose, but the political facts were of massacres and plagues. There was something seedy about the place: "seediness has a very deep appeal . . . It seems to satisfy, temporarily, the sense of nostalgia for something lost; it seems to represent a stage further back."

Graham went because of the risks and discomforts. He was not seeking self-destruction – that would have been pure folly – but self-discovery. In the 'thirties, English writers "were inclined to make uncomfortable journeys in search of bizarre material," but Graham rejected Brazil, Europe, the mapped parts of Africa, and he turned his back on an Intourist ticket into "a plausible future." He wrote, "My journey represented a distrust of any future based on what we are." But it would be wrong to see his motives as especially high-minded and inspired by the possibility of allegory. He clearly liked the idea of utter awfulness, or perhaps getting lost, of being out of touch (at a time when so many writers wanted to be in touch). He was physically strong and had a growing reputation; he was confident; throughout the early parts of *Journey With Maps* one senses that the author is seeking adventure, and to hell with the comforts of literary London.

So far, so good. But he did not go alone.

Barbara Greene is Graham's first cousin (Christopher Isherwood is also a cousin). While Graham is elusive and even somewhat fictionalized in his own account of the journey through Liberia – as if glimpsed from between the dense overhang of tropical jungle – Barbara is completely straightforward. She is modest and a bit self-mocking; Graham led, she followed – sometimes miles behind. She left all decisions to her cousin. This was an age when men were expected to take command. Graham dealt with the carriers, the cook, the immigration formalities, the bad tempers, the disputes. It must have been a great strain – the strain certainly shows. What started as something of a lark turned out to be an obsession; and, a critical moment, it was Graham who fell ill and was near to dying of an obscure fever. To give him his due, Graham did not make much of this near-fatal illness – "A Touch of Fever" that chapter is called – and there is no self-pity and little self-regard in *Journey Without Maps*.

Land Benighted is quite a different pair of shoes. It is the book that Graham wanted to avoid writing, and at the time he admitted to being "disappointed" that Barbara wrote it. After Graham's almost Conradian push through the African darkness, how deflating it must have seemed when his companion in this trek revealed herself as a pretty young thing, not really a hiker ("I love my creature comforts"), who agreed to walk across Liberia ("wherever it was") because she was a bit tipsy on champagne. She is almost at pains to portray herself as the "Oh, dear!", "What a muddle!" and "Mustn't grumble!" sort of traveling companion, though this could hardly have been the case. When her book appeared in 1938, reviewers remarked on Barbara's pluck. It seemed to be full of the sort of details which, if concerned with another place or time or companion, might have been regarded as trivial. Unlike Graham's, there were no flashbacks to Riga or Nottingham, no quotes from Baudelaire or Eliot. Graham had Burton's *Anatomy of Melancholy* in his luggage; Barbara had Maugham and the stories of Saki. It is a wonderfully telling fact, and as the trip wore on Graham became more melancholy, and Barbara began to sparkle like a light-hearted deb in a Saki story. After weeks in the bush, they came upon a small black schoolmaster, one Victor Prosser who wears "short artificial taffeta trousers in a delicate shade of mauve." Mr Prosser asks Barbara to describe London. She tells him about the underground railway and then is sorry she has done so:

> It all sounded horrible, and I almost felt that I did not want to go back – till, of course, I remembered Elizabeth Arden, my flat, and the Savoy Grill.

Notice that Saki-ish "of course".

What might have seemed trivial or unimportant about *Land Benighted* in the 'thirites, now – over forty years later – is like treasure. What if Waugh had had such a companion in Abyssinia, or Peter Fleming's cousin had accompanied him to Manchuria? What if Kinglake, or Doughty, or Waterton had had a reliable witness to their miseries and splendors? We would not have thought less of these men, but we would have known much more of them.

> Graham had a little twitching nerve over his right eye. When he felt particularly unwell it would twitch incessantly, and I watched it with horror. It fascinated me, and I would find my eyes fixed upon it till I was almost unable to look anywhere else. I did not tell him about it, for I got to know it so well that I was able to gauge how he was feeling without having to ask him.

The social details which Barbara gives about herself – the longing for the Savoy Grill, and smoked salmon and a manicure – fix that aspect of the book in a particular time and give it its privileged pre-war flavor. The trivial, after a time, becomes revealing and even necessary, which is why we put the hairpins and buttons of Roman matrons in museums. But more important than this are the two chief virtues of *Land Benighted*. The first is that it is an intimate portrait of Graham Greene as a young man in a foreign country. It is the quintessential Greene; the 'thirties were a time for him of almost manic energy, when he still believed that "seediness has a very deep appeal" and wrote the books that made his name a resonant adjective. That Greene mood is the mood of *Journey Without Maps*. The other virtue, but it is unintentional, is that *Land Benighted* shows that however light-hearted a departure is, if the traveler is generous, observant, and dedicated to the trip, the traveler will be changed. From a rather scatty socialite at the beginning, Barbara Greene becomes hardy and courageous without ever being tempted into the role of *memsahib*. How easy it would have been for her to accept the traveling style of the missionary widow of Zorzor, who in Graham's book (where she appears as "Mrs Croup") "always travelled in a hammock specially made to carry her weight, with eighteen hammock-carriers. She drove them hard; a ten-hour trek was nothing to her." Indeed, it is at this very odd woman's house (pet cobra, black baby, Biblical pamphlets) that Barbara reflects:

> I was feeling most extraordinarily well. My feet had nearly healed and were getting beautifully hard. The long walks seemed to suit me, and although the heat was almost too much of a good thing, it now seemed to tire my mind only and not my body. I was getting used to being bitten all over by insects and just went on scratching automatically, thankful that although they bit every other part of my body, they never attacked my face.

Barbara had agreed to go to Liberia because "It sounded fun." It wasn't fun. It was almost hell. But after weeks of it, she changed. Habitually she marched behind. Then Graham fell ill, and although he recovered he was still, in her words, "sub-normal." "He looked rather weak, and for the first time I was the one who was marching on ahead." It is an extraordinary reversal. She had come as a companion, to follow and take orders. But her health was better than Graham's towards the end – her spirits were certainly higher – and on the last lap it was she who set the pace. In the course of this reckless trip, she had grown up and even in a small way taken command. She never says so in the book, just as she never boasts of her good health; but it is clear from what she describes of the last part of the trip. She followed obediently, she nursed Graham through his illness, she made a careful record of the journey. It is no wonder that Graham dedicated his book to her.

Barbara is too modest, too self-effacing, to make any claim for her book. It was not an adventure story, she said. It was not knowledgeable. The reader "will learn nothing new." In a delightful aside she says, "It was the little everyday things that pleased me most."

One of these things was Graham's presence. How was she to know that in time he would be regarded as one of the greatest English writers? Just as Graham avoids mentioning Barbara in his book, so Barbara never mentions that Graham is a writer, that she has read his books, or that he is making this difficult journey with the intention of writing a book about it. (He had already received, and spent, his advance of £350.) "I looked up to him," she says, but her role in this trip was every bit as important as Graham's, and just as literary. She is the witness, like the narrator of a novel who sometimes becomes part of the action. She did not know at the time that she was telling a Graham Greene story. In Freetown, Sierra Leone, she took out her diary and analyzed him.

> His brain frightened me. It was sharp and clear and cruel. I admired him for being unsentimental, but "always remember to rely on yourself," I noted. "If you are in a sticky place he will be so interested in noting your reactions that he will probably forget to rescue you." For some reason he had a permanently shaky hand, so I hoped that we would not meet any wild beasts on this trip ... my cousin would undoubtedly miss anything he aimed at. Physically he did not look strong. He seemed somewhat vague and unpractical ... Apart from three or four people he was really fond of, I felt that the rest of humanity was to him like a heap of insects that he liked to examine ... He was always polite. He had a remarkable sense of humour and held few things too sacred to be laughed at. I suppose at that time I had a very conventional little mind, for I remember he was continually tearing down ideas I had always believed in, and I was left to build them up anew. It was stimulating and exciting, and I wrote down that he was the best kind of companion one could have for a trip of this kind. I was learning far more than he realized.

Long after he took the trip, Graham wrote, "My cousin left all decisions to me and never criticized me when I made the wrong one ... Towards the end we would lapse into long silences, but they were infinitely preferable to raised voices."

"Graham," Barbara writes in her book, "would sometimes become rather obstinate, hanging on to some small, unimportant point like a dog to a bone." And then, she adds, "But we never quarrelled, not once."

They had put themselves into a situation in which people nearly always quarrel, or abandon each other, or worse. I once hiked for four days down the same sort of twelve-inch path through a tropical jungle. I had three male companions, and at the end of it vowed that I never wanted to see any of them again. The Greenes walked for many days. They succeeded because as Barbara says in one of her splendid passages she learned to defer; not to kowtow, but to know when to fall silent. The jungle is not really neutral: it is stubborn and it can drive intruders mad. Barbara discovered conflict-avoidance, though she never uses that pompous phrase. She stayed away from contentious subjects. She said, "I expect you're right, really." Soon, every subject was contentious, except the subject of food.

The trip was Graham's idea. Barbara thought of herself as a passenger. But no jungle trek tolerates passengers. Barbara did as she was told, made useful friendships with the carriers, and following at the end of the long file observed Graham meticulously. In the beginning, he frightened her a little. She came to respect him, and then to admire him, and towards the end of the trip a kind of understanding was reached. They are like a man and wife in the best marraiges, with a profound understanding of each other's strengths and weaknesses; passion is gone, but what has supplanted it – sympathy and trust – is far greater.

Barbara judges Graham not by the way he treats her, but by his manner in dealing with the Africans. Graham did not take any of the advice he was given by the coastal colonials. He had been told to be harsh, to distrust, to shout. Instead, he "treated them exactly as if they were white men from our own country. He talked to them quite naturally and they liked him." This got results, "they did everything he wanted them to do." And it earned him Barbara's respect. When Barbara remarks, "he was like a benevolent father," it is like a woman speaking of her husband's love for their children. One must also add that these Africans were being required to venture into a place that was not just strange, but nightmarish: the journey held far greater terrors for them, for they believed in cannibals and devils and people who threw lightning bolts and who could walk through walls and who could kill them with a glance. These Africans had never been on such a trek. They were being led around the back of Liberia and down to the coast. All the paths were new to them, and frightening. It was not only the Greenes who were coming of age as discoverers.

After entering French Guinea, at a very uncertain point in the journey, there is a near mutiny. Graham does not threaten. He is firm; he lectures the men; then he bluffs and turns his back on them. The subtle tactic works better than whips. The men are sheepish; the journey continues. Later, there is a tribal dispute among the men. Graham, who had said, "There is only one thing to do here – get drunk," hears the men quarreling. With the calm and optimism of a little whisky, Graham goes out.

> He listened majestically for a few minutes. Then he gave his verdict firmly, prompted, I suppose, by the faithful Amadu, and lifting up his hand he said, "Palaver finished." Then (swaying, oh so slightly) he walked away. It was a superb performance. We were all astonished. The men had no more to say.

A passage that Graham himself chose for comparison with Barbara's book was the one in *Journey Without Maps*, beginning, "I remember nothing of the trek to Zigi's Town and very little of the succeeding days." He remembered nothing because he had a high fever, and for several days, Barbara thought he was going to die. She kept a close watch on him, what amounted to a vigil, and continued to make notes, which she elaborated in Chapter XII of her own book. The portions of each book are too long to quote here, but a reader would do well to compare them. In any case, the reader of *Land Benighted* ought also to be a reader of *Journey Without Maps*. Few journeys have been so well-recorded, and there are not many discrepancies and no contradictions between the two accounts. Because Graham does not mention Barbara very much, he does not say how much the style and shape of her hiking shorts irritated him. Barbara says they drove him nearly to distraction. But his slipping-down socks irritated her quite as much. As time passes, the socks bother her more and more. It is a measure of her patience that she never mentioned the socks to him. In Monrovia, Barbara says she is going to take her funny shorts back to England ("I could wear them in the country"), and Graham explodes, and "told me with all the wealth of phrase at his command exactly what I looked like in them. It was worse even than I imagined, and hurriedly and humbly I gave the shorts to Laminah."

My favorite comparison between the two books concerns the prostitute they encountered in Zigi's Town.

> A young girl, an obvious little prostitute, hovered round and postured in front of Graham. She was a beautiful little creature, and I felt that at some time she had been down to the coast and that she had known white men. She was cute and intelligent, but over-optimistic, or she would have realized at once that my cousin was beyond noticing anything.

It is rare, as I said, to have two travel books about the same trip; for the best trips, certainly, one is enough. We have one *Eothen* and one *Arabia Deserta* and one *Waugh in Abyssinia*. In the Greenes we have two Liberias. Graham did most of the leading and arranging, so we know the trip from the head of the column; Barbara mainly followed, she did little arranging, but her book is easy-going and her portraits of incidental characters are warmer and chattier. Graham could be severe, but of course the trip was making him ill. On the night Barbara expected Graham to die, she wrote in her diary, "Feeling very fit indeed. This weather agrees with me . . ." Graham wrote often about the rats that jumped and played in his hut and prevented him from sleeping – rats are villainous subsidiary characters in his book. Barbara writes, "The rats were fat and well fed, and apart from the noise they made, they left me in peace. For two or three nights they upset me and after that I grew so used to them that I ceased to notice them, and they bothered me no more."

But what about the prostitute? Barbara had seen her, and she had seen Graham, unshaven, cadaverous, his eyes glazed with fever. He was "beyond noticing anything." Or was he? Was the novelist now so sick that he had turned into nothing more than a weary traveler anxious to be free of this dismal setting he had wished upon himself? In Barbara's book he had become at this point a stumbling wreck, fighting towards the coast and fearing the onset of the rains – single-minded, as the sick so often are. There is a parallel passage, about the prostitute in *Journey Without Maps*. Graham may have been ill, but he was alert:

> I noted, too, a sign that we were meeting the edge of civilization pushing up from the Coast. A young girl hung around all day posturing with her thighs and hips, suggestively, like a tart. Naked to the waist, she was conscious of her nakedness; she knew that breasts had a significance to the white man they didn't have to the native. There couldn't be any doubts that she had known whites before.

Graham's glance told him all he needed to know; after all, he had promised his publisher that he would come back with a book. It is the one instance where Barbara guesses wrong about her cousin. In other respects, she is uncommonly sensible, accurate, and perceptive. Graham lives in her book as he does in none other that I know. Barbara had no thought of writing about the trip until her father fell ill; she chose the opportunity to amuse him on his sickbed. She is extremely modest, but her dignity, bravery and loyalty can easily be discerned in her pages. We are very lucky to have this companion volume, and it is appropriate because no one can read it without reaching the conclusion that Barbara was the best of companions.

Summertime on the Cape

[1981]

When I've had it up to here with people telling me that what *The Guardian* needs is a good comparability study and that, in flood, south Dorset is no worse than Chittagong, and the petrol price is finally bottoming-out, and the Common Market isn't as boring as Canada, and that all you need to appear on television is a speech impediment, and that the aristocrat who disemboweled that schoolgirl (his plea: "But she had the body of a nine-year-old!") ought to have his Red Rover pass endorsed, and wittering on about some gloomy comedian's coronary, and shop assistants replying, "If you don't see it, we don't have it" to every question, including the way to the toilet, and that licensing hours have nothing to do with the fact that most publicans are drunk by 2.30, and that the Royal Family are overworked and underpaid, and that Park Lane is like the Gaza Strip, and dogturds are preferable to cyclists in public parks, and beginning with every sentence, "You Yanks –" and saying that funny old England is changeless, then I figure it's high time I took myself away on a good vacation.

The point is that England is not changeless, and I sometimes think it is no place for children. Though I suppose if children grow up among the geriatric, the frantic and the scheming they will end up knowing a thing or two about survival, even if they do sing the wrong words to "My Country 'Tis of Thee."

Most people go away for a vacation; I go home. And I consider myself lucky that I don't have to live at home, that I am for most of the year on this narrow island. England has the strictness and estranging quality of school. It is an old-fashioned place in which unpredictable suffering is part of the process of enlightenment. It keeps me hard at work because I find there is absolutely nothing else to do in England but work. But the summer is different. Ever since I was an ashen-faced tot, I have regarded the summer as a three-month period during which one swam, fished, read comic books, ate junk food and harmlessly misbehaved. In Massachusetts the sun comes out at the end of May and keeps shining until the first week in September. No one talks about the weather. There is no talk of weather in places that have a reliable climate. Once I recall staying in London in

August. I spent nearly the whole month in Clapham on a roadside with a dozen crones in overcoats, waiting for a 49 bus.

There is no bore like a vacation bore, but I think it is worth mentioning why I happen to like this handle-shaped piece of geography, swinging from the crankcase of the Bay State. It is largely a return to childhood, to a setting I understand and one which I associate with optimism. Americans still believe that all problems have solutions and that one deserves to live happily and uncrowded; they believe in the sanctity of space and can be surprisingly generous. This is very soothing.

The really serious traveler is the healthy intrepid person who, with a free month at last, and some money, and badly in need of a break, picks himself up and goes home. The casual traveler is another species entirely. For him, the journey is a form of neurosis that provokes him to leave at a moment's notice – and he may never return. But the rest of us, for whom travel is the experience of There-and-Back, are capable of the longest journeys precisely because we have homes to return to. And when early summer drops its clammy hand on London, and the English start crossing the Channel, and the idea of travel is in everyone's mind, I pack my bags and go back to Massachusetts.

"Pack my bags" is merely a metaphor for pulling myself together. I don't need to carry any bags home. I have a house on Cape Cod. My closets there have enough clothes in them; my tennis racket is there, my bathing suit, my other sneakers, my second-best razor, my pajamas. I am better equipped in East Sandwich than I am in London. I have an electric can-opener at my Cape Cod house, and a jeep, and a sailboat. I also have things like toothbrushes there. This allows me to go home empty-handed.

But traveling light like this can raise problems at Customs. Customs Officers in Boston often demand to know why I am entering the USA after a prolonged period abroad, carrying nothing but a book and my passport.

"Is this all you have?"

"Yes, sir."

If your entire luggage consists of one book, they take a great interest in the book. Last year it was Johnson's *Dictionary*, and the Customs Official actually began leafing through it, as if looking for clues to the meaning of my mission.

"You mean, this is *all you have*?"

"Yes, sir."

On one occasion, the officer said, "I think you'd better step over here and do some explaining." I was carrying an apple and a banana. I had no suitcase. He confiscated the apple, but let me keep the banana.

It is roughly an hour from Boston to Cape Cod, but once I have crossed the Sagamore Bridge everything is different. It is then that summer begins. A person who is tired of London is not necessarily tired of life; it might be that he just can't find a parking place, or is sick of being overcharged. But anyone who grows tired of Cape Cod needs his head examined, because for purely homely summer fun there is nowhere in the world that I know that can touch it.

Its geography is simple and explicit. It has the odd flung-out shape of a sandbar, with an excellent but boring canal at one end and at its furthest, wildest shore, Provincetown, the haunt of extroverts and practitioners of the half-arts such as soap-carving and sandal-making, where women with mustaches stare stonily at men with earrings. The Mid-Cape Highway, Route 6, runs through woods and salt marsh and dunes to Provincetown. To the right of this highway, and parallel, is Route 28, with a bar or a pizza parlor, or a fast-food joint, or a motel, every ten feet; to the left of the Mid-Cape Highway is Route 6A, "The King's Highway," with its roadside orchards and cranberry bogs, its antique shops, and pretty churches. The town of Hyannis is in the middle of all this. Hyannis is partly rural and partly honky-tonk; it has the airport, the seaport and the shopping mall, and most of the Cape's better restaurants. But Hyannis is the ugliest town on the Cape – it is hard to tell where it begins or ends, it is such a blight on the landscape – and it is one of the ugliest in the world, though it may be the only place in the world where you can buy a potholder with the late President Kennedy's face printed on it. Cape Codders forgive Hyannis its gimcrack look, because Hyannis is so useful a place – it's where you rent things, buy things and get things fixed and go to the movies. You can't have movie theaters and charm, anymore than you can have condominiums and rusticity. "What a place for a condo!" is the developer's war cry. The Cape is under assault at this moment and there is no question in my mind but that in time the Cape will be nothing except mile after mile of tasteful cluster development, so tasteful you will want to scream and go away.

The motels along Route 6A are straight out of *Psycho. Cabins*, the signs say, and nearly always, *Vacancy*. Strange gray outhouse-looking buildings lay huddled in the pines, each one solemn and weather-beaten, as if concealing the victim of a late-night strangulation or Prom-goers who have just discovered the facts of life. It is my belief that the most comfortable restaurants may be found along Route 6A, the liveliest auctions, the best second-hand bookshops, golf courses, and the freshest fish. It is possible to spend the whole summer on Route 6A without ever leaving it – shopping at the supermarket in Sandwich, swimming on the northside beaches, eating and drinking at any one of a score of places. The best whale-watching boat on the Cape, the *Speedy VII*, leaves from

Barnstable Harbor. "I suppose you could call this non-directive whale-watching," the on-board naturalist says as he urges the pilot towards a quartet of leaping fin-backs, or the geyser-gasps of whale spouts in the distance, or the magnificent sight of a humpback whale thrashing its vast tail against the green Atlantic. The whale-watchers are almost always successful; only one trip in fifty fails to uncover at least one whale. Long ago, there were so many whales in Cape Cod Bay they were harpooned from the beach off Sandy Neck and at the mouth of Barnstable Harbor. They were dragged ashore and flensed and boiled in the dunes.

Cape Codders are not particularly hospitable people, and yet in spite of this resentment of outsiders, it is noticeable that most activities on the Cape are designed for the amusement of visitors. The golf courses and tennis clubs and fishing outfits invite the enthusiastic tourist to join them. From Memorial Day until Labor Day, the Cape is a hive of activity, and most things are possible: you can charter a boat or a plane, hire a Gatsby-like mansion, go windsurfing or eat great meals. In the fall and winter it is different. *Closed for Season* signs go up, and the streets and the road-shoulders are messier. There are no tourists around, so why should we pick up the litter? That seems to be the reasoning. Cape Codders know that they live off tourists and so, in an offhand way, they welcome them; the Cape Codder does not become really fearful until he meets someone who wants to take up residence. In general, the Cape Codder is an inbred and rather puritanical skinflint, with a twinkle in his eye. An old Barnstable man once tried to win an argument with my brother by howling, "My family's been here for four-hundred years!"

Never mind. The only thing that matters on the Cape is that you stay a while. A week is not enough, two weeks are adequate, three are excellent, a month is perfect. This isn't travel, remember; this is a vacation. After a week or so, it is possible to develop a routine. Working in the morning – I write until noon in my study, undisturbed; then lunch at the beach, a swim, a sail; a trip along the shore in my rowboat at sundown; then a shower, a drink and the evening meal; lobsters or spaghetti at home, or a trip to a nearby restaurant. On the Cape, every good restaurant makes its own clam chowder (or even better, scallop chowder). On the whole, it is plain cooking with sensational ingredients: what could be plainer than a starter of steamed clams, a main dish of boiled lobster with salad, and dessert of strawberries? It hardly qualifies as cooking, and yet it is a wonderful meal.

After dinner, it is part of our routine to play parlor games. We have a card game in which each side must cheat to win ("Kemps"), a coin game for eight players ("Up Jenkins"), a word game for ten ("The Parson's Cat") and the most elaborate game of all, called simply "Murder", which requires up to twenty people and – ideally – a fifteen-room house for proper play – younger contestants can get the collywobbles in this frightening game. If there is an auction on – there is an auction in practically every town in the Cape – it is worth going to. The Sandwich Auction and Robert Eldred in East Dennis are two of the best; inevitably, some of the items are junk, but just as many are valuable, and some are treasures.

Morning is the best time for blueberry picking, and the best place is at the corner of Route 6A and Willow Street in West Barnstable. On rainy days, most people take to their cars and drive slowly towards Province-town, stopping at antique shops. This is a fairly dreary way of passing the time – dreary, because everyone else is doing it, and Cape traffic on a rainy day can be maddening. Much better, if the weather is foul, is to leave the Cape altogether for the Islands, where the sun might well be shining.

An ideal Island trip is the one to Martha's Vineyard. Boats leave from Hyannisport and Falmouth. The lazy or infirm can take a bus or taxi to Gay Head at the other side of the Vineyard; the energetic – but it doesn't take that much energy – ought to rent a bike and cycle to Edgartown, among the prettiest villages in New England. It is just a twenty-five cent ferry ride from here to Chapaquiddick, and about five miles across this wooded sandbar to the long beaches which are marvelously empty. Nantucket is distant; there is not much point making the long boat trip unless you spend a few days. But Martha's Vineyard is easily accessible, full of interest and beauty spots. What difference does it make that the locals are cantankerous rustics and sailors, and the summer people are howling snobs from New York?

As the summer passes, the odors of the Cape become more intense, the sting of salt marsh, the gamy smell of tomato vines, the mingled aromas of ripe grapes, cut grass, skunks and pines. Plovers begin to appear on the shore, feeding side by side with the Greater Yellowlegs and the Ruddy Turnstones. The snowy egrets are watchful on the tidal mudflats and by riverbanks. Cars with Florida licence plates pass by, full to the windows with suitcases and clothes: they'll be back next year. Through the thinning foliage – the Gypsy Moths have left their mark – comes a train whistle of the Cape Cod and Hyannis Railroad winding along from Hyannis to Sandwich – this is the best glimpse of rural Cape Cod, and the train is run proudly and well. The beach plums have swollen, and the marsh grass is high and local stores are holding "Back-to-School" sales – and I get sad thinking that the summer is about to end.

At the end of the summer I find myself surrounded by some very strange objects. There is a pewter teapot that wasn't here in June, nor was the rifle, nor the rocking chair with geese carved on its arms. Nor the telescope, the miner's lamp, the ewer. It is all auction loot. Why did I buy that commode? Here is a bird's skull from the beach, some feathers and green glass sucked smooth as a stone by the tide. Around Labor Day I think: How lucky we are to know this place!

In July last year I bought a 1925 "Angelophone" wind-up phonograph at an auction for $50. This was a great bargain, and so were the records – a stack of them I bought for a few dollars. I have the original album of *Oklahoma*, Bing Crosby singing "Danny Boy" and "MacNamara's Band," Cab Calloway singing "Chattanooga Choo-choo" and the Andrews Sisters' version of "One Meat Ball." I also have Peggy Lee singing "Mañana." A fortune in memories for fifty bucks! But no, I don't have the one called "Old Cape Cod" and it's just as well, because I hate the song anyway. But I do have Gene Autry singing "Mexicali Rose." I wind up the machine and put it on, and notice a slight blush of autumn in the maples. A perfect summer is a dream of childhood: idleness, and ice cream, and heat. Everyone deserves summer pleasures, before the seriousness of September.

The Cape in the summertime is a resting place for the imagination, a release from the confinement I feel in London, and a way of verifying that the excitement I felt during childhood summers was not illusion. I hope my children will have the same fond memories.

In the first week of September, there is a faint chill in the air, the foretaste of what is always a bitter winter of paralyzing snow; the surf is higher and whiter, and the hermit crabs swarm more boldly from the jetty. Yellow school buses appear on roads where there were only dune buggies. We hose down the sailboat and put it in mothballs. Then the flight to London, to the clammy airport where, one September I heard a nasty porter snarl "You're not in America now, mate" to a mildly complaining tourist. I am reminded again that I am a refugee for the winter. I have always associated leaving the Cape with going back to school, and now that I think of it, it was probably my pleasant summers that made me hate school so much. As for the Cape: I'll come back to you some sunny day . . .

His Monkey Wife

[1983]

"This is a strange book," the man wrote of *His Monkey Wife*, beginning the review on a small rectangle of notepaper. It was unlined paper but his sentences were set out in an orderly way, as if his copperplate was for someone at a linotype machine. He went on, "It clearly sets out to combine the qualities of the thriller with those of what might be called the decorative novel. Like most things which are extremely far apart, these two are also surprisingly near to one another." He continued in this elliptical way for four pages and then found the novelist wildly inexact. "From the classical standpoint his consciousness is too crammed for harmony, too neurasthenic for proportion, and his humour is too hysterical, too greedy and too crude."

On the other hand, this review of the novel was written by John Collier himself in 1930, when the book first appeared. It was titled "A Looking Glass," and one of its more bizarre aspects was that though it was carefully written it was very much a private joke: it was never printed anywhere, nor has anyone ever mentioned it before. Furthermore, it was rather dismissive – it contained faint praise but was generally belittling. It must have been the result of an impulse, but when you think about its backhanded generosity, its self-mockery and its extreme poise it is impossible not be curious about its perpetrator.

What sort of a man writes a masterpiece and then writes a sniffy review of it and slides it into a drawer to be found fifty years later by his widow? It is not an easy question, because John Collier is one of the great literary unclassifiables – it is another synonym for genius. Collier had a generous man's modesty, and a great imagination, and no airs. Towards the end of his life he said, "I sometimes marvel that a third-rate writer like me has been able to palm himself off as a second-rate writer."

He was a poet, editor, reviewer, novelist and screen-writer. He was also unknown to the general public. "He eschews fame and has a horror of publicity," Anthony Burgess wrote in his Introduction to *The John Collier Reader* (1972). Like many other people who have no appetite for celebrity, John Collier was a happy man, who lived a rich and contented life. I am not speaking of books but of passions and pleasures. He was an attentive friend and a traveler; he was enthusiastic about boats and food. He liked to cook. He grew roses. He was asked by *Sight & Sound* magazine in 1976 why he had become a script-writer. He admitted that he had been "abysmally ignorant of the cinema . . . I had seen scarcely a dozen films in my life". He had gone to Hollywood because he had fallen in love with a fishing boat in Cassis, near Marseilles in 1935, and so he wrote the script of *Sylvia Scarlett* in order to buy the boat.

There is another aspect to his anonymity that is interesting. He seems faceless and ungraspable and then, after a little probing, you discover his involvement in all sorts of well-known contexts. Mystery men are often like that. Collier was poetry editor of *Time and Tide* in the 1920's, and in the 1930's published a number of short stories in the *New Yorker*. Collier it was who first suggested that Jack Warner buy *The African Queen* to film – and he wrote the first script for it. Some of his macabre stories were dramatized in *Alfred Hitchcock Presents*, Sandy Wilson made a musical out of *His Monkey Wife*, and it was Collier who introduced "the magical-Druidical element" into Franklin Schaffner's film, *The War Lord* (1965). He also wrote the script for the film *I Am A Camera*. So, though he may have been somewhat hidden, the fact remains that he spent the best part of his life working magic.

"John Henry Noyes Collier was born May 3, 1901," his widow Harriet wrote to me, when I asked for the details. "His parents were John George Collier and Emily Noyes Collier. His great-grandfather was physician to King William IV, a great uncle was a physician connected with the Hospital for Nervous Diseases, and there were other doctors, artists, and an Uncle Vincent, who was an unknown novelist (he published *Light Fingers and Dark Eyes* in 1913), who tutored John and was a great influence on him and his career. His mother, a teacher, taught him to read at the age of three, and he read an average of a book a day for the rest of his life. Except for kindergarten, this was the extent of his formal education. He read at the Bodleian and spent a great deal of time in the Reading Room of the British Museum."

His early writing was poetry and reviews. This was in the 1920's – in 1922 he received the poetry prize from *This Quarter*. In the 1930's he published thirteen books – poetry, novels, short story collections, an edition of John Aubrey, and a piece of collaboration entitled *Just the Other Day: An Informal History of Britain Since the War*. His early life divides almost by decades, for after his literary beginnings in the 'twenties, and his assured and varied writing in the 'thirties, he was occupied in the 'forties with films – "a mixed bag," one critic wrote, for they included *Elephant Boy, Her Cardboard Lover, Deception* and *Roseanna McCoy*. "I suspect that what I wrote was far too wordy and far too literary," Collier once reflected, with his customary humility. The 1950's were the beginning of a happy period that lasted until his death in 1980. During this time he wrote more stories and more movie scripts, and with the proceeds he bought a house, Domaine du Blanchissage, in Grasse, France.

His last project was his favorite, a movie script of Milton's *Paradise Lost*. In an interview, Collier said, "I think the theme of *Paradise Lost* is singularly suited to attract a wide audience, and especially the young audience, of today. It is quasi-religious, quasi-scientific, and deeply humanistic, being the thrilling story, with which we can all identify, of how innocent, vegetarian, Proconsul or Pithecanthropus was caught up in the guerrilla war waged by Satan against the authoritarian universe, and how he emerged as moral and immoral, curious, inspired, murderous and suffering Man." The film was not made but the script was published as "A Screenplay for the Cinema of the Mind" in America in 1973. It is an astonishing thing – not quite what Milton intended – and Satan is the hero.

Collier loved unlikely heroes. His stories are full of them, and so are his novels – not only Willoughby Ollebeare in *Defy the Foul Fiend*, but a whole marauding gang of savages in his novel of our tribalistic future, *Tom's A-Cold* (the American title was *Full Circle*) – set in the 1990's. And what is less likely than the main character of *His Monkey Wife*?

"The chimp is civilized" – the flat statement appears in the first chapter. Very soon we begin to realize its implications, for Emily is no ordinary chimp. The laugh is on the scientists "who have chosen to measure the intelligence of the chimpanzee solely by its reactions to a banana." Collier implies that it might be far better to test a chimp's reaction to the poetry of Tennyson or Frances Crofts Cornford. Emily is tremendously well-read – no one in the novel, not even the aesthetes or writers, is so knowledgeable as she or possesses her range of reference. She knows she has no dowry but "she brought with her the treasure of a well-stocked mind ... which, all the books said, was infinitely to be preferred." She has a good nose for literary style, finding in the prose of the divorce laws a stark simplicity of greater merit than the exoticism of the marriage service. On the ship to England from Africa the other passengers want to feed her nuts and they urge her to smoke and do tricks. She tries to engage them in a mute discussion of Conrad's understanding of the sea. She can't win.

That she is a monkey is of small significance to the other characters.
(She is not, we know, a monkey, but rather an anthropoid ape. Collier
uses the words interchangeably, and I have followed his example.) There
are many references to the fact that Amy, too, looks like a chimp. I once
heard that in the seventeenth century a monkey was found in the north of
England and was hanged by the locals, who suspected the poor beast of
being a French spy. Emily is taken to be Arab or Chinese or Irish; most
onlookers conclude that she is probably Spanish – dusky and hot-
blooded. On several occasions men try to pick her up. It is the humans in
the book who behave like monkeys, gibbering and indulging their
frivolous passion for fancy dress. This has the effect of making Emily a
deeply sympathetic character and of giving force to the love story in the
satire. If Alfred Fatigay were not so clownishly obtuse and such a jackass
in all his dealings with Emily, it might even have been a touching love
story.

Throughout the novel all the real feeling is Emily's and all the
insincerity belongs to the humans. After reading a letter Amy has written
to Alfred, Emily understands the bogus nature of Amy's sentiment – but
Alfred remains blind to it. Soon we cease to expect any subtlety or
surprise from the humans in the book; they are stick-figures, being held
up to ridicule, and they come out very badly in comparison with the
chimp.

It is not only the subtlety of Emily's understanding that is impressive,
but also her ability to express it. It is Emily's bookishness that fills this
novel with literary allusions. (One of the great games *His Monkey Wife*
inspires is guessing the sources of the numerous quotations.) I have
mentioned Tennyson and F. C. Cornford; but there are also Vaughan,
Donne, Dowson, Coleridge, Wordsworth and Blake. Emily is romantic-
ally inclined and eager to give Alfred the benefit of the doubt. Love has
made her literary, and so has contempt, for when Amy treats her like a
slave Emily feels "like something out of *Uncle Tom's Cabin*." Collier
made her presence especially effective by giving her thoughts but no voice.
What might have sounded pompous or improbable in direct speech is
persuasive and vigorous rendered as ruminant thought. One of the
funniest scenes in the novel also depends on a literary classic for its effect.
This occurs when Emily brandishes a knife and a copy of *Murders in the
Rue Morgue* in Amy's face, just before the wedding ceremony. It is
unexpectedly fierce of Emily to threaten anyone (love is her excuse), but
even so it is the Poe that makes the point.

His Monkey Wife has been described by Osbert Sitwell (in his
Foreword to Collier's *Green Thoughts*, 1932) as an allegory about "the
growth of the soul, from beast to man," and other critics have suggested
that it is a satire against the New Woman. Anthony Burgess describes the

book as a "wayward masterpiece" and a "sport" and said that thematically "anything will do." It is a highly adaptable fable, but will anything do? The book is so funny and bright it does not need critical explanation. Sitwell's thesis about its illustrating a kind of moral evolution is not very interesting, and mentions of Virginia Woolf and Mrs Pankhurst, and gibes at George Moore, hardly create enough wind to fill the sails of a feminist argument.

But not anything will do. The book is a laugh, yet it is also a great satire about human weakness. The chimp is weakest at her most human, and strongest and most resourceful at her monkeyest. There is not a human being in the book who is not deficient and deeply silly in a fatal way. Collier's writing is in the tradition of English satire in being cheerfully misanthropic, and not long after writing the novel he declared, "I cannot see much good in the world or much likelihood of good. There seems to me a definite bias in human nature towards ill, towards the immediate convenience, the ugly, the cheap . . . I rub my hands and say 'Hurry up, you foulers of a good world, and destroy yourselves faster'."

Fatigay is perfectly named – he is limp and clapped out, always the solemn fool, and not a patch on "his sensitive pet." It is one of the ironies of the novel that none of the characters has any idea of how wonderful Emily really is, or what a fine mind she has. This is particularly true of Alfred. He never discovers how perceptive and high-minded she is. The chimp is civilized, an omnivorous reader and a woman of the world, but it is for her pet-like qualities that Alfred admires her. He comes to love her at last for her being a good pet, for her constancy and devotion. Human love is shown to be no more than selfish condescension. Emily is the worthiest character in the book. If this were not so, the satire would be quite different. The last irony is that a novel that delights in being unphysical ends on a note of triumphant carnality.

Among other things, the novel is a chronicle of Emily's success. In the course of four years, Emily rises to such a highly paid position as a star dancer in London that she is able to transform Alfred, who has been brought to a pitiful condition – gnawing cauliflower stems for sustenance and chattering in Piccadilly.

It is when he becomes most monkey-like that Emily shimmers out of the Ritz and offers him a new life. Redemption is the proper word but it is out of place in a discussion of this glancing novel. In important points in the narrative Emily takes the initiative – saving Alfred from Loblulya, learning to read, managing the marriage ceremony, and carrying Alfred away from the brink of oblivion. At last it is she who suggests that they return to Africa together. One of my favourite asides in the book is Collier's mention that Alfred is the only person ever to have returned to Boboma after having once left it.

From the first sentence of the novel the reader is aware that he is in the presence of a magician. This is Collier's strength as a writer. He casts a spell and he does so always with a smile. His style is effortless, always enjoying itself as it weaves its magic. The book is full of asides, parodies, half-quotes, and Collier's literary rope tricks, in which before our eyes he levitates a number of clauses and then he disappears leaving a long sentence dancing in the air. The second sentence in Chapter XII contains 354 words.

If *His Monkey Wife* is a disturbing book it is because the chimp is so innocent, so winsome, so undemanding, relying on the power of romantic love in an atmosphere of human failure. She is civilized in the way man ought to be; she is man before the Fall, before Satan and God hatched the idea of sin. She is also a terrific vaudeville act. The ending – one of the greatest last paragraphs of any novel – is a good shock; it is perfect, in fact. It gives order to the disturbance, and it reminds me of Collier's remark about his script for *The African Queen*, in which he chose to deal with Allnut and Rose in his own way. "A happy end?" he said. "Bet your life it was."

Being a Man

[1983]

There is a pathetic sentence in the chapter "Fetishism" in Dr Norman Cameron's book *Personality Development and Psychopathology*. It goes, "Fetishists are nearly always men; and their commonest fetish is a woman's shoe." I cannot read that sentence without thinking that it is just one more awful thing about being a man – and perhaps it is an important thing to know about us.

I have always disliked being a man. The whole idea of manhood in America is pitiful, in my opinion. This version of masculinity is a little like having to wear an ill-fitting coat for one's entire life (by contrast, I imagine femininity to be an oppressive sense of nakedness). Even the expression "Be a man!" strikes me as insulting and abusive. It means: Be stupid, be unfeeling, obedient, soldierly and stop thinking. Man means "manly" – how can one think about men without considering the terrible ambition of manliness? And yet it is part of every man's life. It is a hideous and crippling lie; it not only insists on difference and connives at superiority, it is also by its very nature destructive – emotionally damaging and socially harmful.

The youth who is subverted, as most are, into believing in the masculine ideal is effectively separated from women and he spends the rest of his life finding women a riddle and a nuisance. Of course, there is a female version of this male affliction. It begins with mothers encouraging little girls to say (to other adults) "Do you like my new dress?" In a sense, little girls are traditionally urged to please adults with a kind of coquettishness, while boys are enjoined to behave like monkeys towards each other. The nine-year-old coquette proceeds to become womanish in a subtle power game in which she learns to be sexually indispensable, socially decorative and always alert to a man's sense of inadequacy.

Femininity – being lady-like – implies needing a man as witness and seducer; but masculinity celebrates the exclusive company of men. That is why it is so grotesque; and that is also why there is no manliness without inadequacy – because it denies men the natural friendship of women.

It is very hard to imagine any concept of manliness that does not belittle women, and it begins very early. At an age when I wanted to meet girls – let's say the treacherous years of thirteen to sixteen – I was told to take up a sport, get more fresh air, join the Boy Scouts, and I was urged not to read so much. It was the 1950s and if you asked too many questions about sex you were sent to camp – boy's camp, of course: the nightmare. Nothing is more unnatural or prison-like than a boy's camp, but if it were not for them we would have no Elks' Lodges, no pool rooms, no boxing matches, no Marines.

And perhaps no sports as we know them. Everyone is aware of how few in number are the athletes who behave like gentlemen. Just as high school basketball teaches you how to be a poor loser, the manly attitude towards sports seems to be little more than a recipe for creating bad marriages, social misfits, moral degenerates, sadists, latent rapists and just plain louts. I regard high school sports as a drug far worse than marijuana, and it is the reason that the average tennis champion, say, is a pathetic oaf.

Any objective study would find the quest for manliness essentially right-wing, puritanical, cowardly, neurotic and fueled largely by a fear of women. It is also certainly philistine. There is no book-hater like a Little League coach. But indeed all the creative arts are obnoxious to the manly ideal, because at their best the arts are pursued by uncompetitive and essentially solitary people. It makes it very hard for a creative youngster, for any boy who expresses the desire to be alone seems to be saying that there is something wrong with him.

It ought to be clear by now that I have something of an objection to the way we turn boys into men. It does not surprise me that when the President of the United States has his customary weekend off he dresses like a cowboy – it is both a measure of his insecurity and his willingness to please. In many ways, American culture does little more for a man than prepare him for modeling clothes in the L. L. Bean catalogue. I take this as a personal insult because for many years I found it impossible to admit to myself that I wanted to be a writer. It was my guilty secret, because being a writer was incompatible with being a man.

There are people who might deny this, but that is because the American writer, typically, has been so at pains to prove his manliness that we have come to see literariness and manliness as mingled qualities. But first there was a fear that writing was not a manly profession – indeed, not a profession at all. (The paradox in American letters is that it has always been easier for a woman to write and for a man to be published.) Growing up, I had thought of sports as wasteful and humiliating, and the idea of manliness was a bore. My wanting to become a writer was not a flight from that oppressive role-playing, but I quickly saw that it was at odds with it. Everything in stereotyped manliness goes against the life of the mind. The Hemingway personality is too tedious to go into here, and in any case his exertions are well-known, but certainly it was not until this aberrant behavior was examined by feminists in the 1960s that any male writer dared question the pugnacity in Hemingway's fiction. All the bullfighting and arm wrestling and elephant shooting diminished Hemingway as a writer, but it is consistent with a prevailing attitude in American writing: one cannot be a male writer without first proving that one is a man.

It is normal in America for a man to be dismissive or even somewhat apologetic about being a writer. Various factors make it easier. There is a heartiness about journalism that makes it acceptable – journalism is the manliest form of American writing and, therefore, the profession the most independent-minded women seek (yes, it is an illusion, but that is my point). Fiction-writing is equated with a kind of dispirited failure and is only manly when it produces wealth – money is masculinity. So is drinking. Being a drunkard is another assertion, if misplaced, of manliness. The American male writer is traditionally proud of his heavy drinking. But we are also a very literal-minded people. A man proves his manhood in America in old-fashioned ways. He kills lions, like Hemingway; or he hunts ducks, like Nathanael West; or he makes pronouncements like, "A man should carry enough knife to defend himself with," as James Jones once said to a *Life* interviewer. Or he says he can drink you under the table. But even tiny drunken William Faulkner loved to mount a horse and go fox hunting, and Jack Kerouac roistered up and down Manhattan in a lumberjack shirt (and spent every night of *The Subterraneans* with his mother in Queens). And we are familiar with the lengths to which Norman Mailer is prepared, in his endearing way, to prove that he is just as much a monster as the next man.

When the novelist John Irving was revealed as a wrestler, people took him to be a very serious writer; and even a bubble reputation like Eric (*Love Story*) Segal's was enhanced by the news that he ran the marathon in a respectable time. How surprised we would be if Joyce Carol Oates were revealed as a sumo wrestler or Joan Didion active in pumping iron. "Lives in New York City with her three children" is the typical woman writer's biographical note, for just as the male writer must prove he has achieved a sort of muscular manhood, the woman writer – or rather her publicists – must prove her motherhood.

There would be no point in saying any of this if it were not generally accepted that to be a man is somehow – even now in feminist-influenced America – a privilege. It is on the contrary an unmerciful and punishing burden. Being a man is bad enough; being manly is appalling (in this sense, women's lib has done much more for men than for women). It is the sinister silliness of men's fashions, and a clubby attitude in the arts. It is the subversion of good students. It is the so-called "Dress Code" of the Ritz-Carlton Hotel in Boston, and it is the institutionalized cheating in college sports. It is the most primitive insecurity.

And this is also why men often object to feminism but are afraid to explain why: of course women have a justified grievance, but most men believe – and with reason – that their lives are just as bad.

Making Tracks to Chittagong

[1983]

India, one of the greatest railway nations in the world, is peculiarly visible from its railway trains. I have the idea that much of Indian life is lived within sight of the tracks or the station, and often next to the tracks, or inside the station. The railway is part of Indian culture. It was one of the greatest imperial achievements, and now – a larger system than ever – it still has the powerful atmosphere of empire about it.

People sometimes wonder how the vast overpopulated subcontinent manages to run, and even to prosper. The chief reason is the railway. Trains have been running for a hundred and thirty years, but – dusty and monumental – they often seem as ancient as India itself. In Pakistan they look like part of the landscape. An old reliable network of track brings hope to beleaguered Bangladesh.

I had happy memories of these trains, and after a ten-year absence I wanted to return and to trace a line from the Khyber Pass in Pakistan, and through India, to Chittagong in Bangladesh. I wanted to take as many trains as possible. It was to be neither a vacation nor an ordeal, but rather a kind of sedentary adventuring – an imperial progress on the railways of the old Raj.

From the corner seat in a railway car it was possible to see an enormous amount of this land; moving east from the stony cliffs of the Northwest Frontier in Pakistan, then cutting into India on an express across the Punjab and traveling up and down, linking the hill stations of Simla and Darjeeling with the long straight journeys of the plains – via Delhi, the Taj Mahal, and the holy city of Benares. After Calcutta I could nip into Bangladesh and go south to the end of the line, in Chittagong. I imagined my itinerary on a map as resembling my own elongated signature written in railway lines across the top of India.

I started from Jamrud, a deserted station, a short distance from Jamrud Fort which, having been built in 1823, is just a hundred years older than the Khyber Railway. It was an early morning in July, and very hot – the monsoon was weeks overdue.

Once a week, this train descends the 3,500 feet from the highest point of the Khyber Pass, carrying the refugees and travelers who can afford the seven rupee train fare. The train is required to climb such steep inclines that it is powered by two steam engines – one at the front and one at the rear of the five coaches – both belching smoke and whistling as it makes the journey to and from Landi Kotal.

"Once there was no trouble here," a man told me as we clattered across the plain. "There was no water, no trees. Only small villages. Then a dam was built and water came to the valley in a stream, and since then there has been constant fighting."

Tempers were very bad: the months of drought had scorched the face of the land and made it so hot that people had moved out of their houses and set up their string beds under trees – I counted fourteen beds under the dusty leaves of one large tree. To cool themselves, men sat on the banks of the stream trickling beside the railway tracks and they chatted, keeping their feet in the water.

There were over thirty-five thousand people in the Kacha Garhi Refugee Camp, and nearly as many in the one at Nasserbad not far away. Driven from their homes in Afghanistan by the war, they lay in hammocks, they cooked under trees, they waited for the daily shipment of food; they watched the train go by.

Across the ten miles of gravel are the high grey-brown mountains which mark the border of Afghanistan, and the black smoking train makes its way across the dead land.

This was always a tribal area, the people were always dressed like this, and always armed, the train was always pulled by smoking screeching steam engines, and the night-time noises were always human voices and the clopping hooves of the tonga ponies, and when – hours late – the train pulls into Peshawar Cantonment Station, the passengers hurry in various directions – to "Lower Class Exit" or "First Class Exit," to "Woman's Waiting Room" or "Waiting Room for Gents." It is pitch dark and a hundred and ten degrees. As in the old days most people make straight for the bazaar.

"This is the Qissa Khawani Bazaar," said Ziarat Gul in Peshawar. Mr Gul was a powerfully-built and kindly soul who was known locally as "Gujjar" – "Buffalo Man." He was pointing at a labyrinth of alleys too narrow for anything but pony carts.

"This means 'The Storytellers' Bazaar'. In the old times all the *kafilas* (caravans) came from Persia and Russia and Afghanistan, here to Peshawar. They told stories of their journeys."

But Peshawar is once again a great destination. Now the travelers are Afghan refugees and the stories in the bazaar concern the heroism of Pathans ambushing Soviet convoys. There are said to be more than a million of them, and many of them bring goods and food to sell at the bazaar – carpets and jewelry, embroidery, leatherwork, cartridge belts, pistol holders, rifle slings, almonds, dates, prunes, and fresh fruit. The bazaar has never been busier or more full of hawkers, and everywhere are the beaky craggy faces of the travelers, the turbaned men and shrouded women, the rifles and pistols, and the tea-drinkers huddled around samovars – storytellers again.

Once I had come to Peshawar and asked for a bed-roll for the train and was told they had none. This evening I inquired again and was told they had one – but only one: "You may book it." I gladly did so and then stood with it under a whirring fan. Most of the larger railway stations in Pakistan and India have ceiling fans on the outdoor platforms, which is why the people waiting are spaced so evenly – clustered in little groups at regular intervals, and the humming fans make one feel one is trapped in a food processor.

It was an air-conditioned compartment and in its grumbling way the machinery actually worked. I was soon traveling under a bright moon through Nowshera and across the Indus River at Attock. We passed through Rawalpindi and Jhelum, too, but by then I was asleep.

Just before Wazirabad at dawn there was a knock on the door of my compartment. "You wanting breakfast?"

I could have been wrong of course, but it seemed to be the same brisk man who had asked the question ten years ago: it was the same bad eye, the same dirty turban, the same lined face. And the breakfast was the same – eggs, tea, bread on heavy stained crockery.

Scattered showers of the monsoon had begun to appear. They had darkened Lahore, once the princely city of Akbar and Shah Jahan, now the capital of Punjab. It was cooler here and the rice fields had water in them; planting had begun; the grass was green. Here the soil was mostly clay and so brick-works had sprung up, each one with a steeple-like chimney. Little girls, some looking as young as six or seven, were digging mud and clay out of pits for bricks and carrying it in baskets on their heads. In sharp contrast to this, little boys were playing gaily in the grass or else swimming in ditches. It is the absurd puritanism of the country that requires little girls modestly to remain clothed and do laborious work, while naked boys can frolic all the livelong day.

The decrepitude near Shahdara Bagh was interesting, because not far from Shahdara Station is one of Pakistan's most glorious buildings, the Tomb of Jahangir, with its vast park – grander than the Shalimar Gardens – and the marble mausoleum inlaid with gems; all of it in a perfect state of preservation. Surrounded by palms, it lies outside Lahore, another marvel on the northwest railway.

When India was partitioned in 1947, so was the railway, and there were no through trains to Pakistan. But the tracks were not removed, and the steel rails still connected Wagha in Pakistan with Atari, the Indian border town. And then in 1976, the trains began to run again. Very little had changed on this line; the steam locomotives, like all steam locomotives in India, looked filthy, ancient, and reliable; they are great sooty thunder boxes, and there are eight thousand of them still operating in India; and the travelers, no matter what their religion or nationality, still privately celebrated the fact that they were Punjabis. The coaches were battered, and the train was very slow. This was the International Express.

The Customs and Immigration bottlenecks were set up there at Lahore Station – platform one – and four officials, one after the other, peered at me and said, "Profession?" I said I was a writer. "Ah, books."

The train left on time, which surprised me, considering that the thousand or so people on board had all had their passports stamped and their luggage examined. We traveled across a plain towards India. After an hour every man we passed wore a turban. We were nearing Amritsar, spiritual capital of the Sikhs, and we were among the great family of Singhs. *Sikh* is from the Sanskrit word *Shishya*, "disciple" – they are disciples of a tradition of ten gurus, beginning with the fifteenth century Guru Nanak who taught monotheism, espoused meditation, and opposed the Hindu caste system. Sikhs herded goats, Sikhs dug in the fields, Sikhs processed the passengers on the International Express. This was Atari Station and the operation took several hours: everyone ordered off the train, everyone lined up and scrutinized, everyone ordered back on. Then the whistle blew and the black smoke darkened the sky, and we proceeded into India.

But it was not only black smoke in the sky. The clouds were the color of cast iron; they were blue-black and huge. It is usually possible in India to tell whether it will rain from the whiteness of the egrets – they look whitest when rain is due; and these dozens flying up from the rice paddies near Amritsar were brilliantly white against the dark clouds massing over us.

We arrived just before one o'clock at Amritsar, and as we pulled in, passing buffaloes and scattering the goats and ducks and children, the storm hit. It was the first rain of the monsoon – pelting grey drops, noisy and powerful and already, only minutes after it had begun, erupting from drains and streaming under the tracks.

The rain in its fury put the Indians into a good mood. It was the sunny days and blue skies – intimations of drought – that made them bad-tempered.

Because of the rain, only rickshaws were running in Amritsar. Cars lay stranded and submerged all over the inundated city. I sat inside, deafened by the rain, and studied the Indian Railways Timetable, and after a while I became curious about the route of a certain train out of Amritsar. This particular mail train left Amritsar at ten in the evening and headed south on the main line to Delhi; but halfway there it made a hairpin turn at Ambala and raced north to Kalka where, at dawn, it connected with the railcar to Simla. It was an extraordinary route – and a very fast train: instead of going to bed in the hotel, I could reserve a sleeper, and board the train, and more or less wake up in the foothills of the Himalayas, in Simla.

It was not a popular train, this Simla Mail. Its odd twisted route was undoubtedly the result of the demands of the imperial postal service, for the British regarded letter writing and mail delivery as one of the distinguishing features of any great civilization. And Indians feel pretty much the same.

"Use the shutters," the ticket collector said, "and don't leave any small articles lying around."

The whistle of the Simla Mail drowned the sounds of music from the bazaar. I was soon asleep. But at midnight I was woken by rain beating against the shutters. The monsoon which had hit the Punjab only the day before had brought another storm, and the train struggled through it. The thick raindrops came down so hard they spattered through the slats and louvers in the shutters, and a fine spray soaked the compartment floor.

The Guard knocked on the door at 5:20 to announce that we had arrived at Kalka.

It was cool and green at Kalka, and after a shave in the Gentlemen's Waiting Room I was ready for the five-hour journey through the hills to Simla. I could have taken the small pottering "Simla Queen" or the express, but the white twenty-seat railcar was already waiting at the platform. I boarded, and snoozed, and woke to see mists lying across the hills and heavy green foliage in the glades beside the line.

Two hours later at five thousand feet, we came to the little station at Barog, where every day the railcar waits while the passengers have breakfast; and then it sets off again into the tumbling cloud. Occasionally the cloud and mist was broken by a shaft of light and it parted to reveal a valley floor thousands of feet below.

Solan Brewery, on the line to Simla, is both a brewery and a railway station. But the station came afterward, for the brewery was started in the nineteenth century by a British Company which found good spring water here in these hills of Himachal Pradesh. In 1904, when the railway was built, the line was cut right through the brewery.

The opinion of the Indian in the hill station is that the plains are disorderly and crime-ridden. It is believed that as soon as they are above three or four thousand feet people tend to behave themselves. "People on the plains indulge in bad behavior, indiscipline and mischief," a man at

Simla station told me. He was a train Guard, but he was full of complaints about lowland vandalism and tardiness and "mischief – especially political mischief" on the railways.

"You're very frank, sir," I said.

"It is because I have resigned," he replied.

The residents of Simla are often visited by relatives. "They always say, 'I'm coming for two or three days,' but after three weeks they're still here. And there is something about this air that excites them and makes them difficult."

The man speaking was an army colonel. He had a remedy for unwelcome guests. He made lists of sights that were not to be missed in Simla. Each one was a day's walk from his house and it was usually at the top of a steep hill. After a few days of this sightseeing the starch was taken out of his guests and they were fairly glad when it was time to go.

The most knowledgeable railway buff I met in Simla was a man who, over a period of years, had traveled all over India on trains visiting race tracks. He seldom stayed overnight. He would hurry to Lucknow on a night train, gamble all day at the track, and then catch the sleeper to Calcutta and do the same thing. I said it seemed a difficult thing to do, all that railroading. No, he said, the difficult thing was putting on a sad face and hailing a tonga and then riding Third Class so that no potential thief would guess that he had five thousand rupees of winnings in his pocket.

I glided down from Simla in the cozy little blue train to Kalka and then in the late evening boarded the sleeper for Delhi. It was air-conditioned, and the bed was made – starched sheets and a soft pillow. There was no better way to Delhi.

At seven the next morning I looked out the window and saw the outskirts of Delhi, simmering under the grey lid of the sky.

At Old Delhi Station, it seemed to me that the unluckiest railwayman in this season of heat was a fireman on a steam locomotive. Rambling around the station yard I discovered an even more exhausting job: boilermaker. The boilermaker is essentially a welder, but because he deals with all aspects of the boiler he is often required to use his welding torch inside the boiler or the firebox.

Today it was 103° at the Old Delhi loco shed, but Suresh Baboo, a boilermaker, crawled out of a locomotive's firebox to tell me that he was not deterred by a little thing like heat.

He was a railwayman Grade Two and earned one thousand rupees a month ($100) of which four hundred was his "Dearness Allowance" ("Because in Delhi, food and living are very dear").

Was this enough to live on? Not in Delhi. "We are asking for an increase in the Dearness," said Suresh Baboo.

"For some reason – probably because of the British tradition – morale among railwaymen is very high," said Mr K. T. V. Raghavan, Chairman of the Indian Railway Board. His position in the hierarchy of the Indian Civil Service shows the importance of the railway in India: he is the second most senior civil servant in the country.

Mr Raghavan impressed me by speaking of the special nature of the railway in India. It was not merely a way of going to and from work, but rather in India a solution to the complex demands of the family. Birth, death, marriage, illness, and religious festivals all required witnesses and rituals which implied a journey home. Indians, Mr Raghavan said, only *seemed* to be restless travelers; in fact, most of them were merely showing piety and carrying out religious or domestic duties.

In Delhi I found the best organized railway station in India. This was Hazrat Nizamuddin Station, just south of the city and a short walk from Humayun's Tomb.

There were flowers and shrubs in pots on the platform, and every day on the orders of the Stationmaster, Mr G. L. Suri, ant powder was sprinkled along the walls. Mr Suri proudly took me on a tour of the station. He hadn't been recommended to me by the Railway Board – I had simply stopped on one of the one hundred and eighty trains that pass through each day and noticed how unusual it looked. How was it possible to keep a station so clean in the hot season?

Mr Suri said, "I do my duty – I get satisfaction from it. Somtimes I work sixteen hours a day. I do not accept excuses." He nodded and added softly, "And I am very tough."

The Janata-Madras Express passes through Hazrat Nizamuddin Station, and of course it stops, because "Janata" means "People" and the People's Express stops everywhere. It is probably the slowest express in the world.

It would be several days before this long rumbling steam train arrived in Madras. It was cheap – all second class – but it was not really for long-distance passengers; it went fourteen hundred miles, stopping at every station – just like a country bus – and most people only went a few miles.

In India, it is easy to tell the long-distance travelers. They are heavily laden, and always carry a big steel trunk. At railway stations in India one sees the family grouped around the trunk – they sit on it, sleep beside it, use it for a table, and when their train draws in they hire a skinny man to wrestle it on board.

"My mother was typical," a man told me on this train. "She carried all her jewelry and all her saris – thirty or forty of them. She brought glasses to drink out of, cooking utensils, plates and the trays we call *thali*. She

took the essential household. All Indians do this. The trouble was that my
mother used to take all these things even if she was only going away for a
day or so."

It seemed that the trunk was an Indian's best defense against being
robbed, contaminated, or stranded: it made them completely portable
and very safe. At any moment, using the trunk, an Indian could set up
house.

"You're not going far," I was reminded.

No, only to Agra — six hours on this slow beast; but six hours was
nothing on an Indian train, where some people might say, "When do I
arrive? Let me see. Today is Thursday and tomorrow is . . ."

I was sitting across from Bansilal Bajaj, who was on home leave from
Abu Dhabi — every two years he got two months' leave, and he spent a
month of that on Indian Railways, going up and down the country.

"In Abu Dhabi all we do is work. I am in the catering and cleaning
business, but I am no more than a machine. When I come back to India I
am human again."

It was a lovely evening, very clear, just after a heavy rainstorm of the
monsoon. Now there was not a cloud in the sky, and in the west it was the
color of a tropical sea — greeny-blue, reflected in perfectly still pools and
paddy fields. There was a sweetness in the air and for a number of miles no
people — just color and empty space and darting birds.

Just after dark the lights in the train failed, and we traveled clattering
through pitch-blackness, with the steam engine puffing and wheezing,
and the whistle blowing off-key, and the only lights were the sparks from
the smokestack, sailing past the window like fireflies.

It was almost nine by the time we arrived in Agra. The town is nothing.
The Agra Fort is substantial. Akbar's Mausoleum of Sikandra has
character, and the Moti Masjid (the "Pearl Mosque") has personality;
but the Taj Mahal is something else. Just looking at it you are certain that
you will never forget it. It is not merely a visual experience, but an
emotional one — its pure symmetry imparts such strong feeling; and it is a
spiritual experience, too; for the Taj Mahal is alone among buildings I
have seen. It is not merely lovely; it looks as if it has a soul.

The Ganga-Yamuna Express to Varanasi was like a certain kind of
Asiatic prison cell.

It was a long night. Dawn broke at Kanpur, and two hours later at
Lucknow it was very sunny and bright, a noontime heat, though it was
hardly half-past seven in the morning.

All the paddy fields were brim full. The rains were dangerously strong in Hardwar and had flooded Delhi, but here beside the line of the Ganga-Yamuna Express they had guaranteed a great rice crop and had given the landscape a serene lithographed look – the palms very still, the buffaloes obedient, the Indians up to their shins in water. An emblematic mother weeding vegetables with her infant in the middle of another field under the shade of a big black umbrella.

For miles, for hours – for days on these plains – you see nothing else at this time of year: men, women, and children planting, or plowing or tending the crop, and all of them working under the blazing sun and burned as black as their buffaloes.

The villages were mud huts and grass roofs, like a glimpse of central Africa in the province of Uttar Pradesh, except that in the center of every frail village was always a substantial stone temple. None of these villages were sign-posted but sometimes a tiny station or a halt displayed the name. One sun-baked station in the middle of the hot plain was Rudanli. Three horse-drawn tongas were waiting at the platform, and some people looked hopefully up from their tin trunks. The Ganga-Yamuna Express did not stop.

We were going the long way to Varanasi, taking "the Faizabad Loop," via Ayodhya where monkeys on the platform sat on the inkblots of shade. We passed through Shahganj, where rice planters stood scanning the blue sky for clouds; and then after Jaunpur we joined the main line.

Varanasi Station has the contours of a Hindu temple, built in the Mauryan style, and like a temple it is filled with holy men and pilgrims. It is also full of sacred cows. The cows at Varanasi Station are wise to the place – they get water at the drinking fountains, food near the refreshment stalls, shelter along the platforms, and exercise beside the tracks; they also know how to use the cross-over bridges and can climb up and down the steepest stairs.

"We are installing cow-catchers," the Station Superintendent told me – but he did not mean the traditional ones, on the engines, he meant fences to prevent the cows from entering the station.

The flocks of goats at Varanasi Station are on their way to the Ganges to have their throats cut and be dumped into the river as a sacrifice; the beggars are testing the piety of the pilgrims; and those small narrow bundles that are part of so many of the travelers' luggage are in fact human corpses, headed for the cremation fires on the ghats. Because nothing that is holy in India can be regarded as dirty, holy Varanasi with its fifteen hundred temples is one of the filthiest of Indian cities and positively stinking with sanctity. I met an Indian medical student who had just arrived in Varanasi. He was on his way to the Ganges to take his ritual bath. He said he was definitely planning to bathe in the Ganges, among the dead goats and monkeys and corpses of beggars who died at the station and were taken in rickshaws to the river and thrown in uncremated.

"Oh, yes," the medical student said. "I will immerse myself."

"What about the health aspect?"

He said, "It is a question of mind over matter."

From a distance in the early morning, Varanasi looks wonderful, and the most glorious sight of it is from the Howrah Mail as it crosses the Dufferin Bridge which spans the Ganges just east of the city.

The Howrah Mail, one of India's best trains, leaves Varanasi at five-thirty in the morning, just as the passengers from Delhi are yawning and peering out the window and getting their first glimpses of the holy city. And the people waiting on the platform at Varanasi are watching the train with admiration, because this train represents luxury – it has three chair cars, and sleeping cars, and a pantry car, where food is cooked and dished up in trays which are distributed around the train by waiters. The Howrah Mail is efficiently air-conditioned; it is famous for being fast and is nearly always on time. From the high vantage point of the bridge the whole populous riverbank and all the ghats can be seen gilded in the light of the rising sun, and its splendor is intensified because the distance blurs the city's decay, and at this time of day – the early morning – the river is filled with people washing, swimming, and generally going about their prayers.

From here – the outskirts of Varanasi all the way to Calcutta – the land is waterlogged and fertile, an endless rice field. At noon the train stops at Gaya, where Buddha received enlightenment.

Gaya also marks the beginning of a very strange landscape. Sudden single hills are thrust out of the flatness like massive dinosaurs petrified on the flat Bihari plain; and other hills are like pyramids, and still more like slag heaps. They don't seem to belong to any range of hills and have a comic plopped-down look.

It was wet and cool and jungly four hours later when we entered West Bengal, and when the train stopped some blind beggars got on. The Ticket Examiner asked them to beg in a different part of the train and they meekly agreed.

This Ticket Examiner was a woman – one of three or four women who work on the Howrah Mail. "And there are many women working on Indian Railways." Her name was Ollie Francis. "I was a Christian," she said. "But then I married Mr Ningam and so I became a Hindu. It was not an arranged marriage. I married for love."

She had seven children, the eldest eighteen, the youngest five. She missed them when she made this Calcutta run, but her relatives helped look after them. She had worked for the railways for twenty years.

What Ollie liked best about the Howrah Mail was its speed – less than fourteen hours from Varanasi to Calcutta. As the train drew into Howrah Station, the daylight was extinguished by smoke, and rain mixed with fog; frightening numbers of people were making their way through the mud and the lamplight.

Howrah is very large; but like Calcutta it is in a state of decay. Enormous and noisy, a combination of grandeur and desolation, the wonder is that it still works. Calcutta is one of the cities of the world that I associate with the future. This is how New York City could look, I think, after a terrible disaster.

The monsoon that beautifies and enriches the countryside had made Calcutta ugly and almost uninhabitable. Rain in India gives all buildings, especially modern ones, a look of senility. The streets were flooded, there were stalled cars everywhere, and people waded among the drowned dogs.

"Calcutta's future is very dark," Professor Chatterjee told me in Calcutta one afternoon. Professor Chatterjee was an astrologer. He then told me (after a brief examination of my palm) that I would live to the age of seventy-eight, have another child (a daughter) and be given problems by people of small size.

The part about small people was certainly true. It was a small man who refused to find me a bedroll, and another small man who demanded that I double his tip, and yet another who overcharged me in a taxi, and a fourth little man who insisted that I get in touch with his brother in California to settle some family litigation that was long overdue; and four small porters squabbled so furiously over carrying my suitcases that I ended up carrying them myself in order to keep the peace.

In Calcutta I reflected on my traveling across the subcontinent by train, my going from station to station. The stations had everything — not only food and retiring rooms and human company, but also each station possessed the unique character of its city, its peculiar stinks and perfumes.

I had wanted to take a train to Assam, to Nowgong and Silchar, and then to descend into Sylhet and move sideways into Bangladesh. But this was now impossible. There was fighting in Assam, civil strife between Assamese and Bengalis, and the Nagas had never really been pacified. If I needed proof of that I had only to look at my fellow passengers on the Kamrup Express: they were men from the Indian Air Force and the Army; they had unfinished business in Assam.

Even New Jalpaiguri and Darjeeling are regarded as Disturbed Areas; foreign travelers needed a special permit to visit these places, and when it is shown at the railway station in Jalpaiguri your passport is stamped, just as it would be if you were crossing into another country.

In India there is nothing remarkable about a train that is slow – particularly one that is making a long journey through such remote provinces. But in one respect, the Kamrup Express to New Jalpaiguri was unusual: it had a dining car. For hours after we left, relays of men – only men – sat in the dining car squashing rice and *dhal* in their fists and flinging it into their mouths. Meanwhile, the kitchen staff boiled cauldrons of lentils and crouched between the cars strenuously peeling potatoes.

At dawn everything was different and serene. The landscape was dry here, but the trees were green, and not far away were the dim blue shapes of mountains to the north and northwest. We were scheduled to arrive at seven-fifteen. At seven-thirty we stopped at a tiny station near the village of Dhumdanj, which was no more than a few cows and a few families and one buffalo.

Two hours had passed. This is an aspect of train travel that must not be overlooked: the unexplained stop in the middle of nowhere; and the unexplained delay – hours during which only a dog barks, and someone shuts off a radio, and a child emerges from the tall grass beside the track to sell tea in disposable clay cups. You don't know whether you will leave in two minutes or two days, so it is unwise to stray very far from the train. The sun moves higher in the sky. A child begins to weep. Then an unexplained whistle and a few seconds later the train moves, and five hundred Indians run alongside, trying to board. We left Dhumdanj.

Everyone calls the train to Darjeeling The Toy Train. It is a narrow-gauge mountain railway, with the sort of small blue steam engines that other people put into transport museums; a real jewel, a tremendously ingenious piece of engineering – a true original. If it is inconvenient it is because in the hundred years in which it has been running it has never been improved and hardly been maintained. It was bravely built and it looks so clever and powerful that it seems an impertinence to do anything to it except ride it and let it run. It actually looks indestructible.

On this railway line dogs sleep between the tracks, and children play on the tracks and roll toys along them, and the tracks are also put to practical use by men who push huge logs along them – skidding them downhill on the rails.

The four coaches are nearly always full, if not with legitimate travelers then with joy riders – the train is part of the life of the long series of mountainsides that connect Siliguri to Darjeeling. Some people only ride a hundred yards, others are going miles. It is full of businessmen, farmers, Buddhist monks, and schoolchildren. Every ticket is made out in duplicate, though none of them costs more than a few cents.

The train passes by the houses, a few familiar inches from the windows. It passes close enough to the shops and stalls for a train passenger to reach out and pick an onion or an apple out of a basket on the shop counter.

The valleys and these hillsides are open to the distant plains, and so the traveler on the toy train has a view which seems almost unnatural it is so dramatic. At Sonada it is like standing at the heights of a gigantic outdoor amphitheatre and looking down and seeing the plains and the rivers, roads and crops printed upon it and flattened by the yellow heat. There are wisps and whorls of cloud down there, too. But up here it is dark green and wet hill country, where nearly everyone has rosy cheeks.

After Sonada we came to Jor Bungalow Station and then Ghoom, the highest railway station in Asia at 7,407 feet (2,257 meters). The mist shifts slightly and farther along, towards Darjeeling, it is possible on a clear day to see the long irregular ridge of rock – Kanchenjunga, massively white in the great folds of snow-covered rock.

The so-called "Batasia Loop" is the famous descent in which the train appears to be tying itself into a knot while at the same time whistling to clear its own caboose out of the way, and after three or four curves it continues on its way, gliding into Darjeeling, still following the main road and bumping past the shops and sharing the thoroughfare with the Buddhist monks and the bullock carts.

Darjeeling is unlike Simla. It is not an Indian resort but rather a Nepali town. It is a solemn place, full of schools and convents and monasteries. It is barer than Simla, not as populous; it is muddier, friendlier, very oriental looking and rather un-Indian in aspect. Simla has visitors, Darjeeling has residents; Simla is Anglo-Indian, but Darjeeling is Oriental. It is not posh. It is a hospitable place.

The curse of the town is its traffic – an endless procession of honking jeeps and trucks. It seemed to me that most of Darjeeling's problems would probably be solved with a modern version of the train, which was finished just a hundred years ago. It was a great solution then, and it still serves the town, for many people commute from places like Ghoom to jobs in Darjeeling – to the shops, to the government offices, and even to the stranger occupations in Darjeeling such as the carver of yak bones and the clerk who stands under the sign "Licensed Vendor for Ganja & Bhang." Ten grams of ganja (marijuana) cost thirty cents.

The railway needs to be improved, yet the wonder of it – like the wonder of much else in India – is that it still operates. India is a complex place. The phones seldom work, the mail is unreliable, the electricity is subject to sudden stoppages. There are numerous natural disasters and there are eight hundred million people. It seems almost inconceivable that this country is still viable, and yet there are times when one gets glimpses of its greatness. Towards the end of my Indian journey I decided that India runs primarily because of the railway. It is an old-fashioned solution, but India has old-fashioned problems.

India's relations with Bangladesh have never been cordial, but perhaps on the theory propounded by Robert Frost that good fences make good neighbors, India has recently announced its plan to secure its national boundary with Bangladesh with a two-thousand-mile barbed-wire fence. Trains have not crossed the border for some time. I flew to Dhaka and took the Ulka Express south.

This train was on the world news the day I boarded it: it was the only link between Dhaka and Chittagong – every other road was under five feet of water, and scores of people had drowned in the torrential rains. But the monsoon comes every year to Bangladesh, and it is always severe. Its damage comes so regularly it is not remarkable. The feeling on the Ulka Express was that Bangladesh was having another unlucky week.

It was not immediately obvious that the rain was a disaster. Today the sun was shining, and this whole southern part of Bangladesh had been turned into a spectacular lake – hundreds of miles of floodwater. And the only things showing in all that water were the long straight rails of the railway track.

The Ulka Express, fifteen coaches long – one was First Class – was pulled by a Diesel engine. I would have gone Second but I would not have found a seat, and I was not prepared to stand for nine hours.

At Tongi Junction I saw another train pull in. There were perhaps fifty people clinging to the sides of the engine and hanging from the carriages and sitting and standing on the coach roofs. These seemingly magnetized people had the effect of making the train look small. They completely covered it and of course the paying passengers were jammed inside.

It made me curious about seating arrangements on the Ulka Express. I leaned out the window and saw that, apart from my coach, the whole train was exactly the same – people everywhere, holding on to the sides, the engine, and crowding the roofs. To the sound of a young beggar boy's flute, the train rattled south.

In the hot, stricken country the only thing that moved was the railway. But there was no panic. At Akhaura ("Change Here For Sylhet") a man stood up to his waist in a flooded field thoughtfully washing his cow, and farther on boats had penetrated to villages – the large boats were beamy, like old Portuguese frigates, and the smaller ones were gracefully shaped like Persian slippers.

"You will see where President Zia was assassinated in Chittagong," Mr Shahid said as we rolled along. It was as if he was passing on a piece of tourist information. He did say that I should have taken the Karnafuli

Express — it did not stop often and therefore fewer people clung to its sides.

At Comilla I met a young man who had just opened an office to encourage Bangladeshis to enroll in a Voluntary Sterilization program.

"They need incentives . . ."

What sort? I wondered.

"We have tried money and clothes as a sort of reward, but it is not enough. We need something more substantial. There is no problem with middle-class people. I have two children myself and I think that is a good number. The problem is with the poor. But this is a democratic country, and so we do not make sterilization compulsory."

Was he making any progress?

"Very slow progress," he said.

The worst of the floods were south of Comilla, at the town of Feni. With a kind of gloomy resignation some people resolutely bailed out their houses and fields, and others took baths. The children in the area were swimming and diving and having a wonderful time. The floods had also brought fish to these hungry people, and where the banks of rivers had been breached fishermen were enthusiastically using nets, scoops, lines, buckets, and ancient-looking fish traps.

The day continued hot, but the flood did not abate. Chittagong lay just ahead, simmering under the sun.

Introducing Jungle Lovers

[1984]

Jungle Lovers was the result of my departure from Africa. In 1968, after five years in Malawi and Uganda, I decided to leave for good. I had a definite reason. There was a political demonstration in Uganda's capital, Kampala, where I was teaching at Makerere University. Violent demonstrations were not new to me – but I had never been the focus of the violence. Today the issue was white-controlled Rhodesia, and I happened to be driving into town and was taken by surprise. The Africans parading on the main street saw me – and my pregnant wife next to me – and attacked the car while we were seated in it. All the windows were broken and the steelwork hammered and dented by iron bars. An Indian helped us to safety and we hid in his shop while the Africans set about damaging the car. Later, we sneaked home, and I noticed there was broken glass all over the city.

Many of the Africans who had set upon us were my students – so they said on Monday morning. They were not apologetic. They simply said that Africans were being persecuted in Rhodesia, and that whites . . . And here I stopped their explanation. Was I a white man to them, just a color, nothing more? They looked sheepish and did not reply. They had that morning prepared essays on something – perhaps a Shakespeare sonnet or a Hemingway short story. They wanted to get on with the class. I could not see the point of it. I wanted to discuss mob violence. They said it was over with – and could they please read their essays? Didn't I realize they had an exam to take?

I could not see the point of their exam. I could not understand their hurry. I disliked being a white man – after five years that was what it had come to! I decided there and then to quit my job and, as soon as our baby was born, to leave Africa. I had lost my confidence in these students. I needed different students and a new country. I remember thinking: *I have no business to be here.*

Late in 1968 I got a job teaching at the University of Singapore. The Singapore authorities had got wind of the fact that I had published three novels and, taking the philistine view that writers were troublemakers, they insisted that I sign a paper saying that I would not write or publish anything about Singapore while I was under contract. They also put me on the lowest salary scale. I wondered what they were trying to hide.

I discovered: nothing – or very little. Singapore was a small, humid island-city that called itself a republic. It was dominated by puritanical Chinese who were getting rich on the Vietnam war. My students said they wanted to emigrate to Australia. I taught courses in Jacobean literature, seventeenth century revenge-tragedies. Again I questioned whether I was cut out to be a teacher in the tropics. Of course, I wasn't, and I saw writing as liberation.

I could not write about Singapore, so I wrote about Africa – this novel. The weather was very hot, I could only work at night or on weekends, I kept my writing a secret from my employers, and in the middle of this book I contracted dengué fever: it took me more than two years to finish the novel. No novel before or since took me that long. But I had to keep at it, I had nothing else to write – and I was forbidden to write about Singapore. At last I finished it and sent it off, and it appeared in Britain and the United States at about the time I left Singapore (and teaching) to write my Singapore novel, *Saint Jack*.

That was in 1971. Now, rereading *Jungle Lovers* I am struck by its peculiar humor and violence. Some of it is farce and some tragedy. I suppose the insurance man and the revolutionary were the two opposing sides of my own personality. After all, seeing education as protection, I was a teacher in Malawi; but I was deported from the country in 1965, charged with covert revolutionary activities (I had been accused of passing messages from rebel ministers to disaffected Malawians). There are many moods in the book – I had wanted to write an ambitious novel – but the underlying feeling is affectionate and skeptical. I had gone to Africa in 1963 believing in political freedom and the possibility of change. I still believe in political freedom; but five years doesn't change much, and even now more than twenty years later I think the institutions I satirized in this novel may be still as farcical. It seems to be a novel of futility and failed hopes. Well, that was my mood on leaving Africa. I was younger then. Now I should say that it takes a long time for change to be brought about, and change ought always to come from within. Outsiders, even the most well-intentioned in Third World countries, are nearly always meddlers.

Nowadays, people my age are asked: *Where were you in the 'sixties?* Americans went various ways. They clung to universities, or "dropped-out" and became part of the counterculture; or they were sent to Vietnam. Some, like me, spent the 'sixties in the Third World – it was a way of virtuously dropping out and delicately circumventing Vietnam. I was in my twenties in the 'sixties, and I think this novel is very much of its time. Many African countries had just then become independent;

colonialists were going home; volunteer teachers – and insurance agents and revolutionaries – were arriving and wondering what would happen next. No one realized that the darkness they found was the long shadow of Africa's past.

A number of things interest me in this novel. A very minor character, Wilbur Parsons, I used later in a short story, and a professor who writes about Parsons' poetry I used in yet another story. Several times in the novel, the vice-president of the Hartford Accident and Indemnity Company is mentioned. This man is of course the most literary insurance man America has produced: Wallace Stevens. While I was writing the novel, the Singapore government was in the throes of renaming things – streets, parks, squares, buildings. I began to see that naming is the great passion of all new governments and that, in history, often only names change and all else remains the same. So this novel is full of street names. In Malawi they have been changed, but they were once as strange and English as Henderson and Fotheringham.

When I went to Malawi in 1963 it was called the Nyasaland Protectorate and was administered by Britain. In rural areas, women and children often dropped to their knees, out of respect, when a white person drove past in a Landrover. African men merely bowed. The country became independent in July, 1964, and four months later there was an attempted coup d'état – sackings, shootings, resignations. The President-for-life, Doctor Banda, had spent much of his working life in Britain and did not speak any African language well enough to give speeches in anything but English. He had an interpreter for talking to his people. It was, some months, very cold in the country – I had expected Africa to be hot. Most Africans I met were rather pious members of the Church of Scotland, but they also believed in ghosts and witches. There were rural redneck Portuguese on Malawi's long border with Mozambique. They had come out from Salazar's Portugal to be barbers and shopkeepers in the African bush. There were stubborn, mustached English settlers who said they would never leave Africa; and nuns, lepers, guerrillas, and runaways. Malawi had a once-a-week newspaper and a terrible radio station: it was a country of constant rumors. Many of the Africans spoke English with a Scottish accent, because their teachers were Scots, following in the steps of the great Scottish explorer, David Livingstone. In the deep south of the country the Africans often went stark naked; in the north they wore English flannels. I tried to put some of this oddness into my novel.

Dead Man Leading

[1984]

V. S. Pritchett, a master of the short story, once wrote, "The masters of the short story have rarely been good novelists." But *Dead Man Leading* is an extremely good novel. It has an intensity, a passionate strangeness, that sets it apart from Pritchett's other novels, and except for its vivid language it has little in common with his short stories. In setting and mood it is wholly original. It is certainly the best of the five novels Pritchett has written (though I am an admirer of *Mr Beluncle*), and yet it is practically an unknown book. It was published in 1937. "This novel was more imaginative than my earlier ones," Pritchett wrote in *Midnight Oil*, "but it came out not long before the war started and that killed it."

When I read it the first time I was immediately reminded of *Brazilian Adventure*, by Peter Fleming, which appeared in 1933. Pritchett told me that he had been influenced by that travel book – the search for the explorer Fawcett who went missing in Brazil in the 1920s – but that he had also thought of his fellow writers, the restless novelists who, in the 'thirties, poked around the world inviting privation. He explained in his autobiography that he had read the lives of the African explorers and the accounts of missionaries' experiences ("Missionaries always write down the practical detail") and he found a common characteristic to be an "almost comical masochism." It was *Green Hell*, and Stephen Gwynn's biography of Scott of the Antarctic (1929) and – he told me – "memories of childhood fancy" that heartened him to begin writing. He summed up his intention in the novel by saying, "I attempted a psychology of exploration."*

* "Exploration is the physical expression of the Intellectual Passion," Apsley Cherry-Garrard wrote at the end of *The Worst Journey in the World* (1929). This masterpiece of travel writing, which is an account of the Scott Antarctic expedition of 1910–1913, describes many instances of severe hardship and a satisfaction in enduring it that amounts almost to pleasure. Another explorer, Fridtjof Nansen, wrote, "Without privation there would be no struggle, and without struggle no life –" This was also Scott's feeling; in one of his last letters ("To My Widow") as he lay freezing to death in the tent on the Ross Ice Shelf, he wrote, "How much better it has been [struggling against blizzards] than lounging in too great comfort at home." Pritchett knew these sentiments from Stephen Gwynn's *Captain Scott* (1929).

It is that and more, and is especially remarkable for having been written before Pritchett went to Brazil. He says he knew the literature of the Amazon and he created his own Amazon: "I constructed a small model of my bit of the river in the garden of the cottage we had rented in Hampshire." I am usually doubtful about the novels written by people who have never traveled in their setting. "And he'd never set foot in Africa!" readers say of the author of *Henderson the Rain King*, but no one who has been to Africa has to be told that; and internal evidence in the Tarzan stories shows their author to have been similarly handicapped. This is another reason *Dead Man Leading* is exceptional. Apart from the orangutan with its gulping Lear-like laugh in Chapter Fourteen – the mostly silent *pongo pygmaeus* lives ten thousand miles from the Amazon – the novel is completely convincing. And of course Pritchett himself is a great traveler; he eventually went to Brazil and was able to confirm that he had invented the truth.

The narrative is not hard to summarize: it is the account of an expedition in search of a man who disappeared in the jungle seventeen years before. "The Johnson mystery," it was called: what really happened? The question is not answered in a conventional or predictable way, because the men on the expedition are of such conflicting character. Indeed, the achievement of the novel is that it portrays an exquisitely physical landscape along with minutely detailed portraits of the inner life of the men lost in it. In one sense it is as concrete as can be, and yet it is also full of subtlety and suggestion.

At the center of the expedition (but the resonant word "quest" would be more accurate) is Harry Johnson – it was his father, Alexander Johnson the missionary, who vanished. Rev. Johnson had often been away for long periods. He had four sons. They were proud of their courageous father and dutiful towards their mother. Harry says that his mother brought them up to hate women, and "It was necessary for each of them to be the missing father – to be immaculate, her husband." Harry is only in his thirties, but already he is an explorer-hero who has mapped Greenland, the Arctic, the tropics; he is the subject of admiring anecdotes. He has a stubborn and solitary nature. "I think I may be very different from other people," he says to Lucy in an early chapter, and soon after, she has an equally tantalizing but more specific perception of him: "The frightening thing was the closed door in his heart and the fanatic behind it."

Lucy is a fascinating person, and fully human – her decent fear of setting sail in a terrible wind shows just how dangerous Harry's masochism is. The whole of Chapter Three is brilliantly done, a passionate battle of wills in what is less a love affair than a struggle for supremacy. Although Lucy does not go on the expedition her presence is continually felt, and she is often referred to. Harry is as obsessed by her as he is by his father.

What is surprising in the novel is how closely connected the characters are. Even that marvelous reprobate, Calcott, claims a relationship with Harry's father. It is a novel of the jungle, but it is not a novel of savagery – no cannibalism, no blowguns, no shrunken heads. Indeed, it sometimes seems like a version of English society feverishly disintegrating in the tropics.

The leader of the expedition, Charles Wright, is Lucy's stepfather. But Wright was first attracted to Lucy and only afterwards married her widowed mother. So Wright is a potential father-in-law to Harry. Gilbert Phillips, the journalist who goes along on the expedition, is a friend of both Harry and Lucy – and Lucy was his lover before she chose Harry. In the course of the search for the missing explorer these facts, and others, are revealed. It would not be fair to the reader to state everything baldly here, except to say that where relationships exist there is passion and desire; and Pritchett sees the explorer as something of a sexual misfit.

For Wright, the Brazilian jungle has the enticement of a woman, and the treetops have for him the look of "fantastic millinery." He had seen the Johnson country – "he would remember the sun upon the wall of trees like the light on a woman's dress" – and regarded it as his own, something virgin and private: "He had seen its face and its dress. He longed to be in its body. The talk of the missionary's country and the mystery of his disappearance was talk of a rival and an attempt to enhance her attraction which he could admire as a connoisseur of discovery and adventure but which . . . made him alert for any sign of betrayal."

The novel is full of rivalries, and it may also be said that nearly every character in this account of an expedition is traveling in a different direction, mingling flight with pursuit, and usually suffering the satisfactions and frustrations that we associate with lovers. This is another reason Calcott is so welcome. He is a necessary element in the Englishness of it all – not a bloody gentleman, as he says. And he is also full-blooded and funny, unreliable, boasting, and populating the Amazonian town with his dusky children. I am inclined to think that it is the inclusion of Calcott that gives this novel its greatness, for otherwise it would be too intense and too sad; and it does not become truly tragic until this odd clown enters the narrative. The seance in which Calcott figures is one of Pritchett's triumphs as a writer.

One reads *Dead Man Leading* and one is struck again and again by how easy it is to imagine this remote landscape. The men and their obsessions seem much odder than their setting. It is one of Pritchett's most visual pieces of fiction, and it is visual in a particular way. It is not merely the clarity and strength of the images; it is, most of all, their familiarity.

He speaks of the brown water of the river resembling strong tea, and a sky like a huge blue house; the forest is faint, like "a distant fence", and the jungle at another point is bedraggled and broken, "as if a lorry had crashed into it"; there is a creek "like a sewage ditch" and some birds rising up "like two bits of charred paper" and a bad rainstorm making "the intolerable whine of machines" and a forest odor "like the smell of spirits gone sour on the breath." It is what English explorers would see – either a kind of tempting purity and allure in the liquefaction of the jungle's clothes, or else a way of discovering memories and establishing among all these relationships that the imagery of the Amazon is the imagery of England. This is emphatic in the last paragraph:

> He went with her to the door. Nothing could have been more like the river and the jungle and the sudden squawk of birds to his unaccustomed sight and ear, than the street light-daubed in the rain, the impenetrable forest of lives of people in the houses and the weird hoot and flash of the cars. He went back to his room, wishing for a friend.

It is impossible in a short introduction to do full justice to this novel. It has real excitements – the desertions, the chance meetings, the overwhelming hardships; and it has pleasures – the byplay between Calcott and Silva, the glimpse of the jaguar in Chapter Ten, the rainstorm in Sixteen, the surprising but surely inevitable ending of the quest. And there are the numerous perceptions, almost casually noted, but so telling: "He spoke abruptly and hastily to Silva, treating him with that laconic contempt which conceals the gratitude one feels to an accomplice" and when Wright lies dying and Johnson watches, "There enters with the handling of the sick a kind of hatred, a rising of life to repel the assault of evil." It is an extraordinary book, in all respects precise and wise.

What Maisie Knew

[1984]

If it were not for Henry James's art – his subtlety, his grace, his handy euphemisms – this very modern story about aimless lives and messy marriages would be practically untellable. Even so, and for all its unexpected humor, it is painful and at times pathetic. In these pages are many instances of characters blushing at something said or glimpsed – he (or she) "coloured a little," is the usual expression. They have a great deal to color about. The antique word "sordid" suits much of the action perfectly. It is a novel about the aftermath of a bitter divorce. Self-interest, battle and greed figure in most of the characters' motives, and so there are many pairings-off, many quarrels and partings. These people do not think they have enough love, sex, money or happiness. It is no wonder they "colour." They "throb," too. And they make noises suggestive of smoldering, like the fumbling sounds rising up a staircase, "the deepening rustle of more elaborate advances." It is a novel of thrusting hands.

It is most of all a novel about a small unselfish girl and the ways in which she is passionately victimized by adults. Maisie is a factor in her parents' divorce settlement. Each of her child-hating parents, in an arrangement made out of pure spite, agree to keep her for six months at a time and then toss her back to the other. It is not the keeping but the tossing back that pleases them. Maisie is very young – five when it begins. The parents take lovers; each parent remarries; the new spouses take an interest in their step-daughter and then in each other, and finally, in a sexual tangle that may be unique in English fiction, the separate step-father and step-mother become lovers. The natural parents have gone on to new attachments. Meanwhile, Maisie watches each move closely. "Her little world was phantasmagoric" – like a magic lantern show – "strange shadows dancing on a sheet." She is at last compelled to choose her future.

The novel is highly patterned and orderly. It has been compared to a stately dance. As if that is not off-putting enough, it has also been compared to a bedroom farce. Yet there are no bedrooms in the James novel – certainly no beds. It makes for a certain archness in this book. James himself called it an "ugly little comedy." He implies in many places in the text that Maisie is incorruptible. But she grows, she changes, and in the course of this novel we witness "the death of her childhood."

The idea came to James, as so many others did, at a dinner party, when one of the guests described an unusual divorce settlement. James set it out fully in his notebook: "The court, for some reason, didn't as it might have done, give the child exclusively to either parent, but decreed that it was to spend its time equally with each – that is alternately. Each parent married again, and the child went to them a month, or three months, about – finding with the one a new mother and the other a new father. Might not something be done with the idea . . ?" He proceeded to invent complications and consequences, and he finished his synopsis, "with the innocent child in the midst."

It was his innocent-child phase. It was the period of *The Turn of the Screw* (1898), with its pair of terrified tots. There are blameless kiddies in *The Other House* (1896), and one each in *The Pupil* (1890) and *In the Cage* (1898), and the anxious virgins of *An Awkward Age* (1899). James's biographer saw a peculiar symmetry in this: at a harrowing time in his career (his play *Guy Domville* had been a humiliating failure late in 1895), James began to write about childhood, and he depicted all its stages, from roughly the age of four through puberty and adolescence, finishing with the threshold of adulthood, Nanda at eighteen. Professor Edel sees a great deal of James in Maisie: "Maisie's bewilderment and isolation is James's . . . but the world's cruelty and hostility are recreated into a comic vision of benign childish curiosity." It is true James is nearly always complimentary in describing the child, and though he says in his Preface that Maisie resembles other small children in being inarticulate, he insists on the numerous perceptions and rich visions of her childhood.

That same highly receptive mind acquires experience through the "immense sensibility" that James attributes to fiction-writers in his essay, "The Art of Fiction." It is not difficult to imagine Maisie (or James himself) in those same terms, with "a kind of huge spider's-web of the finest silken threads suspended in the chamber of consciousness, catching every air-borne particle in its tissue. It is the very atmosphere of the mind; and when the mind is imaginative – much more when it happens to be a man of genius – it takes to itself the faintest hints of life, it converts the very pulses of the air into revelations."

Maisie begins as a parrot, and is entirely innocent of the physical implications of the affairs around her; but she grows in the novel, and though she is still young when the novel ends she has come into flower. I don't think of Maisie as one of James's little lisping waifs, but rather as a girl whom circumstances have forced to behave like a woman. Sir Claude says, near the end, "One would think you were about sixty –" Most critics seem to think of the novel's action taking place over two or three years. I think it is more, perhaps six or seven, filling out Maisie's body and giving her desires of her own. James wanted time in the book to be fluid. "I must handle freely and handsomely the years," he wrote in his notebooks, "be superior, I mean, on the question of time."

He noted his first idea in 1892. A year later he returned to his notebook and elaborated a bit. He had earlier wondered whether Maisie's parents should die so that Maisie could go her own way with new parents. He now decided that his killing them off would mean evading more interesting consequences; he would let them live, he asserted, for the sake of irony and complication. He had named the parents "Hurter", as unambiguously as if he were labeling a humor, and he thought it would be a story of about five thousand words.

Late in 1895 he told the editor of the *Yellow Book* to expect a story of about ten thousand words. The "Hurters" were now the "Faranges". (He got many of his characters' names from the social pages of *The Times*, where the weddings, births and deaths are announced.) In his notebook entry for December, 1895, he set out the structure of the story in detail – his notebooks are full of *Maisie* ruminations, and as a result we know more about its composition than any of his other novels. He began to see how symmetrical a story it was; he was determined to make it subtle, to blur its edges. He became interested in the possibilities of the governesses, particularly Mrs Wix, whom he calls "the frumpy governess." He saw the core of the drama as "the strange, fatal, complicating action of the child's lovability," and considering the powerful material and the steamy incidents he made another bold decision: everything – every important action or word in the novel – would take place in the child's presence. He said, "That is the essence of the thing."

He got going on the actual writing of the story in the summer of 1896, roughly four years after he had heard the divorce story over dinner. All that time he had been puzzling out the details in his notebook. He was a great rehearser of his novels and he used his notebooks to remind himself of what he knew and to correct his impressions. In October 1896 he told himself, "I have brought this little matter of Maisie to a point at which a really detailed scenario of the rest is indispensable for a straight and sure advance to the end." He proceeded for a number of pages to summarize the plot and he prefaced his summary with a remark on the form he wanted the book to have. He saw the symmetries, the parallel lives and reduplicated actions and he warned himself not to slacken in his "deep observance of this strong and beneficent method – this intensely structural, intensely hinged and jointed preliminary frame."

He was the man who said that many great novels were "loose and baggy monsters," but *Maisie* is anything but that. It is a most precise novel; it is finely balanced and four-square with a recurring situation that might be summed up in the sentence, "What are *you* doing here?" It is clear from the notebooks that James was certain he was onto something and that the elements of his story, if they were treated artfully, would yield him a fascinating novel. He pondered the matter, but always pleasurably and with confidence: *Maisie* was a novel made out of calculation and conscious decisions. It contains some of his best comedy and some of his most melancholy insights. Nearly every critic has seen it — James saw it himself — as a pivotal book. It shows the onset, the sudden dappled shadow, of his later manner. It is the book in which, at Chapter Seventeen, I think — though the matter is open to dispute — he got writer's cramp and began to dictate to a secretary, and the purification of that eloquent humming and hawing is for most readers the essential Henry James. Though it is less a novel than an enlarged story, and it is in many senses an in-between book, *Maisie* embodies everything that James excelled at in fiction.

Whatever love, warmth, brightness, or humanity is in the book is due to the presence of Maisie; she is the whole point. And it is not really that she is a sweet child with the function of triggering a mechanism to soften our hearts. In most respects she is shrewder and more clear-sighted than the adults around her. What is most curious — it is certainly one of the sticking-points in the book for me — is her angelic nature, which is in complete contrast to her parents' nastiness. How can two such utterly empty people have been responsible for bringing this lovely child into the world? There is a great deal of name-calling in this novel: "abominable little horror," "horrid pig," "fiend," and so forth, but where these severe names are used to describe Beale or Ida Farange the reader can only agree that pig and fiend are about right.

Maisie is said (by Sir Claude) to have a "fatal gift of beauty." We know where this comes from, for, if nothing else, she has inherited physical beauty. Her parents, ugly in every other way, are physically striking. (The ugliest characters in the novel, Mr Perriam and the Countess — the former Ida's lover, the latter Beale's — are also the wealthiest.) Beale is tall, luxuriously bearded, and has a habit of showing his large glittering teeth. He is boisterous, vulgar, showy, priapic and materialistic. He cannot tell the truth. He has dreadful friends who, in the context of this book, seem like child-molesters. We are given to understand that Beale is intensely clubbable and probably a gambler. He is certainly a liar. He is a failed diplomat, hollow at the core, and like many spineless people rather prickly and devious.

This novel is full of counterparts — balancing scenes and perfect echoes.

Ida Farange is so similar to Beale she is almost shocking – but she has more lovers. We are told explicitly about her bosom, which becomes one of the landmarks of the novel, like a familiar headland, heaving one minute, cushioning Maisie's head the next, with its "wilderness of trinkets." On the question of her cleavage James tells us that she wears her dresses cut "remarkably low" and there is explicit salacity in "the lower the bosom was cut the more it was to be gathered she was wanted elsewhere." She has the talkative person's moodiness and bad temper, but she has a compensating charm. Like her ex-husband, she is flashy (she "bristled with monograms"), very tall, vindictive and has awful friends. Seven of her lovers are named in the book; we see quite a bit of three of them, and she is said to have "quantities of others."

In choosing Maisie's parents, James invented a couple who are both handsome and extraordinarily unpleasant, and his artful touch was to make them unpleasant in exactly the same ways. In one respect Ida is different from Beale: she is physically violent and given to sudden lunges – at least where Maisie is concerned. We are told that Ida is addicted to extremes – either she is silent or else wildly gesturing. Usually we see her in motion – "she surged about." The verb is perfect for this amazing woman. I spoke earlier about this being a novel of thrusting hands. One thinks of all the hands in all the plackets. But it is also Ida's thrustings. Maisie is "hurled," "tossed," "snatched," "thrust," "dashed," and "ejected" by her mother at various points in the novel; most of all she is pushed. Ida is a tremendous pusher – and why should she not be? After all, she is a champion billiard player.

This is one of the brightest touches – Ida the billiard champ. It was "her great accomplishment" and we are told of her "celebrated stroke." One of her infidelities is disguised as a match she is playing abroad, and in an aside James – unconsciously of course – makes one of the clearest statements of her sexual character and leaves us with a bewitching image of "other balls that Ida's cue used to send flying."

One could easily overwork this pretty motif, but it seems apparent that the billiard cue is a potent example of Ida's masculinity, and virtually all we need to know of her virile ambition and her competitive instincts. It is as if James is determined to make her identical to Beale, for the billiard cue is not just a convenient phallicism but also a weapon and a career.

Billiards is also the perfect game to illustrate the typical movement in the novel. The three balls – one red and two white – represent both the characters and the action. It is a novel of threes – three characters battling at any one time (and Maisie is always one of them), three parks (Hyde Park, Regent's Park, Kensington Gardens), three settings (London, Folkestone, Boulogne). Ida will have had three husbands and Beale three wives; and Maisie comes under the protection of three men – her father, the Captain and Sir Claude; and three women – her mother, Mrs Beale and Mrs Wix. If one were to search for a word to describe the way in which Maisie passes from person to person, colliding and rebounding, the best term would come from the game of billiards: she does not simply go – she caroms.

How Maisie manages to be so bright and brave – so sensible without being prissy or pious – is a question we cannot answer on the evidence provided. We know about her spotless soul and her kindly nature. But James in describing the slam-bang of her upbringing has given us every reason for her turning out crazy, vengeful or anti-social. As it is, she never puts a foot wrong. She is stimulated by the bustle of these sinners, and she has a child's fearful thrill at the prospect of change. I don't think the reader is ever really worried that she will be spoiled or harmed: this could be the single weakness in the novel. Even when she is described repeatedly as a "pet," a "poor little monkey," a shuttlecock or a football, we see her as fully human, putting on a courageous smile and offering reassurance or advice: "You're both very lovely," "You're free," "Don't do it for just a little . . . Do it always." Often, she is no more than parroting another character's words, but her detachment and her directness ("Mamma doesn't care for me") and her good sense give her a confident aura of independence.

We know Maisie is a child, and James is artful in conveying her childish perceptions in appropriate imagery: the adult faces in close-up with eyebrows like skipping ropes (Miss Overmore) or eyebrows like moustaches (Mr Perriam) or her being in Boulogne "among the bare-legged fishwives and the red-legged soldiers" – a shy and not very tall girl would naturally notice the legs of foreigners rather than their faces. For the others Maisie's sensitivities are pretty much ignored. True, if they were taken into account and pandered to there would be no novel; but they say such wild things to her! It is bad enough that, for example, she sees her mother flirting with the odious millionaire, Mr Perriam (James portrays his Jewishness like a particularly nasty vice), but the rest is stated too: he is "in and out of the upper rooms." Maisie is told everything, often very bluntly, and the fact that many of the crude accusations are distortions or plain lies only makes matters worse. But Maisie continues to gaze on this disorder and noise with understanding eyes and peace-making instincts.

One of the disappointments that Maisie's parents have to face is that their daughter is totally unlike them. It seems clear that they would have been happier if she had been a burden – an armful – who would have been unwelcome in the enemy camp. But she is not. Maisie is tactful, compassionate, forgiving, and oddly objective. She notices that her unreliable mother had never been loved but only disliked by everyone, and she pities her for it. Maisie is no use in battle, and what her parents get is just what they deserve – a reproach to their stupidity, a kindly child who does not need them and who has a perfect memory: long after they have gone on to new people Maisie is still stubbornly there to remind them of their jilts. Maisie herself is independent: she can live perfectly well without her parents – perhaps too well. She is unscathed. Today, the emphasis in such a novel would be on the harm the divorce had done to her – "the needless destruction of a young life," that sort of thing. James does not see this. He is pleased with himself, he is proud of Maisie; his tone is bright as he savors what he takes to be huge and harmless ironies. Why should a child who is indestructible need the protection of parents or any adults?

But Maisie does not wish to live alone. The trouble is that the two characters in the book with whom she has a genuine sympathy – and more than that, an attraction bordering on attachment – both pose problems for her. Mrs Wix is not so bad as she first appears, nor is Sir Claude so good as Maisie believes him to be. The conundrum, which is the plot of *Maisie*, is established fairly early on (you can see the short book in this longish one), but the length of the book – its amplitude, as James might say – depends on the ambiguity of Mrs Wix and Sir Claude. James lets them linger so that Maisie will understand the hopelessness of her situation.

Mrs Beale, the former Miss Overmore, is not very important to the conundrum, I don't think. Her only virtue is that she loves Maisie, in spite of the fact that she is a paid governess, a manhandled mistress and only briefly a step-mother; but in other respects she is not very interesting – not half so interesting or so passionate as Ida. Mrs Beale's main function is first to be seduced and married by Beale Farange, and then to show him up and cast her spell – flesh and promises – upon Sir Claude.

Maisie sees Mrs Wix as a mother. It is her first impression, and an essential one. Mrs Wix is wall-eyed, badly dressed, dim, dogmatic and sad. She is probably a widow and her own daughter was killed in a road accident. She is "safe" – the sort of woman who is described as a dear old thing – but she is also a worrier. Her worrying is quite in key with her religion – it is probably true to say that worrying is at the bottom of her religion, almost an article of faith. Much has been made by critics of Mrs Wix's poor vision, and her reliance on "straighteners" – her spectacles. Like Ida's billiards and bosom, it is a wonderful metaphor and provides plenty of opportunity for speculation, but in this rich novel it is necessary to know what has been stated before one can begin to know what is being suggested; and the various implications of the strabismus and the eyeglasses seem to me less important than Mrs Wix's dogmatism or motherliness, or her sorrowful cry, when she envisages Maisie taken from her, "What will become of me?" It is an example of the singlemindedness of the novel that even Mrs Wix doesn't see that the principal concern ought to be: What will become of Maisie?

By degrees, Mrs Wix asserts herself – losing her cranky certitude and growing less irritating as she becomes familiar, but never, I think, becoming a wholly reliable refuge for Maisie. She can hardly be that, for in a clumsy way she too has fallen for Sir Claude, and persists in her rivalry and pathos (Maisie remembers the cry and says at the end of Mrs Wix "Where will she go? . . . What will she do?"). One of the problems of the novel – for me at least – is that there is no let-up in Mrs Wix's rather terrifying zeal or her moralizing. And of course the more this frumpy old governess in her snuff-coloured dress suppresses her squinting love for Sir Claude the more horribly she bangs on about morality. It is excellent psychology on James's part, but it gives the later stretches of the novel an atmosphere of arid arguing about irreconcilable differences.

It is crucial to remember that Sir Claude is young. Maisie calculates that he is of a different generation from her mother. He is probably in his twenties – a scandalous liaison for Ida, but it brings him closer in spirit to Maisie. He is quite firm in his determination to be a father – we understand that his marriage to Ida fails because she dislikes children, and his love for Mrs Beale is fuelled by the thought that she will bear him a child (and he has been influenced by her love for Maisie). None the less, Sir Claude is a most ambiguous character, and it is one of the triumphs of the novel that James puts us in Maisie's position and makes us overlook – almost – Sir Claude's weaknesses. He is not a villain and yet there is something roguish about him. We see him peering with interest at the backs of bonnets during church services, and distracted by a black-haired lady with a lapdog in the Folkestone hotel, and in Boulogne talking with Maisie but keeping his eyes on "the fine stride and shining limbs of a young fishwife who had just waded out of the sea with her basketful of shrimps" (James leaves us to imagine the damp clinging blouse on the snouts of her breasts, and her skirts hitched-up against her flanks). Sir Claude has a roving eye, which is amazing, considering the tangle he is already in as a result of his amorous nature. He is very generous, open-hearted and kind. He alludes a number of times to his fear – afraid of women, he says, afraid of Ida, afraid of Mrs Beale; but no, we are told, in one of the helpful suggestions that occur frequently in this lucid novel, that he is probably afraid of himself, of his weakness for women, his sentimentality. He is a cheerier and younger but just as devastating Edward Ashburnham from Ford Madox Ford's *The Good Soldier*, always doing his duty while at the same time fantasizing about an ambitious elopement.

Sir Claude's magic works on most of the women we see in the book, including Maisie. He is forgiven everything – never blamed, never seen as unfaithful, never depicted as a tempter. And he might be, because, for much of the novel, his relationship with Maisie is plainly sexual and his tone a kind of bantering intimacy with its "dear boys" and "old mans." At times he talks to her as if she is his mistress or his catamite. He courts her. At one point he undresses her efficiently – but in the presence of Mrs Wix. He says "I'm always talking to you in the most extraordinary way" – he means bluntly; he is surprised by his frankness, and so he should be. In an earlier place he says significantly, "I should be afraid if you were older."

In his notebooks and in his Preface to this novel, James is emphatic about the ironies that attracted him and continued to sustain his interest in this story. It is true that the novel has a heroine, but it does not really have a villain. Beale and Ida are merely a little ahead of their time in making their divorce much more imaginative than their marriage. It is an indulgent novel about right and wrong, not good and evil. "Morality" is something Mrs Wix harps on, but James repeatedly draws our attention to the fact that morality is not the same thing as love and that only an old-fashioned conscience is likely to muddle the issue. In any case, Mrs Wix by the end is biased and pretty passionate herself, and one never quite believes that she has awakened Maisie's "moral sense." The implication is that James is joshing the notion of conventional morality – finding it limited, narrow and harsh; indeed, finding it a source of irony.

The idea of money – or poverty and wealth – provides many ironies, too. It is at the very heart of the bargain that Ida has struck with Beale. A satisfactory financial settlement would have meant no quarrel and no battle over Maisie: Maisie stands for the money Beale cannot raise – the £2,600 that Ida wanted refunded to her. We are given the impression that the Faranges married for money and were disappointed in each other's fortunes. Money is a factor in their divorce and something of an aphrodisiac in their love affairs. Libido alone cannot keep these liaisons going. It is specifically noted that Miss Overmore is a lady and yet "awfully poor," which is obviously part of her failure with Beale. Mr Perriam's wealth guarantees his success with Ida, but eventually he has been exposed as a crook. At the end of the novel Ida and Beale are living off other people – money matters to them enormously – and at the same time the moneyless Sir Claude, Mrs Beale, Mrs Wix and Maisie debate the question of morality in Boulogne, while the idea of money is at the back of everyone's mind – everyone except Maisie.

Maisie is the eternal exception. It is easy to see why James found her so beguiling and why he is at such pains in his Preface to explain how she redeems the story and makes the sorriest incident easy to take. She is at once the freest and most dependent character in the novel – that is, spiritually free but in fact tied down. The idea of freedom becomes part of the conundrum in the plot. And the repeated word "free" acquires low associations and nuances of immorality as the narrative proceeds until, at last, Mrs Beale's declaration, "I'm free!" has a genuinely vicious sound. Freedom means doing exactly what you want, which is fine for Maisie's natural goodness, and essential to the others' restless greed; but freedom is a condition that strikes terror into the heart of Mrs Wix, whose Christian conscience tells her that freedom creates occasions of sin.

Maisie knows better. Her innocence and decency allow her to find peace in the notion of freedom. It is her fascination and impartiality that aid her in knowing, and knowing gives her the detachment and calmness that enable her to understand. She doesn't blink, she doesn't take sides, she remembers, she is uncommonly curious, she is tactful, she is solitary: she has the makings of a writer. Even here, she often seems like a grown-up novelist rendered small and fitted into a frock and given a taste for chocolates and an ability to play dumb. One of Maisie's great skills is being able to pretend not to know: "She practised the pacific art of stupidity." And when Mrs Wix says, "Well, my dear, what you *don't* know ain't worth mentioning!" we can only agree. "Oh yes, I know everything!" Maisie says to her father, when he asks her about her "brute of a mother". It is not quite true – Maisie is trying to please him – but in the course of the book her knowledge increases. No one bothers to conceal anything from her.

As she was condemned to know more and more, how could it logically stop before she should know Most? It came to her in fact as they sat there on the sands that she was distinctly on the road to know Everything. She had not had governesses for nothing: what in the world had she ever done but learn and learn and learn? She looked at the pink sky with a placid foreboding that soon she should have learned All.

It is her knowledge of human affairs that makes the last chapters so melancholy. She is less animated as she grows in experience, and when she and Sir Claude seem to be bargaining awkwardly at the end like passionate uncertain lovers, the implications are not lost on Mrs Beale, whose outrage has a shrillness that makes her sound like a sexual rival. "I love Sir Claude – I love *him*," Maisie replies to the furious Mrs Beale. It is a plaintive cry. It is the strongest wish Maisie voices in the whole novel – in Sir Claude she would have a father and a lover. Of course the wish is unfulfilled, and for the simple reason of bad timing: Maisie is too young in years. Sir Claude lets her down; Mrs Wix, who is now superfluous as a protector, gathers her up; and the novel ends on a note of failure and thwarted hope. Maisie now knows everything, and that knowledge is the death of childhood.

Sunrise with Seamonsters

[1984]

The boat slid down the bank and without a splash into the creek, which was gray this summer morning. The air was wooly with mist. The tide had turned, but just a moment ago, so there was still no motion on the water – no current, not a ripple. The marsh grass was a deeper green for there being no sun. It was as if – this early and this dark – the day had not yet begun to breathe.

I straightened the boat and took my first stroke: the gurgle of the spoon blades and the sigh of the twisting oarlock were the only sounds. I set off, moving like a water bug through the marsh and down the bendy creek to the sea. When my strokes were regular and I was rowing at a good clip, my mind started to work, and I thought: I'm not coming back tonight. And so the day seemed long enough and full of possibilities. I had no plans except to keep on harbor-hopping around the Cape, and it was easy now going out with the tide.

This was Scorton Creek, in East Sandwich, and our hill – one of the few on the low lumpy terminal moraine of the Cape – was once an Indian fort, Wampanoags. The local farmers plowed this hill until recently, when the houses went up, and their plow blades always struck flints and axe heads and beads. I splashed past a boathouse the size of a garage. When they dug the foundation for that boathouse less than twenty years ago they unearthed a large male Wampanoag who had been buried in a sitting position, his skin turned to leather and his bones sticking through. They slung him out and put the boathouse there.

Three more bends in the creek and I could see the current stirring more strongly around me. A quarter of a mile away in the marsh was a Great Blue Heron – five-feet high and moving in a slow prayerful way, like a narrow-shouldered priest in gray vestments. The boat slipped along, carrying itself between strokes. Up ahead on the beach was a person with a dog – one of those energetic early-risers who boasts "I only need four hours' sleep!" and is probably hell to live with. Nothing else around – only the terns screeching over their eggs, and a few boats motionless at their moorings, and a rather crummy clutter of beach houses and *No Trespassing* signs, and the ghosts of dead Indians. The current was so swift in the creek I couldn't have gone back if I tried, and as I approached the shore it shot me into the sea. And now light was dazzling in the mist, as on the magnificent Turner "Sunrise with Seamonsters".

After an hour I was at Sandy Neck Public Beach – about four miles. This bay side of the upper Cape has a low duney shore and notoriously shallow water in places. The half a dozen harbors are spread over seventy miles and most have dangerous bars. It is not a coast for easy cruising and in many areas there is hardly enough water for windsurfing. There are sand bars in the oddest places. Most sailboats can't approach any of the harbors unless the tide is high. So the little boats stay near shore and watch the tides, and the deep draft boats stay miles offshore. I was in between and I was alone. In two months of this I never saw another rowboat more than fifty yards from shore. Indeed, I seldom saw anyone rowing at all.

Sandy Neck proper, an eight-mile peninsula of Arabian-style dunes, was today a panorama of empty beach; the only life stirring was the gulls and more distantly the hovering marsh hawks. A breeze had come up; it had freshened; it was now a light wind. I got stuck on a sand bar, then hopped out and dragged the boat into deeper water. I was trying to get around Beach Point to have my lunch in Barnstable Harbor – my forward locker contained provisions. I was frustrated by the shoals. But I should have known – there were seagulls all over the ocean here and they were not swimming but standing. I grew to recognize low water from the posture of seagulls.

When I drew level with Barnstable Harbor I was spun around by the strong current. I had to fight it for half an hour before I got to shore. Even then I was only at Beach Point. This was the channel into the harbor, and the water in it was narrow and swiftly moving – a deep river flowing through a shallow sea, its banks just submerged.

I tied the boat to a rock and while I rested a Ranger drove up in his Chevy Bronco.

He said, "That wind's picking up. I think we're in for a storm." He pointed towards Barnstable Harbor. "See the clouds building up over there? The forecast said showers but that looks like more than showers. Might be thunderstorms. Where are you headed?"

"Just up the coast."

He nodded at the swiftly rushing channel and said, "You'll have to get across that thing first."

"Why is it so choppy?"

His explanation was simple, and it accounted for a great deal of the rough water I was to see in the weeks to come. He said that when the wind was blowing in the opposite direction to a tide, a chop of hard irregular waves was whipped up. It could become very fierce very quickly.

Then he pointed across the harbor mouth towards Bass Hole and told me to look at how the ebbing tide had uncovered a mile of sand flats. "At low tide people just walk around over there," he said. So, beyond the vicious channel the sea was slipping down – white water here, none there.

After the Ranger drove off I made myself a cheese sandwich, swigged some coffee from my thermos bottle and decided to rush the channel. My skiff's sides were lapstrake – like clapboards – and rounded, which stabilized the boat in high waves, but this short breaking chop was a different matter. Instead of rowing at right angles to the current I turned the bow against it, and steadied the skiff by rowing. The skiff rocked wildly – the current slicing the bow, the wind-driven chop smacking the stern. A few minutes later I was across. And then I ran aground. After the channel were miles of watery shore; but it was only a few inches deep – and the tide was still dropping.

The wind was blowing, the sky was dark, the shoreline was distant; and now the water was not deep enough for this rowboat. I got out and – watched by strolling seagulls – dragged the boat through the shallow water that lay over the sand bar. The boat skidded and sometimes floated, but it was not really buoyant until I had splashed along for about an hour. To anyone on the beach I must have seemed a bizarre figure – alone, far from shore, walking on the water.

It was mid-afternoon by the time I had dragged the boat to deeper water, and I got in and began to row. The wind seemed to be blowing now from the west; it gathered at the stern and gave me a following sea, lifting me in the direction I wanted to go. I rowed past Chapin Beach and the bluffs, and around the black rocks at Nobscusset Harbor, marking my progress on my flapping chart by glancing again and again at a water tower like a stovepipe in Dennis.

At about five o'clock I turned into Sesuit Harbor, still pulling hard. I had rowed about sixteen miles. My hands were blistered but I had made a good start. And I had made a discovery: the sea was unpredictable, and the shore looked foreign. I was used to finding familiar things in exotic places; but the unfamiliar at home was new to me. It had been a disorienting day. At times I had been afraid. It was a taste of something strange in a place I had known my whole life. It was a shock and a satisfaction.

Mrs Coffin at Sesuit Harbor advised me not to go out the next day. Anyone with a name out of *Moby Dick* is worth listening to on the subject of the sea. The wind was blowing from the northeast, making Mrs Coffin's flag snap and beating the sea into whitecaps.

I said, "I'm only going to Rock Harbor."

It was about nine miles.

She said, "You'll be pulling your guts out."

I decided to go, thinking: I would rather struggle in a heavy sea and get wet than sit in the harbor and wait for the weather to improve.

But as soon as I had rowed beyond the breakwater I was hit hard by the waves and tipped by the wind. I unscrewed my sliding seat and jammed the thwart into place; and I tried again. I couldn't manoeuver the boat. I changed oars, lashing the long ones down and using the seven-and-a-half-foot ones. I made some progress, but the wind was punching me towards shore. This was West Brewster, off Quivett Neck. The chart showed church spires. I rowed for another few hours and saw that I had gone hardly any distance at all. But there was no point in turning back. I didn't need a harbor. I knew I could beach the boat anywhere – pull it up over there at that ramp, or between those rocks, or at that public beach. I had plenty of time and I felt all right. This was like walking uphill, but so what?

So I struggled all day. I hated the banging waves, and the way they leaped over the sides when the wind pushed me sideways into the troughs of the swell. There were a few inches of water sloshing in the bottom, and my chart was soaked. At noon a motorboat came near me and asked me if I was in trouble. I said no and told him where I was going. The man said, "Rock Harbor's real far!" and pointed east. Some of the seawater dried on the boat leaving the lace of crystalized salt shimmering on the mahogany. I pulled on, passing a sailboat in the middle of the afternoon.

"Where's Rock Harbor?" I asked.

"Look for the trees!"

But I looked in the wrong place. The trees weren't on shore, they were in the water, about twelve of them planted in two rows – tall dead limbless pines – like lampposts. They marked the harbor entrance; they also marked the Brewster Flats, for at low tide there was no water here at all, and Rock Harbor was just a creek draining into a desert of sand. You could drive a car across the harbor mouth at low tide.

I had arranged to meet my father here. My brother Joseph was with him. He had just arrived from the Pacific islands of Samoa. I showed him the boat.

He touched the oarlocks. He said, "They're all tarnished." Then he frowned at the salt-smeared wood and his gaze made the boat seem small and rather puny.

I said, "I just rowed from Sesuit with the wind against me. It took me the whole goddamned day!"

He said, "Don't get excited."

"What do you know about boats?" I said.

He went silent. We got into the car – two boys and their father. I had not seen Joe for several years. Perhaps he was sulking because I hadn't asked about Samoa. But had he asked about my rowing? It didn't seem like much, because it was travel at home. Yet I felt the day had been full of risks.

"How the hell," I said, "can you live in Samoa for eight years and not know anything about boats?"

"*Sah*-moa," he said, correcting my pronunciation. It was a family joke.

My brother Alex was waiting with my mother, and he smiled as I entered the house.

"Here he comes," Alex said.

My face was burned, the blisters had broken on my hands and left them raw, my back ached and so did the muscle strings in my forearm; there was sea salt in my eyes.

"Ishmael," Alex said. He was sitting compactly on a chair glancing narrowly at me and smoking. " 'And I only am escaped alone to tell thee.' "

My mother said, "We're almost ready to eat – you must be starving! God, look at you!"

Alex was behind her. He made a face at me, then silently mimicked a laugh at the absurdity of a forty-two year old man taking consolation from his mother.

"Home is the sailor, home from the sea," Alex said and imitated my voice, "Pass the spaghetti, Mum!"

Joe had started to relax. Now he had an ally, and I was being mocked. We were not writers, husbands, or fathers. We were three big boys fooling in front of their parents. Home is so often the simple past.

"What's he been telling you, Joe?" Alex said.

I went to wash my face.

"He said I don't know anything about boats."

Just before we sat down to eat, I said, "It's pretty rough out there."

Alex seized on this, looking delighted. He made the sound of a strong wind, by whistling and clearing his throat. He squinted and in a harsh whisper said, "Aye, it's rough out there, and you can hardly" – he stood up, banging the dining table with his thigh – "you can hardly see the bowsprit. Aye, and the wind's shifting, too. But never mind, Mr. Christian! Give him twenty lashes – that'll take the strut out of him! And hoist the mainsail – we're miles from anywhere. None of you swabbies knows anything about boats. But I know, because I've sailed from

Pitcairn Island to Rock Harbor by dead reckoning – in the roughest water known to man. Just me against the elements, with the waves threatening to pitch-pole my frail craft . . ."

"Your supper's getting cold," father said.

"How long did it take you?" mother said to me.

"All day," I said.

"Aye, captain," Alex said. "Aw, it's pretty rough out there, what with the wind and the rising sea."

"What will you write about?" my father asked.

"He'll write about ocean's roar and how he just went around the Horn. You're looking at Francis Chichester! The foam beating against the wheelhouse, the mainsheet screaming, the wind and the rising waves. Hark! Thunder and lightning over *The Gypsy Moth*!"

Declaiming made Alex imaginative, and stirred his memory. He had an actor's gift for sudden shouts and whispers and for giving himself wholly to the speech. It was as if he was on an instant touched with lucid insanity, the exalted chaos of creation. He was triumphant.

"But look at him now – Peter Freuchen of the seven seas, the old tar in his clinker-built boat. He's home asking his mother to pass the spaghetti! 'Thanks, mum, I'd love another helping, mum.' After a day in the deep sea he's with his mother and father, reaching for the meatballs!"

Joseph was laughing hard, his whole body swelling as he tried to suppress it.

"He's not going to write about that. No, nothing about the spaghetti. It'll just be Captain Bligh, all alone, bending at his oars, and picking oakum through the long tumultuous nights at sea. And the wind and the murderous waves . . ."

"Dry up," father said, still eating.

Then they all turned their big sympathetic faces at me across the cluttered dining table. Alex looked slightly sheepish, and the others apprehensive, fearing that I might be offended, that Alex had gone too far.

"What will you write about?" mother asked.

I shook my head and tried not to smile – because I was thinking: *That.*

It had all been harmless ridicule, and yet the next morning I got into the skiff at Rock Harbor and felt my morale rising as I rowed away. I thought about the oddness of the previous day: I had ignored a Small Craft Advisory and had been tossed about in a difficult sea; and then I had gone home and had a family dinner. I had not been able to describe my rowing experience to them – anyway, what was the point? It had been private.

And in poking fun at me, Alex had come crudely close to the truth – all risk-taking has a strong element of self-dramatization in it: daredevils are notorious egomaniacs. Of course it was foolish to be home eating and bumping knees with the aged parents after such a day! So, the next day, which was perfect – sunny and still – I went out farther than I ever had and I rowed twenty-two miles.

It was my reaction to home, or rather to the bewildering juxtaposition of this boat and that house. The absurdity of it all! I was self-sufficient and private in the boat, but from this protection at sea I had gone ashore and been half-drowned by the clamor and old jokes and nakedness at home. Now it was satisfying to be going – like running away. It was wonderful at last to be alone; and if I had courage and confidence it was because I had become attached to my boat.

"See you named it after a duck," a lobsterman called out as I passed him that day. He was hauling pots out of the soupy water.

Goldeneye was carved on my transom and shining this sunny morning, gold on mahogany.

"Killed plenty of them right here!" he shouted. "What with this hot weather we probably won't see any until January!"

He went back to emptying his pots – the lobsterman's habitual hurry, fueled by the anxiety that the poor beasts will die and deny him his $2.70 a pound at the market in Barnstable.

But even in his frenzy of work he glanced up again and yelled, "Nice boat!"

It was a beautiful boat, an Amesbury skiff with dory lines, all wood, as well-made and as lovely as a piece of Victorian furniture, with the contours and brasswork and bright finish of an expensive coffin. Every plank, every separate piece of wood in a wooden boat, has its own name. What you take to be a single part, say, the stem, is actually the false stem, the stem piece and the breasthook; and the frame is not merely a frame but a collection of supports called futtocks and gussets and knees. We can skip this nomenclature. *Goldeneye* is pine on oak, with mahogany lockers and thwarts, and a transom like a tombstone. It is fifteen feet long.

Mine is the deluxe model. It has a sliding seat for sculling, out-rigger oarlocks, and three rowing stations. It is equipped to sail, with a dagger-board, a rudder and a sprit rig. I have three pairs of oars and two spare thwarts. It is a very strong boat, with a flat and markedly rockered bottom and the most amazing stern, tucked high to prevent drag and steeply raked, tapering at the bottom, which makes it extremely seaworthy for its size. The high waves of a following sea don't smash over it and swamp it but rather lift it and help it escape the swell.

"We used to make those for $35 each in Marblehead," an old man told me in Harwichport. "That was years ago."

That certainly was years ago. This skiff cost me $4,371 at Lowell's Boat Shop in Amesbury. I could have had it made for half that, or less, but I wanted the extras. Most good wooden boats are custom-made – no two are strictly alike. They are made for particular coasts, for a certain number of people, for the size and shape of the owner, for specific purposes. "If you were sea-mossing you'd say, 'Put on an extra plank,' " I was told by John Carter, curator of the Maine Maritime Museum. It was Mr Carter who told me that this sort of boat had no business on Cape Cod. It is a North Shore boat, made for the waters off Cape Ann, where a shoal draft and a flat bottom are helpful in the tidal rivers. The dory style of boat wasn't a suitable fishing boat for the Cape; here, people fish farther out and often in very rough water.

Lowell's Boat Shop originated this skiff's design in the 1860's and made thousands of them. It was a working boat – for hauling pots, hand-line fishing, and ferrying; and it was for river rowing on the Merrimack and also in protected harbors, like Salem. Rowing was one of the great American recreations, and the rowing age stretched roughly from the end of the Civil War until the invention of the outboard motor, in the 1920's. The outboard motor, which is one of the ugliest and most bad-tempered objects ever made, changed the shape of boats and made them also ugly and furiously turbulent. It is not very difficult for the average twin-engine cabin cruiser to swamp a thirty-foot sailboat. Motorboats are the rower's nightmare because the shoebox-shape creates a pitiless wake. I tend to think that only a motorboat can swamp a skiff.

My skiff had an old pedigree. It was based on the dory that was designed by Simeon Lowell in the early eighteenth century, and it is related to the French-Canadian *bateaux*. There are family resemblances – and certainly connections – between it and the flat-bottomed boats you see in India, and the skiffs depicted in Dürer engravings. There are sampans on the Karnafuli River at Chittagong in Bangladesh which are certainly skiff-like. John Gardner, who wrote a history of this style of boat, found an Amesbury skiff in "Big Fish Eat Little Ones" (1556) by Brueghel the Elder.

The shore had begun to look as featureless as the sea had once done. The sea seemed passionate and enigmatic and the charts showed the sea bottom to be almost comically irregular – here, at Billingsgate Shoal, miles from Rock Harbor, I could stand up; and farther on I could lean out of the skiff and poke crabs scuttling along the sand. I saw the shore as something shrunken and impenetrable. I had never expected to be indifferent to it, but I had grown impatient. It was the result of that awkwardness I had felt at going home. I rowed, and I stared at the receding shore as I had once stared at the brimming ocean. The shoreline was a smudged stripe: tiny boats, frail houses, timid swimmers – small-scale monotony.

A mile or so southwest of Billingsgate Light there was a large rusty ship in the water. This was the *James Longstreet*, a Second World War Liberty Ship that had been scuttled here to be used as a target ship. I was told in Orleans to look for it. A few Cape Codders set themselves up in successful scrap businesses by sneaking out to the ship at night in the early days and stripping it of its copper and brass. During the Vietnam War, ARVN pilots flew up from Virginia and dropped sand bombs on it. It was big and broken, russet-colored this bright day, and listing from the weight of its barnacles.

I shipped my oars off Great Island – the Wellfleet shore – and ate lunch. And then I made a little nest in the bow and lay there and went to sleep. It was hot and dead still and pleasant – like dozing in a warm bath, with a little liquid chuckle at the waterline. I was two miles out. I woke up refreshed, put my gloves on and continued, occasionally glancing at the long empty beaches and wooded dunes. My destination had been the Pamet River, but it was only two-thirty and I could see the dark tower of the Pilgrim Memorial where the top of Cape Cod hooked to the west.

Excited by the prospect of rowing so far in a single day, I struck out for Provincetown. I found Pamet Creek and Corn Hill on my chart and calculated that I had only about seven or eight miles to go. A light breeze came up from the west and helped me. But water distorts distance: after an hour I was still off Pamet Creek and Corn Hill, and Provincetown looked no closer. I may have been about three miles from shore. I began to suspect that I had not made much progress, and that gave me a lonely feeling that I tried to overcome by rowing faster.

Just before four o'clock a chill swept over me. The sun still burned in the sky, but the breeze had freshened to a steady wind. It was not the gust I experienced yesterday that pushed me back and forth; this was a ceaselessly rising wind that lifted the sea in a matter of minutes from nothing to about a foot, and then to two feet, and whitened it, and kept it going higher, until it was two to four, and so steep and relentless that I could not keep the boat straight for Provincetown. I thought of Alex saying: *The wind and the murderous waves! Please pass the spaghetti, mother.*

I could only go in one direction – the way the wind was blowing me. But when I lost concentration or rested on my oars the boat slipped aside and I was drenched. I had no doubt that I would make it to shore – the wind was that strong – but I expected to be swamped, I assumed I would go over and be left clinging to my half-drowned boat, and I knew that it would take hours to get to the beach that way.

The discouraging thing was that I was nearer to Provincetown than to the Truro shore. So I was turning away. I rowed for an hour, pulling hard, and at times I was so tired I just yanked the oars, keeping the high sea behind me. Every six seconds I was smacked by an especially high wave – but even the sea's crude clockwork didn't sink me, and it gave me a special admiration for the boat's agility. The wind had beaten all the Sunfish and the windsurfers to the beach at North Truro, but there were children dodging waves and little dogs trotting along the sand, and people preparing barbeques. I pulled the boat up the beach and looked out to sea. Nothing was visible. That unpredictable place where an hour ago I was afraid I might drown now looked like no more than a frothy mockery of the sky, with nothing else on it.

"She was a hooker," the young man was saying. "She walked into the place and said, 'I can take all you guys on.' Everyone knew her – 'Snowflake', they call her."

We were traveling on the coast road back to my Jeep. I had had to hitchhike – there was no other way to go – and I was picked up by two beer-drinking men in a jalopy. Their town was in the news for being the location of a particularly notorious rape trial.

"Then, after about eight or nine guys screwed her on the floor of the bar she freaked out and went crying to the cops. 'They raped me,' she says. But it wasn't rape – it was just a gang-bang. You sure you don't want a beer?"

It was so sudden after my long empty day that it was as if I were leading two lives – one on water and the other on land – with nothing to connect them, even though they were only minutes apart. This sort of travel made for a simultaneity that amounted to surrealism.

I had come to dislike the disruption of going ashore. The following day I rowed across the crook of the Cape to Provincetown, but I did not beach the boat. I tied up to someone else's mooring and had lunch on the water; and then I rowed towards Long Point Light and around the harbor; and I feathered my oars and procrastinated. Music and voices carried from the shore, the depressing hilarity of vacationers, shrill all-male "mixers" and party-goers queening it at the far end of Commercial Street; and glum couples kicking along the sand; and sunbathers, leather freaks, whale watchers, punks. At last, at sundown, I rowed in and blew up my inflatable boat roller until it became a four-foot sausage, and jammed it under the bow and wobbled *Goldeneye* up to a town landing.

I was watched by thirty-four men having a terrific time on a hotel veranda.

"Come on up and have a drink, darling. We don't have AIDS!"

I was ashore once again.

That became the rhythm of this trip: skimming on the water and almost hypnotizing myself with the exertion of rowing; and then, at the end of the day, being startled by the experience of touching land again. There was a serenity – something silken – in the worst wind, and the behavior of water was always fascinating and wayward. But this pretty skiff aroused a harassing instinct among bystanders. They shouted at me, they yodeled, they threw stones.

Long-distance rowing in a wooden boat attracts attention. It is one of those mildly frantic, labor-intensive activities, like operating a spoke-shave or pumping a butter churn. It is difficult to indulge in physical exertion and not seem like an attention-seeker – most joggers are accustomed to being yakked at. Very few onlookers are indifferent to someone getting exercise in public, and there is something in the very sweat and single-mindedness of running or rowing that inspires admiration in some people and ridicule in others. An old square-faced hag in a motorboat nearly sank me as she swerved past the tip of my oar in order to shriek, "Guess you're not in a hurry!"

That was in Pleasant Bay. I had started at the top end of Meeting House Pond and had rowed south down what they call The River into Little Pleasant Bay. I stayed on the outgoing tide and kept on, past Chatham Light to the tip of Nauset Beach and into Stage Harbor. Some of the worst Cape currents sweep between Nauset and Monomy Island, but I could cope with them much better than I could the inshore barracking of "Good exercise!" or "Faster, faster!" or "One-two! One-two!" I got it from people in other boats; I got it from swimmers and beachcombers; I got it from fat facetious people at the boat ramps. It was usually well-intentioned, but it was nearly always unpleasant. It was like having my bum pinched.

And there were the kids in motorboats. When I was young the roads of Massachusetts were full of hot rodders – pale pimply adolescents in jalopies. In a general sort of way, a car represented freedom, and driving – especially driving in a dangerous manner – was a form of self-expression. *He wrapped himself around a tree* was always said with a tinge of admiration. In those days, too, sex was impossible without a car, and I doubt whether there are many of my generation who didn't have their first sexual experience in a car. We were the first generation of adolescents to drive cars in any great numbers – Driver Training, with its leering instructors, started when we were in high school. Driver Training was the state's answer to hot rodders, and when the roads improved and most of the main roads were highways, policing was stricter, drinking laws were enforced, and the jalopy – useless on a highway – became a thing of the past. At that point, hot rodding turned into an aquatic sport.

Every year, off Cape Cod, swimmers are beheaded by kids in motorboats; people wading have their feet chopped off, and other unsuspecting souls are mutilated in even more grotesque ways. There are spectacular collisions – boats ramming each other, or plowing into docks, or flipping over. Often the engine dies and if the boat is not swamped it is taken by the wind and the current into the open sea. You need a driver's licence for a harmless little moped, but any twelve-year-old with a free afternoon is at liberty to whisk himself around in the family motorboat: there is no law against it, there are no laws at all about motorboating – there aren't even rules. There is boating "etiquette", but virtually the only people who observe it are people in sailboats.

I was on the southern side of the Cape. It is densely populated, full of pretty harbors and ugly bungalows – and blighting the once-charming towns are the fast-food places and the pizza parlors, the curio shops, the supermarkets. On the bay side of the Cape there are miles of empty beach and barren cliffs; but here the shore has been entirely claimed by developers; the shoreline is a cluttered wilderness of fences. Here and there are grand houses, even mansions, but there is little solitude. In a way, the mansions are responsible for the overdevelopment, for it was the boasting ostentation of the newly rich that attracted the seedy developments. The pattern is repeated all along the Cape, but it is at its ugliest at Hyannis where the dynastic Kennedys – still breeding after all these years – are the chief attraction. The Cape is a subtle landscape: there are few places on it to which people naturally gravitate – no mountains, no valleys, only harbors. So the settlement has been based on social insecurity – people have planted their bungalows around the mansions of rich families (much as they have in Newport), proving once again that all classes have their snobberies.

And everyone there seemed to have a motorboat – especially the teenagers. Boys in baseball caps, girls in bikinis, they went in circles, beating the ocean into a fury.

I rowed as fast as I could – dodging the sea traffic and the shouters – from Stage Harbor in Chatham to Wychmere in Harwich. The prevailing southwesterly wind was always opposing my progress. I continued to Bass River, but this time did not go to my parents' house. I slept at my own house now, and my routine was to sneak the boat into the water early and head west. I rowed to Hyannis and was surprised by the strong current and the protruding rocks. The Cruising Guide said, "Out here, too, a brisk afternoon southwester blowing against an ebb tide can kick up a short breaking chop, unpleasant in any boat and possibly dangerous in a small open boat." But I stayed afloat. I crossed Lewis Bay. I rowed to Hyannisport and Wianno; and there, where overdressed people sheltered behind hedges, grimacing at the sea with expensive dentures, I stopped. Rowing around the Cape had become routinely pleasant. I needed another challenge.

I had been rowing through Nantucket Sound. It is a reasonably safe stretch of water near the shore; but a few miles out it is another story entirely. It has been called the most dangerous water on the New England coast. There are shoals, tidal streams, stiff winds, sudden fogs. They are bad, but worse are the currents. The tide ebbs to the west and floods to the east – twelve separate charts in the Eldridge Tide and Pilot Book are needed to demonstrate the complex changes and velocity in the currents, and at their worst they surge at four knots, creating little maelstroms as they swirl past the deep holes in the floor of the Sound. It is like a wide wind-swept river, which flows wildly, changing direction every six hours; and the most unpredictable part lies just between Cape Cod and the northwest coast of Martha's Vineyard where, a bit lower down, the current has proven such a ship-swallower the waters are known as The Graveyard.

I decided to row across it in my skiff.

What had most impressed me about offshore rowing was how alienating it could be. It really was like leading a double life: there was no connection between being in the rowboat and being on the Cape, and it was always somewhat disturbing to go ashore. There was a pleasing secrecy in rowing this boat – or boating in general. It only seems like a conspicuous recreation; in fact, boating is a private passion – you are hidden on the ocean, which may be why boat owners are independent, stubborn, finicky, and famous for doing exactly as they please. There are few sea-going socialists.

I had never tried to explain my trip to anyone. It could not be rationalized; it could only be stated. I said what I was doing but not why. *Must be good exercise*, people said. And then, when I discovered that things were different out here, and unrelated to life on land, I decided to keep it a secret. I began to understand the weekend sailor, the odd opinionated boat owner, the person urgent to set sail; I think I even began to understand those idiot kids in their motorboats. We were all keeping the same secret.

But in *Goldeneye* I believed I felt it more keenly: I was nearer the water's surface, I was victimized more by the weather and the tides, I was moving under my own steam. These were all crucial factors in rowing across Nantucket Sound, where if I did not make careful calculations I would probably fail.

From the Eldridge Tide Table I determined that, for an hour or so, four times a day, there was no current in the Sound. My idea was to find a day when this slack period occurred in the early morning, and then rush across, from Falmouth Harbor to Vineyard Haven. If the wind was light and visibility fairly good, and if I rowed fast, there would be no problem. A certain amount of luck was required, but that imponderable made it for me a more interesting proposition.

I chose the fourth of September, the Sunday before Labor Day: Eldridge showed it to be just right from the point of view of the current, and the day seemed appropriate – it was regarded on the Cape as the last gasp of summer. The forecast was good – sunshine and light breezes. I was not confident about succeeding, but I knew that I would never have a better chance; conditions were as near to ideal as possible. Consequently, I decided to take my son Marcel with me. I liked his company, and he was strong enough to help with the rowing. If we made it he could take some of the credit; if we failed, I would take all the blame.

We left Falmouth Harbor in the early morning. It was a mile to the harbor mouth, where the breeze was just enough to stir the bottom half of the American flag on the flagpole there. Once past the jetty it was too rough for the long oars and the sliding seat. I put in the extra thwarts, handed Marcel a pair of oars, and using the two rowing stations we headed into the mist.

The Vineyard was hidden in the haze of a hot summer's morning. We pulled, talking a little at first, but in a short time fell silent. It was hard rowing, it took total concentration; and we were both nervous – but each of us was at pains to conceal it from the other. The waves regularly hit us on the starboard side, and the spray on Marcel's back dried to white smudges of salt. Now the Cape shore had a veil of mist across it, and out of it came the ferry *Island Queen* with a bone in its teeth. It was just astern of us and then it changed direction. I knew it was headed for Oak Bluffs, so I could guess where Vineyard Haven was, in the mist.

About an hour after leaving Falmouth Harbor we were rowing in the black water of the Sound, and neither the Cape nor the Vineyard was visible. In this misty isolation I felt a foolish thrill that was both terror and pleasure. I stopped rowing in order to savor it. Marcel said, "We'd better hurry." Another hour and we were off West Chop Lighthouse – the Vineyard had become gradually visible, like a photographic image developing on paper in a tray of water, acquiring outlines, then solidity,

and finally color. A cabin cruiser went slapping past, and the bow of
Goldeneye hit a four-foot curbstone of water, and we were drenched. But
we had almost made it; and sheltered by the Vineyard, the water was flat
enough for my long oars and my sliding seat. Marcel curled up on the
stern locker and went to sleep as I rowed the two and a half miles to the
head of Vineyard Haven harbor.

It had not been bad – I counted it as a small victory, and I was so
heartened by it that I decided to row back after lunch. It was an ignorant
decision. I had forgotten about the currents; I didn't know that the rising
afternoon winds on the Sound can be devastating; I did not realize how
tired we were from the morning trip. And I had thought that West Chop
was just another comic Cape name.

I soon learned. The current had begun to run west, and the wind had
picked up and was blowing to the east, fringing the three-foot sea with
foam. About half a mile off the lighthouse we were powerless to resist the
tipping wind, and the current took us into the chop – West Chop. The car
ferry *Islander* went by, leaving vast corrugations on the water. We were
no longer trying to get across to Falmouth; we were merely trying to stay
afloat.

"Know what I think?" I said.

Bam went another wave, soaking us again.

"That we should turn back," Marcel said.

Immediately we turned the boat, and we rowed as hard as we could;
but it was two hours before we were back in the harbor and on a friendly
beach. Now the fear was gone, and all that was left of my worry was
exhaustion. And the experience of the day was so strange it could only be
compared to the abruptness of a nightmare – it was the experience of
absurdity and danger, the surrealism of the unknown near home.

The next day the weather report was dire: a gale was expected, small
craft warnings, heavy seas. Everything looked fine in Vineyard Haven,
but I was unsure about a safe return to the Cape in the skiff. I decided not
to risk Marcel's life and sent him back to the mainland on the ferry. As I
felt I still had some time to spare, I rowed over to Bill Styron's dock.

He was sitting on the porch of his house with his son Tommy. The sun
high in the clear sky exaggerated with brilliance the whiteness of his house
and the green of his lawn. We talked awhile over glasses of lemonade.
Tommy praised my boat, and I urged him to row around the harbor.

"He works among homeless people in New York – waifs," Styron said,
after his son had gone.

Styron is the friendliest of men. He is watchful but unsuspicious, and
not in the least severe. He is so human, such an imposing physical
presence, it is hard to think of him as literary, or even bookish. He is
happy, apparently unmethodical and patient; he takes his time. I think of

him as living a charmed life, having had everything he has ever wanted. Easy-going people who have intelligence are usually merciful: Styron is that way. It gives him tremendous grace.

"I must say," he went on, "I'm fetched by the idea of someone his age who doesn't want to go into banking."

Tommy in *Goldeneye* was dissolved in the intense glitter of the sun on the water. It was a perfect day.

"I've been to France three times since I saw you in Paris," Styron was saying. "I've had my fill of it for a while. One of the times I was on the Film Jury at Cannes. That was a real circus. The Soviet juror wanted to give the prize to Monty Python's *The Meaning of Life*. It seemed to me a silly film. But that's what the English are best at, isn't it? They're good at farce and low comedy. They're through with tragedies, I guess."

I said that to succeed at writing tragedy you had to take yourself pretty seriously, and the English didn't do that anymore. We Americans took ourselves very seriously indeed, which was why tragedy was so common in our novels and plays: it was an aspect of our innocence and our optimism. We were still interested in the texture of our character, still wondering about the future. The English had just about ceased to care. Their cynicism had turned them into bizarre jokesters.

Rose Styron, dressed for tennis, crossed the lawn and walked onto the porch. We talked about bird watching, and India, and Northern Ireland. "Please stay for lunch," Rose said.

I said I had to row to Falmouth: I had set myself that task today.

"We're having *sushi*," Styron said.

"You must get sick of people dropping in all the time," I said.

"We love it," Rose said. "I encourage people to drop in. Oh, the other day my daughter said, 'Mother! Ricardo Montalban has just climbed up the dock – he's crossing the lawn!' I looked out and saw it was Senator Dodd on the grass!"

"Stay for *sushi*," Styron said.

But I said I had to go. We all walked down to the dock, as Tommy brought the skiff back.

"Sure you don't want to go to Falmouth?" I said.

"Not today," Styron said. He clapped his hands on his belly. "I'd just be extra weight."

"We'll both row," I said. "It'll take us three hours." I was getting into the boat.

Tommy said, "With him rowing it would take four!"

They waved me off and I rowed, watching them walk down their dock to lunch. It was one o'clock. An hour later I was at the buoy that marked the harbor entrance, and making no progress. I was pushed by the wind, pulled by the current. Within minutes I was in West Chop again, but

much farther out than I had been the day before. I put in the short oars,
but the chop was too fierce to row through – I couldn't row at all, I
couldn't even steady the boat. The oars were bending and I thought it was
likely that I might break one as I fought the current. Some boats passed
me, riding high; they glanced at me and moved on. The wind was strong.
Another hour went by: three o'clock – I was nowhere, still pulling. The
Styrons had finished their lunch, and Bill was writing – he was an
afternoon writer. He was working on a series of linked novellas, about the
Marines. I thought of him saying, "I'm fetched by the idea . . ." I had
never heard a northerner use that old word in that pleasant way. The
waves thudded against my wooden skiff. "Stay for *sushi*." I'd said no. The
Styrons had seen me go and probably said: That seems a good idea.

I was blown aside and tugged towards shore, and it was another hour
and a half before I got back to Vineyard Haven. Then I admitted to myself
that I had almost been swamped – and it wasn't seamanship but only luck
that had prevented it. I might have drowned. I certainly had been
frightened: they had been the worst waves I had seen all summer. But
there was no link between anything out there among the seamonsters and
lunch at the Styrons in this still harbor. It was almost six: I had spent half
the day going nowhere. It would be dark soon – this sunset like the last
hour of summer light for me.

I fretted in the harbor for a while, and then nerved myself and asked a
boat owner for a tow back to the Cape. "I'd be glad to," the man said, and
tied *Goldeneye* to his cabin cruiser. I joined him at the wheel and he
remarked on the high waves and strong wind. He wasn't bothered. He
had a big boat and a deafening diesel engine: we were safe. I had been
saved by the sort of boat I had been cursing all summer.

Goldeneye was crusted with salt again. Everything in it – the charts, the
tide tables, my food – was wet and had to be thrown away. I found the
boat ramp at Falmouth clogged with rubbish – plastic bottles, some rope,
a smooth swollen rat. I winched the boat onto the trailer and headed
home.

"Here he comes," Alex crowed. There were ten people in the dining
room. "Big dramatic entrance! Look everybody, it's Ishmael! 'Aw, it was
the schooner Hesperus that sailed the wintry sea!' " And then he took me
aside. "What the fuck took you so long?" he said. "You were supposed to
carve the turkey."

Afterword

Soon after I went to Africa I began writing what I thought of as Letters from Africa to *The Christian Science Monitor*: "The Edge of the Great Rift," "Burning Grass," "Winter in Africa," "The Cerebral Snapshot," and "State of Emergency" all appeared in that paper. My editor there was a woman who rejoiced in the motto-like name Mrs Silence Buck Bellows. I mentioned in one piece that I taught night-school in the dark – English language lessons at any rate – in order to save lamp-oil; then checks were sent to me by *Monitor* readers – several thousand dollars. We started a scholarship fund with it. When Mrs Bellows turned down a piece I wrote about fishing ("We don't approve of killing fish," she said) I wrote no more for this newspaper.

"Leper Colony" appeared in *Evergreen Review*. "Scenes from a Curfew" was one chapter of a book I wrote about a month-long curfew that was imposed on Kampala, Uganda. The book was never published. A version of this piece was first published in my book *Sinning With Annie* (1972). "Tarzan is an Expatriate" was published in the Ugandan magazine, *Transition*; it ceased publication when the editor, Rajat Neogy, was jailed for sedition in 1970. "Cowardice" appeared in *Commentary*. "Seven Burmese Days" was published in *The Atlantic* under the title "Burma". "The Killing of Hastings Banda" first appeared in *Esquire*; "A Love-Scene After Work" – thinking out loud about quitting my job in Singapore – in *The North American Review*; the first part of "V. S. Naipaul" appeared in the anthology, *People* (Chatto & Windus, London); the second part in *The Telegraph Magazine* (London); "Kazantzakis' England" in *Encounter*, under the title "You Orientals!", "Malaysia" in the English edition of *Vogue*, and "Hemingway: Lord of the Ring" in *Encounter*.

When I wrote *The Great Railway Bazaar*, I included a chapter on Afghanistan, but I was persuaded to leave it out. There are no trains in Afghanistan. "Memories of Old Afghanistan", this chapter, first appeared in *Harper's* under the title "In Darkest Afghanistan." "The Night Ferry to Paris" was published in *Travel & Leisure*; half of "Stranger on a Train" appeared in *The Observer* (London) and the other half was the first Thomas Cook Travel Lecture, which I gave in London in 1981; "An English Visitor" first appeared in *The New Statesman*, "Discovering Dingle" in *Travel & Leisure*; "The Exotic View" was commissioned by Mr Arthur S. Penn in New York for a collection of nineteenth century photographs, which was never published; "Homage to Mrs Robinson" first appeared in *Playboy*. "My Extended Family" was commissioned by *The Sunday Times* (London) for their Pleasures of Life series, but was never published; "A Circuit of Corsica" was commissioned by *Travel & Leisure* but turned down by them and finally published by *The Atlantic*. "Nixon's Neighborhood" appeared in *The Radio Times* (BBC, London), and Nixon's *Memoirs* in *The Sunday Times*. "The Orient Express" was commissioned by *Horizon*, rejected by them, and published in *Holiday*.

"Traveling Home: High School Reunion" was written for my own satisfaction, and it later appeared in *The New York Times Magazine*. When I wrote a play about Kipling in 1979 and could not get it staged I decided to write about this American period in Kipling's life. It is appearing here for the first time. "John McEnroe, Jr" was first published in *The Radio Times*; "Christmas Ghosts" in *The New York Times*, "Henry Miller" in *The Sunday Times*, and "V. S. Pritchett" in *The New York Times Book Review*. "Dead Man Leading" formed the introduction to Pritchett's novel, published by Oxford University Press. "The Past Recaptured" was the Foreword to *The World As It Was*, a book of old photographs, edited by Margarett Loke, and "Railways of the Raj" was the Foreword to a book of the same name (Scolar Press, London). "Subterranean Gothic" appeared in *The New York Times Magazine* under the title "Subway Odyssey". I am grateful to Faber & Faber for permission to use an extract from T. S. Eliot's *East Coker*. "Easy Money – Patronage" was my Gertrude Clarke Whittal Lecture at the Library of Congress (April, 1981) and was later published in a slightly different form by *Harper's* magazine. "Mapping the World" was the Foreword to the Annual Report, 1982, of The Hongkong and Shanghai Bank.

"The Last Laugh" was the Introduction to the posthumous collection of S. J. Perelman's pieces, published by Simon & Schuster. "Graham Greene's Traveling Companion" was the Introduction to Barbara Greene's *Too Late to Turn Back* (1982, but first published in 1938 under the title *Land Benighted*). "His Monkey Wife" was the Introduction I wrote for John Collier's novel, published by Oxford University Press in England, and "Being A Man" first appeared in the column "About Men" in *The New York Times Magazine*. "Introducing *Jungle Lovers*," I wrote for a German edition of the novel (published by a Munich insurance company, Bayerische Rücksversicherung Aktien-gesellschaft, as a Christmas present for their clients). "Making Tracks to Chittagong" was published in *The National Geographic* in a different form, under the title,

"By Rail Across the Indian Subcontinent." "What Maisie Knew" was my Introduction to the Penguin edition of the Henry James novel, and "Sunrise with Seamonsters" appeared in a shorter form in *Vanity Fair* under the title, "Rounding the Cape."

Most of the pieces here first appeared in a slightly different form. English magazines have the lightest editorial hand, American magazines the heaviest, occasionally making so bold as to rewrite one's work. "I think our readers would like it better our way," an editor at *Mademoiselle* told me once over the phone, as she ran her blue pencil through one of my paragraphs. For the *Monitor* of course I avoided all mention of death, a concept that is at odds with Christian Science. *The New York Times* is unexpectedly fastidious, and even at times prissy ("Please don't use the word 'stinks' "). In my subway piece the graffiti I noted, "*Guzmán – Ladrón, Maricón y Asesino*" appeared on my proofs without *Maricón*. "We don't use that word in this newspaper," I was told. I pointed out that it was in Spanish and that it was part of a true quotation. This did not matter: it was not fit to print. I agreed to the cut but was left to ponder this newspaper of record, in the most violent city in the world, averting its eyes when it saw something it did not like; and printing the words "thief" and "murderer," but not the noun "gay."

MORE ABOUT PENGUINS, PELICANS, PEREGRINES AND PUFFINS

For further information about books available from Penguins please write to Dept EP, Penguin Books Ltd, Harmondsworth, Middlesex UB7 0DA.

In the U.S.A.: For a complete list of books available from Penguins in the United States write to Dept DG, Penguin Books, 299 Murray Hill Parkway, East Rutherford, New Jersey 07073.

In Canada: For a complete list of books available from Penguins in Canada write to Penguin Books Canada Ltd, 2801 John Street, Markham, Ontario L3R 1B4.

In Australia: For a complete list of books available from Penguins in Australia write to the Marketing Department, Penguin Books Australia Ltd, P.O. Box 257, Ringwood, Victoria 3134.

In New Zealand: For a complete list of books available from Penguins in New Zealand write to the Marketing Department, Penguin Books (N.Z.) Ltd, Private Bag, Takapuna, Auckland 9.

In India: For a complete list of books available from Penguins in India write to Penguin Overseas Ltd, 706 Eros Apartments, 56 Nehru Place, New Delhi 11019.

A CHOICE OF PENGUINS

☐ *Further Chronicles of Fairacre* **'Miss Read'**　　　£3.95

Full of humour, warmth and charm, these four novels – *Miss Clare Remembers, Over the Gate, The Fairacre Festival* and *Emily Davis* – make up an unforgettable picture of English village life.

☐ *Callanish* **William Horwood**　　　£1.95

From the acclaimed author of *Duncton Wood*, this is the haunting story of Creggan, the captured golden eagle, and his struggle to be free.

☐ *Act of Darkness* **Francis King**　　　£2.50

Anglo-India in the 1930s, where a peculiarly vicious murder triggers 'A terrific mystery story . . . a darkly luminous parable about innocence and evil' – *The New York Times*. 'Brilliantly successful' – *Daily Mail*. 'Unputdownable' – *Standard*

☐ *Death in Cyprus* **M. M. Kaye**　　　£1.95

Holidaying on Aphrodite's beautiful island, Amanda finds herself caught up in a murder mystery in which no one, not even the attractive painter Steven Howard, is quite what they seem . . .

☐ *Lace* **Shirley Conran**　　　£2.95

Lace is, quite simply, a publishing sensation: the story of Judy, Kate, Pagan and Maxine; the bestselling novel that teaches men about women, and women about themselves. 'Riches, bitches, sex and jetsetters' locations – they're all there' – *Sunday Express*

A CHOICE OF PENGUINS

☐ *West of Sunset* **Dirk Bogarde** £1.95

'His virtues as a writer are precisely those which make him the most compelling screen actor of his generation,' is what *The Times* said about Bogarde's savage, funny, romantic novel set in the gaudy wastes of Los Angeles.

☐ *The Riverside Villas Murder* **Kingsley Amis** £1.95

Marital duplicity, sexual discovery and murder with a thirties back-cloth: 'Amis in top form' – *The Times*. 'Delectable from page to page . . . effortlessly witty' – C. P. Snow in the *Financial Times*

☐ *A Dark and Distant Shore* **Reay Tannahill** £3.95

Vilia is the unforgettable heroine, Kinveil Castle is her destiny, in this full-blooded saga spanning a century of Victoriana, empire, hatreds and love affairs. 'A marvellous blend of *Gone with the Wind* and *The Thorn Birds*. You will enjoy every page' – *Daily Mirror*

☐ *Kingsley's Touch* **John Collee** £1.95

'Gripping . . . I recommend this chilling and elegantly written medical thriller' – *Daily Express*. 'An absolutely outstanding storyteller' – *Daily Telegraph*

☐ *The Far Pavilions* **M. M. Kaye** £4.95

Holding all the romance and high adventure of nineteenth-century India, M. M. Kaye's magnificent, now famous, novel has at its heart the passionate love of an Englishman for Juli, his Indian princess. 'Wildly exciting' – *Daily Telegraph*

A CHOICE OF PENGUINS

☐ *Small World* **David Lodge** £2.50

A jet-propelled academic romance, sequel to *Changing Places*. 'A new comic débâcle on every page' – *The Times*. 'Here is everything one expects from Lodge but three times as entertaining as anything he has written before' – *Sunday Telegraph*

☐ *The Neverending Story* **Michael Ende** £3.95

The international bestseller, now a major film: 'A tale of magical adventure, pursuit and delay, danger, suspense, triumph' – *The Times Literary Supplement*

☐ *The Sword of Honour Trilogy* **Evelyn Waugh** £3.95

Containing *Men at Arms*, *Officers and Gentlemen* and *Unconditional Surrender*, the trilogy described by Cyril Connolly as 'unquestionably the finest novels to have come out of the war'.

☐ *The Honorary Consul* **Graham Greene** £2.50

In a provincial Argentinian town, a group of revolutionaries kidnap the wrong man . . . 'The tension never relaxes and one reads hungrily from page to page, dreading the moment it will all end' – Auberon Waugh in the *Evening Standard*

☐ *The First Rumpole Omnibus* **John Mortimer** £4.95

Containing *Rumpole of the Bailey*, *The Trials of Rumpole* and *Rumpole's Return*. 'A fruity, foxy masterpiece, defender of our wilting faith in mankind' – *Sunday Times*

☐ *Scandal* **A. N. Wilson** £2.25

Sexual peccadillos, treason and blackmail are all ingredients on the boil in A. N. Wilson's new, *cordon noir* comedy. 'Drily witty, deliciously nasty' – *Sunday Telegraph*

A CHOICE OF PENGUINS

☐ *Stanley and the Women* **Kingsley Amis** £2.50

'Very good, very powerful . . . beautifully written . . . This is Amis *père* at his best' – Anthony Burgess in the *Observer*. 'Everybody should read it' – *Daily Mail*

☐ *The Mysterious Mr Ripley* **Patricia Highsmith** £4.95

Containing *The Talented Mr Ripley*, *Ripley Underground* and *Ripley's Game*. 'Patricia Highsmith is the poet of apprehension' – Graham Greene. 'The Ripley books are marvellously, insanely readable' – *The Times*

☐ *Earthly Powers* **Anthony Burgess** £4.95

'Crowded, crammed, bursting with manic erudition, garlicky puns, omnilingual jokes . . . (a novel) which meshes the real and personalized history of the twentieth century' – Martin Amis

☐ *Life & Times of Michael K* **J. M. Coetzee** £2.95

The Booker Prize-winning novel: 'It is hard to convey . . . just what Coetzee's special quality is. His writing gives off whiffs of Conrad, of Nabokov, of Golding, of the Paul Theroux of *The Mosquito Coast*. But he is none of these, he is a harsh, compelling new voice' – Victoria Glendinning

☐ *The Stories of William Trevor* £5.95

'Trevor packs into each separate five or six thousand words more richness, more laughter, more ache, more multifarious human-ness than many good writers manage to get into a whole novel' – *Punch*

☐ *The Book of Laughter and Forgetting* **Milan Kundera** £3.95

'A whirling dance of a book . . . a masterpiece full of angels, terror, ostriches and love . . . No question about it. The most important novel published in Britain this year' – Salman Rushdie

PENGUIN OMNIBUSES

☐ **Victorian Villainies**   £5.95

Fraud, murder, political intrigue and horror are the ingredients of
these four Victorian thrillers, selected by Hugh Greene and Graham
Greene.

☐ **The Balkan Trilogy** **Olivia Manning**   £5.95

This acclaimed trilogy – *The Great Fortune, The Spoilt City* and
Friends and Heroes – is the portrait of a marriage, and an exciting
recreation of civilian life in the Second World War. 'It amuses, it
diverts, and it informs' – Frederick Raphael

☐ **The Penguin Collected Stories of**
  Isaac Bashevis Singer   £5.95

Forty-seven marvellous tales of Jewish magic, faith and exile. 'Never
was the Nobel Prize more deserved . . . He belongs with the giants' –
Sunday Times

☐ **The Penguin Essays of George Orwell**   £4.95

Famous pieces on 'The Decline of the English Murder', 'Shooting an
Elephant', political issues and P. G. Wodehouse feature in this
edition of forty-one essays, criticism and sketches – all classics of
English prose.

☐ **Further Chronicles of Fairacre** **'Miss Read'**   £3.95

Full of humour, warmth and charm, these four novels – *Miss Clare
Remembers, Over the Gate, The Fairacre Festival* and *Emily Davis* –
make up an unforgettable picture of English village life.

☐ **The Penguin Complete Sherlock Holmes**
  Sir Arthur Conan Doyle   £5.95

With the fifty-six classic short stories, plus *A Study in Scarlet, The
Sign of Four, The Hound of the Baskervilles* and *The Valley of Fear*,
this volume contains the remarkable career of Baker Street's most
famous resident.

PENGUIN OMNIBUSES

☐ *Life with Jeeves* **P. G. Wodehouse**   **£3.95**

Containing *Right Ho, Jeeves, The Inimitable Jeeves* and *Very Good, Jeeves!* in which Wodehouse lures us, once again, into the ever-green world of Bertie Wooster, his terrifying Aunt Agatha, his man Jeeves and other eggs, good and bad.

☐ *The Penguin Book of Ghost Stories*   **£4.95**

An anthology to set the spine tingling, including stories by Zola, Kleist, Sir Walter Scott, M. R. James, Elizabeth Bowen and A. S. Byatt.

☐ *The Penguin Book of Horror Stories*   **£4.95**

Including stories by Maupassant, Poe, Gautier, Conan Doyle, L. P. Hartley and Ray Bradbury, in a selection of the most horrifying horror from the eighteenth century to the present day.

☐ *The Penguin Complete Novels of Jane Austen*   **£5.95**

Containing the seven great novels: *Sense and Sensibility, Pride and Prejudice, Mansfield Park, Emma, Northanger Abbey, Persuasion* and *Lady Susan*.

☐ *Perfick, Perfick!* **H. E. Bates**   **£4.95**

The adventures of the irrepressible Larkin family, in four novels: *The Darling Buds of May, A Breath of French Air, When the Green Woods Laugh* and *Oh! To Be in England*.

☐ *Famous Trials*
   Harry Hodge and James H. Hodge   **£3.95**

From Madeleine Smith to Dr Crippen and Lord Haw-Haw, this volume contains the most sensational murder and treason trials, selected by John Mortimer from the classic Penguin Famous Trials series.